D0510109

RESEARCHING
HOSPITALITY
and TOURISM

For Penny – my one and only love and soul mate

2ND EDITION

RESEARCHING
HOSPITALITY
and TOURISM

BOB BROTHERTON

/ **LRC Stoke Park**
GUILDFORD COLLEGE

Los Angeles | London | New Delhi
Singapore | Washington DC

194917   research
          Skills

338
4791
BRO

Los Angeles | London | New Delhi
Singapore | Washington DC

SAGE Publications Ltd
1 Oliver's Yard
55 City Road
London EC1Y 1SP

SAGE Publications Inc.
2455 Teller Road
Thousand Oaks, California 91320

SAGE Publications India Pvt Ltd
B 1/I 1 Mohan Cooperative Industrial Area
Mathura Road
New Delhi 110 044

SAGE Publications Asia-Pacific Pte Ltd
3 Church Street
#10-04 Samsung Hub
Singapore 049483

Editor: Chris Rojek
Assistant editors: Gemma Shields and
    Delayna Spencer
Production editor: Katherine Haw
Copyeditor: Elaine Leek
Proofreader: Christine Bitten
Marketing manager: Michael Ainsley
Cover design: Shaun Mercier
Typeset by: C&M Digitals (P) Ltd, Chennai, India
Printed and bound by CPI Group (UK) Ltd,
    Croydon, CR0 4YY

© Bob Brotherton 2015

First published 2015

Apart from any fair dealing for the purposes of research
private study, or criticism or review, as permitted under th
Copyright, Designs and Patents Act, 1988, this publicatio
may be reproduced, stored or transmitted in any form, or
any means, only with the prior permission in writing of th
publishers, or in the case of reprographic reproduction, i
accordance with the terms of licences issued by the Cop
Licensing Agency. Enquiries concerning reproduction ou
those terms should be sent to the publishers.

Library of Congress Control Number: 2015939811

British Library Cataloguing in Publication data

A catalogue record for this book is available from
the British Library

MIX
Paper from
responsible sources
FSC
www.fsc.org   FSC® C013604

ISBN 978-1-4462-8754-5
ISBN 978-1-4462-8755-2 (pbk)

At SAGE we take sustainability seriously. Most of our products are printed in the UK using FSC papers and boards.
When we print overseas we ensure sustainable papers are used as measured by the Egmont grading system.
We undertake an annual audit to monitor our sustainability.

CONTENTS

List of Figures and Tables   xiii
About the Author   xiv
Preface   xv
About the Companion Website   xix

1 THE NATURE AND RELEVANCE OF RESEARCH   1

Chapter Content and Issues   1

1.1 Introduction   1
1.2 The Nature of Research   2

    1.2.1 Experience and common sense   4
    1.2.2 Thinking about research   5

1.3 The Characteristics of Scientific Research   6

    1.3.1 Purposeful   7
    1.3.2 Rigorous   7
    1.3.3 Testable   8
    1.3.4 Replicable   8
    1.3.5 Precision   9
    1.3.6 Confidence   9
    1.3.7 Objective   10
    1.3.8 Generalisable   10
    1.3.9 Parsimonious   11

1.4 Types of Research   12

    1.4.1 Exploratory, descriptive and explanatory research   12
    1.4.2 Pure and applied research   14
    1.4.3 Theoretical/empirical and primary/secondary research   14

1.5 The Main Research Approaches   16

    1.5.1 Induction   16
    1.5.2 Deduction   18

1.6 Research Issues, Questions and Problems   18

Chapter Summary   22
Chapter References   22

WITHDRAWN

2 RESEARCH PHILOSOPHIES AND SCHOOLS OF THOUGHT 23

Chapter Content and Issues 23

2.1 Introduction 23
2.2 The Nature of Knowledge and Reality 24

    2.2.1 The 'ologies' 26
    2.2.2 Schools of thought and paradigms 28

2.3 Positivism and Phenomenology 30

    2.3.1 Positivism 31
    2.3.2 Phenomenology 35

2.4 Post-modernism and Pragmatism 39

    2.4.1 Post-modernism 39
    2.4.2 Pragmatism 40

2.5 Where Do You Stand? 43

Chapter Summary 44
Chapter References 44

3 DEVELOPING THE RESEARCH PROPOSAL AND PLAN 46

Chapter Content and Issues 46

3.1 Introduction 46
3.2 Finding and Refining a Topic 47

    3.2.1 Choosing a topic with potential value 47
    3.2.2 Choosing a topic that interests you 48
    3.2.3 Do some exploratory work 49
    3.2.4 Be aware of who is saying what 50
    3.2.5 Refining and focusing the topic 51

3.3 Refining the Research Question(s) 54

    3.3.1 Using what is known already 54
    3.3.2 Be creative 55

3.4 Developing Aims and Objectives 55
3.5 Putting the Research Proposal Together 58

    3.5.1 What should the research proposal contain? 58
    3.5.2 The research proposal and the research process 60

3.6 Ethical Considerations 62

Chapter Summary 65
Chapter References 66

4 SOURCING AND REVIEWING THE LITERATURE   67

Chapter Content and Issues   67

4.1   Introduction   67
4.2   Why is a Literature Review Necessary?   68

    4.2.1   Avoiding the trivial and adding something new   68
    4.2.2   Using what has gone before – opportunities for
            replicative studies   69
    4.2.3   Developing your ideas   71
    4.2.4   Deduction, induction and the literature review   71

4.3   What is the Literature?   72
4.4   What is a Literature Review?   73
4.5   Sourcing, Searching, Accessing and Organising the Literature   76

    4.5.1   Managing the literature search   76
    4.5.2   Reading, note-taking and organising the literature   80

4.6   Evaluating and Reviewing the Literature   86
4.7   Writing the Literature Review   89

Chapter Summary   92
Chapter References   93

5 DEVELOPING THE CONCEPTUAL FRAMEWORK   94

Chapter Content and Issues   94

5.1   Introduction   94
5.2   The Conceptual Framework   95

    5.2.1   What is it?   95
    5.2.2   Why is it necessary?   96
    5.2.3   Where does it appear in a research study?   96
    5.2.4   What does it do?   96
    5.2.5   What does it have to do with concepts, constructs,
            variables and hypotheses?   97

5.3   Constructs and Concepts   98
5.4   Variables   100

    5.4.1   Dependent and independent variables   103
    5.4.2   Intervening variables   103
    5.4.3   Moderating variables   103
    5.4.4   Expressing relationships between variables   103
    5.4.5   Considering variables from different perspectives   107

5.5   Theories and Models   108

5.6   Hypotheses   109

        5.6.1   Causal and correlational hypotheses   110
        5.6.2   Null and alternate hypotheses   111
        5.6.3   Writing hypotheses   111

5.7   Operationalisation   114

        5.7.1   Identifying concept dimensions   115
        5.7.2   Identifying elements and indicators   116

5.8   Measurement and Scales   117

        5.8.1   The nominal scale   118
        5.8.2   The ordinal scale   118
        5.8.3   The interval scale   119
        5.8.4   The ratio scale   120
        5.8.5   Selecting an appropriate scale   120

5.9   Establishing Good Measures   121

        5.9.1   Determining validity   122
        5.9.2   Determining reliability   123

Chapter Summary   124
Chapter References   125

6 CHOOSING THE EMPIRICAL RESEARCH DESIGN   126

Chapter Content and Issues   126

6.1   Introduction   126
6.2   Choosing the Design   127

        6.2.1   Justifying your decision   129

6.3   Experimental Research   130

        6.3.1   Control and manipulation   130
        6.3.2   Artificiality and validity   131
        6.3.3   The influence and significance of experimental
                design principles   132
        6.3.4   What is the relevance of experimentation to
                hospitality or tourism students?   133

6.4   Survey Research   134

        6.4.1   Surveys and sampling   134
        6.4.2   Communicating with the respondents   135
        6.4.3   Advantages and disadvantages of surveys   136
        6.4.4   Types of survey   136
        6.4.5   Survey implementation   137
        6.4.6   Sources and types of error   138

6.5	Comparative Research	143
	6.5.1 Basic approaches to comparative designs	143
	6.5.2 The importance of equivalence	144
	6.5.3 'Intra' and 'inter' comparisons	145
	6.5.4 Comparison and other research designs	146
6.6	Case Study Research	146
	6.6.1 The importance of context	147
	6.6.2 What constitutes a case?	148
	6.6.3 The unit(s) of analysis	149
	6.6.4 The principle of replication	151
6.7	Observational Research	151
	6.7.1 Ethnography	152
	6.7.2 Visual ethnography	153
	6.7.3 Netnography	153
	6.7.4 Is observational research a good option for you?	156
6.8	Action Research	156
6.9	Mixed-method Designs	158
	6.9.1 Which is best – singular or mixed designs?	158
	6.9.2 Mixed methods vs mixed designs	159
	6.9.3 Mixed designs in the real world	159
	Chapter Summary	160
	Chapter References	161
7	**COLLECTING THE EMPIRICAL DATA**	**163**
	Chapter Content and Issues	163
7.1	Introduction	163
7.2	Questionnaires and Questions	164
	7.2.1 The nature of questionnaires	164
	7.2.2 Designing unstructured/open-ended questionnaires	164
	7.2.3 Designing structured/closed questionnaires	166
	7.2.4 Questionnaires and validity/reliability issues	166
	7.2.5 Mixed-design questionnaires	167
	7.2.6 Choosing the appropriate type of questionnaire	167
	7.2.7 Basic questionnaire design and preparation issues	168
	7.2.8 Writing questions	176
	7.2.9 Questions and measurement scales	179
	7.2.10 Standard and non-standard questions	185
	7.2.11 Questionnaire piloting	186

7.3	Interviewing	187
	7.3.1 Why choose interviewing?	188
	7.3.2 Group interviewing	190
7.4	Observation	192
	7.4.1 Observation – validity and reliability issues	192
	7.4.2 Site selection and access	193
	7.4.3 Observational issues	194
	7.4.4 Recording observational data	195
	7.4.5 Observation and interviewing	196
7.5	Projective Techniques	196
	7.5.1 Why use projective techniques?	197
	7.5.2 Types of projective techniques	197
	Chapter Summary	200
	Chapter References	201

8 SAMPLING — 202

	Chapter Content and Issues	202
8.1	Introduction	202
8.2	What is Sampling and Why is it Important?	203
	8.2.1 Sampling and representativeness	203
	8.2.2 Why sample?	205
	8.2.3 Populations	205
	8.2.4 Sample size	208
	8.2.5 Sample selection and population characteristics	211
	8.2.6 Sampling and response rates	213
	8.2.7 Sampling and confidence intervals	216
	8.2.8 Sampling and reality	217
8.3	Quantitative Data Sampling	218
	8.3.1 Simple random sampling	222
	8.3.2 Systematic random sampling	222
	8.3.3 Stratified random sampling	222
	8.3.4 Cluster sampling	223
8.4	Qualitative Data Sampling	223
	8.4.1 Convenience sampling	225
	8.4.2 Purposive, judgemental or criterion sampling	226
	8.4.3 Snowball and expert-choice sampling	227
	8.4.4 Quota sampling	227
	8.4.5 Theoretical sampling	228
8.5	N = 1 Investigations	228

Chapter Summary   229
Chapter References   229

9 ANALYSING QUANTITATIVE DATA   **232**

Chapter Content and Issues   232

9.1   Introduction   232
9.2   General Issues   233

    9.2.1   Coding the data   233
    9.2.2   Setting up SPSS for data entry   235
    9.2.3   Entering data into SPSS   237
    9.2.4   Checking the data   238
    9.2.5   Selecting cases and/or variables   238

9.3   Descriptive Statistics   240

    9.3.1   Frequency distributions   240
    9.3.2   Measures of central tendency   241
    9.3.3   Data range and dispersion   242
    9.3.4   Uses of descriptive data   244
    9.3.5   Scale reliability   245

9.4   Bivariate Analysis   246

    9.4.1   Cross-tabulation   246
    9.4.2   Scatter graphs and correlation   248
    9.4.3   Statistical significance   250
    9.4.4   Regression analysis   252

9.5   Inferential Statistics   253

    9.5.1   Hypothesis testing   254
    9.5.2   *t*-Tests   256
    9.5.3   The chi-square test   260

9.6   Data Reduction Techniques   261

    9.6.1   Principal components analysis   262

Chapter Summary   265
Chapter References   266

10 ANALYSING QUALITATIVE DATA   **267**

Chapter Content and Issues   267

10.1   Introduction   267
10.2   What Kind of Qualitative Data Do You Have?   268
10.3   Basic Principles and Stages in Qualitative
      Data Analysis   271

10.3.1   Unitising and coding   272
10.3.2   Open coding   273
10.3.3   Axial coding   274

10.4 Qualitative Data Analysis Techniques   275

10.4.1   Content analysis   275
10.4.2   Semiotics   276
10.4.3   Computer-assisted qualitative data
         analysis (CAQDAS)   277

10.5 Displaying Qualitative Data   277
10.6 Justifying Qualitative Data Analysis Choices   278

10.6.1   Triangulation   279

Chapter Summary   280
Chapter References   280

11 WRITING UP THE RESEARCH PROJECT   282

Chapter Content and Issues   282

11.1 Introduction   282
11.2 Style, Presentation and the Reader   282

11.2.1   The nature of academics   283
11.2.2   Credibility   283
11.2.3   Academic style   285

11.3 The Contents   287

11.3.1   The introduction   287
11.3.2   The literature review   287
11.3.3   The methodology chapter   289
11.3.4   The results or findings chapter   289
11.3.5   The conclusions   290

11.4 References in the Text and Bibliography   291

11.4.1   Why reference?   292
11.4.2   How to reference correctly   292
11.4.3   Text citations   293
11.4.4   Bibliographic citations   296

11.5 A Final Check   299

Chapter Summary   302
Chapter References   302

Index   303

LIST OF FIGURES AND TABLES

Figures

1.1	The inductive approach to research	16
1.2	The deductive approach to research	17
5.1	Stating the relationship between variables	104
5.2	The stages of hypothesis development	112
5.3	Operationalising a concept	115
6.1	Alternative design options for case studies	149
8.1	A representative sample	204
8.2	Symmetrical population distribution	211
8.3	Asymmetrical population distribution	212
10.1	Budget airline usage and income levels	278

Tables

1.1	Exploratory, descriptive and explanatory research compared	13
1.2	Pure and applied research compared	15
1.3	What types of research activity do managers engage in?	20
2.1	Key features of positivist and phenomenological paradigms	38
3.1	Different ways that research may make a contribution to the literature	48
9.1	Parametric and non-parametric tests for confirmatory analysis	255
9.2	Summarised one sample *t*-test results	259
10.1	Words associated with hospitality	268
10.2	Words used to describe the physical aspects of hospitality in the hotels	269
10.3	Who is the yield manager in the hotel?	272

ABOUT THE AUTHOR

Dr Bob Brotherton is currently a Visiting Professor in Hospitality Management at the NHTV University of Applied Sciences, Breda, The Netherlands. He was formerly a Reader in Hospitality Management in the UK and has been a visiting professor and/or external examiner at higher education institutions in a number of other countries, including Switzerland, Greece, Cyprus, India, Dubai, Turkey and Spain. He has more than 30 years' experience of teaching hospitality management subjects, and around 25 years' of teaching research methods to hospitality and tourism students, during which time he has also supervised a large number of student dissertations/theses, based on empirical research, at BSc, MSc and PhD levels. As an active researcher he has had numerous books, journal and conference papers published, many of which have been based on the results of empirical research he has conducted.

PREFACE

In coming to write the preface for this second edition of the text it remains clear to me that much of what I wrote for the preface of the first edition remains germane and so I offer no apologies for repeating this here. However, although this second edition does follow the same basic structure and philosophy of the first, it also embodies some significant differences, both in terms of revisions and updating to the original text and new additions to this second version, which I will describe later after the rationale for the original, and this, edition that follows.

This text has been designed specifically for undergraduate students undertaking degree programmes in hospitality and/or tourism, though postgraduate students on these types of programmes may also find this material useful. It has been written to assist students undertaking the type of research project frequently required in the final year of such programmes that is associated with the production of a dissertation or research project report. In terms of its structure and contents, essentially it takes you through the issues and decisions that need to be considered and made to conceive, plan, conduct and write up the type of research project you are likely to be required to complete for such a course, unit or module. In this sense it seeks to take you through each decision and action stage of the research process, from identifying a topic and formulating the research question or aim and objectives to writing up the final document.

In compiling this text I have been acutely aware, as a result of my long experience of teaching undergraduate hospitality and tourism students the type of 'research methods' module frequently included within a programme, of the need to provide students with the methodological issues, tools and techniques necessary for conducting a research project, because students often find it a somewhat alien area compared to much of the other content within these types of programmes. On many occasions I have encountered the view from students that all this 'methodology stuff' and research is not as important as other vocational and/or business management material, for which they can see more immediately the relevance and potential usefulness of studying. Often, research and its associated methodological considerations are seen by students as just a task that has to be done to fulfil the requirements of their degree course and that 'all this research stuff' is just an academic exercise that really has no value in the real world after graduation because it's what academics do while practitioners get on with the important business of managing companies.

Of course, this is true to a certain extent, but it is a fallacy to believe that the knowledge and skills developed in studying and undertaking research will not be of practical use in the real world. The intellectual development this engenders is invaluable in its own right but also, beyond this, the business world is rapidly becoming a more complex and dynamic environment within which conventional knowledge and accepted practices become outdated much more frequently. Indeed, in your future as a hospitality or tourism manager, it is reasonably certain that the fundamental basis of existing business models will be challenged and changed because of new ideas, concepts, products, processes and so on much more rapidly than has been the case in the past. In turn, the rationale for change is likely to be derived from research activity, be it conducted by academic, commercial or company researchers, that seeks to challenge the status quo and develop new knowledge and techniques. Similarly, you may well be a manager who receives research reports and has to evaluate their results to make sound business decisions based on this information or, equally, you may have to commission research from professional research organisations and will need to provide them with a brief and evaluate their proposed methodology before agreeing a contract with them. Whatever the reason, a sound, critical knowledge and understanding of research and its associated methodological considerations will be an increasingly invaluable part of the future hospitality or tourism manager's toolkit.

I hope you enjoy reading this book and find it helpful. In writing it I have tried to take you from your real world of experience to the research methodology jargon by providing vignettes and examples to illustrate that perhaps the language of research and research methodology is not as alien as you may feel when first encountering it. I have also tried to indicate and explain why, when designing and undertaking a research project, various aspects of the research process have to be thought through, why decisions have to made in selecting alternative perspectives, research designs, data collection instruments and analysis techniques and, just as importantly, why these have to be logically supportive of and explained/justified to convince the, perhaps sceptical, recipient of the research that it should be regarded as credible.

This, second, edition I hope builds upon the success of the first that has been well received by the market. It has a number of revised and new features as follows. First, to produce this new text a line-by-line review was conducted of the original to improve the readability and flow of the text; to re-structure it into appropriate sections and sub-sections in order to make the content clearer and more easily identifiable; and to update and extend both the substantive content and chapter references to reflect more recent trends and developments in research topics and methodology relating to hospitality and tourism. These changes, I hope, will make the text of the second edition more user-friendly and relevant to contemporary conditions.

Second, this new edition contains a series of Feature Boxes (see below), the content of some of these having been re-formatted from those presented as 'exhibits' in the original text, whilst others are entirely new to this edition. These boxes appear throughout the text at appropriate points to add additional explanation and examples to the points being covered in the main text focusing on both conceptual and more practical issues and tasks associated with the research process. They are readily identifiable within the text using different and distinctive clipart images for each to indicate the type of box they are. For the use of this clipart my thanks must go to Wolfgang Spraul at Openclipart.org (www.openclipart.org) who kindly agreed to my request to use the images from their website in this way.

The new Feature Boxes in this edition are:

- Key Concepts – These outline and explain key concepts you need to be aware of.
- Technique Tips – These provide guidance, hints and tips for using/applying a range of research techniques.
- Key Decisions – These should help you to focus on the key things you need to decide upon, both conceptual and practical, within the research process.
- Research Reality Scenarios – These are hypothetical vignettes designed to de-mystify some of the aspects of the research process you may find to be rather opaque at first sight. They essentially contain 'short-stories' designed to help you understand issues that are often cloaked in jargon.
- Research in Action – These provide concrete, case study type, examples of the application of principles and techniques derived from real life hospitality/tourism research studies. They illustrate the use/application of methodological principles, concepts, techniques and practices that are covered in the main text associated with each.
- Research Action Checklists – These are probably self-explanatory; they are checklists designed to help you review whether you have covered all the issues or tasks related to a particular aspect of the research process.

Third, this edition is also extended and supported by virtue of a 'companion website', something the first edition did not benefit from. This provides a significant extension to the text itself and is designed to further support your understanding of research methods issues, concepts and practices. Details of the content of this companion website are provided in the section that follows this preface.

I hope that all of this illustrates considerable time, effort and thought has gone into producing this second edition to make it an even more valuable resource for you, the reader. I believe there is considerable added-value embodied within both the revised and extended text of the second edition itself and the new companion website compared to the first edition. This should all help you to comprehend the nature and practice of research more fully and completely, which is the object of the exercise.

Finally, I must once again record my thanks to my wife, Penny, who has endured with her usual cheerful stoicism my preoccupied mind and absence from her life while at the computer keyboard writing for long periods.

My grateful thanks must go to two first-class librarians, Scolah Kazi and Zafar Imam Khan, from The Emirates Academy of Hospitality Management (Dubai), who used the 'dark arts' excellent librarians seem to possess to assist me in obtaining copies of journal articles that were not always readily available from common sources that were then used to help develop the main text and provide examples of various techniques and procedures in practice.

I would also like to extend my thanks to Martine Jonsrud and Gemma Shields, the Editorial Assistants at SAGE, who helped me enormously from the original proposal through to the completion of the final manuscript, to Isabel Drury, the Digital Content Editor, for all her assistance with the development of the companion website; to Katherine Haw, the Senior Production Editor, for making the production process as smooth as possible, and to Chris Rojek, the Commissioning Editor, who was not only a significant influence in commissioning the first edition of the text but who also encouraged me to produce this second edition and helped to secure its passage through the SAGE commissioning process.

Bob Brotherton
September 2014

ABOUT THE COMPANION WEBSITE

The site (**study.sagepub.com/brotherton**) contains the following material for each chapter of the book, much of which is entirely new and was not contained in the text of the first edition at all:

- **Further Reading References** – Although these were included in the original text, an opportunity has been taken to move them to the website and to thoroughly revise, update and extend them, where appropriate.

- **Sage Journal Papers** – The publisher has kindly agreed to make available to you, via this website link, three articles for each chapter that have previously been published in Sage journals. These contain real examples of the application of research principles and practices covered in the chapter concerned to help further illustrate how these have been applied and used in actual studies.

- **Chapter Features** – These are essentially all the figures, tables and feature boxes extracted from the text and made available as PDFs via the website.

- **Video Resources** – This contains links to video material available on the internet that should help you to further develop your understanding of particular principles, concepts, approaches and techniques.

- **Web Links and Online Reading** – This is fairly self-explanatory in that it contains links to material contained on other websites relevant to the content of the chapter concerned. Once again this helps to extend the type and range of material available to you and, in doing so, provides further opportunities for you to strengthen your knowledge of the aspects covered in the main text.

- **Test Questions** – Each chapter has a series of 10 self-test or review questions that you can use to test your understanding of the material covered in a particular chapter.

1

THE NATURE AND RELEVANCE OF RESEARCH

Chapter Content and Issues

The nature of research.
Experience, common sense and theory.
Thinking about research.
The characteristics of scientific research.
Good and bad research.
Pure and applied research.
Theoretical/empirical and primary/secondary research.
Exploratory, descriptive and explanatory research.
Inductive and deductive approaches to research.
Issues that require research solutions.
Some problems that may be encountered.

1.1 Introduction

The purpose of this chapter is to provide you with a clear understanding of what research is and what it is designed to do. To achieve this, we will explore the nature of research in terms of its main purposes, functions and characteristics. We will also examine different types of research and focus on how these might be used to address or solve theoretical or practical problems, as well as the two basic approaches used to design and conduct research. We will also consider the features that characterise research regarded as good or bad and highlight some of the problems and issues that can arise in any research project, regardless of its scope and size. At the end of this process, you should not only have a clearer understanding of these issues but should also feel more confident that undertaking research is perhaps not quite as daunting as you may have believed and developing research skills is not just something you have to do because it is required on your course but that these skills will actually be useful to you when you become a practising manager.

1.2 The Nature of Research

Research is often seen by students on hospitality or tourism courses as a necessary evil to be confronted. This is especially the case when tutors inform students that they will have to undertake an undergraduate research project or dissertation. This type of activity may be viewed as something different, larger and much more challenging than the normal pattern of learning on a programme and, because it is outside the normal experience of attending lectures and seminars, writing relatively short pieces of coursework and/or sitting the examinations that tend to characterise most modules or units on a programme, there may naturally be some apprehension about having to undertake such a venture.

In many respects, hospitality and tourism courses, and the people engaged in them, have strong practical and applied emphases. Indeed, it is perhaps unlikely that you see yourself as a traditional high-flying academic who naturally wishes to engage in theoretical or applied 'research' within a chosen academic field or discipline. That sort of thing may be seen as okay for the physicists, chemists, computer scientists, economists and historians of this world, but you might be asking what relevance does it have to the more practical and pragmatic world of hospitality and tourism? Well, before we go on to consider this question, read the material contained in the Research Reality Scenario box – Do I Need to Be Einstein to Do It? – as this may help to demystify some of the misgivings you may have about doing research.

Research Reality Scenario	**Do I Need to Be Einstein to Do It?**

Sarah has just started her final year as an undergraduate student on a BA (Hons) International Tourism Management course and she also works as a part-time waitress at the Mexican Sunrise restaurant. She is usually very bubbly and enthusiastic in her work and well liked by regular diners at the restaurant. However, Carlos Ramirez, the restaurant manager, has noticed that Sarah has looked worried and preoccupied during her recent shifts and this is beginning to affect how she deals with the customers. So, he asks her if she can come to see him in his office after her current shift finishes.

Carlos said, 'Hi, Sarah, come in and have a seat and don't look so worried – I'm not about to sack you! It's just that I've noticed lately that you don't appear to be quite your effervescent self with the customers and I wondered if there was a problem I could help with.' Relieved, Sarah said, 'Well, you're right, I am a bit worried about something. When I started the final year of my course, the tutors told me that a major part of this year was going to be taken up with the individual research project and this will account for 30 per cent of my final marks and have a major impact on the degree I get. As if that wasn't bad enough, they then scared us out of our wits by saying it would be the real test of how good we are and, because we have never done anything like this before, we had better get on with it quickly because we will have to deal with things like research philosophy, deduction and induction, hypothesis testing, collecting empirical data and probably use inferential statistics to analyse this. My God, it's like another language and I don't think I can cope.'

Carlos smiled, 'Ah, so that's it. I knew there was something up. Okay, Sarah, let's see if we can't put your mind at rest a little over some of these things. When I was in your position I felt the same. I felt like I needed to be Einstein to be able to do it, but I learned that, really, all this research stuff is not as daunting as you think. A lot of it is new jargon that you haven't encountered before and, once you learn the research language a little, it will not be so frightening. Let me give you an example. Remember when you first came to work here, you were a little lost because of the jargon we use in the restaurant until I explained it for you in terms you were already familiar with?' Sarah nodded. 'Well, it's pretty much the same with research,' Carlos said, and continued, 'You know more than you think you do. Do you remember when I asked you to come up with some ideas on how we could improve the service in the restaurant?' Sarah nodded again. 'Well, you did, and some very good ones as well. So how did you do it?'

Sarah replied, 'I'd already had some ideas from what I'd read and studied on the course, from my experience of working here and I went to suss out how a couple of other restaurants operated. Then I thought, well, if we could do X then that might improve Y because I could see the connection between the two. So, if you remember, we set this up as a trial for a couple of weeks to see if it was true.'

'And how did we decide whether it was or not?' Carlos asked. 'We compared the restaurant's performance before the trial with its performance during the trial and then I wrote this up in a report for you, which proved my original thoughts were right,' said Sarah.

'Exactly,' said Carlos. 'So, let me put this into research jargon for you, because this is what you did, you conducted a piece of research! You began by examining existing evidence on how to organise restaurant service, then you used this to formulate some educated guesses, or hypotheses, on likely causes and effects. What we then did, through our trial, was to set up a type of experiment to test your hypotheses to see if they were correct or not. How did we find these out? By analysing the restaurant's performance figures, or data, and then we came to the conclusion that this information indicated the original hypotheses were correct. So, when you wrote up these findings in the report, this gave us the rationale for changing the service system.'

'Wow, when you put it like that, I guess I do know more than I thought I did and maybe it's not going to be such a worry after all. Thanks, Carlos – you've put my mind at rest and I think I'll be okay now. It's really very good of you to take the time and trouble to help me in this way.'

'No problem, Sarah', Carlos said, 'After all, I do have an ulterior motive. If you're happier and more relaxed, you'll be back to your old self at work and the customers will be happier again.'

'Ah,' said Sarah, 'what was it you said about Einstein earlier? I think you are smarter than you let on!'

Hopefully this scenario will have helped to convince you that research is less high-brow and complicated than you may have thought! As an aspiring hospitality or tourism manager, you will know that most of your time as a manager will be spent managing, dealing with real-time, practical issues and problems. Decisions will have to be made within tight timescales, often on the spot, and this implies a more prag-matic approach to solving problems and answering questions. Experience, common sense and quick thinking will be important in this type of environment. There may not be time for an extended investigation, reflective theorising and procedures designed to ensure that the answer arrived at is based on sound and comprehensive facts or data and, therefore, the most valid and reliable one available.

1.2.1   Experience and common sense

That said, however, and notwithstanding the value of timely managerial decision-making, not all managerial decisions can be successfully made on the basis of expe-rience, common sense or quick thinking. One of the problems with these as a basis for determining answers, finding solutions and making decisions is that they are likely to have, at best, a fairly shaky evidence base and tend to be idiosyncratic and inconsistent over time.

Let us just consider this issue for a moment. An individual's experience is unique to that individual and is comprised of all the experiences he or she has encountered and how that person has thought about, reacted to and learnt from those experi-ences. Therefore, one person's experience can never be the same as another's. Even if the people concerned share similar past experiences, the ways in which they perceive them and learn from them will differ. Thus, answers, solutions and decisions based on experience will tend to be idiosyncratic because the underlying evidence base – the individuals' experiences and cognitive abilities – used to generate them varies from one person to another.

Similarly, what is common sense? Common sense is a generally accepted view or belief of what is seen to be a sensible way to act or understand certain questions, issues or events. Such a view or belief may indeed be accurate, but, equally, it may not. The problem is that there is rarely, if ever, an opportunity to prove or validate views based on common sense because it is invariably unclear where the origins of the commonsense view in question lie and any evidence base underlying the view is likely to be fragmented, diffuse and indistinct at best. Hence, when challenged, the person using common sense as the rationale or justification for an answer, solution or decision only has recourse to the, rather mythical, strength of the commonsense belief as evidence to support it. Typically the question 'How do you know that is correct or the right way to do things?' is answered with the statement 'Because it's common sense' – an answer that invites the questioner to agree with the common-sense belief of the proponent. What happens, though, if the questioner does not accept this? Can there be a logical discussion, with reference to data that could sup-port or refute the claim, to establish which view is correct? No, of course not. The very nature of a belief is just that – it is something people believe for some reason, but is not something that necessarily can be proved one way or the other. I may believe in God, you may not, but there is no way that we could find irrefutable or incontestable evidence to support either view.

So, although not without value, answers and solutions based on experience or common sense alone may have inherent flaws and lead to inconsistent, if not conflicting, policies and practices if they are the sole basis for managerial decision-making. In addition, where questions arise that cannot be answered by reference to prevailing common sense or accumulated experience, perhaps because they are entirely new or much more complex, we have to resort to other techniques and methods. Among these is research.

1.2.2 Thinking about research

As a practising hospitality or tourism manager, you will have to engage in various aspects of research then – because the questions and problems facing the contemporary manager are increasingly becoming ones that are new and complex and cannot be answered or solved by using experience or common sense alone – but you do actually undertake research in your daily life now. Consider the following issues for a moment: you want to go on holiday, you want to buy a car, you want to find a suitable venue for your twenty-first birthday party, you want to get the best return you can on your savings. How do you decide where to go on holiday, which car to buy, where to hold your party and which form of investment will give you the best return? In a word, research. All of these issues have alternative answers or solutions and you need to find and select the one that fits your needs or criteria the best. How would you do that? Simply by collecting information to identify the options associated with each, then by analysing the information and selecting the best option. In short, you would research the issue in order to identify the most suitable solution.

Many textbooks refer to, or define, research in terms of it being an activity that creates or generates new knowledge or as something that produces a contribution to the existing body of knowledge. The types of words that are commonly used in definitions of what research is include 'discovery', 'investigation', 'new facts', 'advancement of knowledge', 'original insights' – all of which seem to suggest that undertaking research is likely to be a rather daunting task and create the impression that all research is something very difficult, complicated and requires a high level of intellectual ability on the part of the researcher. However, as we have seen above, in the example of undertaking some research to choose a holiday, a car, a party venue and so on, even these simple 'research projects' will involve investigation, discovery and, at least for you as the researcher, the generation of new insights and knowledge. Therefore, it is perhaps preferable to think about research in contextual terms such as these. Indeed, the type of research you will be expected to undertake for an undergraduate project or dissertation, or even a Masters thesis, will be relatively limited in scope and expectations.

By now I hope you are convinced that research is not as difficult as you may have imagined. Of course it has its challenges, but, as indicated earlier, you already do research in your everyday life and the type of research you will be required to do as an undergraduate, or even as a Masters, student is not of the kind necessary to win a Nobel prize. Just in case you are still in doubt, let us consider a couple of views from the literature. Sekaran (2013: 4) suggests that research is, 'an organised, systematic, data-based scientific enquiry or investigation into a specific problem which is undertaken with the objective of finding solutions or answers to it'. By contrast, Wilson (1997: vi) takes the view that 'research is a process of "principled compromise", informed by professional knowledge of the techniques and limitations of research methods, driven by personal energy, and presented with whatever honesty and objectivity that can be mustered'.

Sekaran's view of the nature of research is one that we might refer to as conventional. Although it would be difficult to argue against the value of having a process that had a clear focus and purpose, that was organised and systematic, and based on data capable of being verified or challenged, Sekaran's definition implies that this process is linear in nature and one that can be conducted objectively by using the 'scientific method' to eliminate the influence of subjective values and bias. Wilson's view challenges much of this. His more alternative or, arguably, realistic stance contends that research is inherently subject to personal influence and bias and the idea that a 'method', scientific or otherwise, can somehow create an objective, bias-free process is an illusion. Put simply, because the tools and techniques used to implement the method are chosen by the researcher, and it is the researcher who decides how the results are to be presented, it is inevitable that personal preferences and biases will influence the whole process.

So, who is correct? Is research always objective and value-free or is it subjective and value-ridden? The answer is that, in reality, it tends to lie somewhere on a continuum between these two extremes. Perhaps one way to think about the significance of this is to consider, as some, but not all, researchers do, the objective, value-free view as 'ideal'. Unfortunately, as is the case with most ideals, it is unlikely to be achieved. In that case, you might ask, why bother? The answer to this is that, although you may not be able to achieve what is regarded as the ideal by some, the closer you can get to this the better it will be. This leads us to consider the notions of what constitutes acceptable or 'good' and unacceptable or 'bad' research.

 In this respect you may find it helpful to visit the Video Links Section of the Companion Website (study.sagepub.com/brotherton) to view the 'Battling Bad Science' video via the link provided there.

1.3 The Characteristics of Scientific Research

Logically, good research should reflect the characteristics of the 'ideal' and bad research the opposite. The 'ideal' is variously called scientific enquiry, scientific research or the scientific method and is regarded as having nine general characteristics to distinguish it from other forms of research. Although these are traditionally associated with a positivist philosophy and approach to research (see Chapter 2), interpretivists would also subscribe to the majority of these characteristics, albeit with a slightly different terminology. As we will see, each of these, both individually and collectively, is quite sensible and, if embodied in a piece of research, tends to make it more believable or credible. Whether or not they can all be achieved, however, is another matter, as we have discussed above!

1.3.1 Purposeful

Any research project should have a clear focus that is achievable, as the research process itself is a means to an end. For example, it is a way to obtain answers to a question or solutions to a problem. To make this clear, an overall aim and associated objectives should be specified before the research begins. The aim defines what the overall purpose and output of the proposed research are and the objectives indicate what has to be completed if the aim is to be successfully achieved. For example, the aim of the research might be 'To determine the critical success factors (CSFs) for UK budget hotel operations'. To achieve this overall result, a number of tasks or stages will have to be completed. These will be the research objectives and, in this case, might be expressed as follows.

1. To conduct a literature review to identify the nature of CSFs, both in general and in relation to the budget hotel operations context of the project.

2. To develop a theoretical framework/conceptual model of the CSFs from the literature review and produce associated hypotheses.

3. To collect empirical data from budget hotel companies and other appropriate organisations and/or individuals associated with the project's context.

4. To analyse the empirical data and test the study's hypotheses.

5. To produce conclusions and recommendations for further research.

If these objectives are achieved successfully, then, collectively, they should enable the overall aim to be achieved.

1.3.2 Rigorous

This characteristic is concerned with the quality of the design and how the research is conducted. Essentially, if a piece of research has been conducted in a rigorous manner, it is more likely that it will be seen as credible and the results believed and accepted than would otherwise be the case. To produce a piece of research that is regarded as rigorous requires sound and logically consistent thinking to produce an appropriate overall design (methodology) and the adoption/use of appropriate tools and techniques (methods). A rigorous piece of research will have a sound underlying conceptual basis and will have been conducted in a manner that is both transparent and defensible.

1.3.3   Testable

Testability is concerned with the nature of the question being researched. For the research to be able to answer the question it is designed to address, the question must be answerable. This means that the question, or a hypothesis derived from it, must be written or phrased in a form that will enable it to be tested or proved. Essentially, this means phrasing the issue clearly in either positive or negative terms so that it can be determined whether the proposition can be supported by the evidence or not. Using our example from above, we might produce a series of such propositions or hypotheses relating to the factors that could be critical for a budget hotel's operations to be successful. Having reviewed the literature on this topic, we are likely to have identified a range of factors that it is suggested may be very important or critical for such success. What we would then need to do is test the assertions by collecting evidence to see if it supports them or not.

However, to be able to conduct such tests, we need statements that are testable. For example, one factor that could be regarded as critical for this type of hospitality operation is the cleanliness of the guest bedrooms. So, we might speculate, or hypothesise, that the higher the levels of cleanliness, the more successful the budget hotel would be. Alternatively, we might state that our survey respondents – budget hotel general managers – would indicate guest bedroom cleanliness to be extremely important for the success of the hotel. As we will see in Chapter 5, there are varying forms of hypothesis statements that are capable of being tested and so we may not always want to express them in the form we have used here.

1.3.4   Replicable

If the design and procedures used to undertake a piece of research are transparent and available in the public domain for others to see, then other researchers will be able to replicate or repeat that research to test the rigour of its processes and the accuracy of its findings. This is the same idea as one researcher repeating the same experiment a number of times to see if the same results are obtained. If the results from this process are the same, or at least sufficiently similar, then people are likely to have confidence that they are accurate. I am not suggesting here that you will have the time or resources to repeatedly test your research findings, but you may wish to test previous research findings within a different context as the basis for your project. For example, in previous studies on your topic/research question, other researchers may have designed and used particular data collection/analysis instruments, procedures and techniques, but in a different context. Their studies may have been conducted in other countries to the one you are using in your project and so you may be interested in whether or not these could also be applicable to your country or they may have been undertaken a long time ago and need updating because conditions have changed. Alternatively, these might have been conducted within the context of an industry other than hospitality or tourism and you will then want to test if these would also be applicable to your industry.

Whatever the context, the key issues here are those of comprehensiveness and transparency. For you to be able to replicate someone else's study or for someone else to repeat yours, the process used must be recorded in detail. So, the assumptions made, the hypotheses tested and the data collection and analysis procedures and techniques used must be reported comprehensively and transparently to enable others to test the validity of the findings by repeating the work.

1.3.5 Precision

Because of the scale, scope and complexity of most real-world situations, we are often forced to restrict our research to a sub-set or sample of the full population. Where this is the case, we face an issue concerning the extent to which the findings we obtain from our sample are a true reflection of the population as a whole. If the two are the same, then we can say that they are very precise or accurate. As we may want to generalise the findings from our sample to apply to the larger population, the more precise the findings are, the more we will be able to do this successfully.

There are many issues associated with this, particularly those concerned with sample design/selection, that will be dealt with later in this book (see Chapter 8), but just consider the following example, which is likely to be familiar to you, as an illustration of why precision is important. In all countries there are commercial companies that conduct 'polls' or surveys on behalf of clients. For example, Gallup and Mori are well-known names in the UK. These companies conduct, among others, political polls designed to estimate such things as voting intentions, the popularity of political parties or even specific politicians. So, for example, when an election is due, polls will be conducted to try to predict which political party is going to win. As the UK probably has a voting population of around 40 million people, it would clearly be impossible to ask every voter which party he or she intended to vote for. Therefore, the poll has to be conducted on a much smaller number than this. This may be as low as 2,000 or 3,000 people, which is clearly a very small percentage of the whole voting population. The results from this sample will then be used to predict the overall election results based on millions of voters' behaviour. As you can see, if the results obtained from the sample polled are not precise, then the prediction of the election result is likely to be wildly inaccurate.

1.3.6 Confidence

This is related to precision and is concerned with the likelihood, or probability, that the findings from the sample are correct or, put another way, how confident we can be about the accuracy of the research findings. If we can be 100 per cent confident, then, effectively, we can say that we are certain the same result will be obtained all the time. However, we can never be certain because there is always some potential for error in research work. So, what level of confidence is acceptable?

The general convention is that a 95 per cent level of confidence is the minimum acceptable. This means that the probability of the findings being incorrect is only

5 per cent and, conversely, 9½ times out of every 10 they will be correct. If we can demonstrate that our findings have such a high level of probability of being correct, they are going to appear to be robust and other people will have confidence in them. The importance of this is that we cannot simply expect other people to believe, or have confidence in, our results without presenting some proof to justify our claims in this respect.

1.3.7   Objective

As we have seen earlier, this characteristic is one that has received criticism in terms of whether or not it is really possible for any individual to be truly objective and value-free when designing and conducting research. Whichever stance you accept, the principle here is that the greater the objectivity in the research, the less subjective bias it will have. So, there is an inverse relationship between objectivity and subjectivity – that is, as one increases, the other declines. If the 'ideal' is total objectivity, then the closer you can get to that the better it is.

We probably cannot be perfect, but we can try to get as close to being so as possible. Given that we would probably accept it is not possible to eliminate all our subjective impulses, we should be aware that we are likely to bring these into play and constantly challenge ourselves to either not do this or limit it as much as we can. In addition to this, we should be aware of where our subjectivity has influenced the research and be prepared to recognise this and the impact it may have had.

1.3.8   Generalisable

It is self-evident that all research is undertaken within a particular context or situation, but this does not mean that the findings from this research will be applicable to other contexts or situations that are related or unrelated to the original context in which the research was conducted. However, it would increase the value of the research if it were to be generally applicable rather than relevant only to that one context. Therefore, the ability to generalise from the results of a research project to other contexts is clearly desirable. Thus, the ability to generalise research results widely increases their value.

The problem with this is that, to maximise the generalisability of the research results, considerable thought, time, effort and, often, money, would have to be devoted to the research design and procedures. In the type of research that you are likely to be conducting, this may not be possible for obvious reasons, in which case you may have to accept that the ability to generalise from your findings may be limited at best. The most important issue here is not to over-claim the generalisability of your findings. If the results from your study are clearly limited to a particular company, industry sector, country, culture or time period, then it is important to state this when you write up the findings. Of course you may speculate that the findings could be applicable to a wider context, but you should make it clear that it is precisely this, a speculation, and not a strong or definitive claim to generalisability.

You may encounter this generalisability issue from two possible directions. First, the one described above, where you examine the extent to which your research findings may be capable of being generalised to other contexts. Second, your research may be designed to test the extent to which previous research findings can be generalised to the context in which you are conducting your research. For example, you may take an existing theory or set of research findings that have been derived from other contexts and seek to test the extent to which they are applicable to the hospitality or tourism context you have chosen for your study. This is generally known as a 'replication' study, where you repeat or replicate the original, but in a different context. In principle, this procedure is analogous to repeating an experiment under different conditions to test how robust the original findings are when the original conditions are altered. In short, how generalisable the results may be.

1.3.9 Parsimonious

This characteristic is essentially concerned with simplicity. Any issue being researched is likely to be one that could be influenced by a wide range of factors, but not all of these possible influences will be equally strong or important to the overall answer. For example, you may ask the question 'What determines the level of customer satisfaction in this type of hotel, restaurant, destination, theme park?' When you think about this, it is clear there will be quite a number of factors that could have some influence on the level of customer satisfaction. These might be related to the nature of the product, the abilities and attitudes of staff, accessibility of the premises, price charged, quality of the experience and so on, but they are unlikely to have an equal influence. The question is, which have the largest influence on satisfaction?

Research designed to look for a parsimonious answer would seek to answer this question as well, not just the wider one. Not only would a parsimonious approach to designing the research help to make it more economical and manageable but it would also mean that the results would be likely to have greater practical value. To illustrate this, think of yourself as a manager who has commissioned some research to answer the broader customer satisfaction question above. If the researchers came back to you and said 'There are 15 factors that our research indicates have an influence', how useful would this be? On the other hand, if they came back to you and said 'Our findings show that, of the 15 factors we have identified as ones influencing satisfaction, the results clearly show that, of these, there are two that have a much greater influence than all the others', then it would be much more useful for you to concentrate your resources and efforts on improving those, knowing that, if you did, the chances of achieving an improvement in customer satisfaction and a return on this investment would be pretty good.

To explore further and think about the efficacy of the traditional view of the scientific method and these characteristics, go to the Video Links section of the Companion Website (study.sagepub.com/brotherton) and view the 'Monty Python' and 'The Scientific Method Is Crap' videos via the links provided.

1.4 Types of Research

Research is research, isn't it? Well, yes and no! Research may be regarded as sound and good or flawed and bad. It may be viewed as scientific or unscientific. It may be theoretical or more practical in nature. It can be conducted in laboratories or in real-life situations. It may take place at one point in time or over a period of time. It might be limited to one country or could possibly embrace a number of different countries. It may be designed to test existing knowledge to establish how valid it is or to establish entirely new knowledge. It may be concerned with collecting and analysing quantitative or qualitative data. It could be designed to explore, describe or explain the phenomena in question.

So, where do we start? In the first instance, it may be useful to distinguish between what may be referred to as different types of research purpose compared to judgements regarding the quality of research. Descriptors such as 'good' or 'bad' clearly refer to the quality of a piece of research and are, at least in some respects, subjective, although criteria may be employed to distinguish between research that is regarded as good or bad. For example, research regarded as scientific is more likely to be seen as good research than that which is unscientific. The reason for this is that scientific research will embody the characteristics of scientific research discussed in the previous section of this chapter that, as we saw, are desirable features of any piece of research for a number of reasons.

1.4.1 Exploratory, descriptive and explanatory research

In terms of differing purposes, exploratory research is really self-evident. Where, perhaps, the situation is very new, has been previously inaccessible for some reason or the research problem is too large and complex to address without some initial, exploratory work, an attempt to generate some initial insights and understanding would be of value. In this sense, a piece of exploratory research designed to surface the key issues and questions may be appropriate as it would help to make the situation clearer and, possibly, set the research agenda. Descriptive research will be designed to establish a factual picture of the issue under investigation, whereas explanatory research will be concerned with explaining the why and how of the situation (see Table 1.1 for a comparison of the purposes of the three types of research).

Explanatory research frequently includes descriptive elements but goes beyond this to identify and explore the causes lying behind the effects and the nature of the relationships between the two. Taking our earlier example of the factors that might influence customer satisfaction, a descriptive study would only identify these factors and perhaps speculate about their relationship to satisfaction. In contrast, an explanatory study would seek to differentiate between, and measure, the relative influence of the factors and explain the cause and effect relationship between them. In this sense, the explanatory study clearly has more applied value than the descriptive one.

TABLE 1.1 Exploratory, descriptive and explanatory research compared

Exploratory research	Descriptive research	Explanatory research
Provide first descriptions of the key facts and actors involved in a situation or phenomenon	Accurately and systematically describe a situation, phenomenon or problem	Verify the predictive ability of a principle or theory
Produce an empirically based picture of what is happening	Develop descriptive inferences regarding relationships, processes and mechanisms	Test existing theories and empirical findings to develop better explanations
Collect a large amount of relatively unstructured information to develop a range of ideas to help build tentative propositions	Providing a 'picture' of the what, who, when and where to create a context for further investigation	Specify and explain why and how the mechanism of an underlying process works
Investigate the feasibility of conducting further research into the issues	Identify possible associations and/or correlations	Synthesise differing topics/ issues and/or theoretical perspectives into a more unified structure
Identify the key focus for issues and begin to develop more refined research questions for further enquiry.	Record and document the effects of changes, interventions etc.	Test, develop and refine an existing theory so that it becomes a more complete and useful explanation
Explore the possibilities for new research directions and techniques	Synthesise raw data by classification and categorisation	Enhance the value of an existing theory by applying it to develop a better understanding of a new context or problem
Provide empirical data as a basis for the development of theoretical propositions	Identify linkages in terms of sequences, chains, steps etc.	Generate stronger, more complete, empirical evidence to support or refute an existing theoretical explanation

However, you should not necessarily be led by this to conclude that you should aim to produce an explanatory study rather than a descriptive one. Other things being equal, it would be preferable, but, depending on the existing state of knowledge on the subject, it may be that a good descriptive study is what is required at a particular point in time. For example, although today scientists and doctors are able to prove and explain the relationships and mechanisms between such things as smoking (cause) and lung cancers (effects), it was not the case many years ago. Without earlier, more descriptive, studies that found correlations (non cause-and-effect relationships) between these two things, it is possible that the more detailed, explanatory work would not have taken place.

1.4.2   Pure and applied research

You will also find that the research methods literature will almost universally distinguish between pure, or basic, and applied research as two types of research with very different purposes (see Table 1.2). Pure research, sometimes called 'blue sky thinking', is an activity that has no immediate utility or application to real-life problems. It is designed to contribute new thinking or knowledge to an existing field of enquiry in its own right, without having any other specific purpose. Its role is to expand and/ or improve the body of knowledge, in its broadest sense, within the field concerned. Therefore, it is not utilitarian in nature, although it is quite possible that such intellectual advancements may be translated into more practical circumstances in the future. Pure research is invariably conceptual or theoretical in nature and concerned with intellectual reflection, discovery and invention. It is driven by intellectual interest and curiosity rather than a need to address a particular real-world problem.

Applied research, on the other hand, as the name suggests, is a more practical and focused type of research. It is generally concerned with practical problem-solving and finding solutions to real-world problems. In this sense, it is much more focused and goal-directed than pure research and, therefore, more utilitarian. It has a clear use value and concentrates on the explanation, action and implementation of solutions. This is likely to be the type of research you will be more interested in as it has more immediate relevance to the type of applied course you are engaged on and the challenges you will face as a hospitality or tourism manager.

1.4.3   Theoretical/empirical and primary/secondary research

Similar, but not quite the same, to the distinction between pure and applied research is that between theoretical and empirical and primary and secondary research. The distinction between the latter pairing is one based on the type of data or information to be used in the research project. Secondary research relies on data that already exist – in short, that contained in the literature relating to the issue in question – whereas primary research involves the collection of new data. Another way to think about this distinction is to consider something that is obtained first hand (new) as compared to that which is obtained second hand (old). Although virtually all the research that collects and analyses primary data will also use the same basic procedures for secondary data, secondary research is limited to the use of secondary data alone. Though there is a close connection between these two types and theoretical and empirical research, the two pairings are not necessarily synonymous.

Often, theoretical research is viewed as secondary research in nature and practice and, in the main, this is probably a reasonable view as it tends to take an abstract, conceptual and reflective stance in relation to the existing body of knowledge. Its role is to improve and extend the conceptual and, ultimately, concrete understanding of the issue. This invariably means that existing, secondary knowledge is questioned, tested, re-evaluated and revised. Nevertheless, theoretical research can be conducted by means of the collection and use of primary data and, hence, will be empirical in

TABLE 1.2 Pure and applied research compared

Pure research	Applied research
The pursuit of knowledge is undertaken for its own sake and its value is assessed by academic peers	Research is regarded as 'utilitarian', having a practical use value, and is undertaken in response to a specific problem or issue arising in the real world, being judged on its ability to provide satisfactory solutions
The researcher has, in theory, total freedom to select problems and subjects to research	The selection of research problems and questions is more focused on the problems and concerns of practitioners
The quality of the research is measured by the standards of scholarship and the requirements of academic rigour	Research can be 'quick and dirty' or may accord with accepted scientific standards. Concern may be more focused on the practical rather then the 'academic' value of the work
The key focus lies with the 'credibility' of the research design and the rigour of its implementation	The key focus lies in the extent of the generalisability of the findings to explain and provide solutions for real-world problems
The primary objective is to make a contribution to basic, theoretical knowledge	The primary objective is to generate results that have a practical application and value
Success is measured by the acceptance and significance of the outcomes to peers in the same scientific community	Success is measured by the 'use value' of the outcomes in the real world in that they facilitate greater understanding and enable more effective solutions to be devised

nature. Let us return to the smoking and lung cancer example we used above to illustrate this. By collecting empirical data on the connection between people who smoked and the incidence of lung cancer, researchers began to analyse this data and develop theories to explain the relationship between the cause and the effect, so these theoretical developments were stimulated by the collection of new primary data, at least in the first instance.

Therefore, theoretical research may be conducted by using secondary or primary data. It is not the type of data that is critical here but the purpose of the research – whether it is conceptual or theoretical understanding. On the other hand, empirical and primary research are synonymous in the sense that the former always involves the collection of the latter kind of data, though, as we have seen, such data may be used for theoretical or applied research purposes.

One thing that should be clear from the above discussion is that it is not always easy to decisively separate these so-called different types of research into totally discrete categories. Indeed, most research is likely to involve secondary and primary data, both theoretical and empirical considerations, and to contain descriptive and explanatory elements. The question is not if a piece of research is definitively one or the other, but what its main emphasis and purpose is. This leads us to consider what are often termed the two main approaches to research – induction and deduction.

1.5   The Main Research Approaches

1.5.1   Induction

This is an approach that essentially works by going from the unknown to the known. As Figure 1.1 illustrates, the starting point for an inductive approach to conducting research is the identification of the problem or question to be addressed. In this respect it is synonymous with the deductive approach, but that is where the similarities end, as will become evident as we proceed to examine the two approaches. As the main purpose of induction is to build new theory, rather than test existing theory, its main empirical focus is on collecting data from the real world as a resource to be used in developing explanations or theory. Thus, the collection of empirical data occurs much earlier in the inductive approach than in the deductive approach and its role is different from that found in deduction. The inductive approach is generally regarded as one that favours the use of 'ideographic' methodologies, which we will explore further in Chapters 6 and 7, such as case studies or 'in the field' enquiries – that is, participant or non-participant observation (Gill and Johnson, 2010; Robson, 2011) – because it is rooted in a philosophical view of the world that emphasises social construction, perceptions, meanings and subjectivity as important in understanding and the development of knowledge. As we shall see, this is known as phenomenology or, sometimes, interpretivism or constructivism and, in Chapter 2, this is discussed in more detail.

Having collected the empirical data, the inductive researcher then has to make sense of it by analysing it for patterns, connections, relationships and so on in order to interpret its significance and produce meaningful explanations or theories. Ultimately, although these may be tested by other researchers using a deductive process, that is not the purpose of inductive research. As the philosophical beliefs and types of methods used by the inductive researcher are likely to value

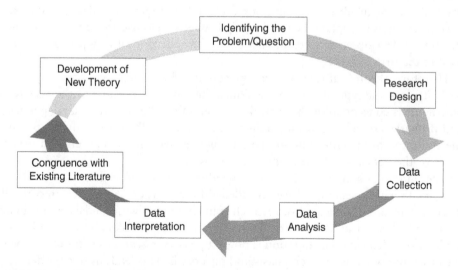

FIGURE 1.1   The inductive approach to research

rich, narrative, descriptive information far more highly than statistical data, inductive research invariably involves the collection of qualitative rather than quantitative data. In this sense, inductive research is frequently seen as synonymous with qualitative research and, as we shall see below, the reverse is true of the deductive approach.

However, some caution should be adopted in uncritically accepting this deceptively simple distinction. Inductive research could be conducted by means of the collection of quantitative data and deductive research by collecting qualitative data. Indeed, many research projects, adopting one or the other approach, are designed to collect both types of data. Inductive research may collect basic numerical data to facilitate the description or indicate the scope and boundaries of the situation being studied. For example, in a case study of a company, the research findings may well include data relating to its size (turnover, capital employed, number of employees or operating units and so on) and perhaps the volume of its operations (output, sales and so on). Similarly, a deductive study designed to discover the volume of a market and understand the preferences of different types of consumers in that market would probably collect quantitative data relating to the size of the market – that is, the number of consumers and qualitative data to explain why they buy certain items and not others.

One question we have not addressed yet is when would it be more appropriate to use an inductive rather than deductive approach to conduct research? Apart from the influence of the researcher's fundamental beliefs regarding the nature of the real world and knowledge, the use of induction would generally be more appropriate when the topic is so new or unique that the existing body of knowledge on it is non-existent or very limited or when it has not previously been possible to gain access to the real-world contexts in question to collect the data. In short, when, for a variety of possible reasons, there is not a sufficient body of knowledge in the literature to sensibly adopt a deductive approach.

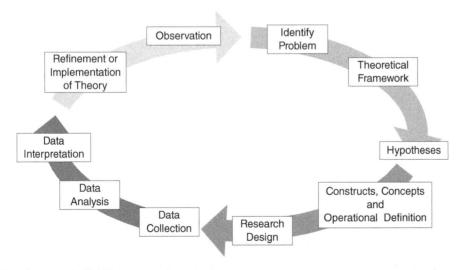

FIGURE 1.2 The deductive approach to research

1.5.2 Deduction

This is the approach to research adopted by archetypal scientists who believe that the world and knowledge are factual and objective. This is based on a set of beliefs known as positivism and we shall explore these beliefs and their implications further in Chapter 2, but as Figure 1.2 shows, this approach takes the existing body of theoretical and empirical knowledge as its primary starting point. It is embodied in the literature existing on the issues being researched and is accessed by conducting a review of this literature (see Chapter 4) to determine the theory, or theories, that will be tested in the research. So, deduction is concerned with testing existing theory, whereas, as we have seen, induction seeks to create new theory.

Once the literature has been reviewed, the deductive researcher will be in a position to develop the theoretical framework that informs and helps to structure and guide the remainder of the research process. We shall consider this in more detail in Chapter 5, but it should indicate to you that the deductive approach is generally more highly structured, focused and constrained, in terms of how the data collection and analysis procedures are designed and implemented, than is the inductive approach. This is highlighted even more when you consider that what the deductive research process will test are the logical consequences of the theory, the hypotheses. As these will be highly specific and relatively limited in number, they focus the design of the data collection procedures and instruments to ensure that only the data required to test them are collected. At the end of the process, once the data have been analysed, the theory tested during this process will either be supported, or confirmed, by the evidence or it may require modification in the light of the evidence or, in extreme cases, it may need to be replaced by an entirely new theory.

1.6 Research Issues, Questions and Problems

We shall consider, in more detail, many of the considerations relating to choosing a research topic and formulating the question(s) or problem(s) to be addressed in the research project in Chapter 3, but here it is worthwhile to briefly reflect on the types of issues and questions that practising hospitality or tourism managers may wish to grapple with or answer and speculate on how they might use research principles and methods to achieve this. Consider the following questions, which are probably the fairly typical issues such managers would be interested in.

- How can we increase the level of satisfaction among the guests who stay in our hotel?
- What would be the best types of location for our new, branded restaurant outlets?
- How can we reduce the level of staff turnover?
- Which advertising media and methods would give us the greatest return for our expenditure?

- What do we have to do in order to attract more visitors to this part of the country?

- Why have fewer people visited our theme park this year than in previous years?

These all represent common practical issues and problems faced by hospitality or tourism businesses. At the same time, however, they all suggest a relationship between at least two things – a cause and an effect. Often, but not always, we know what the effect is, but the cause of it may be far more uncertain. In the questions above, we know that the levels of customer satisfaction are not as high as we would like them to be, the level of staff turnover is too high, some locations are likely to be preferable to others for our restaurant operations, visitor numbers are not as high as we would like or have declined for some reason and certain types of advertising media/methods are likely to be more efficient for our purposes than others, but which ones?

So, we know what the problem is, but not how to solve it. We know what we would like to achieve, but not how to get there. This is the case because our knowledge and understanding are not sufficient to enable us to close the gap. To remedy this, we need to increase our knowledge and understanding to help find the solution. The question then is, how do we do that? We could attempt to simply guess why the effects have occurred. We could commission or employ others – consultants and so on – to investigate the problem for us or undertake some type of more systematic investigation or analysis of the problem ourselves.

Of course, which route is chosen is likely to be influenced by the amount of time, expertise and resources at our disposal. If we had little time and lacked the necessary expertise, but had the resources, we might consider commissioning an outside agency, such as a consultancy company or specialist research organisation, to do the research for us. Although this undoubtedly would produce some answers and solutions, it may be very expensive and not as timely as we might wish for. Buying in external expertise has its value, but, often, we need answers more quickly than they can provide them and may want to develop our own, in-house, knowledge base and expertise for the future. To do this, we need to develop our own research skills. In addition, even if we were to commission an external agency to undertake the research for us, we would want to have an understanding of the principles, techniques and procedures likely to be adopted by such people because we would have to give them a brief in the first instance and to then be capable of critically interpreting their methods and findings. So, either way, this type of knowledge is useful to a practising manager.

To give you some indication of the areas of hospitality and tourism businesses where research is being undertaken by managers in such companies, consultancy organisations and public-sector bodies, I conducted a piece of small-scale, exploratory research when preparing the first edition of this text. This essentially constituted the design and implementation of a survey, using a mailed questionnaire to a sample of 845 members of a UK professional body, the Tourism Society. The questionnaire listed a range of possible areas where research might have been taking place and asked the respondents to indicate if they were involved in any of these.

The overall response to this was a little disappointing, with only 45 questionnaires returned, a response rate of 5.4 per cent, but it illustrates one of the issues discussed earlier. Being dependent on the goodwill of the potential respondents, when they are very busy people and there is nothing of obvious benefit to them in filling in such a questionnaire, can often produce low response rates, over which we have little or no control. The obvious problem this raises here is the validity of the results. Put simply, how can we be sure that the 95 per cent who didn't respond would have made similar choices to those of the 5 per cent who did? The answer is, of course, that we cannot, so the results need to be viewed with some degree of caution in terms of whether or not they are representative of the types of research activity being undertaken across the hospitality and tourism industries as a whole. In addition to this, the composition of the 45 respondents included very few managers from private hospitality or tourism companies. Most of the people who responded were from public sector bodies, consultancy companies and trade associations. Therefore, there is a potential problem of bias in the pattern of the results.

TABLE 1.3   What types of research activity do managers engage in?

Area of research activity	Percentage involved
New product/service development	44
Market research	55
Competitor intelligence	26
Site/location feasibility	35
New equipment evaluation	4
Recipe/dish development	2
Menu development	4
Pilot/test studies	17
Employee surveys	26
Customer surveys	42
Raw material/supply sourcing	4
Advertising effectiveness	37
Service quality measurement	33
Benchmarking	44
Environmental scanning	4
Energy management	4
Investment analysis/appraisal	17
IT systems/applications	20
Ecommerce	13
Business process re-engineering	9
Facilities design	9
Other areas:	
economic impacts of tourism	4

Area of research activity	Percentage involved
sales force management	2
revenue planning and management	2
distribution and channel management	2
training assessment	2
tourism master planning	2
tourism sector reviews	2
destination branding	2
visitor management plans	2
customer/marketing studies	2
cultural and heritage tourism	2
consumer choice criteria	2
accommodation quality standards	2
brand research	2
skills audits	2

These issues demonstrate that even a small-scale, simple piece of research can have similar problems to those endeavours that are much larger in scale. The point here is not the existence of the problems *per se*, but how they are recognised and dealt with. Any research you undertake may suffer from similar problems, but this is not necessarily disastrous. As we shall see in Chapter 11, it is what you claim and don't claim in relation to your results that is important. If you produce conclusions and make claims that are not supported by the evidence within your research, then you will be heavily criticised.

Table 1.3 shows that the areas or topics of greatest research activity for the respondents are market research, new product/service development, benchmarking and customer surveys, followed by advertising effectiveness, site location/feasibility and service quality measurement. Bearing in mind the reservations expressed above, and perhaps not unsurprisingly, it would seem that there is a general emphasis on those aspects of hospitality and tourism business directly concerned with markets, customers, competitors and the product/service. These are all areas that tend to be complex, difficult to control and can be problematic to understand and predict, while, at the same time, being critical to success or failure. They are also areas where change can be rapid and innovation may be crucial to succeed. Indeed, if the 'other' areas indicated by the respondents were added to these, this view would be further reinforced as many of them are also concerned with markets, customers and competitors. These are also areas where it is often difficult to be as sure as possible of the relationships between causes and effects. Given that these environments are complex and dynamic, it is invariably problematic to isolate one or even a few factors that are the main causes of the effect/s and, hence, knowledge and understanding of them tends to be less than perfect.

Finally, the Web Links section of the Companion Website (study.sagepub.com/brotherton) has a series of links to further material relating to this chapter that may prove useful in helping you to think about the issues discussed in this chapter.

Chapter Summary

Research is a purposeful activity designed, planned and undertaken to investigate and discover answers to questions and solutions to problems.

It can be exploratory, descriptive or explanatory in purpose and theoretical or applied in emphasis.

It can help to develop our conceptual and practical knowledge and make us better practitioners.

There are two basic approaches that can be adopted to inform the design of research and how it is conducted – induction and deduction.

To design and undertake research that will produce credible results, there are a number of issues to be considered – the characteristics of scientific research.

Although research can be carefully designed, planned and executed, there are invariably elements that we cannot predict or control and, therefore, despite our best intentions, successful outcomes do have an element of luck.

References

Gill, J. and Johnson, P. (2010) *Research Methods for Managers*, 4th edition. London: Paul Chapman.

Robson, C. (2011) *Real World Research*, 3rd edition. Chichester: John Wiley.

Sekaran, U. (2013) *Research Methods for Business: A skill-building approach*, 6th edition. New York: John Wiley.

Wilson, D. (1997) 'The insidious erosion of ethics', *The Times Higher Education Supplement*, 16 May: vi.

2

RESEARCH PHILOSOPHIES AND SCHOOLS OF THOUGHT

Chapter Content and Issues

What is knowledge and how is it created?
Knowledge and reality.
The influence of different philosophies and perspectives.
The 'ologies' – ontology, epistemology and methodology.
Objectivity and subjectivity.
Independent factual and socially constructed reality.
Schools of thought and paradigms.
Positivism and phenomenology.
Post-modernism, pragmatism and critical realism.
Mixed-method designs.

2.1 Introduction

The purpose of this chapter is to introduce you to issues, debates and controversies relating to the philosophical strands of thought that are the most appropriate for informing and guiding your approach to designing and conducting research. In common with everyday life, there are differences of opinion in the academic world regarding what constitutes knowledge, how this should be established and the most appropriate ways to achieve this end. In the same way that you might decide to follow a particular political or religious philosophy in your everyday life rather than others that are available, academics have to make similar choices in terms of what they believe is the right or correct set of perspectives to adopt. So, by the time you have read this chapter, you will be familiar with these issues and more confident about deciding on the philosophical basis of the approach you will take in your research.

2.2 The Nature of Knowledge and Reality

In Chapter 1, we touched on some of the issues associated with common sense and more scientific approaches to research and the enhancement of knowledge. However, it was a rather limited exploration of these areas and we do need to take things further in this chapter. It might be tempting to think that 'knowledge is knowledge' and that 'reality is reality' or, in other words, that a fact is a fact and what is real is real. Life would be that much simpler if these were true, but unfortunately they are not. Of course there are shared and agreed, or non-contested, facts and views of what is real between people. Indeed, life would be even more difficult if this were not the case. On the other hand, not all 'knowledge' is agreed unconditionally and people do have different views and perceptions regarding the nature of reality and what should properly be regarded as fact or truth.

Before we consider some of the academic thinking and jargon related to these issues, let us consider them in a more easily understandable context. Read the text in the Research Reality Scenario box – Knowledge and Reality – which contains a short, perhaps fairly typical, conversation between a hypothetical general manager and the members of his departmental management team, discussing a problem that has arisen at their hotel, and think about how the different characters react to the so-called problem in terms of their acceptance of it, their perceptions of what could be done to address it and what they accept as factual and real.

Research Reality Scenario	Knowledge and Reality

Bill Soames, the General Manager of the hotel, opens a meeting with the words, 'Welcome to this week's management meeting. One of the main problems we need to discuss this week is the fact that our room occupancy levels have declined quite significantly over the past two weeks. We need to try and do something about this. Who has some ideas?'

'Well, common sense suggests that we could look to discount our rates more to try and attract extra bookings and guests,' ventured Janet Faulkner, the Restaurant Manager.

'Perhaps we should set up a guest satisfaction feedback system to find out what our guests particularly like or dislike and then we could use this to improve things and get more repeat bookings,' offered John Thames, the Human Resources Manager.

'How about setting up a reward scheme – like air miles – so that the more guests stay with us, the more reward points they get to redeem for another stay?' added the Marketing Manager, Justin Bones.

'I think that we should invest in better vacuum cleaners and other equipment so that we can improve the cleanliness and hygiene in the guest bedrooms and make them more attractive,' Carmen Hoyes, the Housekeeping Manager, chipped in.

'Hang on, hang on,' Paul Gestalt, the Rooms Division Manager, cried. 'Are we in danger of seeing a problem here when there isn't one?'

'What do you mean, Paul?', said Bill Soames. 'We obviously have a problem when occupancy levels are going down.'

'Yes, perhaps, but we need to look at this in a wider context,' replied Paul, who went on to explain what he meant by this. 'This is our low period during the year and, if we were to look at the occupancy levels for this period over the last five years, we would see that this always happens at this time. It is a natural consequence of the seasonal highs and lows. All our experience indicates that we will have periods of higher and lower occupancy during the year and we just have to accept it.'

'Well, I'm not sure I agree with you, Paul,' said Caroline Oast, the newly appointed Conventions and Meetings Manager. 'Yes, we all know that high and low periods can and do occur, but, just because they have in the past does not mean that they have to in the future or that we should accept this as inevitable. I think such a proposition can be challenged. For example, not all hotels have this problem at this time of year, so it is not universal, and we could try to boost our meetings and special events business at this time, when other sources of demand for accommodation are lower.'

'Good idea,' Bill replied, 'We'll explore that after the meeting. Now for the next item ...'

Paul remained unconvinced and muttered, 'There's a lot to be said for experience and common sense in these matters, everyone knows that for a fact.'

Clearly different views are expressed in this piece regarding whether there is a problem or not and, if there is, whether it is something that just has to be accepted or can be addressed. Some of the people involved make what may appear to be reasonable suggestions to try to address it, but there are assumptions about both the possible causes of the low occupancy problem – that is, room prices are too high, the rooms are not clean enough, insufficient incentives are being offered to encourage repeat business and so on – and, therefore, what may be appropriate solutions.

These suggestions could have a positive effect on occupancy levels, of course, as could the suggestion of looking to increase meeting and special events business, but on what basis is this problem–solution connection being addressed? Is it being addressed in a subjective or objective manner? Are the managers presenting any evidence to support their solutions or just using guesswork to advocate these? To what extent are experience and common sense driving their thinking? Are they assuming that this is a universal problem or one specific to the hotel concerned – that is, is it seen as a general rule or only one applying to that hotel at that point in time? To what extent are they simply accepting things as being known and factual?

What the conversation reveals is that what is known, or knowledge, and what is regarded as factual, and therefore non-contestable, is not always subject to universal agreement. Similarly, when people suggest, implicitly or explicitly, that there is a relationship or connection between two or more things, they will often be making and using assumptions about the nature of this relationship, but where do they get these assumptions from? They might be based on experience, as Paul states, or on Janet's commonsense view of the influence of price on the demand for accommodation, or on John's speculation that guests might be interested in, and motivated by, some kind of reward scheme, or on Caroline's transference view that what works well in other hotels could work in this one. Paul's assumption is that the factors and conditions that have influenced demand in the past remain the same. Janet's is that demand is sensitive to price. John's is that guests are interested in something more than the basic product and Caroline's is that the factors and conditions influencing demand in other contexts will apply equally in this one.

The problem here would appear to be that none of these proposed relationships, and consequent solutions, have been supported by any kind of objective evidence or logical argument. Therefore all, or none, of these could be correct. So, how do we decide which is and which is not? This is clearly a problem in itself. If we were to use experience as the sole basis for making this decision, it would be problematic because people accumulate widely divergent experiences that will have influenced how they perceive and interpret such situations and, thus, what they believe to be correct or incorrect. Using common sense may generate a consensus, but it may be largely subjective and not amenable to proof one way or the other. Accepting uncritically what appear to be logical propositions, such as Caroline's, may also be problematic, but evidence could be collected to test the view based on this.

What the example highlights is the fact that anyone grappling with questions concerning connections between different factors or events or the causes of observed effects uses, explicitly or implicitly, assumptions about them that are invariably derived from a type of personal viewpoint or philosophy of what is required to know something and the processes that support or justify statements of what should be generally regarded as known or factual.

 To explore these issues further view the video entitled 'Is Anything Real?' available via the Video Links Section of the Companion Website (study.sagepub.com/ brotherton).

2.2.1 The 'ologies'

In the academic jargon, these three things are known as ontology, epistemology and methodology (the 'ologies') and, collectively, they have quite a fundamental influence on how people design and conduct research. Ontology, for example, is concerned with beliefs about the nature of reality. For example, some researchers – particularly those in the physical and natural sciences – believe that there are universal truths waiting to be discovered, while others suggest that reality is more complex and dynamic as it is shaped and interpreted by human action and intellect and, therefore, because of the multitude of differing situations and interactions that this gives rise to, it is more contextually determined rather than universal or contextually independent.

These differing ontologies suggest different beliefs concerning the appropriate way to develop a knowledge of the world and what the researcher's relationship to this process should be. For example, those adopting an ontological position based on a belief in universal truths are likely to advocate and adopt an epistemology that regards neutral, independent and objective inquiry as preferable as this is seen to be an approach best suited to minimising potential contamination and bias. On the other hand, those preferring the ontological position of multiple, contextually determined truths or realities would advocate a very different epistemological stance. For such researchers, the belief that research can be conducted in a neutral, independent and objective manner would be seen as a type of 'fool's paradise'. Therefore, their epistemological position would be that the most appropriate approach to developing knowledge would be one in which the researcher interacted with the subjects of the enquiry in order to understand their perspectives and feelings.

Similarly, differing ontological and epistemological positions suggest different views of what the most appropriate means, or methodologies, are to develop knowledge. Experimentation – particularly experiments conducted in a laboratory – is a very different methodology to participant observation. Those researchers advocating experimentation as the most appropriate methodology to uncover truth would have very different ontological and epistemological beliefs from those advocating participant observation. Taylor and Edgar (1999: 27) succinctly summarise the relationship between ontology, epistemology and methodology in stating that: 'the belief about the nature of the world (ontology) adopted by an enquirer will influence their belief as to the nature of knowledge in that world (epistemology) which in turn will influence the enquirer's belief as to how that knowledge can be uncovered (methodology)'.

To strengthen your understanding of the 'ologies' it would be helpful to access and use some of the resources on the Companion Website (study.sagepub.com/ brotherton). The video links 'Complex Research Terminology Simplified: Paradigms, Ontology, Epistemology and Methodology' and 'Introduction to Epistemology' provide two useful videos dealing with these issues in a very systematic and clear manner.

To illustrate this further, think about the following example. In every democratic country, there will be political parties with different philosophies, policies and assumptions about the type of society that is regarded as preferable. As a result, these parties are likely to take very different stances over the same issues. Excluding the extremes of fascist and communist parties, broadly speaking, it is possible to distinguish between political parties on the right of the political spectrum – conservative or republican – and those on the left – socialist or democrat. So, if we take the issue of a society's economy, we are likely to find that politicians from the right tend to employ the belief and assumption that the free market is the natural and preferable way to organise economic activity because it is a logical consequence of a philosophy that emphasises the desirability of individualism and freedom with minimal state intervention. By contrast, politicians from the left tend to believe and assume that a totally free market is not the most preferable form of economic structure for a society because the underlying philosophy of this type of political stance emphasises more collective and egalitarian values and, to achieve this, more state intervention is required to regulate and modify the dysfunctional aspects of unfettered freedom and individualism in order to ensure greater social justice.

In the political sphere, in common with many others, what is seen to be a problem by one side may not be for the other, what are regarded as the facts by one are likely to be disputed by the other, views of how society (reality) works and should work differ, the policies seen to be desirable and positive to one side may be seen as undesirable and damaging by the other. In short, the point here is that there are a great many situations and issues where disagreements arise over what are regarded as the appropriate basic assumptions, philosophy and approaches to developing knowledge. The importance of this is that if the underlying philosophy, assumptions or processes used to obtain what is being presented as knowledge can be seriously questioned or discredited, the knowledge derived from them also becomes less credible. Thus, although these considerations may appear to be rather abstract, esoteric and to have little immediate, practical value, if the foundations on which the knowledge has been built are weak or inappropriate, then the knowledge will be also. Let us think about this using the analogy of a building. If the foundations of the building are not constructed properly, you may well expect the walls, floors and roof constructed on them to be suspect and unsafe.

2.2.2 Schools of thought and paradigms

As it is self-evident there are groups of people in society sharing different views of the world based on different philosophical, political, religious or cultural beliefs, it should not surprise you to know that such divisions also exist in the world of academic enquiry. Within most academic disciplines there are groups of people who subscribe to different views regarding what is most important in their field and the most appropriate ways to approach and explain these things. They tend to align themselves according to different views of what constitutes knowledge, the shared sets of assumptions derived from this and the approaches to developing knowledge these imply. In short, each different group will tend to have a different view of the most appropriate philosophical stance, or ontology, epistemology and methodology, that should be used to develop knowledge.

Such groups are often referred to as 'schools of thought'. For example, in economics there are, among others, monetarist and Keynesian schools of thought. To illustrate in a simple way the implications of the differences between these two schools of thought, we might consider their views on how to manage an economy. Unsurprisingly, the monetarist school believes that it is money and, more specifically, the supply of money that are the prime determinants of economic activity and outcomes. Consequently, and logically, if it is possible to control and manipulate the supply of money in an economy, usually via interest rates, then the economy itself can be controlled and manipulated. Alternatively, while not denying that money has importance, the Keynesian school believes that other factors are more important than the supply of money in determining the state of an economy and would suggest that the use of fiscal measures (taxation and government expenditure) to manipulate the economy are likely to be more effective than changing interest rates. Therefore, the ontology, epistemology and methodology adopted and advocated by the two schools of thought are different.

Why is this important? It is important for obvious reasons and perhaps some that are not quite so obvious. In terms of the former, a political party adopting the monetarist school of thought as the basis for its economic policies would, as an elected government, introduce very different policies from one based on the Keynesian school. In Chapter 4, we will explore the significance of recognising where a particular researcher or author is 'coming from' when we review the literature relating to our research topic. In some instances, as we shall see, this is obvious, but, in others, it is not quite as transparent. If we read material written from a communist perspective and other material on the same issue written from a conservative standpoint, it will be quite obvious that the two sets of writers subscribe to very different schools of thought over the issue. On the other hand, we may find that within a given school of thought there are sub-schools that adopt variations on the general school of thought they belong to. Again, perhaps the best way to illustrate this is via our political party analogy. Though a conservative party will subscribe to a different school of thought than a socialist one, within each of these parties it is likely that there will be subdivisions based on differing interpretations of the party's underlying philosophy and so on. Typically, we might find some conservative politicians referred to as coming from the far right of the party and others as being more moderate or from the centre ground of the party. In the socialist party, we are likely to find some politicians described as belonging to the far left and others from the centre ground.

The point here is that it cannot be assumed that clearly different schools of thought are internally cohesive or, put another way, all who belong to a particular school share both a unanimous view of the world and a generally accepted method of the most appropriate way to develop knowledge. That said, most schools of thought are not as highly fragmented in these respects as this may imply. Although unanimity may not be present, there are generally accepted methods for conducting research and developing theory within and between schools of thought. These are invariably referred to as 'paradigms' and essentially constitute agreement over the most appropriate way to conduct research among their members. In many fields it is possible to refer to a 'dominant paradigm', which is the one that is most widely accepted and adopted by researchers in that field.

2.3 Positivism and Phenomenology

These are generally regarded as the two main opposing paradigms for conducting research. However, as we have discussed above, the real world does not divide into two such internally cohesive groups. Within each of these there are sub-groups advocating differing interpretations of the basic standpoint as the most appropriate way to design and conduct research. To discuss these here would complicate matters unnecessarily, but you should be aware that such variations influence the views and prescriptions of different authors within each of the two major schools. To illustrate the fundamental differences between the positivistic and phenomenological (also sometimes referred to as interpretative or constructivist) philosophies, read the conversation in the Research Reality Scenario box – Different Strokes. Here, the hypothetical characters take very different approaches to the same issue. Justin Balfour, the Marketing Director, has an academic background in chemistry, while Randolph Strauss, the Marketing Manager, has a degree in anthropology.

Research Reality Scenario	**Different Strokes**

Justin, opening the meeting between the two marketing supremos of the Galactica Fun Park, said, 'Hi, Randolph, we have a bit of an urgent issue to deal with. As you know, the company's Managing Director is getting a bit hot under the collar about some of the complaints we've been receiving from visitors to the park and she is insisting that we investigate the reasons for this so that we can improve their experience.'

'Yes, I've been giving some thought to how we might do that,' replied Randolph.

'So have I,' Justin said, 'so let me tell you where I'm coming from on this one and then you can do the same, Randolph. My view is that we have to investigate this in a manner that will give us a set of results that are accurate, valid and credible enough to stand up to the scrutiny of the MD. To achieve this we need to go about it in a scientific manner. What I propose is that we address the issue of what the most critical aspects of the visitor experience are for determining their level of satisfaction.'

'Sure, I've no problem with that,' Randolph offered.

'OK, then we're agreed on the issue that needs investigating,' said Justin gleefully. Justin went on to say, 'The next question is how are we going to do this? I propose that we design and set up a survey, using a predetermined questionnaire with closed questions to obtain the data we need, and select an appropriate sample of visitors to complete this. Then we can statistically analyse the data and generalise from our findings. What do you say?'

Randolph has different views on how to approach this and outlined how he would go about doing it: 'I'm not so sure that would give us what we're looking for. Let me explain. I see where you're coming from, in terms of taking a rationalistic, reductionist and quantitative view of how to go about this, but I feel that we would get a more valid view of the most important aspects of the visitors' experiences if we approached it in a more holistic way. I think it is difficult to separate out individual elements of the experience and quantify their importance in isolation from the other elements because visitors are likely to judge their satisfaction with the experience as a whole, not by rating each separate part. Also, if we predetermine the questions to be asked and constrain how the visitor can respond to them, we are in danger of being selective in what we ask and so will get only standardised responses, which, by definition, may not be the real responses the people want to give. So, my approach would be less predetermined and involve a range of techniques, such as observing the visitors' behaviour, interviewing them – perhaps both in individual and group contexts – so that they give us their deeper feelings about the experience.'

'Ah,' said Justin, 'I can see we're going to have quite a discussion over how we should proceed on this one!'

As you might expect, given their respective backgrounds, Justin and Randolph have very different views about the most appropriate approach to take and methods to use to address the issue they face. There are, of course, advantages and disadvantages to each of their preferred options, but what this situation highlights is the difference between the stance a positivist (Justin) and a phenomenologist (Randolph) would take in response to the same issue or question. Although they agree that the issue is important and requires some investigation to explore it further, their respective ontological, epistemological and methodological preferences and beliefs push them in very different directions in terms of how they advocate the investigation should be designed and conducted, and the reasons they give to justify these preferences. In short, they subscribe to different paradigms.

This leads us into a consideration of what are generally regarded as the two main philosophies or paradigms – positivism and phenomenology – that influence the way research is conducted. We shall examine the basis of each of these in turn and then summarise their differences.

2.3.1 Positivism

Positivism is a belief based on, and derived from, the view that a 'real' world of tangible social and physical phenomena exists independently – that is, objectively – of how such phenomena are perceived and conceptualised by people and what is required to understand and explain these is impartial, value free, logical, empirical, scientific research. In short, the truth is out there and it can be revealed by applying an appropriate methodology.

As you might expect, positivism is the mindset of the archetypal white-coated laboratory scientist, but it is also a significant, if not the most dominant, philosophy in management research, including that into hospitality and tourism. The positivist assumes that people and/or organisations behave in a self-interested, logical and rational manner. Phenomena and events can be explained by general, or universal, cause–effect laws because knowledge and cause–effect relationships, while probabilistic and conditional, are not contextual. In other words, because there is always room for error and doubt, it is difficult to be absolutely certain that a cause–effect relationship is correct, but we can say there is a very high probability something will be the cause and, if the necessary conditions are present, that this will not be influenced by other contextual features.

Positivism, therefore, contends that the theories and laws established via research must be logically consistent and explain empirical reality. In addition to this, proponents would also take the view that this theoretical empirical consistency should be replicable. This is logical because, if a general law is to be accepted, it must be applicable across a range of different contextual circumstances, so, if the research is repeated or replicated, it should deliver the same results whatever the context. To be capable of achieving this, positivists would take the view that scientific research is the only way to discover the truth and it must be conducted in an objective manner, deterministic in purpose (to determine cause–effect relationships), mechanistic in process and use well-established and validated methods.

Positivists take the view that the 'best', or most valid, way to learn the truth is to conduct experiments. Experimentation – or, more specifically, laboratory experimentation – is the preferred method of the positivist because it enables the research to be designed and conducted with the maximum degree of control. Although it may be unlikely that you will be conducting experimental research in laboratory conditions, this issue of control is important in a more general sense and something you would need to give consideration to if you were undertaking research from a positivistic perspective using other methods, such as a survey. The significance of being able to control the inputs to the research, the processes used and the conditions under which all this occurs is that it enables the researcher to eliminate or, at the very least minimise, the possible contaminating or confounding effects that other influences may have on the results. In addition, because control is complete, it will also allow the researcher to measure the relative effect of different influences that have been designed into the research.

However, because most phenomena and events are not caused by one factor acting in isolation from others, especially in the real world, this complexity makes it difficult to distinguish between the most and least important influences and be certain, or as near as is possible, of what the nature and mechanism of the cause–effect relationship is. For example, we might identify that the numbers of tourists coming to the UK from other countries have been declining in recent years and there is a range of possible influences that could be contributing to this. Our problem is discovering which of these is, or are, the most important or significant. All of them may have some degree of influence, but some are likely to have had a stronger influence than others. If this was something we could investigate using a laboratory experiment, we could take each influence in turn, control the process and conditions and test to measure the strength of its effect. Unfortunately, this is not possible, but there are other ways of doing so, although they are not as ideal in terms of control as experiments. Often, such techniques are statistical in nature (as we shall see in Chapter 9), but there are techniques designed to achieve similar aims with qualitative data (Chapter 10).

The key issue here is the degree of control that can be exerted over the design, process and conditions of the research. The closer we can get to the 'ideal' conditions for control – that is, the laboratory experiment – the more likely it is that we will be able to justify the accuracy of the findings. If you think about this from the reverse direction, it may become even clearer. If there are a range of factors that could be influencing or causing the effect we are investigating, but we cannot isolate or control for the influence of one from the others, it would be difficult to state with any degree of confidence what the relative influence of each is and what the nature of the mechanism (the cause–effect relationship) between each of these and the effect actually is. In these circumstances we may be able to say that there would appear to be a connection, or correlation, between the possible causes and the effect, but we would not be able to state and explain the mechanism that connects the causes and the effect.

Another problem we would have in this situation would be trying to meet the positivist's condition that research must deal with what we can see and measure – that is, real, concrete things. This is not a problem in the context of a laboratory, where we can control everything and observe and measure the outcomes from the experiment, but, in the real world, it usually is. In our example above of the reductions in the numbers of tourists, there are certain things that are concrete and measurable. The numbers of people arriving at border points – that is, airports, seaports and so on – from other countries can be seen and measured fairly easily. The exchange rate(s) between the two countries' currencies will also be known, as perhaps will the travel costs, such as airfares. We could also identify things associated with the ease of travel, such as the number and frequency of flights from the other countries to ours. All of these things would be factual and easily measurable in their own right, but their relationship with the effect may not always be as simple.

To illustrate this, consider how people often behave in terms of buying overseas tourist travel. In many cases, people book their holidays and travel many months in advance of actually taking the trip. This implies that there may be a time gap between cause and effect. In other words, the exchange rate in existence at the time of the visit may not be the one that influenced the decision to make that visit several months before and, hence, the overall number of visitors at that point in time. Therefore, the influence on visitor numbers of a less than favourable exchange rate and, equally, of a favourable one, is likely to have a delayed effect. In the jargon, this would be known as a 'lagged relationship or effect' because of the time delay between the change in the cause and the consequent change in the effect.

Beyond these more objective, concrete, factual influences, we might also reasonably speculate that the degree of hospitality our population extends to such visitors or the quality of the experience they have when they are in our country may influence whether they want to visit or not. These, however, are nebulous terms – they do not exist as such in the real world as they are general and conceptual rather than specific and concrete. So, how do we observe and measure the quality of experience or warmth of hospitality? We cannot do this directly, but, rather, have to do it indirectly by breaking down the concept into the 'real' things that comprise it. This is known as 'operationalisation' and is a task discussed more extensively in Chapter 5, but suffice it to say here that we would need to identify real, tangible things that would influence and indicate the presence of a higher- or lower-quality experience or better or worse hospitality.

In emphasising the importance of obtaining empirical proof to support logical theories, positivists need a mechanism to link the two together. As the deductive approach to research is the one favoured by positivists, the process begins by developing a possible theoretical explanation for the phenomena or event and then requires empirical evidence to be collected to verify, or not, the validity of this. This raises questions concerning the nature of the link between theory and reality and what empirical evidence will be required to establish whether or not this is true. What are we suggesting the nature and mechanism of the link will be, and how do we decide what data are required to test this? The answer is that the positivist examines the theory and its predictions and implications in order to formulate specific relationships that the empirical data would confirm to be true if the theory is correct. These predictions are the logical consequences of the theory and are known as hypotheses. Again, we will examine the nature and role of hypotheses in greater detail in Chapter 5, but their importance to the positivistic approach to research cannot be emphasised strongly enough. For the positivist they are what the empirical aspect of the research process is designed to address and, as such, not only constitute this vital link between theory and reality but also serve to determine the structure and processes adopted to collect and analyse the empirical data. Indeed, their confirmation or otherwise is the purpose of the empirical part of the research project.

Although, as noted earlier, positivism is widely accepted among researchers from many fields as the preferred paradigm or approach to research and the development of knowledge, it is not without its critics and, as we shall see shortly, some of these reject it completely in favour of alternative approaches or paradigms. Among the criticism of positivism is that it is largely a-contextual in nature or, to put it another way, it views people and organisations as isolated from their contexts. This is reinforced by the high levels of artificiality created by the favoured methods of the positivist, particularly in relation to experimentation.

Critics of the positivist approach also point out that researchers cannot be totally objective in the way they conduct research, that objectivity is a myth. As human beings, we cannot avoid being influenced by our beliefs, values and prejudices, whether we consciously realise this or not. This challenges the impartiality claim and is reinforced by the observation that, in the positivist approach, the relationship between the researcher and the subject is one within which the former exerts much greater influence and control than the latter. It is claimed that this can distort the research process and lead to accurate (reliable) but not necessarily truthful (valid) results. For example, people who complete questionnaires can only respond to the questions asked by the researcher. This may generate accurate responses to the questions asked, but may not generate the true feelings of the respondents because they may lie outside the questions asked. Similarly, the subject taking part in an experiment has no input into, or control over, the process and content of the experiment as he or she is merely required to behave in the way the researcher wants.

Finally, it is suggested that positivistic approaches to conducting research, such as experiments and surveys, tend to gather rather superficial information compared to that elicited by means of alternative approaches. This is invariably true because the positivistic philosophy is based on what is often called 'reductionism'. One way to think about this is via the analogy of peeling an onion. As the successive layers are peeled away, we get closer and closer to the centre of the onion until we arrive at its core. Positivists believe that this process of reducing the problem to its essential core reveals the fundamental cause–effect relationships driving the larger entity as a whole. However, it means that, by definition, many of the aspects have to be discarded so that researchers can focus on those regarded as the key ones. Clearly such an approach may have value, but it does carry the danger that the answers it delivers may be more simplistic and partial than the reality it is trying to describe and explain, and hence, be less valid as a result.

2.3.2 Phenomenology

Phenomenological, constructivist or interpretative approaches to research place considerably less emphasis on the need to develop so-called objective research methods and more on the need for interpretation in research. This is a view based on the belief that the real world, and the phenomena and events that occur in this world, are created by the subjective thoughts, actions and interactions of people who inhabit it. In short, it is socially constructed rather than being a separate and independent entity that determines people's behaviour.

At this point you should already be able to see that there are fundamental differences between positivists and phenomenologists. Indeed, they are really the antithesis of each other. The fundamental beliefs (ontologies and epistemologies) of the two paradigms – and the consequent methodologies and methods they advocate as being the most appropriate for undertaking research – are directly opposed. In the same way that it would be unthinkable for a person to simultaneously be a fascist and a communist, you cannot be both a positivist and a phenomenologist at the same time.

Phenomenology, in all its varying guises, developed as an alternative to positivism when researchers in certain fields of enquiry, such as sociology, became increasingly disenchanted with the ability of positivism and its methods to adequately explain the phenomena they were interested in. Although it was generally accepted that positivistic approaches and methods could deliver reliable results – that is, ones that can be repeated or replicated – the criticism was that they may not be valid or accurate in terms of adequately reflecting and explaining real-world phenomena because of the reductionist and artificial manner in which the research is conducted. In other words, while the results may be reliable, they may well be reliably inaccurate as valid explanations.

To counter this flow, phenomenologists reject the ontological, epistemological and methodological foundations of the positivist approach and advocate essentially opposing views on each of these. Phenomenologists are interested in understanding and explaining how people make sense of the world they inhabit and are less concerned with trying to devise and use objective methods to discover deterministic relationships and general laws. By implication, context is an important element in developing this understanding because people exist and interact within contexts. Therefore, rather than trying to eliminate or control for contextual influences, they are seen as being integral to understanding. Similarly, artificially constructed situations or environments, such as those occurring in an experiment or survey, are seen to be threats rather than aids to understanding because they are partial and exclusive rather than holistic and inclusive, with the content and processes they include being selected and controlled by the researcher rather than the subject under investigation. In short, they are artificial rather than naturally occurring situations and conditions.

Not unsurprisingly, therefore, phenomenology advocates an inductive rather than a deductive approach as the most appropriate for undertaking research. This perspective suggests that a more valid understanding of a phenomenon or event is likely to be derived from investigating these in their real-world contexts in the first instance than is possible by theorising about them in isolation and then collecting data on them to test the theory. As the belief is that meanings, understanding and theories can only be developed in a valid manner by studying reality first and then working backwards by analysing and interpreting the data to find patterns and relationships, phenomenology takes the opposite stance from positivism. This approach is often referred to as 'grounded theory'. Put simply, the theory that is developed is based upon, or grounded in, the data collected from the real world. For an example of how this approach works in the context of a real study see Kim et al. (2009).

However, this seems to imply that phenomenology driven research always begins with a blank sheet, at least in terms of theory. The problem with this is that, unless the research topic is absolutely unique, such a stance ignores any previous empirical or theoretical work on the issues in question and is thus in danger of possibly reinventing a wheel that is already known about! In practice, therefore, although the process may work from empirical data collection to theoretical development, the former is likely to be informed and guided by previous research findings from the literature relating to that topic.

In terms of the methods favoured by the phenomenological approach, it is clear that those advocated by the positivists – experimentation or surveys – are generally seen to be inappropriate. As we saw earlier, these methods are essentially a-contextual in nature and embody high levels of artificiality and control, which are features that the phenomenological approach rejects. Because context, realism or naturalistic enquiry and interpretation are crucially important to the phenomenological view, it should not be surprising to find that methods such as case studies and what are referred to as 'field study' techniques – participant or non-participant observation – are the type of methods preferred by phenomenologists. This is because they are more consistent with the philosophical and ontological positions taken by such researchers. As the phenomenological approach takes the recording of the complexities of the situation being investigated as its starting point in order that these may be examined, analysed and interpreted to find patterns and connections, it should not be surprising to find that these types of methods are more appropriate to collecting the type of data required for this process. In many instances, this is referred to as the building of a 'rich picture' of the complex reality being studied.

This, in turn, implies that research undertaken from a phenomenological perspective is more likely to involve the collection of qualitative rather than quantitative data. In general, this tends to be the case, but it should not be assumed that all positivistic research is quantitative and all phenomenological research is qualitative in nature. Qualitative data are collected in some positivistic studies – for example, by interviewing – and there may be elements of quantitative data involved in some phenomenological studies. In short, although it is far more likely that positivists will concentrate on the collection of hard (quantitative) data because of their amenability to measurement and statistical manipulation and phenomenologists will tend to concentrate on soft (qualitative) data because they are more capable of revealing people's feelings, perceptions and meanings, there is nothing inherent in the two stances that precludes the use of either type of data. Furthermore, because there are varying types and degrees of both positivism and phenomenology, it may be more useful to think of the differences in the data collection preferences between them as lying on a continuum rather than being polar opposites. In other words, while the purest forms of each would undoubtedly favour purely quantitative or qualitative data, there are variations that would advocate mixed or multiple methods and varying combinations of each type of data.

Although it is probably reasonable to suggest that phenomenology has a relatively stable and consistent ontological position and identity, a feature it shares with positivism, there are variations in the epistemological stances and methodological preferences amongst its proponents. For a useful discussion of a range of pertinent issues associated with this see Pernecky and Jamal (2010) and for one specifically related to methodological issues in relation to constructivism within tourism studies see Pernecky (2012).

To summarise, Table 2.1 illustrates the main features of differences between and preferences within the positivistic and phenomenological paradigms. It shows not only that there are clear epistemological, ontological and methodological differences between the two but also that these differences are so marked they are fundamental opposites. However, while this is undoubtedly true, as we have noted earlier, reality tends not to be quite so black and white. Differing schools of thought do exist within each of these main types and there are variations in the form of positivism and phenomenology adopted by different groups of researchers. Put another way, you might consider this as people agreeing with the basic philosophy but having differing ideas about the most appropriate style of 'doing science' or scientific research.

TABLE 2.1   Key features of positivist and phenomenological paradigms

	Positivistic paradigm	Phenomenological paradigm
Basic beliefs	The world is external and objective The observer is independent Science is value-free	The world is socially constructed and subjective The observer is part of what is observed Science is driven by human interests
What researchers should do	Focus on facts Look for causality and fundamental laws Reduce phenomena to their simplest elements Formulate hypotheses and then test them	Focus on meanings Try to understand what is happening Look at the totality of each situation Develop ideas through induction from data
Preferred methods	Operationalising concepts so that they can be measured Taking large samples	Using multiple methods to establish different views of phenomena Small samples investigated in depth or over time

Source: Easterby-Smith et al. (2012: 27). Reproduced with permission of Sage

This notion is nicely illustrated by Mitroff and Kilman (1981), who discuss four types of scientist based on differences concerning the two dimensions of the type of input data and decision-making they prefer. The combination of these two dimensions produces four types of researcher:

- academic scientist (AS)

- conceptual theorist (CT)

- particular humanist (PH)

- conceptual humanist (CH).

Viewing these in a simplistic manner, we would conclude that the AS and the CH are very much the archetypal positivist and phenomenologist. The AS looks for certainty and is concerned with precision, accuracy and reliability. He or she prefers details and practical, specific, 'hard' facts and to establish these by means of controlled enquiry and, in particular, controlled experimentation.

The CT is similar to the AS in that he or she has a preference for the same type of data as the AS, but the CT places greater emphasis and importance on the value of imagination and speculation to produce new, innovative insights that generate what may be called 'grand theory'. So, although the two share the same basic philosophy, they differ in what they see to be the most important purpose of doing research. The AS has a preoccupation with the specific and particular as a way of discovering a single definitive answer to an issue, while the CT is more concerned with multiple possibilities. By contrast, the PH and CH scientists are essentially phenomenologists and adopt the beliefs, values and methods advocated by that paradigm and, in common with the AS and CT types, where they differ lies in their specific data preferences.

2.4 Post-modernism and Pragmatism

Over time, people's beliefs about the world, what can be legitimately regarded as knowledge or ways of knowing and the best ways to generate knowledge change. We have already seen that the rise in popularity of phenomenology has been due to researchers adopting different philosophical and operational views from those advocated by positivists. Therefore it should not be surprising that this basic process continues to unfold. Over the last two decades or so, and increasingly since the first edition of this book, the views that those approaches and techniques adopted in 'modernity' are inadequate to explain phenomena in the 'post-modern' world and that the type of 'ideology'-driven stance, typified by the one-or-the-other choice of positivism or phenomenology, are not necessarily the only, or indeed best, choices available to the researcher has resulted in the rise of both post-modern and pragmatic schools of thought and their associated paradigms. Hence, these are additional options open to the researcher beyond the previous dichotomous choice of either positivism or phenomenology as the guiding philosophy and, as such, deserve consideration here.

2.4.1 Post-modernism

Post-modernism is a term that will probably be familiar as it tends to be used in a quite wide variety of contemporary contexts but, as common as it is, exactly what it means is often somewhat opaque. Obviously post-modern thought is based upon a rejection of modern thought and to understand this it is necessary to have some idea of what modern thought means. Modernism and modern thought essentially arise from the progressive movement of societies, particularly in Europe and the USA, from more traditional forms to those regarded as more modern over the course of the nineteenth and twentieth centuries. This 'modernity' was therefore a period within which the dominance of science and rational/linear thinking came to the fore, being typified by the centrality of causation, or cause–effect relationships and mechanisms, to scientific, and indeed more general, thinking. The notion that a relatively stable and recognisable structure, forms of organisation, static relationships and enduring processes existed within society, albeit over a period of quite significant change over the last two centuries, was really central to modern thinking. The idea that reality is fixed and certain, as it is subject to the underlying rational laws, becomes contestable in the post-modern view.

Post-modernists would claim that the world, certainly in the final couple of decades of the twentieth century and into the twenty-first, has become much more uncertain, unstable, less predictable and much more fluid and diversified than was the case previously. In such a world, it is argued, there is a need for phenomena to be viewed in a more fragmented, ambiguous and discontinuous manner because this is how society is developing. People are behaving differently, their identities are becoming more varied and defined by attributes and factors that were not as significant in the past, technology is changing – often radically – the nature of work, organisations and how people interact in everyday life. This all means that phenomena may have varied meanings and significance rather than being seen, in a more rationalistic and linear way, as correct/incorrect or right or wrong. So different views and interpretations are seen as a natural and integral part of the world rather than contradictory. This, in turn, implies that the development of 'grand theory' and universal laws should not be the aim of the researcher but rather the development of more disaggregated or localised perspectives derived from the variety of 'situated' meanings that arise from differing contexts. So it is contextual constructivism and relativity that are important to the post-modernist, not the universalism and absolutism that characterised much modernist thought, especially that advocated by positivists.

As post-modernism is both critical of modernist perspectives and practices it also embraces and encourages a critical and more open-ended approach to research. In this it encourages the researcher to be more reflective and reflexive which, in turn, encourages critical thinking not only about the veracity of interpretations and findings but also about the status quo. As phenomena are regarded as situated both culturally and historically there is no overwhelming reason to simply regard these as given and/or everlasting. Therefore, the 'critique' aspect of post-modernist enquiry is one not simply aimed at critiquing previous findings and theories but one that is employed to critique one's own analysis and the phenomena themselves. The first two of these should be self-evident but the third may require a little more explanation. Rather than simply attempting to describe, explain, analyse and understand the phenomena as a 'given', the post-modernist critiques this reality by considering alternatives to how the phenomena are currently manifested. Put simply, it does not just accept the current situation as something that exists independently of the research process. This of course implies that there is often a political or policy aspect to post-modern work because in considering the alternatives there are prescriptive implications.

2.4.2 Pragmatism

If we see positivism, phenomenology and post-modernism as distinctive, ideology-driven choices, then the choice of one of these tends to imply that the others will be rejected. In short, if we sign up to a particular set of beliefs about the nature of the world (ontology) that then determines what we regard as knowledge and how we can know this (epistemology) and the ways by which this knowledge can be revealed and proven (methodology), we become locked into a particular belief–action system. Although there is nothing inherently wrong with this, and some would say that it has advantages in terms of internal consistency, it does preclude consideration and use of a range of perspectives and methods derived from these mutually exclusive alternatives. However, recently, within the last 20 years or so, an increasing number of researchers have broken with this tradition and have suggested that the adoption of a more pragmatic approach has value.

This is often referred to as mixed-design, mixed-methods or mixed methodology research but these are terms that you should treat with some caution (see Chapter 5) as they tend to be used rather loosely and interchangeably in the literature. So, if authors use these terms you should be clear about exactly what they mean by them in the context of their work. At a very simple level the collection of both quantitative and qualitative data in the same study may be referred to as evidence of the study being one using mixed-methods, or even possibly as one utilising a mixed design, but this could still be based upon a particular research philosophy. It is quite possible for studies based upon either a positivist or phenomenological philosophy to be operationalised in such a way that the collection of both types of data are required to address the research question, even though each may stress the relative importance of one type or another.

By contrast, the true pragmatist would reject a unitary ideology or ontological/epistemological stance and be prepared to recognise that certain aspects of the world may be best approached from the viewpoint of objective realism and universal laws whilst other aspects can be best understood from a more subjective, interpretative perspective and, as a consequence, that using a range of research designs and methods from across the traditional paradigm boundaries might be preferable to signing up to the restrictions that inevitably arise from a more unitary stance. For the pragmatist it is invariably the nature of the research question/s that is the key driver. If the research question requires differing stances, methods and data to be successfully answered then the suspension of a more 'purist' approach to the work may well be appropriate. However, the rise in popularity of what is often called 'critical realism' provides more of a philosophical basis and rationale for the adoption of a pragmatic approach. Critical realists essentially subscribe to the positivist's view that there is an objective and independent reality but also that this reality cannot be entirely understood through objectivity. In this they join with the phenomenologists in agreeing that research and researchers cannot be entirely objective, that subjectivity inevitably plays a part somewhere in the process, and that at least part of this reality is subject to some element of social constructionism where context plays a role. Critical realists take the view that reality is determined both by wider structures in society and by the consequences of human agency. In addition, the 'critical' aspect recognises that our ability to understand this reality is imperfect and we need to be intensely critical of our own subjectivity through critical reflection and reflexivity. For a useful discussion of these issues in greater detail see Platenkamp and Botterill (2013).

So why might you decide to use a 'mixed' approach to your research? One reason may be what is known as 'triangulation'. This is a term derived from navigation, where, to fix your position and/or course accurately, you need to take more than one reading or bearing, typically at least three, and construct a triangle to determine the point you are seeking. In the context of research this translates to the use of more then one methodology or method, theoretical perspective and data sources and/or types. In using a range of differing approaches and methods it is claimed that a wider and deeper understanding may be achieved and that this variety may be complementary, i.e. that findings from one perspective or method may illuminate those from another. However, while this may be the case, the downside to this is that it often makes the research process more complex, time-consuming and difficult to design and put into practice. This means that though a mixed approach may be desirable it is often not feasible for many students undertaking a severely time- and resource-constrained research project for a dissertation.

That said, it might be feasible to use a mixed approach within such a study if the research question/s and the context are sufficiently specific and tailored to the time/resources available. In such circumstances there are basically two choices: either a separated but sequential design or one that mixes the elements together in a concurrent manner. In addition, the choices may not carry equal weight, i.e. one perspective, design or method may be the dominant or primary approach/vehicle with the other assuming secondary importance. Often, but not always, this is expressed as a combination of exploratory or pilot study and the main study. So, for example, in certain circumstances it might be appropriate to undertake an initial qualitative study to discover the things that are important to, say, a small sample of frequent fast food consumers in order to use this information to design a questionnaire to conduct a larger-scale quantitative survey. Here we have a mixed design and methods study where the qualitative element, as important as it is, is the secondary or minor aspect used to support the primary or major element of the study. Alternatively, we might already know what the important factors are from previous studies on the same topic, that we have identified in our literature review, but perhaps not why these things are regarded as so important by these consumers. In this situation we may wish to address this issue by including a number of 'why' questions in our questionnaire to generate the type of open-ended, qualitative data needed to answer this question. Here we have a different 'mix' in that, arguably, the qualitative data are more important than the quantitative data that are being collected simultaneously rather than sequentially.

Although mixed approaches and designs can be used, if appropriate, in any type of research study (see Chapter 6) there are perhaps some designs that naturally lend themselves to this. One in particular, the case study, is often particularly amenable to a mixed approach of one kind or another. Because the context is invariably limited in a case study and is also of central importance to the design of this type of research and because there is likely to be a range of actors and perspectives evident within the context or case it is likely that both qualitative and quantitative data may have an important role to play in developing an understanding of the case situation. To achieve this a range of data sources/types may need to be investigated and different methodologies may have to be employed to do this. That said, the use of a mixed approach is certainly not limited to case study research design. For an interesting perspective on this see the discussion of Q-methodology by Stergiou and Airey (2011) in the context of tourism research that explores this methodology in relation to the quantitative analysis of qualitative or subjective data.

2.5 Where Do You Stand?

Having read this chapter you should now be aware of the different beliefs about the world held by different people (their ontological position), the differing approaches to knowing (epistemology) and the preferred ways of acquiring this knowledge (methodology). So, at this point it may be worthwhile taking a few minutes to synthesise this knowledge by asking yourself what type of researcher you are and what your preferences might be. The Research Action Checklist box – Who Am I? – provides an opportunity for you to think about this.

Research Action Checklist	Who Am I?

- ✓ What are my basic beliefs about the world? Am I a realist, a critical realist or a constructivist?

- ✓ Which philosophical stance do I favour? Positivism, phenomenology, post-modernism or pragmatism?

- ✓ Which type of epistemology would I advocate? Is knowledge best obtained from an objective, external observer stance that sees the world as existing independently of you or from a more subjective, involved observer stance that sees we are part of the knowledge that is being obtained?

- ✓ What type of strategic approach to developing knowledge (methodology) do I favour? The 'scientific approach' or one more closely associated with 'social constructionism'?

- ✓ What type of data do I need to collect – quantitative, qualitative or both?

- ✓ Which empirical methods and procedures would be the best to answer my research question/s – survey, case study, experiment, comparative, observational, mixed?

You may also wish to consult some of the additional resources available via the Companion Website (study.sagepub.com/brotherton). The Web Links section of this contains a series of links to material on positivism, phenomenology, critical realism and pragmatism and the Video Links Section has a link to a video that explains the basis of a pragmatic epistemology.

Chapter Summary

What constitutes knowledge and fact is contestable.

Different people subscribe to different views (schools of thought) concerning how knowledge and facts can be established and the accepted ways of achieving this (paradigms).

Positivism is often regarded as the dominant paradigm and is a philosophical standpoint or belief that a real world of tangible phenomena exists independently and objectively, regardless of how they are perceived by people.

The positivist researcher favours use of the deductive approach to research and also believes that truth can only be revealed by using an appropriate methodology (the scientific method) and the application of this, particularly by means of experimentation, can identify and explain cause–effect laws that are universal.

The ability to control the research process is crucial to the positivist, so as to be able to prove cause–effect relationships, which can only be proved via empirical investigation.

Phenomenology, constructivism or interpretivism, is an alternative paradigm based on the view that the real world is socially constructed by people's thoughts, actions and interactions.

Phenomenologists advocate an inductive approach to conducting research and the use of more naturalistic enquiry methods than positivists, such as observation or case studies.

For phenomenologists, new knowledge is developed, in the first instance, by collecting and analysing in-depth, real-world data rather then testing existing theories.

Pragmatists tend to avoid the 'ideology-driven' choices made by positivists and phenomenologists in favour of a more flexible approach that allows them to select a range of approaches they regard as suitable for the issue under investigation.

References

Easterby-Smith, M., Thorpe, R. and Lowe, A. (2012) *Management Research: An introduction*, 4th edition. London: Sage.

Kim, Y.G., Eves, A. and Scarles, C. (2009) 'Building a model of local food consumption on trips and holidays: a grounded theory approach', *International Journal of Hospitality Management*, 28 (3): 423–31.

Mitroff, I. and Kilman, R. (1981) 'Methodological approaches to social science', in P. Reason and J. Rowan (eds), *Human Enquiry*. Chichester: John Wiley. pp. 43–51.

Pernecky, T. (2012) 'Constructionism – critical pointers for tourism studies', *Annals of Tourism Research*, 39 (2): 1116–37.

Pernecky, T. and Jamal, T. (2010) '(Hermeneutic) phenomenology in tourism studies', *Annals of Tourism Research*, 37 (4): 1055–75.

Platenkamp, V. and Botterill, D. (2013) 'Critical realism, rationality and tourism knowledge', *Annals of Tourism Research*, 41: 110–29.

Stergiou, D. and Airey, D. (2011) 'Q-methodology and tourism research', *Current Issues in Tourism*, 14 (4): 311–22.

Taylor, S. and Edgar, D. (1999) 'Lacuna or last cause? Some reflections on hospitality management research', in B. Brotherton (ed.), *The Handbook of Contemporary Hospitality Management Research*. Chichester: John Wiley. pp. 19–38.

3

DEVELOPING THE RESEARCH PROPOSAL AND PLAN

Chapter Content and Issues

The intellectual and real-world value of a research topic.
Sources of research topics.
Choosing something of interest and value.
Limiting the conceptual and empirical aspects of the research
  topic to make it more manageable and feasible.
Considering the use of replicative studies.
Developing the initial research question(s), aims and objectives
  to focus the work and state a clear outcome.
Producing a research proposal.
How the research proposal relates to the research process.
Ethical considerations.

3.1   Introduction

The 'blank page syndrome' is usually the starting point for a research project and I always hear students say, 'I have no idea what topic I want to explore.' It is difficult to think about and begin to formulate a research proposal, especially one that will be of interest to others and feasible to complete in the time available. However, the task is not an impossible one, as I hope you will begin to appreciate as you progress through this chapter.

To help you get to the point where you have a clear idea of what you are going to research, why this will be of interest and importance, how you plan to investigate it and what the desired end product will be, this chapter takes you through the process of identifying, refining and finally specifying the focus, method(s) and purpose of your research project.

In taking this journey, you will encounter issues associated with possible sources of inspiration that you may want to consider exploring to stimulate ideas on what may be interesting topics and issues to research and how to think about the intellectual and real-world value of any of them. You will also be able to think through the process of narrowing and refining initial ideas into a final format that is more focused and feasible than your starting point and has a clearly stated purpose and outcomes to be achieved at the end of the process.

3.2 Finding and Refining a Topic

Unless you have a long-standing interest in something particular, this is often one of the most difficult issues to resolve because there is such a wide range of possible topics to research in the contexts of hospitality and tourism. Students ask, 'What could I use as a topic and where do I start?' However, before addressing these questions, it may be useful to take a step back, consider the various options and ask yourself, 'Why do I want to do some research on topic X? What is it about the topic that will be interesting and motivating for me?' until something sets you thinking. The research process is a journey and one that does not always progress smoothly, so you will need a topic that will sustain your interest and curiosity until the end, otherwise it will become difficult to keep going and complete the project.

3.2.1 Choosing a topic with potential value

So, what might be possible sources of interesting topics? These are likely to be related either to your own personal experiences – that is, the real world – or gaps you identify from information in the public domain – that is, the theoretical or conceptual world. However, as King et al. (1994) point out, there is no particular rule governing which topic to choose for research. That said, they go on to suggest that research projects should satisfy two criteria. These are, first, that the project should pose, and address, a question that is of importance in the real world. In short, that it has some significance in terms of developing understanding, explanation and possibly prediction and is therefore not trivial in nature. Second, that a project should make a contribution to the scholarly literature relating to the research topic. Essentially, the point they are making is that the research should have value, both a practical value in the real world and an intellectual value in relation to enhancing the existing state of knowledge on the topic.

Both criteria are important, though not necessarily equally so for each piece of research, because, collectively they indicate that the work should have practical and theoretical significance. It is often not difficult to envisage what the practical implications or significance of a research topic may be as these generally will relate to some type of improvement in the real world. On the other hand, anticipating what value the research may have in terms of making a contribution to the existing body of knowledge in the field may be less clear and seem more daunting as it is often interpreted as something high-flying academics or intellectuals can do, but not the average student. The issues here are the nature of expectations and the order of magnitude of the contribution. If you were a professor at a leading university, you may well be expected to produce entirely original, ground-breaking research results, but this is not the expectation people have of an undergraduate or even a Masters-level student. Just think about the word 'contribution' for a moment. It is quite possible to make small or large contributions and for both to have value. Adding something that is new, even if it is quite small, to what was known before constitutes a contribution. Table 3.1 shows some of the possible ways that such a contribution might be made.

TABLE 3.1   Different ways that research may make a contribution to the literature

Type of issue	Example
Select a hypothesis that is viewed as important by the literature but that is one for which no one has completed a systematic study. Any evidence discovered that supports the hypothesis, or not, will be considered to be a contribution	This might be something like 'increased levels of inbound tourism in developing countries help to stimulate economic growth in these countries'
Finding a hypothesis that appears to be accepted in the literature which we contend may be false, or one that lacks appropriate verification, and investigate it	This could be something along the lines of 'The speculation that the banning of smoking in public places, such as bars, pubs and restaurants, will result in a decline in business'
Discover a controversy in the literature and undertake a study to either substantiate one side of the argument against the other, or conclude that the controversy is unfounded	For example, an ongoing debate in hospitality is the conflict between the views that, on the one hand, hospitality has unique features not found in other types of business and, on the other hand, that it does not
Identify assumptions in the literature that have not been questioned and undertake research to determine their efficacy	The commonly held assumption that 'High levels of labour turnover in hospitality/tourism businesses are due to low pay' could be explored
Identify a gap in the existing literature characterised by an important issue that has either been ignored or inadequately addressed and undertake a study to remedy this	An example of this would be my research into critical success factors (CSFs) in hospitality businesses because, although CSFs had been researched in many other contexts, there were no systematic studies on this in a hospitality context
Identify theories, models or evidence existing in another body of literature that could be tested for their applicability and efficacy in another field or domain	An example of this would be the SERVQUAL studies, which were developed and tested in other service industry contexts, but the researchers claimed that this model could be used in any service business context
Replicate a study conducted in one context, or time period, and repeat this in another context or time period	This might be a study conducted in another industrial context, such as banking or retailing, or in another country or culture

3.2.2   Choosing a topic that interests you

In terms of personal interest, it could be that you have found a particular area of your course to be more interesting than others – marketing, say, or human resource management or sustainable tourism or fast food restaurants. If so, this could be a useful starting point for you. Alternatively, you may have particular career interests and selecting a topic related to these would give you an incentive to pursue and complete the work. For example, if your ambition is to pursue a career in high-quality international hotels as a rooms' division manager, a topic related to this may help you to obtain a job in this field. Alternatively, if your dream is to work in the tourism and visitor attractions field, you may wish to consider a topic related to this area. Similarly, you might want to combine an area of academic, or course, interest with one related to future job and career ambitions. For example, if you find marketing fascinating and want to work in tourism destination management, why not combine the two?

Another possible source of interest might be one based on your own experience of a hospitality or tourism organisation that you have worked in. Perhaps there was a particular problem you experienced there or a new development that took place and worked well or not. Alternatively, new legislation or regulation may have recently come into force and you have become interested in evaluating how it has or will affect the operation of a business. The organisation may have introduced new technology or has changed the way it is structured and operates. It may have been taken over by another company that has brought in a different way of conducting business. The organisation may have had particular problems with recruiting and training casual, part-time or seasonal staff that has impacted on the quality of the product or service offered to customers. It may be a 'unique' organisation in the sense that it has been the first to introduce a new way of working, a new technology or a new type of product. In other words, where the effects of recent change or innovation are not yet known or long-standing (apparently insoluble), problems are evident, there may be scope to investigate some aspects of them.

3.2.3 Do some exploratory work

If you are pursuing this route to identifying a topic, it might be useful to speak with other people associated with or involved in that issue and organisation. This is essentially an exploratory exercise, conducted in a relatively unstructured manner, to 'surface' ideas, views and so on. It simply involves having conversations with a number of people associated with, and probably affected by, the situation, in an attempt to obtain a range of perspectives regarding the nature of the issue or problem, the possible cause–effect mechanisms and probable answers or solutions. In some instances, they may give you vital raw material that will enable you to focus and structure the research project.

A good example of this type of process is that provided by Brotherton and Watson's (2000) piece of case study research. This sought to identify if a company's senior and public house managers had shared views regarding what was most critical for successful public house operations. Here, the senior managers' views and priorities were established in the exploratory part of the work. It was then a relatively simple matter to incorporate these into a questionnaire, asking the public house managers what level of importance they placed on each. Then the two sets of results were compared to ascertain the similarities or differences in views between the two levels of management.

In another unpublished student research project, the individual concerned wanted to determine whether or not the factors that the managers of fast food restaurants believed were most important to their customers' satisfaction were regarded as such by the customers themselves. To do this, initial conversations with the restaurant managers surfaced the factors they deemed important and these were then incorporated into a questionnaire for the customers, asking them to indicate how important each was to them. Again, by comparing the two sets of results, the similarities and differences could be identified.

3.2.4   Be aware of who is saying what

Turning to sources in the public domain, here we are talking about information made available to the general public in one media form or another. This might be the printed word – books, journals, magazines, newspapers, trade publications and so on – or audio or visual in nature – television, film, radio, DVD – or a combination of the two, such as multimedia material available on the internet. However, whichever format it appears in, it essentially reports what is and what is not known about the topic in question and helps to make people aware of the debates, points of view, differing interpretations, controversies and so on relating to the area. Therefore, the media in general is often a useful source of stimulation or even possibly inspiration when you are thinking about what a suitable topic might be for your research project.

As the writers/producers – be they academics, journalists or practitioners – of this type of material are invariably experts within their respective fields, they are likely to point out what is known and what is not, what is questionable or contestable, where evidence exists and where it does not, whether there are different perspectives being taken on the issue or issues, and so on. All of this can be helpful when you are trying to identify unanswered questions and gaps in the existing knowledge on the topic. Indeed, in some cases the authors may indicate the key questions and issues that need further research. We shall return to consider many of the issues relating to the literature, in its broadest sense, when we consider the literature-reviewing stage of the research process in more detail in Chapter 4, but it takes place after the topic, aims and objectives have been formulated, so it is much more focused in nature than the kind of initial explorations being suggested here. At this point in the process, the published literature is purely used as a source of ideas to identify the broad topic for the research project.

By looking at this material, your interest and curiosity may be sparked in varying ways. For example, at the time of writing, television news reports have indicated that the threat level from terrorist activities within certain countries is very high. This raises questions such as how is it going to affect tourism to those countries and what is the relationship between people's safety concerns and their willingness to travel to certain destinations? Similarly, we also read in the newspapers that low-cost airlines are extremely successful in helping to increase the volume of international air travel while, at the same time, environmental groups tell us that the carbon emissions this additional travel is generating are helping to speed up the process of global warming and climate change. So, are low-cost airlines a positive factor in helping to open up new tourism destinations and develop visits or volume to them or are they, in the longer term, likely to contribute heavily to climate change, which, in turn, may make some of these destinations less attractive?

3.2.5   Refining and focusing the topic

Once you have carried out these kinds of explorations and identified the broad topic for your research project, the next stage is to refine and focus this into something that is more realistic and feasible. In most instances, the initial idea will be something quite general and potentially large in scope. For example, your initial topic might be as broad as 'marketing in the hospitality industry' or 'new product development in tourism'. If you think about either of these for a second, you will be able to see that their breadth is potentially enormous and, given the time and resources you have to complete the work, this makes them unrealistic and not feasible. Therefore, you need to make the topic more manageable, but how?

The first step is to recognise that this type of broad research topic has two components. They are the conceptual and contextual aspects. Let us take the 'marketing in the hospitality industry' topic to illustrate this.

The 'marketing' aspect is the conceptual component of the topic and the 'hospitality industry' aspect the context within which it is to be explored. Because of their scope, both of these must be refined to produce a manageable project. To do this, it is useful to ask yourself a series of questions about each of them and try to make them more specific. So, for the context, you might begin by asking, 'Which sector of the hospitality industry do I want to use to explore marketing? Am I more interested in hotels or restaurants or contract food service?' If you choose hotels, you might then ask, 'Is it corporate, chain or independent hotels I'm interested in? Is it upscale, exclusive, mid-market or budget hotels that I would like to focus on?' If it is restaurants, you may ask, 'Do I want to concentrate on fast food operations, fine dining or public house restaurants? If I chose one of these areas, would it still be too broad? Would I have to limit it further, say to one particular company or brand, such as McDonald's, or perhaps to one location – fine dining restaurants in London, for example?'

This process should enable you to produce a context that is more focused and realistic than that of your starting point. So, for example, we might move from 'marketing in the hospitality industry' to 'marketing in UK budget hotels'. This considerably reduces the contextual scope of the project because it eliminates all the other sectors of the hospitality industry and other types/grades of hotel from the context of the study. This means that it is more realistic and manageable than before. Indeed, we may even decide to limit it further to something like 'marketing in the two UK budget hotel market brand leaders' or even just 'the market leader'.

However, even though this contextual focusing principle is sound, you need to be aware that, as the scope narrows, it has an influence on the type of research design that is then most appropriate to investigate it. If the context is 'marketing in UK budget hotels', it is likely that the most appropriate research design will be a survey, probably using a mailed or electronically distributed questionnaire. If, however, it is limited to the market leader or the two brand leaders, it is more likely that a single case study or comparative case study design will be used. In turn, this could imply that a standard questionnaire is not the most appropriate way to collect data from the companies concerned and it may be necessary to interview the marketing managers in each and use company documents to obtain the information required. This may raise issues of access and confidentiality and could be a high-risk choice.

The key point here is that the refining of the topic is ultimately not a discrete and isolated part of the research process as a whole. In common with many aspects of the research process, it is, rather, something that requires trade-offs to be made to produce an acceptable balance between the alternatives. In this sense, and because it takes place at the beginning of the process, there is a need for you to do some forward thinking. For example, if you either do not want to undertake a single, or even comparative, case study project or you feel that there may be problems with being able to get the information required to complete such a project, then this needs to be taken into account when the contextual aspect of the topic is being refined.

So, refining the context is important in helping to make the project more manageable, but it is only half the story. We still have a conceptual part to address, as 'marketing' is extremely broad in scope. For example, in our UK budget hotels context, we might concentrate on pricing and sales volume issues, the effects of promotional activities, the effectiveness of alternative distribution channels, the relative merits of different forms of advertising, marketing to different segments of the market, segmenting the budget hotel market and so on. Again, the principle here is the same as that related to the context – the general field is too broad to be feasible unless the context is reduced to a very small unit. If the context were to be a case study of a single company, then it could well be feasible to investigate all the aspects of that company's marketing. Conversely, if the context is defined in a wider manner – say, all UK budget hotels – then to try to investigate all the marketing policies and practices across this broader context would be complex and very time-consuming.

It would be reasonable to conclude from this that there is an inverse relationship between the breadth of the context and the concept. If the context is narrowly defined, in terms of its scope and scale, then there is room for the conceptual element of the research to be wider and more inclusive. Largely because of practical and pragmatic concerns – namely, the time and resources available to conduct and complete the research and how easy it is to gain access to the people or organisations you need to acquire information from – it is generally advantageous to define the context in such a way that you can deal with it satisfactorily within the constraints you face. This really means that you have to think about and make a judgement on the degrees of size (scale) and variability (scope) you can realistically cope with in the time and resources you have available. Other things being equal, this usually means that limits or parameters have to be placed on both of these to make the project feasible.

However, there is not necessarily a simple linear relationship between these considerations. Although, in general, it is true that reducing the context in scale and scope tends to be beneficial for successful completion, if it is reduced to a single or only a few entities, then access becomes a key issue. If you decide to concentrate your research on one organisation – perhaps because you have worked there and are familiar with it – it is absolutely critical that you are as sure as you can be that the information you need to complete the research will be made available to you before you take this option. Just think about this for a moment. If you decide on a project that involves sending out questionnaires to conduct a survey, then the context is wider and more variable but the risk of non-response is being spread. If only half of your sample of, say, 100, complete and return your questionnaire, you have 50 completed questionnaires to work with. Even if the response rate is far lower than this – say only 30 are returned, for example – you may well have enough data to complete the work. On the other hand, if you are dependent on one or two key people in the case study organisation being able and willing to give you their time and release possibly commercially sensitive company documents to you, this is potentially much riskier because they may change their minds, leave the company, have their superiors tell them that the information cannot be released and so on. In short if, for whatever reasons, your key sources of information fail to deliver, then you will have enormous problems.

Therefore, if you intend to focus your project on a very limited context and, hence, information sources, you must be as sure as you can be that the information you need will be available to you once the project starts. To do this, it is vital that you explain to your key sources, in as much detail as possible, what the project is designed to achieve and what specific information you will require from them to complete it. Being too general or vague about both of these at the beginning may cause potentially insoluble problems later.

Experience suggests that many people who are willing to help will readily say yes to a student asking for assistance with a general topic, but, when they are later faced with requests for the release of detailed information, they may decide that it is not possible for a variety of reasons. What they may have agreed to in general or in principle at the outset they may find impossible to deliver on when the detailed request is made.

So, once the topic has been refined somewhat into a more manageable form, the key question or questions that need to be answered can be developed. Taking the examples we have used above, we might now be in a position to phrase our topic as follows: 'The impact that promotional activities have on occupancy levels in UK budget hotels'. Here, the conceptual aspect now has a clear focus – on the promotional aspects of marketing – and the contextual element is clearly limited to one type of hotel operation. Together, these act to screen out a potentially huge amount of other information and concepts. Now we only have to deal with the literature relating to promotion and budget hotels and collect real-world data from the latter.

To reinforce the benefit of this, compare our final formulation of the topic with the one we started with – 'Marketing in the hospitality industry'. It should be obvious that this would be much more difficult to address as it is less specific and larger in scale and scope than the final one. In addition, because it includes such an enormous range of conceptual and contextual considerations, such a topic has huge breadth but very little depth. To adequately cover the breadth, very little detail could be included for each part. Given that, whatever the specific requirements of the research project, there are always constraints or limits on the reporting of the results, such as a maximum word limit for an undergraduate dissertation of, say, 10,000–12,000 words, then, the greater the breadth of material and issues that have to be included, the less room there is for any in-depth analysis of them. In this situation, it is likely that those assessing or evaluating the work will find it to be predominantly descriptive and trivial or superficial in nature as a result. Clearly, attracting such a judgement is to be avoided, for obvious reasons.

3.3   Refining the Research Question(s)

Once you are armed with the refined topic, it is possible to focus the research project a little more by formulating the key question(s) it will address or answer. Bearing in mind the need to retain the idea of conducting a focused and purposeful enquiry, it should be self-evident that the research question(s) should be limited in number. There may only be one or, at the most, two or three. The issue is how do we move from our topic to the research question(s)? There are various ways that this might be achieved.

3.3.1   Using what is known already

Perhaps the most obvious way to initiate this process is to begin by reading the literature on the topic to identify if there are existing theories or hypotheses related to it that could be applied to, and tested within, the context of the topic. For example, for our budget hotels and promotion topic, we might begin by reading some of the general marketing literature on promotional activity to see if there are any general theories or models that we could apply and test within the context of budget hotels. Alternatively, we might examine the literature on budget hotels and find that marketing managers or others have made claims regarding the effectiveness of certain types of promotional activity and want to research this to discover if there is evidence to support these claims. We might find that someone else has undertaken a study on our topic in another country and we could then consider whether or not the results would be the same if this were repeated in the UK. Similarly, we might find a study on our topic that was conducted some time ago and now, because the contextual conditions have changed, this needs to be updated to see if its results and conclusions are still valid.

This initial exploration of the literature does not constitute a critical review of the literature (discussed in Chapter 4) but is more of an initial scan to help us identify possible ways forward in the focusing of the intended project. Some authors refer to this as the initial or preliminary information-gathering stage of the research process.

In this sense, it is less concerned with a detailed analysis and understanding of the literature in the field and more with becoming aware of, and sensitised to, the possibilities it may reveal.

3.3.2   Be creative

Another source of possible inspiration lies within our own thinking or imagination. This may help to generate different ways of looking at a particular issue. For example, hospitality and tourism businesses invariably have a visible customer interface and an invisible backroom operation, but many other types of service business have a similar structure – banks, supermarkets and so on. Are the visible and invisible elements of these businesses the same as, or different from, those found in a particular kind of hospitality or tourism business? Are the organisational and operating structures of a hotel and a supermarket – and, therefore, management issues – the same or different?

To get you thinking even more about this aspect of the research proposal you may wish to view the two videos via the Video Links Section of the Companion Website (study.sagepub.com/brotherton) that deal specifically with developing good research questions.

3.4   Developing Aims and Objectives

At this point you may ask, 'If we have the research question(s) the project will be designed to answer, isn't that enough? Why do we need an aim and objectives as well?' The answer is, even though the question(s) provide a focus for the research and, at least to some extent, give an indication of what the project will be trying to achieve, they are not formulated in what might be referred to as 'output' terms. To illustrate this, consider the question we formulated previously – 'How, and to what extent, do price promotions affect occupancy levels in UK budget hotels?' Though it encapsulates the issue, it does not define what the end product, or aim, of the research project will be. To formulate this, we need to convert the question into another format. In this case we might do this by converting it into the following aim: 'To determine the strength and mechanism(s) of the relationship between price promotions and occupancy levels in UK budget hotels'.

This enables us to answer the research question but it gives an additional degree of focus to help guide the design of the research project and how it is conducted. The work will focus on quantifying the strength of the implied cause–effect relationship between price promotions and occupancy and also on discovering how this relationship actually works – that is, the mechanism involved.

One thing that you should note concerning the conversion of the question(s) into the aim is the change in terminology from a type of general query to wording that is positive and ends-related in nature. The aim, unlike the question, defines more specifically what the research will achieve. Thus, here we are saying that we will 'determine' rather than ask 'how and to what extent'. We define the desired end product of the process, which will make it easier for us, and of course others, to judge whether this has been achieved or not.

The purpose of the work is now to do or produce something quite specific, not just answer a less detailed question. Hence, aims should always be written in the form 'To ... '. This makes it clear that the purpose of the work is to be action-orientated and produce a specific output. The action verb that immediately follows this declaration may vary but it needs to specify the nature of output that is desired and, presumably, regarded as feasible. It may be to 'identify', 'state', 'determine', 'compare', 'analyse' or 'evaluate', for example.

The action verb used in the aim is seen by some to indicate the level of intellectual or academic treatment that the subject of the research is to receive from the researcher. It is often thought that intentions to 'identify' or 'determine' something indicate the pursuit of a lesser purpose than ones to 'analyse' or 'evaluate'. This may be true, but it is not always the case. Indeed, it can be misleading if the remainder of the aim is not taken into account. A consequence of this is that sometimes you may feel that you have to use the higher-level verbs – 'analyse', 'evaluate' – in your aim to indicate that it will be sufficiently academic in nature. You may even be exhorted by a tutor to do this.

Using this logic, our aim above could possibly be seen as rather simplistic and unambitious, perhaps even not at the intellectual level required for a final year undergraduate dissertation. However, to do so would be far from the truth. To determine the strength and mechanism of a relationship between price promotions and occupancy would be a demanding task in its own right. It would certainly not be an unambitious or easy task to accomplish. If, on the other hand, the aim was 'To determine the types of price promotion used by UK budget hotel companies', this would be quite a low-level, descriptive activity with perhaps little value as it would produce trivial outcomes that were probably already known before the work began. Similarly, as we saw in Chapter 1, an aim with the purpose of 'Determining the critical success factors for UK budget hotel operations' is appropriate and worthwhile because, although academic and industry commentators may have already speculated on what these might be, no one had collected the empirical evidence to test these speculations before. Thus, achieving the aim would add something new to the existing body of knowledge in this area. Indeed, to see how this was actually achieved, see Brotherton (2004).

One key aspect to bear in mind when thinking about the nature of an aim for research is the existing state of knowledge relating to the topic and research question. If it is relatively limited, it may be appropriate to design a piece of research that will be more exploratory and descriptive rather than analytical or evaluative. Knowledge tends to develop in small steps, so, if it is very limited within the area chosen, there may be great value in work that provides a more comprehensive and developed view of the issues. Conversely, if the topic resides within an established field of research work, it is unlikely that additional description would add anything of value to this existing body of literature.

Having made clear what the overall purpose of the research is – the aim – we are now in a position to work backwards from it and specify what we need to do in order to achieve this end result. This involves determining the steps or stages and tasks that will be required to achieve the aim. These are known as the objectives and, collectively, they should equate to the aim. In other words, if we achieve all the objectives, then we will achieve the overall aim.

To establish the objectives, we need to ask the question, 'What must we complete or achieve to ensure that the aim can be achieved?' Taking the aim from our example above – 'To determine the strength and mechanism(s) of the relationship between price promotions and occupancy levels in UK budget hotels' – we now need to consider what would be necessary to achieve it and, once again, specify these things in action-orientated terms. So, for example, we might ask ourselves questions such as, 'What type of information will be needed from the literature and the real world?', 'How are we going to identify and collect this information?', 'Which procedures and techniques will be required?', 'When will each task have to be completed?', 'Can we undertake some tasks simultaneously or will they have to be completed consecutively?' and 'Who will we need assistance and/or support from to do this?'

As there are many different ways of expressing objectives, with some emphasising process stages rather than more specific content and differing preferences of individuals and institutions, it is difficult to give definitive advice on the exact type of approach and wording that should be used to formulate objectives. That said, any objective should be action-orientated, specific, achievable and clearly be making a contribution to the achievement of the aim. The Technique Tip box – Specifying a Research Project's Aim and Objectives – provides an example of an aim and its associated objectives for a hypothetical project that illustrates these features.

Technique Tip	**Specifying a Research Project's Aim and Objectives**

Aim

To evaluate the critical success factors (CSFs) for cruise line operations.

Objectives

[1] To conduct a literature review to identify the nature of CSFs in general and in relation to cruise line operations.

[2] To develop a theoretical framework/conceptual model of the CSFs from the literature review and produce associated hypotheses.

[3] To collect empirical data from appropriate cruise line organisations and/or individuals.

[4] To analyse the empirical cruise line operations data and test the study's hypotheses.

[5] To produce conclusions and recommendations for further research into cruise line operations.

3.5 Putting the Research Proposal Together

The research proposal is really the first formal stage in the research process. It is here that you have your first opportunity to bring together and structure your thoughts and ideas concerning what it is you intend to investigate, why this is something worthwhile doing, how you intend to go about doing it, and what you expect to achieve at the end of the process. It is the proposal that articulates all of these things to communicate your intent to another party, i.e. your supervisor and/or a research approvals committee, who can then evaluate what you propose to do and, in the process, help you to refine and focus your initial thoughts by providing comment and feedback based on their previous experience.

 To develop your thinking on this task you may find it useful to view the video dealing with the issues, stages and questions involved in developing a research proposal and plan that is available via the link in the Video Links Section of the Companion Website (study. sagepub.com/brotherton) and the links in the Web Links section relating to this process.

3.5.1 What should the research proposal contain?

There are differing views on what should and should not be included in a research proposal and the format that should be used to present it. Similarly, your institution will undoubtedly present you with what is required and the format for the proposal you have to develop. However, whatever the specifics of these, a research proposal is a statement of intent and should include the following.

- *A title* This will not necessarily be the same as the aim of the project and is not critical at this stage as it can be changed later on if necessary.

- *An aim and objectives* These indicate the overall purpose, desired outcome and stages required to achieve the aim.

- *An introduction, background or rationale for the research* This explains and justifies why the issue(s) to be researched are important, how your work will develop from what is known already and how it may provide a contribution to advancing this knowledge.

- *A research plan* This indicates what you plan to do to achieve the aim. This may or may not include some indication of timings for the start/completion of these activities, but it should always include as much detail as possible on the overall approach and the methods and processes to be used for the data collection and analysis. Again, at this early stage, this may be somewhat speculative, but it can be changed later on when more is known.

- *Some references* These should also be included to indicate that evidence exists to support the statements you have made regarding the importance of the work and the methods and processes you have chosen to undertake it.

The key question to ask when putting the proposal together is, 'Could anyone pick up this proposal and actually do the research?' In other words, is it clear enough for anyone to understand, is it feasible given the likely constraints and resources available and does it have sufficient details to enable someone to go ahead and start the research? Think of the proposal as a brief you are giving to someone to actually do the work. The Research Action Checklist box – Checking Your Research Proposal – provides a series of questions to consider when deciding if your proposal is ready to submit or requires further work.

Research Action Checklist	**Checking Your Research Proposal**

Does my proposal

✓ provide a clear and appropriate context for the research question/s?

✓ make the boundaries/parameters of the research clear and are these appropriate and feasible?

✓ include a clear and focused research question(s) and appropriate aim and objectives?

✓ provide a clear, coherent and persuasive rationale for undertaking the research?

✓ cite landmark studies and researchers?

✓ present accurately and succinctly the major theoretical and empirical contributions from previous studies?

✓ focus sufficiently on the major issues and not include unnecessary detail on the minor ones?

✓ contain appropriate text and bibliographic citations?

✓ make it clear how I am going to design the data collection process and instruments?

✓ indicate what type/s of data will be collected and why?

✓ contain sufficient detail to inform the reader of how the data collection process will be implemented?

✓ specify and explain the sampling strategy and techniques that will be used to select and obtain the sample/s?

✓ indicate and justify the procedures and techniques that will be used to analyse the data?

✓ hang together as a coherent document?

✓ And finally, if someone gave me this proposal would it make sense to me, could I follow it easily and understand exactly what the person was planning to do and why?

One issue students often get hung up on in developing the proposal is, how long should it be? In many cases this may be prescribed but equally it may not. Where the latter prevails there is no definitive answer to the question of what length it should be. Some large and complex research projects may require considerable detail to be placed into the proposal, others of a smaller and simpler nature will probably not. The most important thing to bear in mind here is the notion of 'fitness for purpose'. Your proposal should include what is necessary for the reader/reviewer to understand what it is you intend to do/achieve and how. On the other hand, while there should be sufficient information provided on these issues the addition of further detail that is not necessary at this stage may conspire to make the proposal less clear. The message here is by all means include what is necessary but do this in a concise, logical and well-structured manner. As an example, one institution I previously worked at required its Masters level students to produce a research proposal for their thesis that required no more than two sides of A4 paper!

3.5.2   The research proposal and the research process

The process, and indeed pain, of developing the research proposal should not be seen merely as something that has to be done because your institution requires you to do it as a prerequisite to actually doing the research. Equally, once the proposal is finalised and approved it should not be cast aside and ignored because this aspect of the process is completed. What you believe and think you will need to do to complete the research, which will be embodied in your proposal, hardly ever turns out to be exactly what you will do as the research progresses. When we start this process we do not know everything we will know by the end of it. The proposal is an initial statement of intent outlining what we intend to do and how. Invariably intentions, based on relatively limited knowledge and understanding of the topic and its associated issues, are formulated on the basis of good, and logical, reasons at the time. As the work proceeds, and your knowledge and understanding grows, you may feel that some of these original intentions are a little naïve, too ambitious, impractical etc., and that you need to make changes to, or move away from, some aspects. However, sometimes students feel that this is problematic because this would somehow devalue the original plan or make them look stupid in the eyes of a supervisor. Nothing could be further from the truth.

The research plan embodied in the proposal should be seen as an initial guide not a definitive road map that cannot be amended in the light of new knowledge and/or previously unanticipated constraints. In this sense the plan will evolve over time, in some cases with only very minor changes to the original and in others with more extensive and fundamental changes. Thus, it should really be seen as a guide rather than definitive directions. Think about it in this way, you are setting out on a journey to arrive at the destination – the completion of your work – but you have only an imperfect sketch map when you begin this journey. As you proceed you will undoubtedly make adjustments to your direction of travel as you learn more about the terrain you are travelling over and encounter unexpected obstacles that you need to climb over or go around. Some of the equipment you thought you would need at the outset you find is inappropriate in the light of experience and some you believed you would need to use you now discover that you don't need to, or can't for some reason. Therefore, as you proceed on your journey you make adjustments to your travel plan and resources in order to reach your final destination successfully. In common with many ventures, this illustrates the variance between expectations and reality – things do not always work out as we expected them to do!

See also the video, available via the Video Links Section of the Companion Website (study.sagepub.com/brotherton), dealing with the issues facing a researcher attempting to navigate this journey.

There should never be a problem with making changes to the original plan. Of course, a good, well-thought out and constructed proposal is less likely to require radical changes as the process unfolds but even the best proposals cannot anticipate everything. Naturally you should attempt to produce a good, sound, comprehensive proposal, as this will almost certainly be a better guide than one that does not possess these characteristics, but this does not mean that it will not require some amendments as the research progresses. In my experience, students sometimes fail to grasp this, almost inevitable, reality of the research process. There can be a tendency to feel that admitting an emerging need to change some aspects of the original proposal is tantamount to admitting the original proposal was wrong and that this is going to reflect badly on them and the final mark the work is awarded. This can lead to such problems being ignored and/or to attempts being made by students to hide or cover up these issues in the mistaken belief that this will be to their benefit.

Once again, nothing could be further from the truth. All experienced researchers and research supervisors know that it would be quite exceptional if everything turned out exactly as it was anticipated at the beginning. Indeed, although the process of conducting research is concerned with producing something of value in its results it is also one that provides a learning experience for the person/s who conduct the work. So, to produce something of value at the end of the process does not require that all the expectations embodied in the initial proposal be validated as the process unfolds. The conduct of the process itself invariably creates new knowledge and understanding, including those aspects that do not go to plan. Discovering previously unknown or unexpected nuances in the existing body of knowledge often leads to research questions, aims and objectives being revised accordingly; finding unanticipated barriers and problems for which solutions have to be found, or identifying errors and flaws in the design, data collection and/or analysis aspects that require addressing, these are all aspects that constitute learning.

All of this means that being honest and transparent in recording the adjustments etc. that have been made during the process, and explaining why these were necessary, demonstrates reflection and insight. Rather than being penalised for this you are more likely to receive credit because this shows the development of problem-solving skills and a deeper understanding of the research process. Indeed, you may be explicitly asked to include a section in your final write up on what you have learned from the whole exercise, and even if you are not you will be expected to identify the strengths and any weaknesses in your work, problems that arose and how you dealt with them and what implications your experience may have for other researchers in the future.

3.6 Ethical Considerations

It is increasingly common for research proposals or plans to include an indication of any ethical issues and considerations the conduct of the research may raise. Indeed, showing that these have been considered and that conducting the research will not give rise to any significant ethical implications may be required as a prerequisite for the approval of a research proposal. It is likely that your institution will have research ethics policies, procedures, structures and documentation to ensure that any research conducted within the auspices of the institution, including that for undergraduate dissertations, is designed and conducted in an ethically acceptable manner.

So, what are ethics or ethical considerations and how do these relate to the research process? Ethics is concerned with moral values, principles and actions, such as honesty, integrity, transparency, obligations to others, responsibility and trust. In short, behaving in the 'right' way. Research ethics are therefore concerned with the moral principles that are used to inform the planning, design, conduct and publication of research. Ethics is not just an issue associated with the implementation of the research design in terms of collecting the data, but one to be taken into consideration throughout all the stages in the process, not only to ensure that the dignity, rights and welfare of any human participants are protected but also that the work is designed and implemented in an honest manner.

At its heart any proposed research should be able to adequately address two key ethical concerns, namely 'non-harm' and 'informed consent' (see the Key Concept boxes – Non-Harm and Informed Consent). These are both concerned with how the research participants are chosen and treated and the extent to which they are willing participants who have been provided with all the information necessary to make an informed decision whether to participate or not.

Key Concept	**Non-Harm**

Non-Harm – It is a basic principle of research regarded as ethical that the participants should not be open to any potential harm as a consequence of their decision to participate. This, of course, includes physical harm but it is a much wider concept than that. For example, unless otherwise agreed at the outset, it is a basic tenet of research that participants are not named, or able to be identified, from the data they provide and the way the results are presented. Such anonymity not only protects the privacy of the participant but it also tends to encourage them to provide more truthful responses, for obvious reasons. The non-harm principle also applies to potential psychological and/or social harm. Some topics and questions could be highly sensitive and have the potential to distress or embarrass the participant; some might put them in a difficult position in relation to their superiors/subordinates or social networks; some may cause them to lose face or lose their jobs. Similar issues may arise with corporate participants; although you may be unlikely to ask for, or be given, commercially sensitive information there still may be information obtained from companies/organisations that needs to respect the anonymity principle.

Key Concept	**Informed Consent**

Informed Consent – In many ways this is self-evident, however exactly what information should be provided to potential research participants so that they are able to make an 'informed' decision is not always self-evident. Naturally you would tell people what the research is about, what it is designed to achieve, why it is being undertaken, what the participant will be expected to do, how much time will be required, who, if anyone, is sponsoring the research and what will happen to the results but would you think about how you are going to record and store the data you collect? Apart from potential legal issues associated with data protection/disclosure legislation the anonymity principle equally applies to this. Although you may feel that using personal descriptors to enter your data into electronic, or any other type of, files is not a problem because they are private to you, this may not be the case. If others could potentially access these files without your consent or knowledge then your actions could, albeit inadvertently, cause harm to those individuals or organisations.

In the UK, one of the leading research councils – the Economic and Social Research Council (ESRC) – has produced a document, *Framework for Research Ethics*, containing six key principles of ethical research that it would expect to be addressed in a research proposal (ESRC, 2012: 2–3). The most recent version of this, updated in 2012, shows these to be as follows.

- **Research** should be designed, reviewed and undertaken to ensure integrity, quality and transparency.

- **Research** staff and subjects must be informed fully about the purpose, methods and intended possible uses of the **research**, what their participation in the **research** entails and what risks, if any, are involved.

- The confidentiality of information supplied by **research** subjects and the anonymity of respondents must be respected.

- **Research** participants must take part voluntarily, free from any coercion.

- Harm to **research** participants and researchers must be avoided in all instances.

- The independence of **research** must be clear, and any conflicts of interest or partiality must be explicit.

(Reproduced with permission from ESRC)

Therefore, any research proposal should contain a consideration of ethical principles such as these within its component parts. In short, it is incumbent on the person writing the research proposal to demonstrate that he or she has considered the extent to which the project may be ethically compromised in any of these respects. Often this does not require lengthy explanation or justification, although it may be required for contentious projects. Normally, inclusion of a short statement or series of statements that demonstrate the proposer has thought through any possible ethical implications raised in the proposed research will be sufficient.

Key issues to consider and state would be the potential benefits from the research and the ethical risks it may give rise to. In particular, issues associated with the integrity of the research design and possible risks to participants, including those that may affect their wider context, such as family, community, employer organisation and so on, need to be addressed. More specifically, these areas are likely to involve consideration of the expected quality and accountability (how it can be verified) of the research, how voluntary, informed consent (where possible and feasible) from the participants will be obtained and how issues of confidentiality, privacy and data protection will be addressed.

Depending on the extent of the ethical implications identified in the proposal, it may require anything from a light touch, an expedited approval process if the implications are minimal to a more rigorous approval process conducted via a research ethics committee if they are more significant. If your institution requires you to complete an ethics form to submit with your proposal for approval, then some of the ethical issues will be outlined in this. However, it may not cover ethical aspects of the overall research design and these may still need to be dealt with in the proposal. To give an indication of the issues this type of form may require you to address, see the Research Action Checklist – Ethical Issues to Consider in Planning Research, which contains a sample of things to consider based on the ESRC's ethical framework document, referred to earlier.

Research Action Checklist	**Ethical Issues to Consider in Planning Research**
Have you considered	

    ✓   potential risks to the researcher, participants, the data collected, your institution?

    ✓   what these risks might be and how they can be addressed?

✓   how the data you collect will be protected?

✓   how the participants will be identified and recruited?

✓   how informed consent will be managed and obtained?

✓   how you will ensure that no harm comes to anyone involved in the research?

✓   what will be done to ensure anonymity and confidentiality?

✓   how you will record, store and, eventually, dispose of the data?

✓   the extent to which you may need ethical approval for your work?

✓   if there are likely to be any 'sensitivities' you may need to address?

If you are able to answer 'yes' to these questions, then it is likely that your proposal will only require a light touch approval process. If the answer to any is 'no', then you would need to describe how these ethical issues will be dealt with in the research as it would then be necessary for a Faculty or Departmental Research Ethics Committee to give their approval to the proposal.

For further assistance on ethical issues see the 'Research Ethics Guidebook' link in the Web Links section of the Companion Website (study.sagepub.com/brotherton).

Chapter Summary

To identify a suitable research topic, think about what you are interested in, speak with others and be aware of current controversies.

From a general idea, begin to narrow the conceptual and contextual aspects down to make the topic more focused and feasible.

Get a suitable focus in terms of a question to answer or an aim and objectives to achieve.

Don't ignore the possibility of conducting a replicative study.

Think about what you will need to do and how you are going to do these things to produce the desired outcomes.

Put all your ideas together into a proposal and ask yourself if it is clear and whether it would be sufficient for anyone to be able to pick it up and then do the work.

Use your proposal as a working document – you will undoubtedly need to revise as the research process unfolds.

Do not forget that you will need to address the ethical issues your proposed research may give rise to.

References

Brotherton, B. (2004) 'Critical success factors in UK budget hotel operations', *International Journal of Operations and Production Management*, 24 (9): 944–69.

Brotherton, B. and Watson, S. (2000) 'Shared priorities and the management development process: a case study of Bass Taverns', *Tourism and Hospitality Research (The Surrey Quarterly Review)*, 2 (2): 103–17.

ESRC (2012) *Framework for Research Ethics*. Swindon: ESRC.

King, G., Keohane, R.O. and Verba, S. (1994) *Designing Social Enquiry: Scientific inference in qualitative research*. Princeton, NJ: Princeton University Press.

4

SOURCING AND REVIEWING THE LITERATURE

```
Chapter Content and Issues

The nature of the 'literature'.
Using the literature to help develop ideas and approaches to
    your research.
What is a literature review and why is it necessary?
Sourcing and searching the literature.
Accessing and obtaining the literature.
Managing the literature search.
Reading, note-taking and organising your literature base.
Critically evaluating and reviewing the literature.
The role and placement of the literature review in deductive
    and inductive studies.
Literature and research design relationships.
Writing the literature review.
```

4.1 Introduction

In this chapter, we will explore the searching, sourcing, accessing and reviewing of the literature element of the research process. The body of literature existing on a particular subject, topic or question essentially represents what is already known about it. Put another way, it is the existing body of knowledge or evidence. It is extremely important, when conducting a piece of research, to be critically aware of what this is as it helps to indicate where your research could/should go in order to add something to what is already known. By obtaining, reading and reviewing the existing literature, you become more aware of what is and is not known, who the key researchers in the field are, what methods, techniques and procedures have been used and how this knowledge can be used to help you develop your own ideas. It also ensures that you do not 'reinvent the wheel' and produce trivial work by investigating things that are already known.

In addressing such issues as what constitutes the literature, sourcing, searching and accessing it, why a review of it is necessary, how this should be approached, structured and written, I have taken the view that what is more important to you is the development of an understanding of the principles underlying these issues and why they should be regarded as important to you within your research project. I have also tried to indicate why certain key aspects of the literature review will be seen as important by the people who are going to read and mark your research project. What I have not done is provide extensive information on, and references to, information sources and how to record, analyse and review the literature. The reasons for this are that you are either likely to be aware already of the databases and other sources available for searching for literature in your institution or, if not, you could very easily do so by talking to the library staff, and you are also likely to have received guidance notes from your tutors on the specific requirements they have for this. Of course, another reason is that the space available within your text as a whole will be limited. If you need a much fuller explanation and further help on these issues, the books authored by Fink (2013), Jesson et al. (2011), Machi and McEvoy (2012) and Ridley (2010), all of which concentrate solely on the literature review, would be ones to consult. In addition, the texts produced by Ford (2012) and O'Dochartaigh (2012), focusing on using the web/internet for research, provide more specific advice on this particular aspect.

4.2   Why is a Literature Review Necessary?

Although, as we shall see shortly, the purpose and positioning of a review of the existing literature on a particular subject or topic may vary depending on the stage of a research process, one of the main reasons for conducting it is to demonstrate that you are aware of and have examined the current state of the knowledge relating to the topic you have chosen for your research project. As the vast majority of research topics within a particular field are likely to have been considered to some degree by previous research studies, be they conceptual or empirical in nature, there will invariably be some published literature relating to the topic you have chosen to pursue. In some cases, the quantity of this literature can be enormous. In others it may be rather sparse. In general, it is probably reasonable to say that the newer and more original the topic, the less likely it is that it will have been studied previously by others, so less literature will have been published on it and the reverse will be true for subjects that have been a focus of interest for several years.

4.2.1   Avoiding the trivial and adding something new

Earlier in this book, it was stated that research is conducted to contribute to an increase in the knowledge relating to a particular topic or field of study, to add something new to what is known already. To achieve this and make the research effort worthwhile, logic dictates that we must be aware of this knowledge if we are to add something new to it. If we do not, then we may be guilty of doing over again what somebody else has done perfectly well or, alternatively, producing a piece of research that is trivial and really has little, if any, value. So, we might say that one of the purposes of conducting a literature review is to protect ourselves from the potential criticism of producing trivial work. If we ignore the current state of knowledge and simply produce research findings that repeat those that already exist within the published literature, then we would expect others to tell us that this has been a waste of time because what we are telling them is nothing new. Again, logically, if we are to design a study that will possibly contribute something new to what is known, then we must be aware of what that knowledge is to ensure that the study is innovative in some way.

This highlights another purpose of the literature review: it helps us to design our research study. To take the state of knowledge on a particular topic beyond what is already known, we need to address questions and problems that currently do not have adequate answers or solutions. In this sense, undertaking the literature review helps us to build on the existing knowledge in a logical manner. It also gives us an opportunity to explain and justify the topic we have chosen, to set out the questions or problems we are trying to address and say why the approach we are taking to do so is appropriate, relevant, important and valid. Therefore, if we identify unanswered questions in the existing literature, differing interpretations of the same issues, such as controversies, or other gaps in the knowledge relating to issues that have not yet been explored, then we have the rationale we need to conduct our study.

Similarly, this analysis helps us to build a bridge between what is currently known – the literature – and what it is hoped will be added to this knowledge in the future – the results of our study. As most advances in knowledge occur via relatively small, incremental additions to or revisions of existing knowledge, analysing the literature is important as it helps to establish continuity in the development of knowledge. Put another way, it also helps you to demonstrate that your findings and conclusions do indeed add something new to what was known before. Furthermore, having a good understanding of the current state of play provides clues, and sometimes raw material, to help you focus and design your study. At the very least, a review of the literature indicates the types of approaches, processes, instruments, analytical techniques and contexts that have been used in previous studies. Beyond this, you will also become aware of the conceptual and theoretical positions previous studies have adopted. This means that you do not have to start with the proverbial 'blank sheet'.

4.2.2 Using what has gone before – opportunities for replicative studies

If you are lucky you may find a ready-made research design within the literature that you can use in your study. This is not to say that you can simply plagiarise previous work. It goes without saying that doing so is unacceptable. However, you need to be aware of the difference between plagiarism and replication because the latter is common, quite acceptable and may help you to develop a fairly robust design for your study. Although plagiarism has many forms and connotations, essentially it is cheating as you are copying someone else's work and attempting to pass it off as your own. Replication is different from plagiarism. Although it does involve an element of copying – because you are literally repeating something done before – there are two important differences. First, there is an explicit recognition of the fact that someone else conducted the original work. Second, there is some variation on the original. If this were not the case, then there would be little point in doing it. Let us look at some examples to clarify these important distinctions.

Many researchers studying the issue of 'service quality' in the hospitality and tourism fields during the 1990s (see, for example, Brotherton and Booth, 1997; Frochot and Hughes, 2000; Knutson et al., 1990; Lee and Hing, 1995; Saleh and Ryan, 1991; Stevens et al., 1995) undertook studies designed to assess the applicability of an instrument known as SERVQUAL, which was originally designed to measure the level of service quality experienced by customers in other types of service business environments. The purpose of these studies was to test the extent to which the SERVQUAL concept and instrument could be applied to hospitality and tourism environments or, put another way, to answer the question of whether or not it could be regarded as a concept and an instrument that could be used successfully across all types of service business without having to be modified to fit particular contexts. Although this SERVQUAL era is perhaps coming to an end as the dominant approach to researching service quality, service performance and customer satisfaction, there is still evidence that the use of SERVQUAL, and its numerous variants including LODGESERV, DINESERV, ECOSERV, SERVPERF, has continued from the millennium through to the present day (see, for example, Al Khattab and Aldehayyat, 2011; Bhat, 2012; Bougoure and Neu, 2010; Kim et al., 2009; and Said et al., 2013).

This approach is also relatively common where a study has been conducted in one country and the researcher asks the question, 'Would the results be the same in another country?' Personally I have conducted this kind of study twice in my research (Brotherton and Burgess, 1997; Brotherton et al., 2002). In the first of these, a study to identify the academic research interests of hospitality companies conducted by other researchers in the USA was repeated in the UK to see if the results would be the same. In the second, a study conducted in the UK to identify the critical success factors in UK corporate hotels was repeated in Holland, again to ascertain if the factors regarded as critical in the UK would also be regarded as such in Holland. Indeed the more recent SERVQUAL studies referred to above are also indicative of this process, with many of them seeking to ascertain the applicability of the SERVQUAL approach to hospitality or tourism businesses operating in very different cultural contexts – i.e. Jordan, Kashmir, Malaysia – than those within which the SERVQUAL approach originated and was applied to in the last decade of the twentieth century.

4.2.3 Developing your ideas

Even in circumstances where the methods used in previous studies do not appear to be suitable for your study, this does not mean that they will not have some value. Indeed it is possible that these may help to generate ideas relating to organising the data and/or to use such previous work to help support your thinking, arguments and conclusions. So, even where existing material does not fit your plans closely enough for you to use it, either in its original or a modified form, it is still likely to be useful, as it can help shape your thinking about how you might proceed with your research. This is not only the case in terms of how you might design and conduct the study but also in relation to how you might analyse the data you collect. For example, you may find that previous researchers have tended to use questionnaire surveys to collect their data and have employed particular statistical techniques to analyse these. Not only will this give you some ideas about how you might resolve these issues in your work but it may also help you to see that planning what to do for each stage of the research process should not be done in isolation because decisions made at one point will usually have implications for a later stage. For example, the way that a questionnaire is designed and the type of questions it contains will determine the type(s) of data that it will collect. In turn, the use of certain statistical techniques requires the existence of particular types of data. Therefore, the type of data analysis you intend to conduct should be thought about at the same time as or before the questionnaire is being designed.

4.2.4 Deduction, induction and the literature review

Up to this point in the chapter there has been an implicit assumption made regarding the role, timing and purposes of the literature review. If you have spotted it, then well done. If you have not, the assumption has been that the research to be conducted will have taken a *deductive* approach. As deduction works from what is known to what is unknown and tries to test the validity of the known theory in the research project, the review of the literature must occur before the new research is conducted. However, as you know, if an *inductive* approach is adopted, then matters proceed from the unknown to the known, from reality to the development of theory. In this latter case, at least in principle, the collection of empirical data comes before the review of any literature and the drawing of conclusions.

Therefore, the literature review is positioned differently and has a different purpose in the inductive research process. At best, the review may be conducted alongside or at the same time as the empirical data are being collected. This is often known as a 'grounded theory' approach to research (Glaser and Strauss, 1967) as the development of theory is said to be grounded in, or derived from, the collection and analysis of the empirical data. In other instances it happens after the data have been collected and serves as a comparator for the data and the themes emerging from the analysis of these data. One important point to make here is that induction and how a qualitative study is conducted should not be seen as synonymous in relation to the literature review. By this I mean that it is possible to conduct a qualitative study using a deductive approach, in which case the literature review would precede the data collection process.

4.3   What is the Literature?

Before considering the types and forms of literature, it is perhaps worthwhile at this point to briefly comment on what is meant by 'the literature' relating to a particular topic or field. In essence, this phrase is used to refer to the collective body of knowledge relating to a particular context. In short, it is all that is known and, indeed, unknown about a topic or field. So, when people talk about the 'body of literature' or an 'extant literature' or about making a contribution to 'the literature', they are referring to the current state of knowledge about a particular topic.

In the vast majority of cases this literature will be text, including figures, tables, diagrams and pictures, and will be printed and published in books, journals, magazines, newspapers and so on. Of course, the same or similar material may be published electronically on websites or other types of storage device. Regardless of its form, the important characteristic is the fact that it is in the 'public domain' and, therefore, potentially available for everyone to access. However, in reality, there are always some restrictions on the availability of published information. The most obvious of these is the ability to pay the price of obtaining or accessing the material– to buy the book, subscribe to the journal and so on. This will not generally be an issue for you, as your institution will have paid to obtain books for its library or the subscriptions required for a hard or electronic copy of a journal. Similarly, some information published on the internet will only be made available if a fee is paid. That said, a great deal of the information available on websites can be freely accessed.

Although texts published either traditionally or electronically are likely to be the dominant form of literature you will use for a literature review, it should not be forgotten that there are other forms of information that can be included within the literature relating to a particular topic or field. Depending on the nature of your research project, it may have no, little or great relevance to your literature review. This information tends to be that which is produced in an audio and/or audio-visual format – radio and/or television programmes, film media on tape, CD or DVD, artwork, advertising images and so on.

It is generally accepted that there are three main types or categories of information:

- Primary
- Secondary
- Tertiary.

There is some variation in the research methods literature concerning the definitions and, hence, what should be included in the primary and secondary categories.

Primary information is that which is collected for the first time from the real world – namely, it is new, original and empirical in nature. Thus, information obtained from questionnaire surveys, interviews or observations would be referred to as primary information. This is the type of information you will be seeking to collect during the empirical phase of your research project. Secondary information or data is essentially that originally collected by someone else, either an individual or an organisation, for their specific (primary) purpose(s), but which can be utilised for a second time in the current project. This really constitutes the substantive body of literature pertaining to a given topic or field of enquiry available in the public domain. In addition to books, periodicals (academic, trade or professional), reports, newspapers, website information and so on, it may also come in the form of unpublished dissertations or theses held in libraries, publications produced by government or quasi-government bodies, conference proceedings and company reports, to name just a few sources.

Tertiary information is essentially processed and summarised secondary information that has been distilled into a reduced form to facilitate the identification of the secondary literature that exists and what this may contain. Therefore such sources as indexes, catalogues, abstracts, bibliographies, databases, encyclopaedias and so on constitute tertiary information. These can be a shortcut to identifying the literature that exists within a field and, depending on their format, may be searchable using keywords or phrases to speed up the searching process.

Some writers also refer to what is known as 'grey' or 'intermediate' literature. The exact definition of this, and what is and is not regarded as grey literature, is somewhat variable. However, grey literature is generally characterised by being that which has been produced to be available to a restricted audience, rather than for general public consumption. So, policy and technical reports, working papers and research reports commissioned by an organisation would be part of the grey literature. One of the issues with some, not all, of this type of material is that there may be relatively little, or no, explanation of the methodology and procedures that have been used to generate this information. This raises issues concerning validity and reliability and should encourage you to treat it with some caution and, of course, critically. Reports commissioned by a particular client, those produced from research paid for or sponsored by particular commercial, or indeed non-commercial, interests and anything emanating from a process that has involved elements of political influence may well be subject to certain bias, reflecting the interests of the client or body politic.

4.4 What is a Literature Review?

It is common for academics to refer to the literature review as a 'critical review' of the existing literature, but what does this mean? It does not mean providing a simple regurgitation or restatement of what is contained in the literature. Neither does it mean doing so with the addition of a few linking comments from yourself. Consider the discussion contained in the Research Reality Scenario box – When is a Literature Review a Literature Review? – before we explore these issues further.

Research Reality Scenario	**When is a Literature Review a Literature Review?**

Manuel is a final year undergraduate student on a BA Tourism Management course and his dissertation supervisor (Dr Alistair Brown) has asked him to come and see him in his office to get some feedback on the draft literature review he submitted a week ago.

'Hello, Dr Brown, I hope you have some good news for me,' Manuel said when he arrived for the meeting.

'Come in, Manuel,' replied Alistair, 'I have certainly got quite a lot to say to you.'

'Oh dear,' thought Manuel, 'I don't like the sound of that!'

Alistair began, 'First, Manuel, can you tell me what your understanding is of what a literature review should be?'

Manuel replied, 'Well, I think the idea is to record what is known about the topic to show that I know this and to help me formulate appropriate questions for the research.'

'OK, that's true,' Alistair said, 'but there is a bit more to it than that. I've read your draft and, although you have been very thorough in covering the breadth of the literature relating to your topic, it is too descriptive at present, with very little critical analysis or comment.'

'I thought you might say that,' Manuel said, with an impending sense of more work to do! 'I know we have been told that the review should be critical,' he continued, 'but I'm not sure how to do that. Can you help me please?'

'No problem, that's what I'm here for, Manuel,' Alistair said, helpfully. 'Let me try to help you think about this. First of all, think about the relationships between the issues of who, what, why, when and how in relation to the literature.'

Manuel looked even more confused.

Alistair continued, 'At present, you cover most of these in your review, but in a descriptive and isolated manner. You tell me who has said what, when texts were published, how they arrived at their conclusions and even, sometimes, why. However, what is missing is the underlying analysis of any similarities or differences between the previous studies, a recognition of the philosophical roots of the different authors, whether or not there are any gaps or omissions in the literature you've reviewed, what the strengths and weaknesses of the studies are and how valid and reliable the methodologies used and results obtained might be.'

'Wow,' Manuel gasped, 'that sounds really difficult, I'm not sure I can do that.'

'Okay,' Alistair said, 'I know you can and I'm going to talk you through one part to show you that it's not as difficult as you seem to think.'

'Okay, that's great,' Manuel said, unconvincingly.

'So,' Alistair began, 'let's look at the section on customer satisfaction. Here you say Jones (1999) found in his study that facilities for children were not regarded as being as important as other factors by the questionnaire respondents, but Tolmey (2002) obtained different results from his questionnaire.'

'Yes, is that not being critical?' Manuel asked.

'No,' Alistair replied, 'You are merely reporting a difference without offering any suggestions as to why this was the case. For example, were the two studies conducted at the same time of year, were they undertaken in the same type of tourism business, did they have similar sample sizes and compositions, were the questionnaires administered in the same way?'

'Ah, I see what you mean,' Manuel replied. 'In the first study, a large proportion of the sample were women and family visitors, but in the second they were mainly student coach parties visiting the centres. Also, in the Jones study, the questionnaires were left on the restaurant tables for the visitors to complete, but, in Tolmey's study, a team of interviewers went around to interview the visitors and complete the questionnaires. So, I guess that the different results might have occurred because of differences between the samples and the ways the questionnaires were implemented.'

'Excellent, Manuel – now you're getting the hang of it,' Alistair said. 'If you look at the literature in that way, then you are going to get much more depth into your review and be able to identify and critically comment on the quality and significance of the previous work.'

'Thanks, Dr Brown,' Manuel said, gratefully. 'I see exactly what you mean. The next version will be much better and looking at it that way should also help me to decide what approach I should take in my empirical research.'

'Exactly, you really have got the hang of it now. I'll look forward to seeing the next version, Manuel', Alistair said, pleased that Manuel now understood what he needed to do.

So, Manuel's supervisor makes the point that merely restating, listing and describing previous work does not indicate that the reviewer has engaged sufficiently with the literature. Such an approach is really quite superficial and likely to attract significant negative criticism and comment. For a review to be regarded as critical, there must be evidence of engagement with the literature. This demands more than regurgitation because it involves an element of processing. When you engage with the literature, you study it in depth because you examine it in detail in an attempt to develop a greater understanding of its relevance, validity and significance. This is exactly what Manuel's supervisor was pushing him to do. Alistair wanted him to demonstrate that he had developed an appropriate degree of insight in relation to the sources he had referred to. In this example, Manuel moves on from simply listing and describing previous work to a position where he was beginning to evaluate it by considering the extent to which it might be seen as robust and credible or flawed.

4.5   Sourcing, Searching, Accessing and Organising the Literature

Before you can conduct a literature review, you obviously have to identify what relevant literature exists. This means that, in the first instance, you need to identify possible sources of the literature. The most obvious source is the library, particularly for books, but other sources, such as the internet in general and other online databases, bibliographies and so on, may be as, if not more, fruitful in terms of speed and ease of access. Most institutions now have subscriptions to electronic journals and subject-specific and/or more general online databases and you should check which of these you are able to access at the earliest opportunity. In addition, many publications, such as newspapers and magazines, have their own websites that can be searched for electronic copies of articles.

4.5.1   Managing the literature search

Once the potential sources of material have been identified, the next stage in the literature reviewing process is to conduct what is commonly called a literature search. Depending on the nature of your topic and research aim/objectives, the scope and scale of the literature that might be relevant could be quite limited or vast. Assuming that you have followed the previous good advice to make sure that your project has a suitable focus, the potential breadth and volume of material that would be regarded as relevant to your study should be limited. However, even where you have done this, there are some questions and issues that will have received a large amount of attention from previous researchers and the volume of literature will reflect that.

To help you cope with some of these issues, in an ideal world, you should know exactly what you are looking for before you start the literature search. The problem is, invariably, that this is unrealistic because you probably will not know what literature exists before you start searching to find it. That said, there are some things that you can do to make your life easier. Even if you cannot know exactly what you are looking for at the outset, you can place some limits or parameters on the search to potentially limit the volume of 'hits'. Intuitively, you probably know and practise this already. For example, if you are looking for something on the internet and enter a term or terms into a search engine such as Google, if your terms are quite broad you are likely to get many thousands of results, but if you repeat the search with more specific terms the volume of hits will be reduced.

The same principles apply to searches of online databases, library catalogues, bibliographies and so on. One way to begin to limit the potential terrain for the search is to qualify or delimit your search terms. For example, if your project is investigating service quality in hotels, then instead of simply entering something like 'service quality' as the search term it may be preferable to enter 'service quality+hotels', as this will limit the number of hits to those that focus on service quality literature specifically related to hotel businesses. If your study is limited to the UK or the USA or any other particular country, then you could also add this to the search string. As you make the search more specific and limited in scope then you can expect there to be fewer hits, but they are also more likely to be relevant. Conversely, if you find that by limiting the search terms this generates only very few references, you can always widen these. For example, if you choose to put a date-range limit on your search of the last five years and this delivers relatively few useful hits then you might consider widening this to say the last 10 years.

One way to expand or limit your searching of internet sources, particularly databases, indexes and abstracts, is to use what is known as Boolean logic. This is not as complicated as it may sound! What it does is expand or contract the search terms. For example, if you were conducting a keyword search for material on recruitment, selection and interviewing, you could enhance your chances of finding material connected with all these keywords by formulating the search so that it will find only material containing all three. By entering the search term 'recruitment AND selection AND interviewing' the search is going to deliver in its results only material containing all three of these terms. Alternatively, if you wanted to widen this search to find material with any one of these three terms in it, then you could formulate your search term with 'OR' instead of 'AND' between the keywords. This would then identify material containing at least one of these three terms.

Where the spellings of keywords differ in UK or US English, such as 'behaviour' and 'behavior', you can use 'AND' to ensure you pick up both. However, there is a shortcut for this known as entering a 'wild card'. So, in this case, you could enter 'behavio?r' and this would pick up material with different spellings of the word. Also, to capture variations relating to a particular keyword, there is another alternative to using a string of variations connected by 'AND'. This is known as 'truncation' – using a chopped-down version of the keyword. By taking the basic stem of the word and adding an asterisk, this will produce results relating to the different variations on this stem. So, for example, the search term 'motivat*' would pick up related keywords, such as motivation, motivational, motivating, motivate and so on.

Computerised searches may also be conducted and broadened or constrained using other search criteria. For example, if you know the names of the most important authors of the material you are interested in, you can search using their names. Similarly, many databases and indexes allow searching to take place for a specific year or a range of years that, again, can help you to widen or limit your search. Alternatively, if you know the journals that are most likely to contain the type of information you are looking for, then it may be possible to specify that you want to search for the keywords within a particular journal.

Of course much of this is relatively easy to do using the 'advanced search' option that is usually available in both general search engines such as Google and Yahoo and more specific ones. This option normally provides a number of 'filters' that you can use concurrently. For example, you can use the Boolean logic described earlier along with a date range to limit the time dimension and, in some cases, you will be able to select the journal titles you want to search using the criteria you have specified. If you have identified a particular author who has written a lot of material on your topic then you will be able to search for just the material authored by him/her.

There are also other ways to limit and/or focus a search. If you are interested only in literature published in English, then you may want to specify this at the beginning. If you do not specify a time period for the search, then, potentially, you may get hits going back many years or decades. Sometimes this is necessary, but often it is sufficient to limit your search to more recent sources. It is difficult to suggest a definitive time period to use because this varies according to the nature of the research topic and its purpose but, in many cases, identifying the literature published over the past 20 years is likely to be more than sufficient. This could always be extended at a later stage if the sources reveal, through the references contained in them, there were important studies produced at earlier dates that are likely to be relevant to your study or, if such a extended time range delivers too large a number of hits, you can instead limit the range further as described above.

Nevertheless, although broadening or limiting the range of your search can be useful, it will not help you to identify the material you need if you have used inappropriate terminology in the search terms. As we saw earlier, the spelling of terms can, and does, differ in UK and US English. In addition to this, different terminology can be used for the same things in the UK and USA. For example, in the UK, it is common to refer to the 'hotel industry', but this is known as the 'lodging industry' in the USA. In the UK, we talk of 'fast food restaurants', but these are known as 'quick service restaurants' in the USA. The same issues can arise in the context of conceptual terms. In the literature, some authors use the term 'critical success factors' (CSFs), but others use 'key success factors' (KSFs) to refer to the same thing. Also, because jargon and terminology change over time and differ from one country to another, we need to be careful how such words are used in search terms. For example, some countries distinguish between their hotel and tourism industries, but others do not – they include the hotel industry within the tourism industry. Today, it is common to use terms such as 'downsizing', 'delayering' and 're-engineering' in relation to organisational change, but in the past terms such as 'restructuring', 'streamlining' and 'reorganisation' were used to refer to such activities. Furthermore, because we are so familiar with the use of abbreviations and acronyms, we may write these as our search terms without thinking. They may, or may not, relate to the formulation of the keywords in the database, index or website. So, using 'UK' or 'US' instead of the spelled out versions of these terms may give rise to problems, as may using 'WTC' instead of 'World Tourism Council'.

Another issue to consider is the type of material to search for. As noted earlier, the literature is represented in varying forms and media, but not all of these will be equally relevant or valuable for your particular purposes. Similarly, not all of them will be equally trustworthy or credible. For example, you may expect that material published in an academic journal is more likely to be objective and accurate than that in a company's own publicity literature or a newspaper. Also, remember that there is always a time delay between when work has been completed and when it is written up and published. This is at its shortest for the most frequently published media, such as those that are daily, weekly, or monthly, and at its longest for books, where the text may have been written a year to two years before it is actually printed and published. Even in the case of academic journals, the peer reviewing and publication processes papers go through before they actually appear in issues can be quite extended, possibly as long as those associated with books.

Although a generalisation, it is probably fair to say that one of if not the best types of material to concentrate on in the first instance is that found in academic journals, followed by books. Frequent publications, such as newspapers, magazines, trade journals and so on, do have the advantage of containing very contemporary, up-to-date material, but it is subject to less scrutiny than that found in academic journals and can be influenced by other, subjective, pressures of a commercial and/or vested interest nature. It is also likely to be less detailed because of the pressure for space in such publications. By way of contrast, the material contained in academic journals will normally have been subjected to review and scrutiny by other academics in the field before being accepted for publication and thus will be quite detailed because, in general, the authors of this material will have been required to make clear the aims, objectives and purposes of their work, provide a critical review of the literature, detail and justify the methodology they have adopted in the study, explain, as fully as space allows, the instruments and procedures used to collect and analyse the data and discuss the importance and significance of the findings. This means that the material is going to provide you with a lot of detail and has a high degree of credibility.

Another strategy that is often a useful one to start with is to limit your search to focus on the most recent material that has been published on your topic. There are a number of reasons for this. Clearly it will allow you to be aware of the current state of play in relation to your topic and this is useful in its own right. It will also enable you to see how the current state of knowledge has been arrived at, because overwhelmingly knowledge development proceeds incrementally by building upon what has gone before. This means that the most recent studies in the field will contain a review of, and the references for, prior studies. This essentially provides a shortcut to identifying authors and studies that have been conducted/published previously, thereby allowing you to get an immediate feel for the nature and size of the underlying literature base. Naturally these references can then be followed up to start building the literature base for your study.

After you have searched to establish the literature available, assessed what is relevant for your purposes and acquired it, you must think about the importance of keeping full and accurate citation records for all the material you have sourced and acquired, regardless of whether or not you are sure that all of it will be cited in the final work. The information required for these purposes is detailed in Chapter 11. Some degree of forward thinking at this point about such details can help to save pain and time later, because if you get into the habit of making sure that all the information you may need for citation purposes is recorded on handwritten notes, photocopies or printed versions of electronic documents you will not be caught out when writing up your project.

Finally, the question often arises, when should I stop the search and move on to the next stage in the process? This is a difficult one to answer because the literature bases relating to different research topics and studies are extremely variable. That said, the decision questions contained in the Key Decisions box – When Should I Stop My Search? – suggested by Jesson et al. (2011), may be helpful.

Key Decisions	**When Should I Stop My Search?**

If you can give the appropriate response to the following questions then you may be in a position to consider stopping your search and beginning the next stage in the process:

- 'Have I searched all of the appropriate resources?

- Are there any gaps in the information sources searched?

- Have I used complex search statements as required by individual data-bases?

- Could any improvements be made to the searches?

- Have I identified all the relevant references? ... [and have I obtained all those of relevance?]

- Have I used both full-text and bibliographic databases?'

Source: Jesson et al. (2011: 30)

Note: Additional text in [ ] added by the author.

4.5.2   Reading, note-taking and organising the literature

Reading the material you have acquired is the first step in processing it to extract the key information relevant to your study. How you approach this is likely to be a very personal decision based upon your preferred learning strategy but there are various techniques proffered in the literature to suggest ways of approaching this task. One that is fairly well known is the SQ3R (Survey, Question, Read, Record and Review) technique. Essentially this technique suggests that you spend some initial time scanning or skim reading the material to get a feel for its structure and main ideas. Having accomplished this, the next stage is to ask yourself what the material is all about, i.e. what is its central concern, what is it trying to answer or achieve, what perspective does it take? The idea of this stage is to test your feelings about the paper from the initial skim-reading stage, to see if you have got a clear idea of what the material is saying. The third (Read) stage involves a much more focused and detailed examination of the material and should take as long as is necessary for you to develop a sound understanding of the issues it deals with and a fairly comprehensive understanding of its significance, or otherwise, for your study.

The Record stage, which may become subsumed within the Reading stage, is then designed to highlight the most important content in the material as far as you are concerned. As this 'importance' can take a variety of forms, i.e. it might be conceptual, logical argument, associated with some aspect of the methodology such as the sampling strategy or data collection/analysis techniques and/or procedures used, it may be helpful to have a way of recording such aspects differently. For example, on photocopied material you may use a colour code system to indicate such different aspects or with handwritten notes you might use different headings or notation to indicate this. Finally, the Review stage provides an opportunity for you to ask yourself if you now have a clear understanding of what the material is saying and its significance and also to begin thinking about how it relates to other material you have been reading to surface similarities or differences.

Alternatively, the EEECA model encourages a more conceptual approach to reading the literature. The first stage is to Examine or analyse the topic from more than one direction or perspective. The second, to Evaluate (critically) the material to begin making judgements about it. Next, to Establish the existence of any relationships and to articulate the nature and mechanisms of these relationships. The fourth stage is to start Comparing and contrasting the ideas expressed in the material to ascertain how similar or different they may be to those expressed in other material. Here it is important not only to compare material from contemporary sources but also to think about how ideas may have changed and evolved over time, i.e. we know where we are at presently but how did we get here? Finally, it should now be possible to start developing for/against Arguments based upon the available evidence.

If all of this seems to be rather restrictive, Jesson et al. (2011) propose a much simpler way to begin the process of beginning to read the, probably daunting, pile of material you have accumulated from the literature search, see the Key Decisions box – Deciding What to Read First.

Key Decisions

Deciding What to Read First

As the well-known proverb says, each journey starts with a single step – but the question is what might be the appropriate first step to take? Which article, book or other type of information you have collected should you focus on to begin this journey? Jesson et al. (2011: 49) suggest a quite simple decision process to get this process started:

'The process is guided by two key decisions:

1. Is this reading relevant to your study? Is the information appropriate to the matter under consideration?

If yes,

Continue.

[If no, do not automatically discard it at this point because you never know exactly where your reading and thinking will take you as the process unfolds. You may not think it is relevant at the beginning but as you develop your knowledge and understanding of the topic you may find it relates to aspects you did not know of, or consider relevant at the beginning when your knowledge was necessarily imperfect.]

2. Does this reading add anything to the arguments or information that you have already completed?

If yes,

Continue.

If no,

Add the reference to your bibliographic list. Make a note that it has nothing new to contribute so far, add your reading date and reference details in case you want to return to it again. Then set it to one side in a colour-coded file. You will probably want to take another look at a later date for further examination, as your understanding and insight develops.'

Note: Additional text in [ ] added by the author.

Taking notes is a very personal thing. The approach favoured by one is unlikely to be favoured by another. We all think and are stimulated to think in quite different ways. For some quite extensive text notes will be helpful but for others it might be their own form of shorthand or diagrams and doodles. Using different coloured highlighter pens on photocopied material is one technique often used to indicate material relating to different categories. Using handwritten notes in the margins of such material to produce mini-summaries and/or to cross-reference to other material dealing with the same issue is another option. Producing a handwritten 'summary sheet', similar in style to an annotated bibliography, to attach to the front of each piece of material can be a useful way of distilling the key information you require. In short, there are an almost infinite number of ways to take and organise your notes, just choose the approach that suits you.

Whatever system or approach you favour, Jesson et al. (2011) suggest there are some generic and critical reasons for taking notes from what you are reading as this proceeds. These are contained in the Key Concept box – The Value of Note-Taking

Key Concept	**The Value of Note-Taking**

The five reasons for note-taking outlined below indicate the value of being actively engaged with your material as you read it by beginning to 'process' it as you go along:

- To identify and understand the main points of what you read.

- To develop a way of rephrasing material in your own words.

- To help you reflect and think, concentrate on what is important and to recall easily what you have read.

- To make connections across texts and authors so that you can rearrange them for writing the review.

- To develop your own comprehension of the topic.

Source: Jesson et al. (2011: 59)

In thinking about how you might approach recording and organising your material once again this may prove to be a personal issue, with what suits one person being seen as counterproductive by another. That said, there might be some approaches that could have more generic value, either as they stand or customised to your preferences. For example, the list of questions contained in the Technique Tip box – Getting to Grips with the Literature – are ones that pretty much everyone might want to ask as they begin to process this evidence base.

Technique Tip

Getting to Grips with the Literature

- How do the authors of the articles define their topic? [Who are the key influencers and researchers in the field?]

- What key terms and phrases do they employ? [Are these really different or just saying the same thing in a different way?]

- How have other researchers approached your topic? [What have their philosophical and methodological stances been?]

- What has been the history of research on this topic? [Is it something that has attracted attention only very recently or has a long track record; has interest increased or decreased in more recent times?]

- What are the research controversies within this literature? [What are these based on – fundamentally different philosophical and/or conceptual approaches or alternative methodologies?]

- Where is there agreement and disagreement? [What form does this take, is it a matter of methodological choice and/or implementation, interpretation, strength of evidence in terms of its validity and/or reliability?]

- What specific questions have been asked? [What questions have not been asked and should be?]

- What has been found out? [What has not been found out, discovered or proven?]

- What findings seem to be most relevant? [Why is this the case, what makes some more relevant than others?]

- What remains to be done, that is, what burning questions still need to be addressed concerning your topic? [What has not been answered, either at all or incompletely?]

- Where do you find gaps in the literature? [Are there conceptual gaps or are these to be found in the ways that previous research has been designed and/or implemented?]

Source: Hesse-Biber and Leavy (2006: 56)

Note: Additional text in [ ] added by the author.

However, to jump from the initial reading and processing of your literature base to dealing with such questions may be difficult. Therefore, compiling an annotated bibliography as an intermediate step could help. This is simply just another part of the filtering process designed to help you extract the key information and record it in a form that can be helpful to address some of the overarching questions. The elements that should be included in an annotated bibliography are indicated in the Technique Tip box – Structure of an Annotated Bibliography – but basically what you are trying to do here is add some value to your notes by not only including additional descriptive comment but also some initial analytical and evaluative thoughts. In short, you begin to address issues such as the credibility, consistency, clarity, accuracy, perspective, methodological and evidential strengths and weaknesses of the material.

Technique Tip	Structure of an Annotated Bibliography

[1] The full bibliographic citation containing all the information required for whatever referencing style you are using.

[2] A series of keywords that indicate its focus – in the case of academic journal articles these will already have been provided in the original.

[3] A concise summary of what the material says, including any critical comment on its value. For example – 'This is the third study conducted by Bond that further develops his model of labour turnover in the tourism industry through additional empirical evidence gathered from a survey of small tourism businesses in Spain. There are some concerns about the sampling strategy used (convenience) and the size of sample (n = 20) he bases his data analysis and conclusions on.'

[4] An indication of the standing of the author and the publication itself. For example – 'Bond is a well known and respected researcher and has published widely on this topic and this paper has been published in a well known peer-reviewed journal.'

[5] An identification of any links the material has to other material you have in your literature base. This can be as simple as merely indicating the basic reference/s to the other material or it could be more extensive to include an indication of the nature of these links. For example – 'This material links to Bond's two previous studies on the same topic and takes his ideas further. It also contrasts with the studies by Largo and Goldfinger who adopt different methodologies and heavily criticise Bond's approach.'

[6] A judgement concerning its value to your work. For example – 'This illustrates one strand of the approaches taken to investigating this issue and, in conjunction with Bond's other work and that of Burgess, illustrates one of the three main approaches researchers seem to have taken to this topic. In that sense it is an important one to include in the study but some care should be taken with its methodology which seems to have some potential deficiencies.'

Another technique you may consider using to help you further distil the material into a more concentrated form is what some refer to as a 'literature map'. This is essentially a visual representation of the information you have already processed, although it also constitutes a further step in filtering and organising the material to help you see the links and connections more clearly and succinctly. Indeed this might be seen as something of a natural progression from the annotated bibliography as the latter should contain all the raw material required to construct such a map or diagram. Developing this more holistic view of your material could also be accomplished using a tabular approach. Indeed, you may wish to consider producing the annotated bibliography not as individual, stand-alone entries but within this type of tabular framework. This approach may save you time and effort and also help you to see some of the connections and linkages more quickly and easily.

As you may have gathered by this stage, the processing of the literature is one akin to an inverted pyramid. You start with all the material you have collected from your literature search and begin, stage by stage, to reduce this volume down to more manageable proportions. Additionally, at each stage, you not only reduce the volume and breadth of material but also begin to identify and concentrate on that which is most important and significant, that which is more crucial or critical to your study and therefore must be included. As many topics will have a literature base so large you could not possibly include all of this detail in your review you have to reduce this down to focus on its key aspects, be they conceptual or empirical, or both.

4.6 Evaluating and Reviewing the Literature

We saw earlier in this chapter that it is necessary for you to engage with the literature in order to review it appropriately and that the review should demonstrate insight. This requires some evaluation to take place, but what does this mean?

Evaluation is concerned with making judgements. Of course, we can all make subjective and fairly superficial judgements and we do so every day, but they may have little or no basis in fact and should more properly be regarded as personal opinions. Evaluation is more objective, organised and criterion-related. To illustrate the difference, if I asked you what you thought of two different cars, you might say that one looked sportier than the other or safer or more comfortable and so on. On the other hand, if I asked you to evaluate the two cars against each other, you would probably ask me how and on what basis? In other words, you would be asking me to provide you with some basis for making the comparison, some common denominator that you could use to compare the features and performance of the two cars. In short, you would be asking me to provide you with a framework or criteria that you could use to do this in an explicit and objective manner. So, for example, I might give you a checklist to use for this containing criteria such as petrol consumption, 0 to 60 miles per hour acceleration time, the boot capacity, the braking distance to a stop at 60 miles per hour, the number of airbags in the car and so on.

Translating this into the context of a literature review for a research project, we might think of comparing and contrasting the literature in terms of:

- the philosophical stance taken by different studies – that is, whether it was positivistic or phenomenological;

- the research approach and design adopted – that is, whether it was deductive or inductive and/or was conducted using a survey or case study;

- the type of data collection instruments and processes used – that is, whether closed or open questions were asked and if they were implemented at a distance (posted or e-mailed) or directly (people interviewing respondents face to face);

- how the samples were determined, what the sizes and compositions were and if they were adequately representative or biased;

- the techniques used to analyse the data;

- whether the conclusions derived from the findings were valid or not.

This may appear to be a lengthy and difficult task, and in some respects it is, but you are expected to produce a critical review of the literature and this is what is required to do so. However, not only will this effort produce a review that is much more acceptable than a trivial, descriptive one, it does not necessarily require more time and words. Because you are looking for patterns, themes, consistencies, irregularities, gaps, omissions, strengths, weaknesses and so on in the literature, you do not need to include as much descriptive detail in the review as you would if you were outlining all the studies. In this sense, you may write the same amount of words, but the structure, approach and content will differ. In short, you should include less detail in terms of 'what' the literature says but more about 'why' and 'how' and the quality and credibility of the work.

In a sense you are trying to create what may be referred to as a 'meta-analysis' of the literature. Although this term is usually used to refer to a process that focuses on quantitative data and seeks to determine whether a particular variable has a certain effect by comparing, contrasting and evaluating the results from a range of previous studies there is no obvious reason why the same thinking and process cannot be applied to the literature review because this, in essence, is what reviewing the literature entails. Therefore, organising the literature using some of the ideas contained in Section 4.5.2 may be helpful in facilitating such an analysis and evaluation.

Evaluation is also concerned with making certain value judgements regarding the quality of the evidence embodied in your literature sources. Although you can use reasonably objective criteria to evaluate the quality of the material you are dealing with, this is unlikely to be a simple dichotomous decision. In other words, it will be one dealing with relativity within which material will be judged as being more or less credible, logical, sound or flawed, accurate, believable etc. The Technique Tip box – Evaluating Your Sources – contains some questions that could be helpful in this respect.

Technique Tip

Evaluating Your Sources

Authority and Credibility

Who is the author or authors?

Who are the key players?

Where are they from, i.e. what type of institution?

Are they being sponsored and, if so, by whom?

Could any sponsorship or funding they are receiving be seen to influence their work and results?

Are they well known in the field?

Do they have an established track record of producing high quality work?

Are they recognised and cited by their peers?

Are they publishing their work in the leading peer-reviewed journals in the field?

Is the language used appropriate, i.e. is it logical, balanced and as objective as might be expected?

Accuracy and Believability

Is the research design appropriate and sound?

Has it been implemented appropriately?

What is the nature of the sampling strategy and the sample achieved?

Are the data analysis techniques appropriate and have they been used correctly?

Does the author address issues of validity and reliability in a sound way?

Are any ethical issues recognised and dealt with appropriately?

Does the work build upon previous work on the topic in a logical and consistent manner?

Does it cite the key researchers, concepts and findings from prior studies?

Value and Significance

What does it add to the knowledge and understanding on the topic?

Is its contribution minor or major, is it a breakthrough or just confirmation of previous findings?

What is the nature of the evidence used to support claims and propositions – is it based on empirical evidence, conjecture, anecdote or logical argument?

How convincing is this evidence – is it extensive, strong, logically consistent or not?

How well does it deal with counter-arguments – are these comprehensively refuted with compelling evidence and/or argument?

Does it recognise and comment on errors and omissions (nothing is perfect!) and indicate what the implications of the results are?

Are any new questions generated by the work articulated clearly?

At this point, it is also worth mentioning that there is, or certainly should be, a connection between how you approach and organise the evaluation of the literature and the structure that the written review will take. This, again, is a case of different tasks in the process having implications for each other. In the following section, we consider how the written review might be organised and structured and identify some alternatives in these respects. These have implications for how the evaluation might be organised and conducted. In short, if you plan to organise the write-up of the review using particular sections, it would be wise to think about using a similar structure to evaluate the literature, otherwise you may find that you have quite a bit of work to do to fit the evaluation into the write-up structure. This is one of the many parts of the research process where a degree of forward thinking can help you to connect the sequential stages as smoothly as possible and reduce the amount of extra work you will need to do if you do not work in this way.

As this is one of the tasks that students often find somewhat bewildering and difficult to get their heads around it may be helpful for you to use two links in the Video Links section of the Companion Website (study.sagepub.com/brotherton) that deal specifically with this issue of evaluating and synthesising the literature.

4.7 Writing the Literature Review

Having processed the literature, all that remains is to write up the review. As you will know by now, the purpose, format or style that this may take will differ depending on whether the research process takes a deductive or inductive approach. In the same way, the timing, placement or positioning of the review within the process will also differ. Normally, if the research is to be conducted by means of a deductive process, the literature review will appear in the final written document as a separate section or chapter (see Chapter 11 for more on this). Indeed, as we have seen previously, one reason for choosing a deductive approach is that there is a substantial body of literature in existence, from which established perspectives, theoretical frameworks and models and methodologies can be identified and reviewed to help focus and shape your own empirical research questions and methodology. Where an inductive approach is used, the review may be presented at the end of the study, where it is likely to be used as something to compare and contrast the empirical data with. Here, the review does not direct and guide the empirical research process, but instead provides assistance to help connect the theoretical perspectives emerging from the empirical work to any literature that does exist on the issues. Remember, the purpose of deductive research is to test existing theory, while inductive research seeks to build new theory.

Taking the review in a deductive study first, which is likely to be the favoured approach for most of the research work conducted for undergraduate or postgraduate dissertations, the main questions are: 'How do you organise and structure the writing of the review?' and 'What style should be used to write it up?' Really, there are no definitive answers to these questions because the nature of given bodies of literature and research studies varies enormously. That said, there are perhaps certain principles that you should bear in mind when writing this type of review. We have already established that it needs to be critical and evaluative rather than merely descriptive. It should illustrate that you are knowledgeable about the previous work in the field; help you to identify key assumptions, questions, issues, gaps and omissions in the current state of knowledge; and inform your decisions concerning what data to collect, how these might be analysed and the methods and procedures that might be the most appropriate to do this.

In the next chapter, we will be exploring how the 'product' of this literature review provides vital raw material to help design the conceptual and methodological details for the proposed empirical research and, thus, connects existing and new knowledge in a logical and systematic manner. To provide suitable raw material for this purpose, the review needs to be written in such a way that it becomes possible to identify the key concepts and methodologies in the existing literature.

So, how can this be done? Cresswell (2014) proposes an approach structured on identifying the key factors relating to cause and effect and what relationships are suggested to exist between the two sets of factors. As we shall see in Chapter 5, these are known as the independent (causes) and dependent (effects) variables. His model indicates that the review should begin with an introductory section, informing the reader about the organisation of sections which are contained within the review. This type of introduction should be present whatever specific approach or format is adopted in what follows it. After this, Cresswell (2014) suggests that a section reviewing the literature on the causes, or independent variables, should be present and then one reviewing the effects, or dependent variables. Once these have been established, the next question is either 'How are these connected?' or 'What is/are the cause–effect mechanism(s) or relationship(s) between them?' Therefore, a section dealing with these issues is required next before the review is concluded, with a summary section to highlight the major themes and so on.

Although the logic of this is sound and it may be possible to organise and structure your review accordingly, it is not always that easy to organise the material in this way. If your research topic or question has a number of subdivisions or components, it might be difficult to write the review in this format. Also, this structure does not automatically make it easy to identify and compare and contrast the philosophies and methodologies underlying previous work. A somewhat easier approach may be to structure the review into sections, such as:

- introduction;

- key questions or issues addressed;

- dominant philosophies and approaches;

- main themes and methodologies, gaps, omissions and controversies;

- summary (the current state of play).

Alternatively, you may wish to use more of a 'content' basis to structure the review. By this I mean using major subdivisions within the field. These may be few or more prevalent depending on the nature of the research question(s) and the literature base. For example, in my research on critical success factors (CSFs) in hospitality businesses, the literature could be divided into two main categories – that relating to CSFs in other organisational contexts and that concerning CSFs in hospitality organisations. However, it could also be further subdivided into more specific categories within each of these two broad areas. In the case of the hospitality CSFs literature, it could be broken down into studies concerned with different types of hospitality business (such as hotels, restaurants, pubs and so on), or geographically (North America, Europe, Asia-Pacific), or by the business function forming the context of the study (information technology systems, food and beverage contracts and so on). The point here is that there are usually many ways to structure and organise a written review of the literature, some of which are appropriate for certain studies and others not.

In the previous section, we identified that, when evaluating the literature, some degree of forward thinking regarding how the writing of the review might be structured could prove to be useful for helping to structure the approach to the evaluation. However, it may also be the case that, in the absence of this, the way in which the evaluation evolves will tend to indicate an emerging structure for the written review, as patterns, themes, connections, relationships, controversies and so on become evident.

In terms of what style of writing is appropriate for the review, this is dealt with more extensively in Chapter 11. However, in common with the imperative to make the review critical and evaluative rather than merely descriptive, there is a need for a more discursive style to be used in the review. If the evaluation has identified commonalities and divergences, agreements and disagreements, patterns and themes in the literature, as it should have done, then these should be reflected in the way the review is written. In turn, this implies discussion rather than statement and a flowing text rather than one broken up into a lot of discrete blocks. The reader needs to be able to follow the story being told and you need to lead him or her through it to its conclusions. Think of this like an upside-down pyramid. As the story unfolds, from its broader beginnings to a much more specific and focused end, you should lead the reader from the background context at the beginning, through the main themes, processes and actors, to a clear identification of the most important elements at the end.

Again, although dealt with more fully in Chapter 11, it is worth mentioning here that there are certain academic writing conventions you need to follow when writing the review. As you will be referring extensively, either directly or indirectly, to the published work of other people, it is important to recognise and record this in the text by using, correctly, the referencing system recommended by your tutors. This will avoid any problems of you committing, intentionally or otherwise, plagiarism and suffering the penalties associated with this. It is also wise to remember that what you are writing about in the review is objective 'evidence'. It may be tempting sometimes to insert your own personal, subjective opinions, but this should be unnecessary if you have conducted the evaluation properly as they will be embodied in the evaluations that you have made.

For additional perspectives on planning, conducting and writing up the literature review go to the Companion Website (study.sagepub.com/brotherton) where you will find, in the Web Links section, a series of links to other websites and documents providing hints, tips and guidance on these issues, and, in the Video Links section, a video providing a student view of the experience of the literature review process.

Chapter Summary

The 'literature' may be comprised of various types of published information, including printed media, such as books, journals, periodicals, magazines and newspapers; electronic media, such as e-journals and books, websites, DVDs, CDs, and other forms, such as video, film, audio recordings and so on.

Different forms or types of literature may have greater or less credibility.

A literature review enables you to demonstrate that you are aware of, and understand, the existing knowledge relating to your research topic or question. It also enables you to demonstrate that you have engaged with it by evaluating and reviewing it in a critical manner.

It can help you to decide what type of study – new, replicative, comparative – may be appropriate and/or feasible in the light of what is known already from the literature.

It also helps to form a bridge between what is already known and what you plan to add to this by carrying out your research. In this sense, within the context of a deductive study, it can help to inform your decisions regarding the formulation of the conceptual framework and hypotheses to be investigated in the empirical part of your research and the data collection and analysis methods, techniques and procedures that might be adopted.

In an inductive study, it is used as a resource to assist the data analysis and interpretation.

References

Al Khattab, S.A. and Aldehayyat, J.S. (2011) 'Perceptions of service quality in Jordanian hotels', *International Journal of Business and Management*, 6 (7): 226–33.

Bhat, M.A. (2012) 'Tourism service quality: a dimension specific assessment of SERVQUAL', *Global Business Review*, 13 (2): 327–37.

Bougoure, U. and Neu, M.-K. (2010) 'Service quality in the Malaysian fast food industry: an examination using DINESERV', *Services Marketing Quarterly*, 31 (2): 194–212.

Brotherton, B. and Booth, W. (1997) 'An application of SERVQUAL to a hotel leisure club environment', *The Proceedings of the EuroCHRIE/IAHMS Autumn Conference*, Sheffield Hallam University, pp. 117–21.

Brotherton, B. and Burgess, J. (1997) 'A comparative study of academic research interests in US and UK hotel and restaurant companies', *The Proceedings of the Sixth Annual CHME Hospitality Research Conference*, Oxford Brookes University, pp. 317–48.

Brotherton, B., Heinhuis, E., Miller, K. and Modema, M. (2002) 'Critical success factors in UK and Dutch hotels: a comparative study', *Journal of Services Research*, 2 (2): 47–78.

Cresswell, J. (2014) *Research Design: Qualitative, quantitative and mixed methods approaches*, 4th edition. London: Sage.

Fink, A. (2013) *Conducting Literature Reviews: From paper to Internet*, 4th edition. Thousand Oaks, CA: Sage.

Ford, N. (2012) *The Essential Guide to Using the Web for Research*. London: Sage.

Frochot, I. and Hughes, H. (2000) 'HISTOQUAL: the development of an historic houses assessment scale', *Tourism Management*, 21 (2): 157–67.

Glaser, B. and Strauss, A. (1967) *The Discovery of Grounded Theory*. Chicago, IL: Aldine.

Hesse-Biber, S.N. and Leavy, P. (2006) *The Practice of Qualitative Research*. Thousand Oaks, CA: Sage.

Jesson, J.K., Matheson, L. and Lacey, F.M. (2011) *Doing Your Literature Review – Traditional and Systematic Techniques*. London: Sage.

Kim, W.G., Nee Ng, C.Y. and Kim, Y-S. (2009) 'Influence of institutional DINESERV on customer satisfaction, return intention and word-of-mouth', *International Journal of Hospitality Management*, 28 (1): 10–17.

Knutson, B., Stevens, P., Wullaert, C. and Yokoyoma, F. (1990) 'LODGSERV: a service quality index for the lodging industry', *Hospitality Research Journal*, 14 (2): 227–84.

Lee, Y.L. and Hing, N. (1995) 'Measuring quality in restaurant operations: an application of the SERVQUAL instrument', *International Journal of Hospitality Management*, 14 (3/4): 293–310.

Machi, L.A. and McEvoy, B.T. (2012) *The Literature Review: Six Steps to Success*, 2nd edition. London: Sage.

O'Dochartaigh, N. (2012) *Internet Research Skills*, 3rd edition. London: Sage.

Ridley, D. (2010) *The Literature Review – A step-by-step guide for students*. London: Sage.

Said, A., Shuib, A., Ayob, N. and Yaakub, F. (2013) 'An evaluation of service quality from visitors' perspectives: the case of Niah National Park in Sarawak', *International Journal of Business and Society*, 14 (1): 61–78.

Saleh, F. and Ryan, C. (1991) 'Utilising the SERVQUAL model: an analysis of service quality', *The Service Industries Journal*, 11 (3): 324–45.

Stevens, P., Knutson, B. and Patton, M. (1995) 'DINESERV: a tool for measuring service quality in restaurants', *The Cornell Hotel and Restaurant Administration Quarterly*, 36 (2): 56–60.

5

DEVELOPING THE CONCEPTUAL FRAMEWORK

> ## Chapter Content and Issues
>
> The conceptual framework.
> Constructs, concepts and variables.
> Correlation and causation.
> Hypotheses.
> Theories and models.
> Operationalisation.
> Measurement and scales.
> Determining validity and reliability.

5.1 Introduction

In the previous chapter we explored the issue of 'what is already known' by considering what is involved in carrying out the literature review relating to a research topic. We saw that the output from the literature review constitutes the raw material for formulating the conceptual and methodological approach to the empirical aspect of the research we plan to conduct. In the same way, it also helps us to explain and justify why the design and implementation decisions we are about to make will be appropriate and valid – because they will be based on our objective review of the best evidence available. Therefore, we will be addressing two sets of issues in this chapter. First, the conceptual framework to adopt for a study, which will specify the main factors, or variables, involved in the issue(s) and question(s) to be researched, how and why these are related or connected and what predictions (hypotheses) can be made and tested on the basis of this. Second, how to explain and justify the methodology used to undertake the research.

5.2 The Conceptual Framework

To explore the issues associated with creating a conceptual framework will involve considering questions such as what is it, why is it necessary, where does it appear in a research study, what does it do and what does it have to do with concepts, constructs, variables and hypotheses? Taking each of these questions in turn, we will begin to explore the nature, purpose(s) and roles of the conceptual framework within the research process.

You can also do this for yourself by viewing the video specifically on the conceptual framework contained in the Video Links section of the Companion Website (study. sagepub.com/brotherton).

5.2.1 What is it?

The conceptual framework is sometimes referred to as a theoretical framework or a model. However, it is not necessarily the same as either of these, as you will see later. Essentially, the conceptual framework is a structure that seeks to identify and present, in a logical format, the key factors relating to the phenomena under investigation. Depending on the nature and purpose(s) of the research project, the conceptual framework may be correlational or causal in form.

A correlational framework would be one designed to postulate or suggest possible connections between two or more factors. For example, it might be suggested that there will be a correlation between food hygiene standards and food hygiene qualifications or that cost-reduction programmes will be associated with different levels of profitability. Similarly, a more complex example might suggest that a range of different factors are associated with a particular phenomenon. Consumers' decisions to purchase a particular product or service could be connected to their income, job security, personal tastes, its accessibility, the extent to which it is perceived to be good value, the availability of competing products/services and so on.

On the other hand, a causal framework would be one designed to be more specific about the nature and direction of the suggested relationship(s). Here the conceptual framework is used to present a cause–effect linkage between factors. Using the examples above, we could change each of them into a causal statement by amending how they are stated. We might say that *if* more people obtain food hygiene qualifications, *then* food hygiene standards will rise or companies that implement cost-reduction programmes will experience higher levels of profitability. Note here that the words '*if* ' and '*then*' are italicised in the above statement. The 'if … then …' form of expression is a standard way of expressing causal relationships because such a statement can be tested – that is, we can arrive at a conclusion that confirms the statement is either true or false. In other words, we can say that the hypothesis is either supported by the evidence (verified) or it is not (rejected).

5.2.2 Why is it necessary?

A research study without a conceptual framework would be like a body without a skeleton! The conceptual framework is necessary to provide a logical and coherent structure for any research study, whether it informs its design and implementation in a deductive approach or integrates its results in an inductive approach. In most, if not all, research work, there are two main aspects – a review of existing literature in the field and an empirical investigation. The conceptual framework is the essential link between these two aspects as it serves to establish a logical connection between the existing body of knowledge and the new knowledge your research is trying to generate. Thus, it creates continuity between what has gone before and what is to come.

5.2.3 Where does it appear in a research study?

This depends on the type of approach that is taken to designing and conducting the study. If an inductive approach is taken, where the empirical data are collected during the early stages of the study, the conceptual framework will not be developed until later in the process. In this case, the conceptual framework is a product, or outcome, of the analysis applied to the empirical data (see Chapter 10). Thus, it emerges from this analysis to assist you in establishing any logical links between the interpretation of reality and any existing literature in the field. An example of this can be found in the study conducted by Milman (2011), who collected data on the image of a tourist destination in Turkey portrayed by postcards on sale to the public and, from the analysis of these, proceeded to develop a conceptual framework identifying four discrete types of postcards portraying different types of image.

On the other hand, if a deductive approach is adopted, then the conceptual framework performs a different role and is established much earlier in the process. Here, it is derived from the literature review undertaken during the early stages of the research project. It is this review that informs the nature of the conceptual framework to be used for the empirical part of the research investigation. Therefore, in this case, the conceptual framework is the synthesis of the critical review of the literature and, as such, identifies the key concepts, constructs and variables relevant to the study's empirical investigation. A good example of this type of approach is provided by Slatten et al. (2011) in their study that examines customer experiences in winter amusement parks. This paper really provides a 'classic' example of the process of developing a conceptual model, and associated hypotheses, directly from a review of the literature.

5.2.4 What does it do?

As you will have gathered by now, the conceptual framework has a different role to play in inductive and deductive research. In the former, it is very much a 'product' of the empirical investigation, while, in the latter, it is an essential 'input' into the design of the empirical work. This means that its purpose in inductive and deductive research is different. In induction, its main role is to provide a logical and coherent framework to interpret the empirical data and develop a theoretical understanding of the phenomena being studied. In this sense, it is an 'integrative' mechanism, designed to surface and articulate the underlying concepts, dimensions and variables within the empirical data from which a theoretical explanation for the real-world observations can be developed.

In deductive research, the conceptual framework is used in a more disaggregated manner to test the hypotheses it contains. Here, the framework is broken up into its constituent parts in order that the postulated linkages and relationships may be expressed as hypotheses that, in turn, are then tested in the empirical investigation. Therefore, in this approach, the framework is a major influence on how the empirical work is designed and conducted – that is, the decisions made regarding the methods and processes to be used to collect and analyse the data.

5.2.5 What does it have to do with concepts, constructs, variables and hypotheses?

Concepts, constructs and variables are the building blocks for the conceptual framework. These effectively help to identify the key dimensions and elements relating to the phenomena being studied and facilitate their measurement. Given the potentially enormous number of individual items or factors that could be included in any conceptual framework, there is a need for these to be grouped or categorised into more manageable entities. Hence, concepts are collections of associated events, objects, conditions, situations and so on that are aggregated in order to make life simpler. In this sense, they do not exist in the real world, but are abstractions created by people to simplify the complexities of the real world and, at least in theory, make understanding and communication easier. However, as you will see later, this is not always as straightforward as it might appear.

Constructs are often confused with concepts, but they are not synonymous. Constructs are more abstract than concepts and are used to group related concepts together. Thus, constructs perform the same role in grouping related concepts together as concepts do in grouping more specific factors together. Therefore, the role of both constructs and concepts in developing the conceptual framework is essentially the same. They are mechanisms that help to structure the complexity of the individual elements relating to the phenomena in question. In short, they help to develop a logical and hierarchically ordered structure for the framework. For example, 'quality' is an abstract term, so, to define it, reference has to be made to specific, real factors. Quality itself, in common with many other abstract notions, may be a construct or a concept. We might refer to the concepts of product and process quality to capture the ideas of tangible and intangible aspects of the tourism or hospitality experience. In turn, we might combine these two as conceptual components of a broader construct, such as service quality, to refer to the totality of the experience a consumer has.

Variables are derived from constructs and concepts and tend to be more tangible, observable and specific. Grouping related items together into concepts or constructs may assist conceptual clarity and understanding, but it does not help to measure the effect, relationship or association between the specific elements in the framework. To do this, the constructs and concepts need to be converted, translated or operationalised into specific and tangible items that can be measured as directly and unambiguously as possible. This is the role of variables in the conceptual framework.

5.3   Constructs and Concepts

Constructs and concepts can be easily confused and used, incorrectly, as if they were the same thing. One way to distinguish between the two is to see a construct as something larger and more abstract than a concept or, alternatively, consider that constructs are made up of groups of concepts that are narrower in scope and less abstract in form. Another way of putting this would be to say that a construct is a broader, more abstract, generalisation than a concept. For example, if we took a very broad, generalised term such as 'customer satisfaction', we might imagine that there would possibly be quite a range of factors relating to, or potentially influencing, the degree of satisfaction a customer feels or experiences. Among them may be concepts such as the quality of the product or service they receive, the friendliness of the company's staff they interact with, whether they perceive the purchase to be good value for money or not, the extent to which the product or service met their needs and wants and so on. Similarly, as you probably know, the construct of 'personality' is comprised of personality types, which are concepts, such as introverts and extroverts.

So, a construct is something we 'construct' to represent a combination or collection of other things that can be used to communicate the meaning of this grouping. In this sense, it is a form of communication shorthand that enables us to communicate and share meanings in an economical manner. Although concepts are used in the same way, they are closer to the real world and less extensive in the range of things that they are used to represent. Hence, the very broad term 'personality' would be a construct and the somewhat more limited term 'extrovert' a concept.

Both constructs and concepts help us to simplify a complex world because we can group together related things or items to convey a quite complex idea more simply. In general life and conversation, this usually does not create problems and is a positive benefit, making communication easier and more economical. However, because the meaning of a construct or a concept depends on the nature and extent of the real, tangible things it represents or is associated with, the degree to which the meaning of the abstract term is shared depends on the extent to which different people's interpretations of what this means are the same. The extent to which constructs and concepts can be used as an aid for communication depends on the extent to which people share the same definitions of them.

In many general instances this is not an issue because we learn the meanings of these from a young age as a natural process of our development and socialisation.

However, where more specific language codes are used, such as the jargon associated with academic disciplines or particular industries or professions, there may be constructs and concepts that are not common in everyday language and communication. In addition, there may also be some that are commonly used in the latter, but when used in the former, have different connotations or meanings within the more limited and specific context of their use. Therefore, there is invariably a need, within a research context, to make clear how the construct or concept is defined and what it is being used to represent – that is, what you mean when you use it.

To give you an example of this, I have conducted quite a lot of empirical research into critical success factors (CSFs) in hospitality businesses (see, for example, Brotherton, 2004a, 2004b) using questionnaires. However, because the meaning of the term CSF is one that can be interpreted differently by different people, asking them a series of questions about CSFs is potentially problematic. To try to avoid this, the questionnaires contained a definition of what I meant by CSFs on the front page and the respondents were asked to read this before answering the questions that followed in an attempt to ensure, as far as was practicable, that they all had the same understanding of the term before responding to the questions about it. This is shown in the Research in Action box – Critical Success Factors in Hotels.

Research in Action	**Critical Success Factors in Hotels**

Before attempting to complete the questionnaire it is important, for the validity of this research, that all respondents have the same understanding of the concepts/terms used in this questionnaire. Therefore, we would ask that you take a few minutes to read and digest the definitions and examples provided here, before you respond to the questions, to ensure there is no misunderstanding of our usage of the terminology throughout the questionnaire.

Critical Success Factors (CSFs) are defined here as: the limited number of areas in which results, if they are satisfactory, will ensure successful competitive performance for the company.

CSFs are not Corporate or Business Objectives, they are the factors critical to success in meeting such objectives. In short, they are not ends, but the means to these ends. A useful way to think of the difference between the objectives and CSFs is that the former are usually prefixed with 'To', and the latter with 'By'. The following example should help to illustrate this difference:

Objective – To maintain our position as market leader.

CSF – By improving the standard of our customer service.

As constructs and concepts are abstract inventions, they do not exist in the real world and cannot be directly seen or measured. Also, because they are collections of associated things, they are not unitary (single) elements, but combinations of, potentially, many elements. Therefore, to use them in the empirical part of a research project, you need to convert or translate them into more specific and concrete things. This is generally known as 'operationalising' the concepts or, sometimes, as writing the operational definition for the research and is a task we shall examine later in this chapter. Before we get there, however, we need to explore another aspect of the conceptual framework that is used to accomplish this translation. It is the specification of the variables associated with the concept(s) to be used in the framework.

5.4 Variables

There are four main types of variables that can be found or included in a conceptual framework:

- Independent

- Dependent

- Intervening

- Moderating.

Before we consider each of these, in terms of what they are and the function(s) they perform within a conceptual framework, read the discussion in the Research Reality Scenario box – What Are These Things Known as Variables? – as this may help you to develop a clearer understanding before encountering some of the jargon associated with them.

Research Reality Scenario	**What Are These Things Known as Variables?**

Bill is Assistant General Manager at the Eldorado theme park and has worked in the tourism industry for 10 years, since gaining a Higher National Diploma qualification when he was younger. He is currently studying, on a part-time basis, for an MA in tourism management at the University of Rutland. Penny, the General Manager of Eldorado, has a BA and an MA in tourism management and is keen to help Bill fulfil his potential and gain the MA qualification.

During their regular weekly meeting, Penny has noticed that Bill has seemed less confident than usual and, at the end of the last meeting, asked him, 'Is there something wrong, Bill? You seem to be distracted in some way. Is there anything I can do to help?'

Bill was a little embarrassed, but replied, 'Well, yes, there is something I'm worried about and you probably can help, but I have been too embarrassed to ask you because you might think I'm stupid for not understanding it.'

Penny laughed, 'Come on, Bill, we've known each other long enough for you to know that won't be the case.'

'Okay,' said Bill, 'It's to do with my MA course. We have just started the Research Methods module and the tutor gave a lecture last week on conceptual frameworks and variables that went straight over my head. I'm a practical man, not some academic theorist, so when you get someone rambling on about independent, dependent, intervening and moderating variables and how important these are for doing research, not only does it scare me rigid but also I don't understand the jargon.'

'Ah, I see,' said Penny. 'Well, the good news is it's not as bad as you think and the bad news is that you are going to kick yourself when I explain it because you do know what these are but not in the terms that the academic used. Okay, you can look at me sceptically, but I'll prove it to you. Do you remember last year, when we had the problem of our marketing effort not delivering the extra numbers of visitors we wanted?' Bill nodded. 'And', Penny continued, 'I asked you to investigate this for us to find out why?' Bill nodded again. 'How did you explain to me what was happening?' asked Penny.

Bill replied, 'Well, I said that, although the extra marketing spend and effort should have led to a higher number of visitors, the fact that our marketing messages tended to create some less than positive impressions of the park among potential visitors and that our competitors launched their campaigns around the same time diluted the effect our messages might have had.'

'Exactly,' said Penny. 'Well, let's just think about what you've said for a moment. Getting more visitors was seen to be dependent on increasing the marketing spend and effort, but that relationship didn't materialise in the way we expected it to because of the other factors you identified. So, let's translate that into "variablespeak". The marketing spend/effort we can change separately – independently – of the number of visitors we have. We can manipulate or control this, but we can't control its effects – that is, how many more or fewer visitors it generates, agreed?'

'Agreed,' said Bill.

'So,' Penny continued, 'which is the independent variable and which is the dependent variable?'

'That's obvious,' Bill retorted. 'Because the number of visitors is, at least to some degree, dependent on or influenced by our marketing effort, that must be

(Continued)

(Continued)

the dependent variable and the thing we can change independently of it is our marketing spend/effort, so that must be the independent variable.'

'Spot on, Bill,' Penny exclaimed. 'You see, I told you that you knew what they were and you do. Now let's address the others. You said that our competitors' marketing campaigns diluted or reduced the effect our marketing effort had on increasing visitor numbers. So, what type of variable is that?'

'I guess it was a moderating variable,' Bill replied nervously, 'because it wasn't something that happened as a direct consequence of our extra marketing effort, but had an impact from outside of the relationship between extra effort and visitor numbers.'

'Same again, Bill,' Penny said, 'you've got it in one.'

'Okay,' Bill said, now more confident, 'so the unintended, more negative perceptions our messages created must be the intervening variable in this scenario because they occurred as a result of us activating the campaign and intervened to alter the relationship we expected between the extra effort and higher visitor numbers.'

Penny smiled and said, 'Absolutely. So, do you need any more tuition on this?'

'No thanks,' Bill said. 'You were right, I did know it all along. I just got confused by the different terminology and jargon.'

'That's right,' Penny replied. She then went on to say mischievously, 'So you created a conceptual framework that identified and included all the key variables, specified the nature of the relationship between these, hypothesised what the nature and direction of the cause–effect mechanism was between the independent and dependent variables, identified other variables that acted to alter this prediction and stated how and why it would work.'

Bill laughed and said, 'Now, wait a minute, I'll be thinking of myself as some sort of genius soon!'

So, as Bill discovered in our little scenario, you probably know what these variables are in a less systematic and jargonised, but more intuitive, real-life context. Think about your own experiences as a student. The category of degree you aim to achieve depends, at least in part, on how much time and effort you put into your studies. You would probably see this relationship as one where more time and effort should lead to a better class of degree. What you may also find is that one unexpected consequence of doing this is that you become happier and more confident in your knowledge and abilities and this, in turn, might help you to obtain an even higher class of degree than you predicted. However, on the other hand, your ability to put more time and effort into your studies might be constrained – moderated – by the need to undertake part-time work to help supplement your finances.

5.4.1 Dependent and independent variables

Does this sound familiar? I guess it will do, so let's put it into a more academic format by restating it in terms of the jargon associated with variables. The thing that depends on all the others is the level of degree you aim to achieve. Therefore, it is the dependent variable. It is the variable you are most interested in as all the others are things that are likely to influence this end. The amount of time and effort you put into your studies, we have suggested, will influence, if not determine, the level of degree you are likely to obtain and it is something that you can change or manipulate separately from the final outcome. So that is the independent variable – it can be changed on its own, independently of the others.

5.4.2 Intervening variables

The intervening variable is something that happens as a direct consequence of a change in the independent variable and has an effect on the expected relationship between it and the dependent variable. That effect might be known and expected before the empirical part of the research has begun or may not be until after the effect of changing the independent variable on the dependent variable is known. This effect may be to enhance or lessen that which the independent variable has on the dependent variable. In our case, the effect is positive, it is a beneficial consequence, side-effect or spin-off because the extra time and effort spent on study create more self-confidence and belief, which, in turn, generate a 'greater than expected' outcome – gaining an even higher class degree than was expected or predicted.

5.4.3 Moderating variables

Similarly, a moderating variable is one that moderates the expected relationship between the independent and dependent variables. Once again, it might be positive or negative in nature. In our example, it is negative because having to work to earn money may mean your ability to spend more time and effort studying is limited in some way. In the same way that an intervening variable may or may not be evident before the investigation begins, in some situations the moderating variable may be identifiable from the beginning and in others it only becomes evident when the expected independent–dependent variable relationship does not materialise from the evidence and needs to be explained by identifying what is moderating or affecting it.

5.4.4 Expressing relationships between variables

There are various ways that we can express such suggested (postulated) relationships between the variables. A simple narrative statement may be used, which may look something like the following. If I were to increase the amount of time and effort I spend on studying (independent variable), then I would expect to get a higher class of degree (dependent variable). In addition to this, as a consequence of me putting more effort into studying, I might obtain an even higher class of degree because I will be more self-confident (intervening variable), but this predicted relationship may be affected by the fact that I have to spend some time working to earn extra money (moderating variable).

Alternatively, we might express it in diagrammatic form (see Figure 5.1). A slightly more complex, but nevertheless clear, example of this way of expressing theorised relationships between the independent and dependent variables, along with possible moderating variables, is provided by Hwang et al. (2013). Another option would be to express it as a logical function. For example, we could state that, other things being equal or held constant, the class of degree (D) we expect to get would be a function of (f), or depend on, the amount of time (T) and effort (E) we are prepared to devote to this, giving us the equation $D = f(T,E)$.

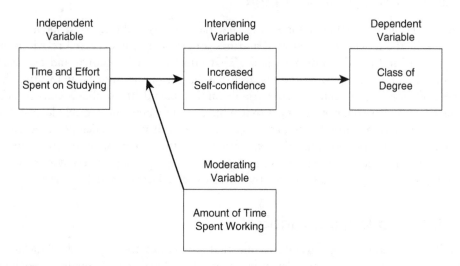

FIGURE 5.1 Stating the relationship between variables

To widen this type of formulation somewhat, we could adopt what Clark et al. (1998) refer to as a 'mapping sentence'. This seeks to combine the independent, dependent and what they refer to as the 'subject' variables. The latter are characteristics of the sample to be used in the research. These are sometimes also referred to as categorical variables. These are characteristics of the sample – different views, behaviour, opinions and so on – that can act to change the expected relationship in some way. Using our degree example, we might express this as follows. A student (male or female) who (works part-time or does not work part-time) will obtain a higher class of degree if he or she (puts more time and effort into studying), but this relationship may be also affected by (he or she developing more self-confidence and belief as a consequence of studying more). So, for example, we could explore the influence of the categorical variable of gender to investigate if any relationship existed between the class of degree obtained by males and females. Similarly, we could compare the class of degree obtained by students who worked more or less and/or put more or less time and effort into studying.

Therefore, if we want to explain something, whether it is just a suggested association between two or more things or a predicted cause–effect relationship, we need to identify the variables involved in that relationship. However, it is not always possible to identify all the four main types of variables before the research is completed and the results of the empirical study are known. The two variables that are most problematic in this respect are the intervening and moderating variables. In some situations, it is possible to identify and specify one or both of these and include them in the study's conceptual framework before the empirical work commences. Where it is reasonable and logical to speculate about a set or chain of events that can be articulated before the relationship is tested, this can be done. For example, it is well known that when governments or businesses change things, such as public expenditure or taxation, marketing spending or product prices, time lags can affect the incidence and timing of the expected effect on the dependent variable(s) in question. In short, the effect(s) of the change do not occur instantaneously or even possibly within a short period of time after they have been made.

In the tourism industry, currency fluctuations and tourism volumes travelling to alternative destinations are a good example of this time lag effect. As many people make their travel or holiday plans and book well in advance of the actual trip, the currency exchange rates in existence at the time of booking, or immediately prior to it, are those most likely to influence decisions about the choice of country or destination when people are choosing between more and less expensive places. Even if currency fluctuations after booking mean that the destination chosen now becomes more expensive and others less so, it is highly unlikely that the customer will cancel the original booking and book the one that is now cheaper because there are financial penalties for this type of cancellation. Also, once the original decision has been made, there is invariably a great reluctance on the part of customers to change because they are also psychologically and emotionally committed to the decision.

However, there are many other situations where either possible intervening or moderating variables or both are not obvious at the outset. Such variables only become evident when the results of the study are available and the expected relationship between the independent and dependent variables has not materialised or is somewhat different to that predicted. In such cases, the variables are identified as a consequence of the study and may be used to explain unexpected or unpredicted outcomes. An example of this is given in the Research in Action box – Identifying Moderating Variables via Data Analysis. This indicates that the ability of licensed house managers to exert direct control over the factors influencing the success of their pub's operations became evident after the data had been analysed and, further, suggested that, using this controllability variable, these factors could be classified as operational or strategic in nature.

**Research in
Action**

**Identifying Moderating Variables via Data
Analysis**

A preliminary analysis of the phase 1 questionnaire results suggested that it
might be possible to subdivide the critical success factor (CSF), critical skills
and competencies (CSC) and critical performance measures (CPM) items
into the categories of *People, Products* and *Processes*. However the factor
analysis* conducted on the phase 2 results did not support such an ex ante
contention as the factors generated by this procedure did not correspond with
such a categorisation. The factor analysis results for the CSF items could be
interpreted in two different ways. First, the CSFs placed into Factor Two – namely,
Location, Size and Range of Products – may be seen to be concerned with the
'physical' nature of BASS Taverns' provision, with those placed into Factor One
more concerned with the 'human' aspects. However, this is an interpretation
we reject because we would expect such a categorisation might reasonably
place CSF 1 (Quality of the Tavern's Premises) in the 'physical' rather than the
'human' category. Thus a more robust way of interpreting these results may
be to regard the CSFs placed in Factor Two to be those largely outside of the
individual Licensed House Managers' (LHMs) control and hence more *strategic*
in nature, whereas those in Factor One are subject to local control and are more
operational in character.

Source: © Brotherton, B. and Watson, S., Shared priorities and the management
development process: a case study of Bass Taverns, *Tourism and Hospitality
Research (The Surrey Quarterly Review)*, 2000. Reproduced with permission of
Palgrave Macmillan.

**Factor analysis* is generally known as a 'data reduction' technique and is
explained further in Chapter 9. It is a statistical technique used to explore the
extent to which the data can be grouped together into separate categories (or
factors) to represent different dimensions of the concept(s) being investigated.

The two variables, or sets of variables in some cases, that must be identified before
a deductive study can be conducted are the independent and dependent variables.
Without these it would be impossible to test a theory and its associated hypotheses.
Of course, in the case of an inductive study, these would be identified as a consequence or product of the data analysis. As we have seen already, the dependent variable is the main subject of the study – it is the thing that we are most interested in or
the outcome we are trying to explain. It, in turn, is a product, outcome or effect of
something else and, therefore, to explain it, we have to identify what causes it and
why. A good analogy here is that of a doctor diagnosing a patient's illness or condition. If you go to the doctor with some symptoms, you would expect the doctor to
tell you what the reasons are for these and prescribe some treatment to cure them. To

do this, the doctor would need to know what things could cause the effects you can see or feel and why these could cause them. In short, for the doctor to provide an appropriate diagnosis of the problem and prescribe appropriate treatment, the possible cause(s) of the effect(s) must be known and the mechanism(s) or relationship(s) between them must also be known.

The number of possible relationships between variables is limited to two. Variables may be related in a positive or negative/inverse manner. Where a positive relationship exists, any change in the two variables moves in the same positive direction, and vice versa for a negative relationship. For example, the more people are willing to eat out in a particular location, the greater the number and/or sizes of restaurants that will be opened – that is, the increase in the size of the market stimulates existing businesses to expand and new ones to open, and vice versa where fewer people eat out. Where a negative or inverse relationship exists, any change in the variables moves in opposite directions. For example, the more restaurants put up their prices, the fewer people will want or be able to afford to eat in them, and vice versa.

5.4.5   Considering variables from different perspectives

As Kumar (2011) has pointed out it is possible to think about variables from the differing perspectives of their causal relationship, the nature of the study's design and the unit of measurement they relate to. As these are alternate views that you may encounter in the literature it is worthwhile spending a little time on each here. Kumar (2011: 66) suggests that in a causal relationship variables may be categorised as those causing a 'change', those that reflect the impact or consequence of this change (outcome variables), those that impact on the link between the change and outcome variables (influence variables) and those that 'connect' or 'link' the relationship between variables. Although different terminology is used here these are effectively equivalents of the four main types of variable referred to earlier, i.e. respectively independent, dependent, moderating and intervening. Similarly, some authors may refer to the moderating variable as an 'extraneous' variable and the intervening one as the 'confounding' variable. Again, this is only different terminology to refer to the same thing.

Perhaps of more relevance are the other two perspectives. From the perspective of the study's design, Kumar (2011: 71) indicates that, in certain circumstances, it is possible to categorise variables as 'active' and 'attribute'. The former are variables that can be changed in some way, while the latter are ones that reflect the characteristics of the study's subjects. Another way of thinking about this would be to regard them as fixed variables or constants on the one hand and those that can be changed in some way. Kumar (2011: 72) also points out that variables can be differentiated from the perspective of the 'unit of measurement' they are based on. So, for example, a variable being measured via the use of discrete categories would be referred to as a 'categorical' variable, while one being measured using a scale with a 'continuous' range, using an interval or ratio scale (see Section 5.8 later in this chapter) would be known as such.

To review and strengthen your understanding of constructs, concepts and variables you may find it helpful to examine the additional resources provided on the Companion Website (study.sagepub.com/brotherton). Here, in the Video Links section, you will find links to video material dealing with the nature and roles of the different types of variables and the relationships these have with research questions. In the Web Links section you will also find links to material dealing with similar issues.

5.5 Theories and Models

A theory is essentially a set of concepts, and associated propositions, that are organised logically and systematically in order to both explain and predict phenomena. In short, it helps us to understand, explain and predict what has happened, what is happening and what will happen. Furthermore, if we can understand, explain and predict, we may also be able to control what does happen. In this way, theories help us to interpret the real world and guide our thinking and actions. We all use theories in our everyday lives, although very often we do this implicitly or even unconsciously as they are embedded, whether we realise it or not, in the way we think and act. They are the generalisations we make about the things we observe or experience and how they are connected or related in order to understand, make decisions and predictions.

There can be a tendency to see theory and fact as opposing forces, but this view does not recognise the interdependency of the two. For a theory to be useful, it must be able to explain and predict. The better it can do that, the more practical value it has. In the same way, to be effective in a practical situation requires an understanding of how the underlying forces operate – that is, we need to have a theoretical understanding of them and their relationships. Where a theory does not adequately explain and provide a sound basis for action in a real-world situation or environment, it does not mean that a theoretical understanding is worthless, just that a better theory needs to be developed.

As our understanding of the world around us progresses, new theories replace older, less useful, ones or existing theories are revised and improved to fit the real world better – often by making them more universal or general rather than being limited to particular time periods or contexts. Indeed, the most useful theories are those that are not limited to the existence of specific conditions. These are often known as general theories or universal laws because they are equally valid and applicable across time and space. Those having a more limited applicability tend to be referred to as context- or condition-specific theories because their value is limited to certain contexts or the existence of certain conditions.

Models or theoretical models are sometimes confused with theories. Although they are related, they are not the same thing. While the role of theory is explanation, the role of models is to represent the logic of the explanation. Such representation of theories may be descriptive, explanatory or designed to simulate the processes the theory is about. In other words, the model may be relatively simple, revealing the structural relationships between its components, or slightly more developed, in that the nature of these structural relationships is explained, or more complex still, with the processes associated with the relationships being simulated. A good example of the development and testing of a structural model, based on a thorough literature review, is contained in Hyun and Han (2012) that sought to examine patrons' 'innovativeness' in relation to chain restaurants and their success. Also, the study conducted by Forgas-Coll et al. (2012), that explored tourist loyalty to destinations, contains a very clear example and exposition of a 'causal' model used as the basis for empirical testing that illustrates how the dimensions, indicators and hypotheses are combined to formulate the model.

5.6 Hypotheses

As we have seen so far in this chapter, theories, models and conceptual frameworks help to link together the constructs, concepts and variables associated with the issue(s) we are seeking to address in our research. What a hypothesis does is state what the logical implication(s) of the theory and so on are if the theory is correct or valid. In other words, a hypothesis expresses a prediction of what we would expect to find if the theory proves to be sound. Given that 'good' theories are not only able to explain why things occur but also predict outcomes, we need a mechanism that allows us to test whether or not the theoretical explanations and predictions can be supported by evidence from the real world.

This mechanism often takes the form of a hypothesis or series of hypotheses. We could view a hypothesis as a type of 'educated guess' about a problem's solution. We know the theory and what this suggests or implies should be the case, but we need a link to be able to test it to see if it is true. Alternatively, we might see this as us having suggested or asserted that there will be certain relationships between the concepts in our conceptual framework and/or theoretical model, but which we cannot confirm at this point in time because these assertions have not yet been tested. Either way, the common denominator here is the idea of being able to test the guess or assertion. Therefore, we need a statement that can be tested and that is the role of the hypothesis. A very clear example of how hypotheses can be developed from the prior establishment of a conceptual model is provided by Mlozi and Pesamaa (2013) in their study of adventure tourist choice in Tanzania.

Depending on the extent to which the theory we are dealing with has been developed previously and/or our ability to be more or less specific in wording the hypothesis, we may be looking to test an association, connection or a more definite cause–effect relationship. Hence, our hypothesis might be tentative or prescriptive in how it is written. Similarly, we may or may not know or be able to logically speculate about the direction of the relationship between the two or more variables in our hypothesis. All of this means that we can have hypotheses that are either correlational or causal in nature and correlational hypotheses may be directional or non-directional in form.

5.6.1   Causal and correlational hypotheses

By definition, a causal hypothesis will be directional as we are specifying and testing a cause–effect relationship. A correlational hypothesis is one suggesting or postulating a connection or association of some kind between at least two variables. For example, the theory may suggest that there is some relationship between the amount of money paid to employees and the volume of effort they are prepared to put into their work. If this were to be specified in a non-directional form, then we would simply hypothesise that the two are connected in some way – that is, we would use the wording of the previous sentence. On the other hand, if we could be more specific about this, we might be able to specify it in a directional form, such as, in companies where employees are paid more then the volume of work they produce seems to be higher. Here we are suggesting a directional relationship in the way the hypothesis is written – that is, where there is higher pay, employees seem to work harder, but this is still only an association, in the sense that the two seem to appear together and our guess or hypothesis suggests that one might come before the other.

However, to turn this into a causal hypothesis, we would have to state it in more definite terms. For example, if employees are paid more, then this will increase the volume of work they do. The key words here are 'if' and 'then' or, put another way, given the existence of one thing, the other will occur or happen. Here we are specifying that a change in the causal, independent variable(s) will definitely create the effect in the form of the dependent variable. In other words, that the effect will follow the cause. For us to be able to specify this type of hypothesis, we need to consider whether or not we can meet what are called the three conditions for causality. This may sound complicated, but it is really quite logical and simple (see the Key Concept box – The Conditions for Causality).

Key Concept	**The Conditions for Causality**

The first condition is that what is regarded as the cause must happen before the effect, otherwise it could not be regarded as a potential cause. This is known as the 'temporal' or time condition.

The second is that there are not any other possible cause(s) of the effect. If there are other variables that can cause the same effect, either in conjunction with the one we are specifying or independent of it, then the cause–effect relationship specified in our hypothesis would only be, at best, partially true and, at worst, false or erroneous. This is known as the elimination of alternative causes condition.

> The third is that the condition of covariation can be met. This simply means that both variables, or sets of variables, in the cause and effect categories vary together – that is, when prices change, there is always some change in consumer demand for the product or service.

So, we might hypothesise that having a 'happy hour' in a bar, when drink prices are lowered, will lead to either more customers visiting the bar and/or existing customers buying more drinks during this period than they would otherwise. This would clearly satisfy the temporal condition – prices are lowered before the rise in demand occurs – and the covariation condition – both prices and demand change or covary. The only problem we might encounter here is that it may be difficult to eliminate other possible causes of the rise in demand beyond that of the reduction in drink prices. In other words, would the rise in demand have happened anyway, or for some other reason, if we had not changed the drink prices? This is possible. To test for this, we could operate the happy hour for a period of time and then stop it to see what effect these changes have on demand. If demand drops back to the level, or very near to that which existed before we started the happy hour, then this may give us some evidence to strengthen the belief in the cause–effect relationship between drink prices and quantity purchased.

5.6.2   Null and alternate hypotheses

Both correlational and causal hypotheses can be stated in negative or positive terms. The literature in general refers to these as the 'null' and 'alternate' forms of the same hypothesis. This means that one of the two ways of stating the hypothesis will be confirmed by the research data. The null form would state that the independent variable (cause) does not have a relationship with, or effect on, the dependent variable (effect). The alternate form states the reverse – that is, the independent variable does have a relationship with or effect on the dependent variable. These are the only two possible outcomes for a hypothesis – either the two sets of variables are related in some way or they are not. Therefore, if the results of the research confirm the truthfulness or validity of one of these and suggest it should be accepted on the basis of this evidence, then the other must automatically be rejected. Either form can be used, as they are the reverse of each other, but it is common for the null form to be used in many research studies because the sceptical proposition that there is no connection or causal relationship between the variables is one favoured by the scientific method.

5.6.3   Writing hypotheses

Writing a hypothesis, or a series of hypotheses, is a relatively simple task. By now you know what a hypothesis is and the different forms it may take, so to actually compose one should be quite a simple process. That said it is not always a 'one-stop' process because we often move from our initial thoughts and ideas for the research towards a situation where we know more about the topic/issues we intend to investigate and, hence, we are able to be more specific about what it is we want to test. Figure 5.2 illustrates such a process. Here you can see we move through three stages to develop the final hypothesis we are going to use for the research. This is quite typical of the process in that we tend to begin with a general idea, refine this as we develop our knowledge of the topic and then finally come to a point where we can be more specific and focused in formulating a hypothesis that is capable of being tested.

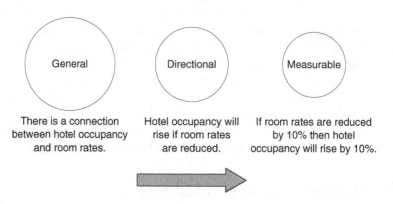

FIGURE 5.2 The stages of hypothesis development

Essentially what is happening here is that we are moving from a situation where we have limited specific and substantive knowledge of any potential relationships to one where we are much more informed about this and are able to be more specific about what this relationship might be and, crucially, be in a position to explain why this relationship may be one worth testing because we now have the theoretical basis to articulate the mechanism by which this relationship works. We might also see this in more common terms. We begin with an initial guess about what the relationship might be, and then convert this into more of an informed or educated guess by refining the proposition, and finally are able to produce a statement that is evidence-based and consistent with the logical predictions that can be derived from the theory. Obviously we want to write 'good' hypotheses, but this raises the question of what is a 'good' hypothesis? The Key Concept box – The Characteristics of a Good Hypothesis – illustrates the basic principles lying behind this question.

Key Concept	The Characteristics of a Good Hypothesis

Good hypotheses:

1. are written as statements not questions.

2. are objective and do not include any subjective terms, personal opinions or value judgements.

3. suggest or postulate a relationship between at least two variables.

4. are derived from, and linked to, the literature on which they are based.

5. should be stated in a direct, explicit and concise form and be 'uni-dimensional', i.e. they test only one relationship at a time.

6. are testable – you should be able to accept or reject the hypothesis on the basis of the empirical evidence.

7. should be non-trivial – they should be statements of some importance or significance.

8. must be internally consistent – the logic expressed in them must be sound.

9. connect the theoretical and real worlds by framing aspects of the former in such a way that these can be measured and tested in the latter.

10. tell you exactly what type of data needs to be collected for them to be tested.

Finally, although all the advice and prescriptions relating to hypothesis development that come before this point are naturally pertinent and valid, there can be situations where the types of standard format stated may not be possible, or indeed, the most appropriate. One such instance where this may be the case are studies involving past events. For example, a study designed to assess or evaluate the impact on employment in the air travel industry of the introduction and operation of Air Passenger Duty (a tax levied on each passenger carried by an airline) over the last decade would find it difficult to formulate an 'if–then' type of hypothesis in a positive form. In such circumstances it may be perfectly acceptable to deviate from the accepted norms of hypothesis writing and to use a form more appropriate for the circumstances. So here, for example, instead of trying to fit the proverbial square peg into a round hole it is likely to be preferable to word the hypothesis in a different manner, such as: Air Passenger Duty has had no effect on the level of employment in the air travel industry over the last 10 years. Of course it would be possible to state this in an 'if–then' format but this would have to be negatively worded, for example: if Air Passenger Duty had not been introduced then the level of employment in the air travel industry would be the same as it is today. However, this is rather inelegant and it also negates many of the other principles discussed earlier.

5.7 Operationalisation

In compiling our conceptual framework, we have brought together theoretical insights, relationships and predictions, identified the key constructs, concepts and variables required to formulate the framework and considered the hypotheses derived as a logical consequence of the framework, which will be tested in the empirical part of the research. We also referred earlier to the need for abstract and intangible constructs and concepts to be converted or translated into something more concrete and tangible to help us collect empirical data in order to measure it. This is known as operationalising the concepts or, alternatively, as creating an operational definition or series of definitions of the concept(s). Whatever form an operational definition takes, the basic purpose is the same: to establish explicit and unambiguous meaning and assist in the empirical measurement of the concept(s) concerned.

One way to think about this is to consider what you would need to do to 'operationalise' (put into practice) an idea or concept someone expresses to you. The idea or concept is likely to be fairly general and lack details. It is rather like a skeleton without flesh. To put the idea or concept into practice, therefore, you would have to translate the principle into practical terms. For example, the concept underlying the TGI Friday's restaurant experience may be expressed as something like 'the provision of casual, informal dining that entertains and provides good value for money'. Sounds like a great idea, but what are the implications of this in terms of the type of restaurant, colour schemes, decor, service style, menu items, presentation of the menu, the type of staff needed, type of server–customer interaction and so on? All of these aspects would have to be considered in order to develop an operational plan to deliver the concept, because they would all need to work together to deliver an experience consistent with the concept.

Similarly, think about the concept of budget or low-cost travel or hotels compared to those of a full-service airline or hotel operation. The end products are different because the concepts underlying the operations differ. The two forms of hotel or travel provision are designed to deliver different types of customer experiences. While this is quite easy to see and understand where the concepts are very different, it can be less clear where the concepts are similar. Indeed, even when dealing with the same concept, different people may interpret what this means in operational terms in differing ways. So, one company's view of the type and style of provision that should reflect the idea of a budget airline or hotel brand may differ from another's.

This all means that it cannot be assumed everyone will translate or operationalise a concept in the same way that you do. The meanings associated with a concept cannot be assumed to be constant and consistent for different people, organisations or cultures. In short, *you* may know what you mean when you use or refer to a particular concept, but how can you be sure that other people will interpret this in the same way? One way to solve this problem is to make your definition explicit rather than implicit – that is, to provide an operational definition.

5.7.1 Identifying concept dimensions

We saw earlier in this chapter that abstract concepts are collections or combinations of things associated with a concept and the sum of their components. To operationalise them, we need to subdivide them, breaking them down into their constituent components. Because they are comprised of related categories or groups of components, this allows us to identify the major 'subheadings' included under any conceptual heading. These are commonly known as the main 'dimensions' of the concept. For example, if we take the concept of consumer demand, we can say that all the factors likely to influence this could be placed into the two main dimensions of price and non-price factors. The former is self-explanatory, but the latter could include such things as people's income level, their tastes, fashions, the prices of complementary and/or competing or substitute goods, marketing and promotional messages and so on.

Figure 5.3 illustrates how the concept of 'quality' can be divided into two main dimensions of 'product quality' and 'service quality'. It would be logical to assume that any assessment or judgement of the overall quality of, say, a restaurant meal experience would be influenced by the quality of both the physical and service aspects of the experience. However, the terms product and service quality are still abstract and, potentially, variable in terms of how people perceive and give meaning to them, so any attempt to use them to collect data, by asking people to rate the quality of the restaurant product and/or experience, may be flawed.

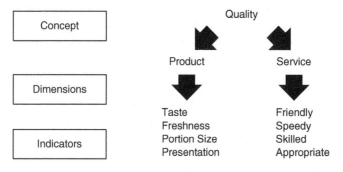

FIGURE 5.3 Operationalising a concept

5.7.2   Identifying elements and indicators

This problem means that we need something else that is potentially less ambiguous and easier for people to respond to. These are known as 'indicators' or 'elements' of the dimension. They are specific, tangible occurrences or attributes of the dimension and it is these that we use to formulate the question we put to people. So, as Figure 5.3 shows, if we want to collect data from restaurant customers to obtain their judgements on the quality of the food product they have received, we need to ask them questions about the taste of the food, its freshness, the portion size, its presentation and so on. These are much more specific and concrete things for people to consider and respond to than simply 'product quality' and so are far less likely to generate widely differing interpretations of what they mean or refer to on the part of the people answering questions.

   To put this another way, if I asked you to give me your opinion or judgement of the quality of the food product you had received in a restaurant, I'm sure that you would be able to give a response or answer to this question, but how would you be able to do so? You would probably think about some or all of the specific considerations mentioned above or perhaps even add others as you formulated your judgement. Although you could give me an answer, the problem for me would be that I would not know what you used as a basis for it and whether or not this was the same as that of the other people who had answered the question. In these circumstances I would not know, and could not claim, that all the answers had been consistent and given using the same definition of the term. This would mean that there would be some, perhaps considerable, doubt over the reliability of this data as a whole. The point here is the one made earlier, that if the definition is made as explicit and tangible or concrete as possible, then the likelihood of different people interpreting this in different ways will be reduced. In turn, this should make the whole set of answers as reliable as possible.

   Before we consider the major types of empirical research designs that can be used to plan and organise the collection of the empirical data in Chapter 6, we need to explore the issues associated with developing valid and reliable measures because it is important to realise that the quality of the data to be collected using any of these designs will, in large part, depend on the quality of the preparation for doing this and an important part of that preparation relates to the issues explored in this chapter. If the conceptual thinking and planning – in the form of identifying the underlying theory, the associated concepts and variables, how these are connected, what predictions can be made and what is required to operationalise them – are not given adequate consideration, then what follows – the empirical part of the project – will be more difficult and probably less valuable than it could have been. In other words, if the foundation for the empirical research is not constructed well, then everything built on top of this may be less than robust.

 See the video specifically on operationalisation available via the appropriate link in the Video Links section of the Companion Website (study.sagepub.com/brotherton).

5.8 Measurement and Scales

Once the variables relating to the constructs and concepts to be explored in the empirical part of the research have been identified and operationalised, the next task to be faced is the development of valid and reliable ways to measure them. This necessitates a consideration of the type of measurement scale that might be most appropriate for collecting the data and measuring the variables in the desired manner. However, before we consider the main types or levels of measurement scales, there are two conditions that should be met by any type of scale.

The first of these is known as the condition of 'collective exhaustion'. This means that the content of the range or scope of the scale should be sufficient to collectively exhaust any other possible responses. In everyday language this means that it covers all the possible answers. This may sound complicated, but it is really quite straightforward. For example, a scale containing response options for only three-, four- and five-star hotels would not be collectively exhaustive unless the sample was restricted to these three categories of hotel as there are other types of hotels, such as those with two or no stars or using grading criteria or symbols other than the star rating system. Similarly, a scale relating to the age of the respondents that only had the categories 18–30, 31–40 and 41–50 would not be collectively exhaustive as there could be respondents younger than 18 or older than 50. In some cases, as we will see later in this section, where the range of potential variation in the variable is very large, a more open-ended way of collecting the data may be used to avoid having to have a huge range of possible response categories to cover all the possible options. Where this is not the case, the age categories problem above could be solved by adding two other catch-all categories to each end of the range – under 18 and over 50. In the hotel star-rating case, we could solve the problem by adding a category of 'other (please specify)'.

The second condition is known as mutual exclusivity. Again, this is simpler than it may sound. It means that the categories used in the scale should not overlap. The importance of this is that a person responding to the question cannot then give a response to more than one of the items in the scale. For example, if a question asked, 'How many times have you flown on a budget airline in the past six months?' and gave the options of none, 1–5, 5–10, 10–15 and more than 15, there would be a potential problem. Because the 1–5 category overlaps with the 5–10 and the 5–10 category overlaps with the 10–15, if there were people who had flown five or 10 times, then they could indicate this in two different categories, but we would not know how many people who had flown five times had ticked the 1–5 or 5–10 boxes or, indeed, how many who had flown 10 times had indicated this by ticking the 5–10 or 10–15 boxes. Once again, there is a simple way to avoid this problem – make sure that the response options or categories are separated. So, in our example simply changing the categories to 1–5, 6–10, 11–15 would make them mutually exclusive. Then, people who had flown five or 10 times could only record this in one of the categories, so the problem has been eliminated.

It is generally accepted that there are four basic types and/or levels of measurement scale:

- Nominal

- Ordinal

- Interval

- Ratio.

5.8.1 The nominal scale

This scale is used to name, group or classify either respondents' characteristics or substantive answers into different groups or categories. In the jargon, it places the values of the attributes into separate groups or categories and, because of this, is sometimes known as the basis for measuring 'categorical' variables. This means that the values used to measure the variable will be contained in a range of mutually exclusive and collectively exhaustive categories used in the scale. This is a relatively simple type of measurement scale because all we can deduce from it is that the members of a particular group or category share at least one thing in common. For example, they are all male or female, single or married, burger or pizza restaurants, museums or theme parks. If the question relates to a more substantive aspect, it would mean that they buy or don't buy the product, have travelled on a budget airline between one and five or six and 10 occasions in the last six months, have visited the tourism destination before or have not.

However, despite its simplicity, questions using the nominal scale can generate useful information on the characteristics of the respondents included in the sample that will allow you to describe the composition of the sample – a feature that we shall see is important in Chapter 8 when we consider sampling issues. This information can also be used to explore possible differences between categories of respondents when the data are analysed. We shall consider this in more detail in Chapter 9, but, to give you an idea of how useful it might be, we could combine our age categories with those relating to how frequently people fly with an airline to establish whether or not there is any connection or relationship between people's ages and the numbers of flights they go on. If we found that people between 18 and 30 were far more likely to fly than those younger or older, we might then choose to target marketing campaigns at this age group. That said, the type of data provided by the nominal scale is limited in terms of the extent that we can manipulate or analyse it using statistical techniques. In itself, nominal data are only amenable to calculating either the frequency (the total) and/or the percentage of the responses in each category, but they can still be used to explore possible associations between variables. This, again, is something that we will return to in Chapter 9.

5.8.2 The ordinal scale

The second type or level of measurement is the ordinal scale. This is used to place the attributes of the variable into some form of order – from highest to lowest, more to less, top to bottom, best to worst and so on. For example, you might use this type of scale to ask questions about people's perceptions, their experiences, behaviour or intentions or to elicit a judgement about a product or service. It could also be used to ask companies how they rate themselves and their competitors on a range of factors, such as service quality, price, brand recognition, standardisation or customisation of service delivery, accessibility of unit locations and so on.

This type of information can be valuable, but there is an underlying issue with ordinal data. The distances between the orders or levels in the scale tend to be viewed as being equal, but this assumption cannot be substantiated. Intuitively, you might be tempted to think that the gap between 1 and 2, and 2 and 3 in an ordinal scale represents the same amount of difference, but this may not be the case. For example, if you asked someone who had visited a range of tourism destinations to rate or rank these destinations from best to worst, the basis on which they would make these judgements would not be known to you. They might decide in their own minds that the destination ranked as the best, or number 1, was far and away the best compared to that recorded as number 2, but that the one recorded as number 3 was only very slightly less desirable than number 2.

5.8.3   The interval scale

The third type of measurement scale is the interval scale. This is widely used in both academic research and life in general and you will probably be quite familiar with it, even though you may not realise it is called an interval scale. This scale has a standard interval between the range of points in the scale and the interval usually has a value of one. In addition, the nature of each point in the scale is defined and this allows the magnitude of the difference between each point to be measured. If this sounds complicated, don't worry, it is not, as you will see.

You are likely to be familiar with what are often referred to as three-, five-, seven- or nine-point scales that range from, say, terrible to excellent, from totally disagree to totally agree or never to always. Regardless of the specific form the scale takes, the principle is the same – it provides a range of possible 'defined' responses or response options to a question or statement from totally negative at one end to totally positive at the other. The important word here is 'defined' because this enables you to know the nature of the opinion or judgement that has been made relating to the number it corresponds to in the scale. This is something we noted above will not be known in the case of an ordinal scale because the intervals are not defined for the respondent who is putting things into a rank order between say 1 and 5 or 1 and 10.

The agree/disagree type of interval scale is commonly known as a 'Likert' scale and defines the points, in a five-point scale, as follows – totally disagree, disagree, neither agree or disagree, agree, totally agree. This form requires people to respond to a statement because it asks them to indicate the extent to which they agree or disagree with it. Where you want to ask a question, rather than provide a statement, and ask to what extent the respondent believes something is important or not important, then the points would take something like the following form – not at all, not very, fairly, very, totally.

Although the wording of the response options differs in these two examples, they both provide a balanced range of points for the person to express their agreement or disagreement with the statement or opinion of the importance or unimportance of the factor. They do this because they have an equal number of negative and positive options and one in the middle that is neutral. This allows the person to express either a totally or strongly negative or positive opinion or one that is indifferent or neutral. To obtain greater detail in the positive or negative responses – known as more precision – the scale would be extended to a seven-, nine- or even greater, point scale because this would allow more negative or positive options to be included.

5.8.4   The ratio scale

The ratio scale is a more open-ended scale. It normally has a zero starting point and, at least theoretically, could extend to infinity. As it is open-ended, it does not contain categories, groups, ranks or points in the same way that the scales we have looked at above do, so it collects what is often referred to as ungrouped, unclassified or raw data. This invariably means that ratio data has to be grouped or organised after they have been collected whereas the other scales group the data as they are being collected. This is not necessarily a detrimental feature because it provides more flexibility to group the data in different ways after collection, but it is often easier, where feasible, to build this organisation of the data into the scales used to collect them.

The ratio scale is generally used where the variable is known or expected to vary continuously across a range and frequently where the full range of variation is not known or could be quite extensive, as discussed earlier. For example, asking nominal scale questions about how many part-time and full-time staff are employed in the companies a questionnaire is sent to could be problematic if they range from small to very large because the range of categories that would need to be provided would be very large. In these circumstances, it would be more economical to use a ratio scale to obtain the exact numbers and group these data afterwards.

5.8.5   Selecting an appropriate scale

So, the scales each have their advantages and uses and which one you choose to use is a matter of judgement and relates to the type of data you need to collect. However, there are certain issues that should be borne in mind when making this choice. First, it is generally not a good idea to select a scale that is more complicated than the one necessary to collect the data you need, as this tends to make the writing of questions and input of data for analysis more time-consuming. Second, as we will see in Chapter 9, the use of certain types of statistical analysis techniques requires you to have collected certain types of data. This means that you need to do a little forward thinking and consider what you intend to do at the data analysis stage, letting this inform your choice of measurement scale(s) for collecting the necessary data.

Finally, the two considerations above give rise to a tension between the use of simpler and more complex scales because the first suggests that you adopt a more economical approach, while the second suggests that you use the more statistically powerful scales to open up more data analysis options later in the process. The balance to be struck between these two is one that needs some thought. My comment on this would be that it is always possible to do less, in analysis terms, with richer data, but you cannot do more with the more basic kind of data. Therefore, it may be advisable to aim higher rather than lower when thinking about which scale to use, especially in the case of substantive questions.

5.9 Establishing Good Measures

Whichever scale or scales are used in developing an instrument to measure the variables, the measures used should be as good as possible. This means that they should be as accurate or valid, as precise and as reliable as you can make them. Accuracy or validity is concerned with the extent to which the measure(s) conform with, or actually measure, the truth. This means that they should be able to provide data that measure what it is supposed to measure and give an accurate reflection of reality. Precision is concerned with the amount of detail to be included in the measure. A measure that is very precise will be able to provide very fine detail – that is, one that is able to measure in millimetres would be more precise than one able only to measure in centimetres. Alternatively, a nine-point interval scale would provide more precision than a three-point scale.

Reliability refers to the consistency of the measure when it is used over time or in different contexts. If a measure is highly reliable, then it can be used across a wide range of contexts and time periods because it will produce 'stable' measurements. However, a reliable measure may not necessarily be an accurate or valid one. It is quite possible for consistent measures to be obtained but for them to be consistently inaccurate or invalid. Similarly, a measure may be valid, but not reliable as it may measure accurately but is not able to achieve this consistently across different contexts or time periods. Therefore, you should not see validity and reliability as being the same thing.

The key questions here are how do you know if your measure is valid and reliable and how do you choose an appropriate level of detail or precision? There are certain issues you can consider regarding these aspects when designing the measure before it is used and there are others used to test the validity and/or reliability of the measure after the data have been collected. In terms of validity, the basic principle is to try to ensure that the measure actually measures what it is designed to measure. To do this, it must be logically consistent with the operational definition of the variable(s) and cover all the aspects of the concept(s) you wish to measure.

Of course one way to choose and use measures that are valid and reliable is to adopt, either in the original or a modified form if necessary, measures used in previous studies and that have been found to be both valid and reliable. An example of this can be seen in a study by Slatten et al. (2011) where a conceptual model, associated hypotheses and the measures used in the questionnaire survey were strongly based on ones that had been used before and where the study sought to extend the external validity of these by applying them to the uncommon setting of a winter amusement park in Norway. In a similar vein, Ladhari (2012) provides an example of a study designed to test the validity and reliability of an existing scale (The Lodging Quality Index – LQI) within a different context, i.e. Canada, from the one where it was originally developed, the USA.

However, sometimes this is not possible and a new measurement scale has to be developed for the purposes at hand. For an account of this type of process in action see the study conducted by Pranic and Roehl (2013) that sought to develop and validate a customer empowerment scale related to hotel service recovery. Alternatively, the study by Kim and Eves (2012) provides another example of the processes associated with developing and validating a new measurement scale.

5.9.1   Determining validity

To demonstrate that a measure is valid, there are different tests of validity you can use, ranging from the more subjective to more objective, evidence-based confirmations. The simplest, and weakest, argument to use to convince others that a measure is valid is known as 'face validity'. This is similar to the idea of accepting something at face value – it looks or seems to be okay. However, this is a subjective judgement and so others may not see things in the same way. Also, it means any claim that the measure is valid cannot be supported by any kind of objective evidence or testing.

'Content validity' addresses the issues referred to above of logical consistency and coverage. In other words, to claim that a measure has content validity, you would need to demonstrate, perhaps by logical argument, that the measure consistently and completely represents the concept being measured and covers the full range of meanings of the concept.

'Construct validity' depends on the quality of the operational definition used in the research design – that is, how adequate (in terms of coverage) and appropriate (in terms of value) it is. This can be established by means of convergence – a process known as 'convergent validity'. This may involve comparing the results obtained from your measure with those previously obtained from another, established, measure for the same construct(s). If the two sets of results are the same or sufficiently convergent, then this would provide evidence for your measure having the property for convergent validity.

Another way of trying to establish the construct validity of a measure could be to claim 'discriminant validity'. This refers to the extent that it is possible to separate or discriminate between the concept you are measuring and others in the theory it relates to. If this can be done, then it indicates that the measure is measuring the target concept and not any others. In other words, the measure is not confusing the measurement of the concept by including items that measure aspects of other concepts – it is measuring only what it is intended to measure and nothing else. This might be claimed via logical argument prior to the collection of the data and/or after the data have been collected by using an appropriate statistical test. For example, a test known as factor analysis (see Chapter 9) could be used to do this.

In circumstances where the measure is seeking to use a criterion to differentiate between groups that are known to be different or predict something that, it is hypothesised, it should be able to predict, 'criterion-related validity' might be used. There are two types of criterion-related validity corresponding to these two situations. First, 'concurrent validity' would be used to validate a measure designed to differentiate between groups that are known to be different. This may involve the use of another independent measure, for which data already exist, to compare the results from your measure with those from the other to ascertain whether they correlate sufficiently or not. Second, 'predictive validity' would be used to claim that your measure is valid in being able to predict the effect of the criterion in the future – that is, the criterion is measured after a passage of time.

5.9.2   Determining reliability

The reliability of a measure can be claimed in two main ways before the measure is used. First, by adopting a previously used and proven measure. If previous research has been undertaken and the researcher(s) concerned have been able to prove the reliability of the measure(s) they have used, then your measure can be claimed to be reliable on the basis that evidence already exists to indicate that the measure is reliable and yours is the same. Second, you can go through a process of testing or trialling your measure before you actually use it to collect data for the project. This essentially means repeating the use of the measure in a series of tests or trials to establish whether or not it behaves in a consistent manner. However, whether you are fortunate enough to find an existing measure you can use or have the time to engage in testing or trialling your newly devised measure, you can only really confirm the reliability of the measure used in your specific research context after it has been used.

There are various procedures and tests that can be implemented to determine how reliable your measure has been. If it has been used to collect qualitative data and designed to help you make judgements based on observations of, say, audiovisual material, text or pictures, there is an obvious danger of subjective bias if you are the only person making the judgements, because only one person is interpreting the data by applying the measure. Other people analysing the same data with the same measure may come to differing conclusions. This is known as the 'equivalence' problem and one way to address this would be to use what is know as 'inter-rater reliability' testing. This simply means using more than one person, independently, to apply the measure and produce the results or make the ratings. If the results obtained from two or more independent raters are the same, then the measure would be regarded as reliable, the opposite being the case if the reverse were true.

To establish the stability aspect of a measure's reliability requires that the measure be repeated over time. This is commonly known as the 'test, retest' method. It is similar to the pre-usage testing or trialling process referred to above, but here it is conducted within the context of the research project itself rather than as a preoperational trial. This method is commonly used in laboratory experiment contexts, but may be more difficult to employ in other circumstances. For example, to repeat a postal questionnaire survey may be very time-consuming and expensive and there would be no guarantee that the same people would respond a second time.

One widely used technique for establishing the internal consistency of multi-item measures (those using a number of items relating to each concept for the subject to respond to) is called 'split-half' reliability. This is used for quantitative data and seeks to establish the extent to which the pattern of responses to a given set of items correlates – that is, the greater the degree of correlation there is between the items in the set, the greater the internal consistency, or reliability, of that set of items. We shall explore this further in Chapter 9, but note here that the most widely used test to establish this is known as Cronbach's alpha coefficient. Given that a perfect correlation between two or more items would have a value of 1.0 and items not correlated at all would have a value of 0, it is not hard to see that the closer the value is to 1, the closer, or better, the correlation is and, hence, the greater is the internal consistency of the items.

If you would like to see examples of how many of these issues associated with establishing validity and reliability in the development of measurement scales are dealt with in actual hospitality/tourism studies I would recommend consulting the journal paper downloadable links included in the Sage Journal Papers section for this chapter on the Companion Website (study.sagepub.com/brotherton). In addition, the Bangor University link contained in the Web Links section deals specifically with the issues of measurement, validity and reliability.

Chapter Summary

Developing a conceptual framework helps to synthesise the literature review and inform the empirical research design to effectively link the conceptual and empirical aspects of the research project.

The conceptual framework may be correlational or causal.

In the deductive approach, it precedes the empirical work, but, in the inductive approach, it is an outcome or product of the research process.

The conceptual framework brings together in a logical manner the constructs and concepts that the research is concerned with and enables key variables to be specified.

The four main types of variable are the independent, dependent, intervening and moderating variables.

Hypotheses are derived from the conceptual framework. They can be correlational or causal in nature and expressed in positive (alternative) or negative (null) formats to suggest that a relationship exists or does not.

To measure the constructs, concepts and variables in the conceptual framework, they have to be translated or operationalised from abstract – intangible – concepts to concrete – tangible – indicators.

Any measures based on the four basic types of measurement scale – nominal, ordinal, interval and ratio – should be as accurate, valid, precise and reliable as possible.

References

Brotherton, B. (2004a) 'Critical success factors in UK corporate hotels', *The Services Industry Journal*, 24 (3): 19–42.

Brotherton, B. (2004b) 'Critical success factors in UK budget hotel operations', *International Journal of Operations and Production Management*, 24 (9): 944–69.

Brotherton, B. and Watson, S. (2000) 'Shared priorities and the management development process: a case study of Bass Taverns', *Tourism and Hospitality Research (The Surrey Quarterly Review)*, 2 (2): 103–17.

Clark, M., Riley, M., Wilkie, E. and Wood, R.C. (1998) *Researching and Writing Dissertations in Hospitality and Tourism*. London: International Thomson Business Press. Chapter 5.

Forgas-Coll, S., Palau-Samuell, R., Sanchez-Garcia, J. and Callarisa-Fiol, L.J. (2012) 'Urban destination loyalty drivers and cross-national moderator effects: the case of Barcelona', *Tourism Management*, 33 (6): 1309–20.

Hwang, J., Kim, S.S. and Hyun, S.S. (2013) 'The role of server–patron mutual disclosure in the formation of rapport with and revisit intentions of patrons at full-service restaurants: the moderating roles of marital status and educational level', *International Journal of Hospitality Management*, 33: 64–75.

Hyun, S.S. and Han, H. (2012) 'A model of a patron's innovativeness formation toward a chain restaurant brand', *International Journal of Contemporary Hospitality Management*, 24 (2): 175–99.

Kim, Y.G. and Eves, A. (2012) 'Construction and validation of a scale to measure tourist motivation to consume local food', *Tourism Management*, 33 (6): 1458–67.

Kumar, R. (2011) *Research Methodology: A step-by-step guide for beginners*, 3rd edition. London: Sage.

Ladhari, R. (2012) 'The lodging quality index: an independent assessment of validity and dimensions', *International Journal of Contemporary Hospitality Management*, 24 (4): 628–52.

Milman, A. (2011) 'The symbolic role of postcards in representing a destination image: the case of Alanya, Turkey', *International Journal of Hospitality & Tourism Administration*, 12 (2): 144–73.

Mlozi, S. and Pesamaa, O. (2013) 'Adventure tourist destination choice in Tanzania', *Current Issues in Tourism*, 16 (1): 63–95.

Pranic, L. and Roehl, W.S. (2013) 'Development and validation of the customer empowerment scale in hotel service recovery', *Current Issues in Tourism*, 16 (4): 369–87.

Slatten, T., Krogh, C. and Connolley, S. (2011) 'Make it memorable: customer experiences in winter amusement parks', *International Journal of Culture, Tourism and Hospitality Research*, 5 (1): 80–91.

6

CHOOSING THE EMPIRICAL RESEARCH DESIGN

Chapter Content and Issues

Choosing the most appropriate research design and being able to
justify your choice – theoretical and practical considerations.
Designs for quantitative and qualitative data.
Issues of validity, reliability and credibility.
Survey, experimental, observational, case study, action, comparative
and mixed research designs.
Control and artificiality versus freedom and naturalistic enquiry.
Dealing with the potential for error.
Implementation and process issues and choices.

6.1 Introduction

In this chapter we will consider the main types of research design that are available
for you to choose from to plan and organise the collection of the empirical data you
need to answer your research questions or test the hypotheses you have previously
established. None of the alternatives is perfect or equally applicable to all research
questions and projects – they each have strengths and weaknesses. In making the
decision as to which one to use for your purposes, there will be both logical, or
methodological, and practical, or pragmatic, considerations to take into account and
you will need to be able to explain and justify the choice that you make.

This is important because the way you choose to collect your empirical data is a
key indicator of how appropriate and robust your method has been. Put another
way, if you were asked to judge whether someone's conclusions were sound or
flawed, you would need to consider whether the method they had used to arrive at
those conclusions was sound or not. Alternatively, if you wanted to build a house,

you would want to have sound foundations to build it on, otherwise it might fall down! The same is true in research projects. If you want others to have confidence in the validity and reliability of your research findings, then you must convince them that the method you have used to generate those findings has been appropriate.

Your research design is essentially a procedural plan indicating how you are going to approach, structure and organise the collection of the empirical data you need to obtain the answer/s to your research question/s. This will necessarily include the tasks that need to be accomplished and how these will be achieved within the overall approach or framework you have decided to adopt. This effectively operationalises your research project. It is the bridge between the theoretical/conceptual world you have been operating in so far and the real or empirical world you are about to enter in the next phase of your project. However, as we will see later in this chapter, being able to articulate how you are going to do this is one consideration but another as, if not more, important is dealing with the 'why' issues. In other words, selecting a particular research design to use is one issue but, as we will see later, it is not just a case of making this choice without being able to explain and justify it. Making a choice is one thing but convincing others that this choice is the most sensible and credible involves a little more thought.

6.2 Choosing the Design

To illustrate this, consider the discussion in the Research Reality Scenario box – Which Design to Choose? – before you go any further.

Research Reality Scenario	Which Design to Choose?
The members of the senior management team of the Travel Delight tour operating company are having their weekly team meeting to discuss how to proceed with a possible major investment in new information and communications technology. John Deeside, the Managing Director of the company, is a very intelligent and experienced man who did not go to university when he was young. In his hand-picked team are Patrick Hampshire, the Finance Director, who has a PhD in physics; Shirley Rutland, the Human Resources Director, who has a MA in anthropology; Dominic Cornwall, the Marketing Director, who has a BA in business studies; Carla Sussex, the Operations Director, who has a BA in tourism management; Bill Somerset, the IT Director, who has a PhD in information systems; and Sophia Kent, the Public Relations and Communications Director, who has an MSc in psychology.	

(Continued)

(Continued)

'Okay,' said John, starting the meeting, 'this is a big project and one we can't afford to get wrong because it could either make or break the business. So, we all feel that updating our IT and communications system is a good idea, but we don't know if it will work in the way we expect or deliver the improvements we want. At this stage we are really guessing and hoping, but that's not good enough to commit $20 million to! I, and the Board, need some hard evidence before we can consider going ahead. That's where you guys come in. Let me hear your ideas and I'll see if I'm convinced.'

Patrick makes the first contribution: 'Well, if we really want to have some hard and credible evidence, we need to set up a controlled experiment to test our hypotheses and establish the cause–effect relationships and mechanisms.'

'Yes, I agree in principle,' Sophia chipped in, 'but we're not in a situation where we can set up a controlled laboratory experiment – it would be too expensive, time-consuming and difficult to implement and, anyway, it might also be too unrealistic in terms of the real context we're dealing with. So, what I would suggest is that we set up a programme of interviews with employee and customer groups to discuss and get their feedback on what we are planning. That would enable us to capture the perceptions and concerns of the key players and take these into account when designing and implementing the new system.'

'Possibly, but, on the other hand, what we could do', Dominic suggested, 'is put together a questionnaire survey so that we could ask a representative sample of the employees and our customers what their views, concerns and priorities are in relation to this type of technology. That would give us data on, and an insight into, what the key issues might be.'

'Interesting, if different, views so far,' said Patrick. 'What do the rest of you think?' Shirley ventured, 'One way to get a real insight into how people are going to react to changes in technology and the way things work would be to go into the situation(s) these are going to impact and observe how the employees and customers currently interact with how we are doing things now. This would give us an idea about how they perceive the current situation, how relationships work now and what are seen to be the norms.'

'That would be useful,' Carla added, 'but it wouldn't tell us how the employees and customers might react to the changes we are planning. So, what I would suggest – perhaps in addition to what Shirley has proposed – would be an approach that would enable us to get an understanding of the current situation, introduce changes in technology in one or two areas of the business and then evaluate the effects and impact of those with a view to rolling the technology out across the company later when we've learnt what the issues and problems might be.'

Finally, Bill got the chance to have his say: 'This sort of change is never easy, is it, but, so far, we seem to be concentrating on the users and interfaces. As important as these are, they really are secondary to the architectural and technical aspects of the system. If we don't get these aspects right, it won't work anyway. So, I suggest we concentrate on modelling and trialling the system in miniature to begin with to make sure that it's set up right and works well, then we can consider some of these other ideas.'

'Wow,' exclaimed Patrick, 'I knew this was not going to be easy, but you guys have really given me some things to mull over. What has come out of this is that we need to give this some considerable thought over the coming weeks before we make any decisions on how to proceed. Perhaps we could start by formulating and agreeing what our aims and objectives are for introducing the changes, as this will enable us to specify what information we need to achieve these and then that might give us a clue about what may be an appropriate way to gather the information we need to make a final decision.'

This discussion reveals a real, practical, managerial problem that needs some form of research-related activity to help the management team arrive at a considered, evidence-based decision. However, the route they could take to achieve this end may vary according to the ideas put forward because there are different approaches, ways or designs that can be adopted to collect data and arrive at conclusions. Some of these may be more or less preferable depending on the circumstances, but they all have their advantages and disadvantages. In short, none is perfect and none is totally useless. Therefore, the reasons behind any decision concerning which one to select – and, by implication, which ones to reject – need to be considered and articulated in relation to the purpose(s) of the exercise itself – that is, the decision needs to be explained and justified. The point is that the way in which the data are collected is one consideration lying behind whether or not other people will see the process adopted to arrive at the findings and conclusions as having sufficient credibility to give them confidence in the outcomes that flow from this.

6.2.1   Justifying your decision

In selecting which design to use, a key issue is whether or not you will be able to justify your decision in the methodology section or chapter of the project or dissertation. If you can do so, then you will probably have thought the alternatives through and are able to present a good argument to justify your choice. If you cannot, then you will have made the decision on the wrong basis and could be in trouble!

This does raise the question, however, how can you justify your decision? The basic principle to be considered when answering this question is fitness for purpose or, in other words, is the chosen design the most appropriate one to enable you to collect the data required to answer the research question(s) or test the research hypothesis? If you are following a deductive process, you will have developed, as a product of your literature review, your conceptual framework and associated hypotheses (remember Chapter 5) as the basis, or raw material, for informing your choice and the implementation of the empirical research design to be adopted. Therefore, you should be able to demonstrate a logical and consistent connection between these two elements in your methodological explanation and justification. In short, you should be able to show that your empirical design choice is the most appropriate for achieving your research purposes, as defined in the conceptual framework.

The other source of evidence, in addition to this argument of logical consistency, is previously validated methodology. By this I mean evidence from prior, published research studies conducted by other researchers who have investigated similar phenomena using empirical research designs and data collection methods or procedures that have proved to be successful and robust. If others have previously demonstrated that particular approaches have been found to be valid and reliable, then their work can be used as evidence to support your choice of design.

To help you think this decision through, the rest of this chapter explores the alternative designs available to conduct the empirical data collection phase of a research project. However, before we progress to these, I want you to have one very important principle firmly established in your mind. You must always remember that the choice of any empirical research design is a contingent one. What does this mean? It means that all the various options have strengths and weaknesses and advantages and disadvantages, and that the choice of design should not be based upon the relative merits of one versus another but on the basis that the one chosen is the most appropriate for the task at hand. How is this determined? Quite simply the choice of empirical research design is governed by what it is being used to achieve. It is a means to an end, not the end in itself. Given that the purpose of choosing any design to help structure the collection of empirical data is to answer the research question, achieve the research aim/objectives and test any hypotheses it is clear that this must be the primary 'touchstone' for your choice. In short, you need to ask yourself the simple question: which design will be the most appropriate to help me answer the research question/s I am seeking answers to, or to achieve the research aim/objectives I have specified, and/or to test the hypotheses I have established?

6.3   Experimental Research

Experimental research designs are derived from the historical legacy of what have been viewed as the 'best' ways to implement the scientific method within the physical and natural sciences. Indeed, the adoption of the positivist philosophy, deductive approach and experimental method is the hallmark of traditional scientific enquiry in these fields. In terms of the method, experimentation, particularly laboratory experimentation, is seen by many, though by no means all, as the ideal design for conducting empirical research. This gives rise to the questions why is this the case and, if it is, should you seek to use experimentation as the favoured design for your empirical work?

6.3.1   Control and manipulation

The reasons for experimental designs being seen as ideal are that they facilitate 'controlled enquiry' in terms of the manipulation of the inputs, conditions and processes and valid and reliable measurements of the data or output. An experimental situation, particularly in a laboratory, enables the researcher to control everything and thereby eliminate anything that could contaminate or confound the process. In this sense, it is often the method most capable of meeting the conditions of causality that we discussed in the previous chapter and, hence, is the most suitable for testing hypotheses to demonstrate cause–effect relationships and mechanisms (see Jones, 1999).

As a consequence of this, other empirical research designs often used by researchers taking a deductive approach to their research – particularly surveys and comparative/replicative methods – tend to adopt the same or very similar principles to those of the experimental method. The problem associated with them, however, as we will see later in this chapter, is that, because they are not implemented in as highly controlled conditions as experiments are, the ability to control and manipulate is more limited and therefore the potential for error to occur is greater.

6.3.2   Artificiality and validity

Regarding the second question above, not all phenomena, issues or questions can be addressed easily by using experimental designs and they are the very antithesis of the phenomenological/inductive school of research, which rejects not only the philosophy and approach underlying the experimental method but also the manner in which it is put into practice. As experimentation is invariably conducted in either a totally artificial environment (the laboratory) or one that is quasi-artificial (an experiment set up in the real world) within which the researcher exerts a high degree of control and manipulation, it is argued that this artificiality compromises the validity of the work because it is contrived and unnatural. In the case of laboratory experiments, internal validity – that is, accuracy and truthfulness within the boundaries or parameters of the laboratory conditions – is considered to be high, but these conditions are, in themselves, contrived and artificial and may not be transferable to the real world. Conversely, where experiments are conducted in the real world, external validity – that is, accuracy and truthfulness within the real-world conditions in which the experiment takes place – is said to be high because these are occurring in more, but not totally, natural conditions. Nevertheless, because the extent and degree of control that are possible under these conditions are reduced, there is a greater potential for errors to arise, which, in turn, may compromise the internal validity of the results. So, how do you decide? The Key Decision box – Choosing Experimentation? – highlights some of the fundamental considerations in this respect.

Key Decisions	Choosing Experimentation?
Whether you should choose experimentation as the method for your research will depend on whether it is the most desirable and feasible way in which to answer your research questions and hypotheses. Of course, this raises another *(Continued)*	

(Continued)

question – how do I decide whether it is the most appropriate and feasible way or not?

This is not an easy question to answer in a few words, but, if your research is going to adopt an inductive approach or is exploratory in scope, is not being conducted to establish cause–effect relationships, requires data to be collected from a wide variety (particularly in geographical terms) of people or organisations, or is concerned with phenomena that are not easy to simulate and control, then it is likely that an experimental design will not be the most desirable or, indeed, feasible method for your purposes.

On the other hand, if your project does demand that the cause–effect relationships and mechanisms be explored or it is conducted in a limited and controllable environment or is concerned with testing or trialling new principles, practices or products, then use of an experimental design may be appropriate.

6.3.3   The influence and significance of experimental design principles

There are numerous types of experimental research designs, ranging from the simple to the more complex and powerful, but because this type of design is one that is rarely applicable to most undergraduate or postgraduate research issues and questions in hospitality or tourism – often for practical reasons of time and resources available to undertake the research – a detailed consideration of these designs is not included here. If this is the design you require, however, then excellent sources to consult for more detail and guidance are Jones (1999) and Sekaran (2013). Both of these deal with the design considerations and Jones also includes examples of, and references to, the application of experimental designs to published research studies conducted in hospitality. To see how a range of experimental designs have been used in physical, quasi-experimental or scenario-based, and online environments relating to hospitality and/or tourism the studies conducted by the following researchers would give you useful insights: Gueguen and Jacob (2012), Jeong et al. (2012), Kuo and Cranage (2012), Lee and Gretzel (2012), Levy (2010), McQuilken et al. (2013), Wu and Mattila (2013).

 And, if experimental design is the choice for you, it may be helpful to visit the Companion Website (study.sagepub.com/brotherton) where you will find a video dealing with experimental and quasi-experimental designs and a link to more extensive and detailed assistance for using experimental designs in the Video and Web Link sections respectively.

However, regardless of whether or not you intend to adopt an experimental design for your empirical research, the basic principles of experimental research design are useful to know if you intend to take a deductive approach for your project because, as stated earlier, other designs utilising this approach have been developed using and adapting the principles of experimentation. As discussed previously (Chapter 5), before we can proceed to the stage of collecting empirical data using the deductive approach, we need to identify and operationalise the concepts and variables we wish to measure, specify the relationships between them in the conceptual framework and develop hypotheses to enable us to test these proposed relationships. This is what an experiment is designed to do within a predetermined and controlled environment.

To conduct an experiment, the researcher exerts a considerable degree of control over its inputs, format and processes to try to ensure that any potential errors are eliminated or, at the very least, minimised so that valid results can be obtained. Similarly, publishing the details of the method(s) used facilitates future, independent testing of the reliability of the measurement instruments as others repeat, or replicate, the experiment. Although the ability of the researcher to exert the same degree of control within a survey or comparative research is more limited than it is for experimentation, this does not mean that these designs do not exhibit similar or equivalent characteristics to those used for experimentation as they are modified to fit the different contexts and conditions under which these designs are implemented.

This will become evident in the sections that follow on these designs, but, to illustrate this point, consider what is involved in designing and conducting a questionnaire survey. As well as all the conceptual and measurement considerations and decisions made by you as the researcher, the survey design also involves making decisions concerning the selection of a sample to give the questionnaire to, the writing of the questions, the method to be used in implementing or administering the questionnaire and, finally, the recording methods and analysis of the data obtained from the questionnaire – all of which are under your control as the designer and implementer of the survey.

Furthermore, given that you will want to make these decisions to help generate as much valid and reliable data as possible, your ability to 'design in' as much control over the content and processes involved to minimise potential error will be important. So, although the context of a survey is different from that of an experiment, many of the principles involved in the design and implementation of research based on both of these are essentially the same – it is the extent to which these can be achieved and how they are addressed that differs.

6.3.4 What is the relevance of experimentation to hospitality or tourism students?

Finally, there can be a tendency for students of hospitality or tourism management to take the view that experimental research is okay for physicists, chemists, biologists, geneticists and other laboratory scientists in white coats, but it is not relevant to people preparing for a career as managers in the hospitality or tourism industries. While this is true in the sense that you are not envisaging a career as a laboratory scientist, it would be wrong to assume that you will never encounter the experimental method in these industries. One obvious application lies in new dish and menu development, where experimentation is commonly used to develop and refine such new products. Another lies in testing out new ideas or concepts that are as yet unproven. For example, the cost of launching a new product format, rebranding or making process or system changes can be very significant and potentially disastrous if they fail.

Therefore, it is common for companies to set up experiments – although they are perhaps more frequently referred to as 'test units', 'trials' or 'pilot operations' – to establish whether a change will work before it is applied to the whole organisation. Similarly, where companies believe that changes in work practices, customer flow management or organisational restructuring will be beneficial, but would be disastrous if that belief was unfounded, they may use the experimental approach to test the beliefs first by making the changes in one part of the organisation to see if the evidence supports the belief or not. This is akin to talking about testing a hypothesis.

6.4   Survey Research

Survey research is a very common and popular form of empirical research design that is widely used by academics, commercial research organisations and companies. For example, you may have heard of polls conducted by organisations such as IPSOS MORI or Gallup reporting the level of support for a political party or predicting election results as they are commonly featured on television news programmes or in newspapers. Similarly, such programmes, in their coverage of topical issues, frequently refer to the results from a survey conducted on a particular newsworthy topic, such as health or the environment.

Hospitality and tourism companies and organisations also conduct surveys to gather information on issues that are important to them. For example, many companies have some form of customer feedback or satisfaction survey questionnaire that they use to collect data on the customers' experience of the product or service. These are often left in a hotel room, placed on restaurant tables, given to customers on a flight, mailed out to tourists after they have returned home, sent by email to the customer's email address and so on. Companies may also use surveys to obtain feedback from employees to ascertain how happy and satisfied they are.

6.4.1   Surveys and sampling

Whatever the specific form and purpose of a particular survey, it is essentially a technique to communicate with and collect information from a 'representative sample' of individuals or organisations, mainly using verbal or written questioning. The key words here are 'communicate', 'representative sample' and 'questioning'. The issue of what a representative sample is will be considered in more detail in Chapter 8, but the principle of this is that, in most cases, it is not possible to survey the entire population of individuals or organisations, often for reasons of time and cost, so a sample is selected from the overall population and the answers derived from this sample are then generalised back to the population as a whole.

This may sound complicated, but it is not, at least in principle. For example, for an organisation like Gallup to predict the voting intentions of, say, 40 million voters in the UK, it may only need to conduct a survey, usually by telephone, using a sample of around 3,000 people. As long as the characteristics of the sample mirror those found in the voting population as a whole, it should be sufficiently representative for the results obtained from the sample of 3,000 people to be generalised to the voting population as a whole and, hence, for the election results to be predicted. On the other hand, if the sample were not sufficiently representative of the voting population as a whole, then, when the survey results from this sample are expanded, or extrapolated, to the population, the prediction based on these would turn out to be wildly wrong. In short, error in the sample selection is magnified when the results are generalised back to the wider context. From this it should be clear that the issue of sample selection for a survey is critical if generalisation and prediction are desired, as they invariably are, from the survey results.

6.4.2 Communicating with the respondents

So, we have to get the size and composition of the sample right for a survey, but the other key issue is asking the sample respondents the questions. We all know that a survey questionnaire asks us to answer or respond to the questions or statements it contains to give its authors the information they require, but what is often forgotten in this process is the fact that the questionnaire itself is a communication vehicle. In some senses, this is obvious as it communicates the questions to the potential respondent, but communication is not always as successful as we would like or anticipate and there is the potential for both manipulation and/or error.

Communication is a two-way process. The sender of the message has to make the meaning as clear and unambiguous as possible so that the receiver understands it in the way it was originally meant and then he or she can respond appropriately to close the loop. The problem is that this process does not always work in the way we had hoped or anticipated. I am sure that you will have experienced situations where misinterpretations and misunderstandings have occurred when you have tried to communicate, either orally or in writing, with someone else, even though you may have felt that your original message and its meaning were entirely clear.

Similarly, it is possible to manipulate the communication process by phrasing questions or statements in such a way that they lead the respondents' perceptions in the direction you want in order that they give you the answers you want. Once again, we will consider this and other issues relating to the writing of survey questions and questionnaire design in more detail in Chapter 7. However, it is worth making the point here that a survey has to be carefully planned and constructed if it is to be regarded as a sound vehicle for collecting empirical data and for the results obtained from it to have credibility.

6.4.3   Advantages and disadvantages of surveys

A survey may be appropriate for your research project, but, in common with all the other possible designs discussed in this chapter, it is not necessarily better than others and should not be regarded as an automatic choice. Surveys have their advantages and disadvantages, as do all the other designs. Perhaps the main advantages of surveys are that they can be relatively quick and easy to design and implement compared to other empirical design options. Surveys also, if designed and conducted properly, can deliver reliable results and the nature of the data obtained from questionnaires is frequently, although not always, amenable to statistical manipulation, which, in turn, can make objective comparisons easier to achieve.

The main disadvantages are that the survey interview or questionnaire is a contrived and artificial situation. As the survey respondents can only respond to the questions they are asked and, in many cases, only in the format prescribed in the questionnaire, this places parameters on the nature and type of response that can be given. Also, people's responses to survey questions tend to reflect what they are prepared to say, or reveal, about their true feelings on the issue and not necessarily what they really feel or believe. These issues together raise questions concerning the validity of the data collected.

6.4.4   Types of survey

Surveys can be used for many research purposes, but most of them can be grouped under one of two headings – replication and new studies. Where previous studies have used survey methods to obtain data and you intend to repeat or replicate one of them in your study, there are often good reasons to choose the same method, instrument and procedures as the original work. As you will see later in this chapter, such a project would be essentially comparative in nature – that is, you want to repeat the study to compare the results of your study with those of the original and it is easier to do this when the methods used in the two studies are either identical or very similar. This would be the case whether your study was being conducted to update the original work that had been undertaken some time ago and was now regarded as not being representative of contemporary conditions or you wanted to repeat a study originally undertaken in another industry, country or cultural context within the hospitality or tourism industry. For example, a survey of the most important influences on hotel guest satisfaction may have been conducted in the USA and you want to repeat it in the UK to see if the hotel guests in each country have the same views, or a survey on museum visitor expectations may have been conducted 20 years ago and you want to update the results.

Alternatively, a survey of banking customers may have found that they could be grouped into certain segments according to their age and lifestyle and you want to undertake a survey of airline passengers to see if the same segmentation applies to that context, or you want to explore the tourism attraction preferences of independent travellers in Spain in your project and have found a previous survey that addressed the same issues in a study conducted in Greece, so you are interested to know if the findings from the Greek study are the same as yours.

Although it is not always possible to exactly replicate the original survey question-naire, because of differences in terminology or issues that have changed over time, it is usually possible to produce an alternative version that is equivalent, but not exactly identical, to the original. In the case of 'new' studies, a survey might be used to explore a gap, or gaps, in previous work that has been identified in the process of conducting the literature review on the topic or to take a new angle or perspective on the same issues.

Surveys can be used for descriptive or analytical purposes, though they tend to be more commonly used for the former than the latter. An analytical survey would be one concerned with the collection of data to test hypothesised cause–effect relation-ships and ascertain the mechanisms underlying such relationships. So, for example, although questions may be asked to determine the what, when, how often and how many aspects of people's behaviour or actions, an analytical survey would also want to ask the why questions as well. These would be absent from a descriptive survey as its purpose would be to identify the characteristics of the sample and relate these to their preferences, attitudes or actions to ascertain similarities or differences. Another way of distinguishing between these two types would be to see the descrip-tive survey as essentially one that is designed to obtain and record facts, whereas the analytical survey is more concerned with producing explanations.

Either of these types of survey could be conducted on what is known as a cross-sectional or longitudinal basis. Which is chosen is simply an issue of time. A survey conducted on a cross-sectional basis is one undertaken at a particular point in time and, therefore, the effects of changes in context, conditions, attitudes, preferences, behaviour and so on over time are not taken into account. A longitudinal study, however, explicitly incorporates the effects of time as the survey is repeated at inter-vals and the results from successive implementations are compared to assess the impact of change over time.

One, albeit imperfect, way to think about the difference between the two is to consider the cross-sectional survey as a still photograph that captures an image at one point in time and the longitudinal one as a film or video that follows evolution or development over time.

To see how these considerations play out in practice, access the video material via the link on the Companion Website (study.sagepub.com/brotherton) dealing with the question of whether to use a survey or not and, if so, how to ensure that it is designed appropriately and/or see the surveysystem.com link in the Web Links section, which will lead you to material dealing with the same issues.

6.4.5 Survey implementation

A survey can be implemented in various ways. These are sometimes described as directly, semi-directly or indirectly, but I prefer to think of these alternatives as either direct – face-to-face interviewing – or 'distributed' – where the questionnaire is sent, or distributed, to the potential respondents by either postal, telephonic or electronic means. It is the telephone survey that others regard as the semi-direct method of implementation because the person asking the questions does have some real-time contact with the respondent, as opposed to the respondent merely receiving a written questionnaire in the post or accessing it electronically. It is not direct because the two are not physically in the same location and it is mediated by the telephone.

Your choice of survey implementation method is likely to be dictated by considerations of time and cost, which, in turn, are frequently determined by the geographical dispersion of the survey sample. Where the sample is dispersed over a wide geographical area, the time and cost involved in travelling to all the locations where the respondents are will probably be prohibitive, so a distributed method is likely to be more suitable. On the other hand, if the sample respondents are limited geographically to one or a number of locations close to you, then it may be feasible to use a direct, face-to-face, interviewing method of implementation.

There are no major advantages *per se* to using either a direct or distributed strategy to implement a survey, but there are implications for the design and content of the survey questionnaire. We shall consider these issues further in Chapter 7, but they revolve around the communication issue of questioner–respondent interaction. Where a survey is distributed by one of the means identified above, there is no direct contact between the two parties, which means that any ambiguity and potential for different interpretation must be eliminated from the questionnaire before it is used. If the recipient does not understand what is being asked, how to respond or is confused by the wording of questions or other instructions in the questionnaire, there is no opportunity for any of these issues to be clarified by the questioner. On the other hand, although it is good practice and desirable for even questionnaires used in direct contact with the respondent to be as free as possible from such contaminating errors, it is possible to interact with the respondent to explain or clarify any uncertainties and so on. However, there is then the potential, if it is not done consistently and carefully, for this to influence or bias the nature of the responses.

6.4.6   Sources and types of error

In common with all the research designs, surveys are not perfect and there are various sources of error that can arise to potentially contaminate the data obtained from a survey questionnaire. Errors can occur in the sampling strategy and procedures used to determine and select the survey sample. We will explore this subject more in Chapter 8, but let us look briefly at the sorts of errors that can occur now so that you can bear them in mind before you progress too far in the design of your project.

First, if the sample is selected in anything other than a random manner or the random selection procedure is not applied correctly, then bias may be designed into the sample itself. Second, systematic (non-sampling) errors can exist. These are usually associated with problems in the questionnaire. For example, if a question can be interpreted in different ways by the respondents, then it will be virtually impossible to tell which interpretation has been used by which respondent to guide their responses and, as they have effectively been responding to a different question, this effectively will invalidate the data relating to that question – all the data collected on that question will be useless. Therefore, as you might imagine, this is a pretty serious problem. To avoid it occurring, it is usually recommended that the questionnaire is tested, or trialled, before you implement it, but more advice on this is given in Chapter 7.

Third, errors can arise from respondents. For example, the non-response form of error can be a major problem. This can happen simply because questionnaires are not completed and returned by the respondents, or when questionnaires are returned but some of the questions have not been answered by all of the respondents. A simple example will illustrate the nature of this problem.

If you mailed out questionnaires to a sample of 100 companies and only 50 were completed and returned, the response rate would be 50 per cent. Not only does this reduce your actual sample to half the size you originally determined that you needed but it also raises the issue of how to know if the 50 companies who did not respond would have responded in the same way to the questions as the 50 who did. The fact is that you cannot know, which begins to threaten your ability to generalise from the results. As you have probably surmised, there is an inverse relationship between a survey's response rate and the degree of non-response error. In other words, as the response rate increases, the level of non-response error decreases and vice versa. Therefore, the key to reducing the non-response error is to try to obtain as high a response rate as possible.

Technique Tip	**Improving Survey Response Rates**

There are various tactics outlined below that you can use to try to achieve a better response rate, but none is foolproof.

✓ Make the questionnaire as easy and quick to complete as possible.

✓ Ensure that a date for completion and return is clearly communicated to the respondents.

✓ Include a 'selling' message with, or in, the questionnaire to motivate the receiver to complete and return it.

✓ Offer some form of inducement the respondent might value, such as a copy of the results.

✓ Provide a reply-paid envelope to eliminate there being a cost involved in returning the questionnaire.

However, all of these tactics serve only to possibly improve the initial response rate. Once you have passed the return deadline and not all of the questionnaires have been received, there are other things you can try in a bid to improve the final response rate. For example, it may be possible, if you have the information, to contact the respondents who have not returned their questionnaires by telephone to remind and/or encourage them to do so. Alternatively, you could send out another copy of the questionnaire to those who have not returned theirs with a message exhorting or encouraging them to complete and return it.

Another source of non-response error can occur where the sample is self-selected. In other words, the respondents choose to complete the questionnaire for various reasons of their own. A good example of this type of problem is often to be found in situations where companies leave questionnaires out for their guests or customers to complete if they choose to do so or they issue questionnaires to their customers but leave it up to them as to whether or not they complete these.

The customer feedback/satisfaction questionnaires seemingly so beloved of hospitality, tourism and other businesses are a prime example of this. Often hotels will leave this type of questionnaire in their guest bedrooms, restaurants may place them on their tables and holiday companies may hand them out to passengers on their return flights. In each of these cases, but particularly the first two, the people most likely to complete the questionnaires will be those who are either very happy or very unhappy with their experience because they wish to praise or complain about it. Thus, the sample obtained as a result of a survey organised in this way is likely to be highly biased and the data are very unlikely to be representative of the views of the hotels' guests or restaurants' customers as a whole. In short, it is really rather a pointless exercise. The message here is clear: if you choose to place or leave your questionnaires in a location for people to pick up and complete or ignore, then you have no control over the selection and composition of the sample and cannot justify claims that the sample is representative. You will recall from earlier in this chapter that it is absolutely crucial for a sample to be representative if you want to generalise from the survey's results.

In the case of questionnaires that are returned but not every respondent has answered all the questions, you have to make a judgement as to whether the level of response to individual questions is sufficient to regard the data as credible or not. There is no easy rule for doing this, but, if from 50 questionnaires returned, only five respondents answered question 10, then you might reasonably conclude that, with a 90 per cent non-response rate to this question, it would not be sensible to draw conclusions from this data. On the other hand, if, of the 50 questionnaires, 30 respondents had answered question 10, then this 60 per cent response rate may well lead you to the opposite conclusion.

The issue here is one of representativeness. If more than half of the respondents have answered the question, you may well feel that this is likely to be more representative of the sample as a whole than if only, say, 10 per cent answered the question. Therefore, the key to making the decision to include and use data on individual questions where not all the respondents have answered them is how confident you feel about being able to claim, and justify, that the amount of data you have is sufficient to be regarded as representative of the sample as a whole.

Response bias is another potential source of survey error. This arises either as a consequence of deficiencies in the questions asked or from the behaviour of the respondents. Where questions are worded in ambiguous terms and can be misunderstood, then errors will probably arise. Similarly, where respondents, for some reason, decide to provide answers that misrepresent or deliberately falsify their true feelings on an issue, the validity of the data becomes questionable. This begs the question, why would they want to do this?

It is thought that where questions are asked about issues that are potentially sensitive to respondents, the responses they give may be contrived in some way to protect themselves or perhaps portray them in a more favourable light. For example, if a company is asked to rate itself in terms of the quality of its products compared to those of its competitors, it is likely that the person responding on behalf of the company will wish to portray his or her company in a favourable light, so might not give a true or accurate answer. Similarly, if a person is asked questions that are associated with his or her self-image, then these too could well attract biased responses.

Finally, errors can creep into the administrative aspects of survey implementation. Where a direct implementation strategy is used, with more than one interviewer conducting the survey interviews, it is possible that the interviewers will behave in different ways when presenting the questionnaire to respondents. Some may offer additional information or explanations, others may not; some may prompt the respondents, and others not. Whatever the nature of the differences, they contaminate the implementation process because the bases on which the respondents are providing answers differ and this makes it problematic to aggregate and compare their responses.

It is also possible for interviewers to cheat when completing questionnaires. It has been known, particularly in commercial research situations where interviewers are paid, for them to cheat by completing the questionnaires themselves! The remedy for interviewer error, of the unthinking helpfulness kind, is to ensure that the interviewers are well briefed and trained before the process begins to try to make certain, as far as is reasonably possible, that they all implement the questionnaire in the same manner. To reinforce this, instructions to the interviewers can be written into the questionnaire – 'do not provide any additional explanation for these questions', 'only ask the question as it is written – do not add anything to this', 'do not prompt the interviewee' and so on – to try to ensure that they all behave in the same way. The Research in Action box – The Nature of Hospitality – contains some examples of this taken from the questionnaire used to interview hotel guests that was implemented by two different interviewers in the two different hotels used for this study.

Research in Action	**The Nature of Hospitality**
This research study (see Brotherton, 2005) was essentially a comparative case study, within which two independent samples of hotel guests from two	
	(Continued)

(Continued)

different four-star hotels in close proximity to one another were surveyed. Having negotiated access with the respective general managers, guests in each hotel were interviewed by two interviewers who both used the same questionnaire to conduct the interviews. Prior briefings were given by myself to each interviewer to stress the need for consistency in conducting each interview and the importance of following the instructions contained in the questionnaire in order to ensure, as far as was reasonably possible, the absence of potentially contaminating prompting or help for some respondents but not others. Some examples of these 'embedded' instructions are provided below.

Section One

Ask the following questions exactly as they are. **DO NOT** provide any explanations or further clarification.

Question 5

a) If I asked you to describe the *Physical Aspects* of hospitality in this hotel as a **season of the year**, which one would you choose?

| **Interviewer Note** – Only allow the respondent to choose one of the seasons. |

Autumn   q

Winter   q

Spring   q

Summer   q

Obtaining Some Personal Details

Thank the interviewee as indicated below and ask the final questions relating to his/her personal characteristics. Don't ask Question 6, just complete this yourself – it should be self-evident! Be sensible here with the 'age groups' question (Question 11). If the interviewee is obviously young or old do not go through all the age groups. If you are unsure start with the one you feel might be closest to the one that the person is likely to fit into. Similarly, be sensible with Question 10. If the respondent's appearance obviously fits one of the categories just record this and don't ask the question.

Note: Question 6 concerned gender (male/female). Question 10 was concerned with the respondent's ethnic origin.

Once the survey has been completed and the questionnaire data are available for processing, errors can arise in keying this data into computers for analysis. This can be as simple as pressing the wrong key or two keys together when entering the data. Therefore, once the data have been entered, it is good practice to review the data sheet, or its equivalent, to check that there are no rogue entries that should not be there.

6.5 Comparative Research

Although all research involves comparisons of various kinds, the difference between comparative research designs and others that include varying amounts of comparison is that the former has a specific comparative purpose from the outset – it is a central part of the rationale for conducting the research in this way, not just a by-product of its design. It is overt and explicit rather than implicit.

Even though research conducted using one of the other designs discussed in this chapter may reveal similarities and/or differences when its data are analysed, the difference between them and a comparative research design is that the latter is specifically used to address one or other of these similarities or differences. In short, it is a design used to discover and explain differences or similarities between phenomena in either a spatial or a temporal context – that is, between different spatial entities, such as companies, industries, countries and so on at the same time, or between different time periods, such as today and 10 years ago. The former is generally referred to as a cross-sectional type of study and the latter as a longitudinal one. Examples of cross-sectional studies are provided by Presbury et al. (2005) and Getz et al. (2010), with longitudinal designs used by Guchait and Hamilton (2013) and Jung and Yoon (2013).

Such comparative studies can help to test the extent to which a theory can be generalised across different time periods and/or contemporary contexts. For example, comparative research designs might address questions such as the following.

- Can a theory of consumer behaviour developed in the context of the American domestic tourism industry be applied to the same industry in China?

- Are the factors that determine the volume of air travel today the same as those 10 years ago?

- Why do some hospitality companies seem to have very low levels of staff turnover when others have very high levels?

- Why are some tourism companies very profitable while others in the same line of business are not?

- Why do some female managers in the hospitality industry achieve high managerial positions but others do not?

In each of these cases, a comparative research design would be suitable to try to identify the answers to these questions or reasons for these differences.

6.5.1 Basic approaches to comparative designs

There are two basic approaches that can be taken when designing comparative research. First, the positive approach, which is concerned with identifying similarities in the independent variables associated with a common outcome or dependent variable. For example, we could ask, in those companies that have very low levels of staff turnover (the common dependent variable), are there similar reasons evident (independent variables) to explain this? In other words, are the same outcomes in different situations caused by the same things?

Second, there is the negative approach, which involves explaining different or divergent outcomes by identifying the major, common reasons for these variations. For example, using the same context as above, we might identify companies with very different levels of staff turnover (the outcome or dependent variable) and ask why this is the case – that is, what common independent variables may explain this difference? In this approach, the aim is to try to identify the main or most influential independent variables contributing to the different outcomes, and then explain why these same variables can generate different outcomes. In this example, it may be due to varying abilities on the part of the companies to pay appropriate wages or salaries or to motivate their employees sufficiently. The issue here is how well the companies perform in relation to the same independent variable that influences the outcome – that is, the underlying cause of different levels of outcome is the same, but, where performance regarding this variable is good, the outcome is more positive and vice versa. The same principle would apply if the study were comparing individuals or groups.

6.5.2   The importance of equivalence

Because comparative research inherently deals with different contexts or time periods, one of the key issues in designing any form of comparative research is that of equivalence. With either spatial or temporal differences in the research context, conceptual and/or measurement differences are likely to arise. This gives rise to a major problem in making direct and valid comparisons between different contexts because, to make valid comparisons, a common denominator is required. For example, the way in which tourism, the tourism industry and tourism expenditure are defined – and, hence, measured – in different countries differs, making direct comparisons of the tourism statistics these countries produce problematic. Similarly, if we wish to track changes in tourism arrivals to a country over time, we might be faced with the problem that the definition of a 'tourist arrival' and the way statistics on this have been collected and analysed could have changed during the time period we want to look at.

The point here is that, to make valid comparisons, we need to be able to compare like with like or as close to this ideal as possible. This does not mean that we need to seek out identical entities – because, by definition, there would not be any differences between them – or, at the other extreme, entities that are totally different in every way – they would have no similarities at all, so there would be no basis for making comparisons. It is the entities between these two extremes, possessing both differences and similarities that are sufficiently similar to be regarded as being equivalent, that are interesting.

This is not a context issue because, often, we will want to study very different contexts, but one that is conceptual in nature and concerns measurement. It becomes most problematic when the research contexts include different countries, cultures and languages – cross-national/cultural or international studies – and less so when the context is more limited and homogeneous – companies within the same line of hospitality or tourism business (Brotherton, 2003).

In the former contexts, because of such influences, the same concept can have very different connotations and meanings in each context, which has the effect that there is no common denominator or reference point to make the comparisons with. This means that making valid comparison is very difficult as there is a lack of conceptual equivalence – that is, we are not comparing like with like. In the latter contexts, because of the relative homogeneity of the situation, there is likely to be a shared or common denominator to make comparisons with, making it less problematic.

One way to illustrate this issue is to consider the simple example of measurement. Where the concept and practice of measurement are the same – that is, the same system and calibrations are used across the contexts, then a common denominator exists. However, where one context uses, say, imperial measurements and another uses metric ones, there is no common denominator and, to establish equivalence, one set of measures has to be converted into the other. The same is true in the case of different currencies, where the exchange rate between them establishes equivalent values. To have a common denominator in this case would require all currencies to be expressed in terms of their value relationship to one currency. In many instances, this is achieved by expressing different currency values and volumes in US dollars, as this provides a common currency to facilitate comparisons between countries.

6.5.3 'Intra' and 'inter' comparisons

These observations should indicate to you that comparative studies undertaken on an 'intra' (within), as opposed to an 'inter' (between), contextual basis are less likely to face such equivalence issues. So, studies designed to compare companies within the same line of business or individuals performing the same job in similar companies would be easier to design, in terms of conceptual and measurement equivalence, than would studies designed to compare service systems in fast food restaurants and banks (see Brotherton, 2000). However, this should not be taken to mean that studies designed to compare different contexts are to be avoided. Indeed, there is often great value in comparing issues, practices and problems in hospitality or tourism contexts to those found in other types of industry because any similarities found across different contexts could help to make the theoretical explanations for the phenomena more general and less context-specific. Indeed, the greater the variations between the contexts used for comparative purposes, the greater the ability to generalise from similar results obtained from them. By contrast, where the contexts are very similar, similar results may be transferable between these contexts but not necessarily generalisable to other, very different, contexts. In such cases, the results and explanations are contextually limited as they are not capable of being applied to, or across, a range of different contexts (Brotherton, 1999b).

6.5.4 Comparison and other research designs

Comparative research designs may be associated with any of the other types of empirical research designs discussed in this chapter, depending on whether they are of a case or variable-orientated nature. In the next section, we will explore some of these issues as they relate to multiple case study and/or units of analysis designs, where more than one case study may be used so as to make comparisons between the two or more cases or, where there is only one case study, it is subdivided into two or more units of analysis, which are then used to make comparisons within the case itself. Similarly, in observational research, more than one situation chosen for observation may be used to facilitate comparisons between the observations for each.

In variable-orientated approaches, too, some experimental research designs are specifically comparative in nature – different experimental and control groups being established to compare the effects of the experimental treatment with that implemented in the control groups. Surveys may also be designed for specific comparative purposes. For example, different samples may be selected to receive the same survey instrument or questionnaire in order that the results from these samples can be directly compared. A good example of this is provided by the Getz et al. (2010) study of festival management in four different countries wherein the same survey procedure is repeated across the four contexts to facilitate direct comparison between the samples.

In addition, the University of Haifa link in the Web Links section of the Companion Website (study.sagepub.com/brotherton) is a site that contains a quite extensive collection of material relating to comparative research methodology.

6.6 Case Study Research

Some commentators see case study research as a design that is most appropriate for initial, exploratory research, often of a qualitative nature. It is a design viewed by many researchers who take a positivistic standpoint as one that is 'completely value-less at worst and markedly inferior to other methodological choices, such as experimentation and large N surveys, at best' (Brotherton, 1999a). On the other hand,

> those researchers with a more phenomenological or interpretivist orientation would argue that case study research, frequently in conjunction with ethnographic and field methods, is at the very least extremely valuable for developing 'grounded' theoretical insights through an inductive process and may be seen as a type of research capable of providing valid theoretical generalisations beyond the specific case(s) considered in the study. (Brotherton, 1999a: 115)

An example of this in practice is provided by Skaalsvik's (2011) study that used an inductive approach to identifying and classifying service failures in the context of cruise line operations.

In this sense, empirical research designs adopting a case study approach are invariably seen as empirically limited because they are normally (but not exclusively) conducted within a context that is relatively small in scope and may or may not be representative of the wider world it is a part of. This frequently means that attempts to generalise the findings from a piece of case study research to a wider empirical reality are fraught with difficulty because the case context may be atypical of the population as a whole and the volume of data collected is likely to be relatively small, which could preclude the use of statistical extrapolation procedures that are based on the existence of a large amount of data. However, this is not the purpose of case study research, as we will see later in this section.

6.6.1   The importance of context

Case studies are generally seen as valuable for exploring an issue in depth within a specific context, using qualitative data to assist in the development of insights and theory, but not usually as a means of testing existing theory. The research methodology literature in general portrays case studies as suitable for research based on a phenomenological philosophy, using an inductive approach to collect and analyse qualitative data to develop new theory. Although case studies may be useful and appropriate for achieving this, they can also be used in a positivistic, deductive and more quantitative context. For example, it is possible to use a case study to test the applicability of an existing theory to the particular conditions within the case situation – that is, if the theory has been developed as a result of large-scale survey work in the first instance, using large organisations as the sample to verify it, then it may be a worthwhile exercise to carry out a case study of a small organisation to test the extent to which the theory fits this type of organisation. Alternatively, if the organisation selected for the case study was atypical or even unique, then it could be used as the basis for exploring whether the theory is generally applicable to all types of organisation or might require some modification under certain conditions.

The point here is that case study research designs may be more applicable to the type of study you have in mind than the literature might have led you to believe. Given the nature of hospitality and tourism educational programmes, it is quite possible that you have close contact with a particular company, in the form of a work placement or part-time employment, and this could constitute a useful context in which to undertake your research. That said, you should exercise caution when doing this. Simply seeing a company you have access to as an easy route to obtaining information is not a good enough reason to choose it and a case study approach to collect your data. The empirical design you choose is merely a means to an end and it should always be selected on the basis that it is the most appropriate and feasible way to obtain the data you need to answer your research question(s) and test the hypotheses you have established. Taking what you may see as the line of least resistance can be disastrous, both in terms of being able to justify this choice and in practice when the people in the company who told you that there would be no problem giving you access to the data suddenly leave or decide that it is not now possible!

One reason for choosing a case study design could be that you need to study the particular phenomena within a situational context because they are interrelated and inseparable – that is, the boundaries between them are not clear. Indeed, this is a key feature of a case situation and one that can be referred to as a 'bounded context', where the phenomenon in question is evident. In short, the premise here is that the phenomenon can only be understood when it is studied in conjunction with the conditions in which it occurs.

This is the opposite of survey research, where specific contextual conditions and variations in these are very much secondary considerations at best because the aim of the survey is to generalise from its results to differing contextual conditions and produce findings that are generally, if not universally, applicable. Hence, while research designs such as experimentation and surveys seek to deliver theoretical and empirical insights that are not determined or limited by the specific conditions existing in any particular context, case studies explicitly recognise that such conditions are an integral part of any explanation.

6.6.2   What constitutes a case?

If a case study design is chosen as the most appropriate design for your research, then the first issue to resolve is the definition of what constitutes the case. In some instances, this may be quite straightforward, but in others it can be more complicated. If it is a particular company or operating unit within a company, the boundaries of the case can be quite clear. If, however, the case is based on particular types of people or events, it can be more difficult to delineate or find these boundaries. For example, if your study involved a case of hotel general managers, airline marketing managers, international sporting events or major festivals, then it would be more difficult to decide which types of these should be included in, or excluded from, the definition or boundaries of the case because there are many of them and they vary considerably.

Sometimes students are confused by the question – is my research a case study or not? It is not always immediately clear that the design being considered can be regarded as a case study. The Key Decisions box – Could my Research be a Case Study? – indicates a number of characteristics and considerations that should help you to decide the answer to this question.

Key Decisions

Could my Research be a Case Study?

If you can answer yes to the following questions then your research might be suitable to be regarded as a case study:

- Is the study going to be one that aims to develop a narrative, or story, about a particular organisation, type/s of individuals, event or geographic area?

- Will it focus on a specific context and a particular activity and/or solutions within that context?

- Will the study have a clearly defined boundary?

- Is the intent to develop in-depth knowledge and explanation within a particular context?

- Will it be necessary to include historical (antecedent) aspects for the present situation to be understandable?

- Will you need to collect/use a range of different types of information to develop a full understanding of the phenomena within the context in question?

6.6.3   The unit(s) of analysis

One thing that can help you to make decisions on what to include and exclude is the notion of the study's 'unit of analysis.' This is the main focus of the study and there may be one or more unit(s) of analysis. Case studies regarded as 'holistic' in nature have a single unit of analysis, whereas those known as 'embedded' have more than one. The other issue here is whether the design is to include a single case or whether it should have more – multiple cases – for comparative purposes.

Yin (2013), one of the leading writers on case study research, puts these two sets of considerations together to produce a typology matrix that generates four distinctive types of case study research design (see Figure 6.1).

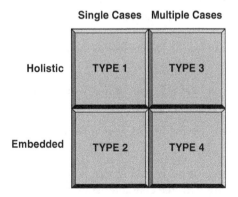

FIGURE 6.1   Alternative design options for case studies (Yin, 2013: 39. Reproduced with permission of Sage)

As Figure 6.1 shows, both single and multiple case study designs can have either a holistic or embedded unit of analysis. Type 1 designs are a single case with a holistic unit of analysis, while Type 2 designs have a single case context but more than one unit of analysis. The primary difference between these two is that the Type 2 design explicitly includes a comparative element by having more than one unit of analysis.

To illustrate the differences between the two types, consider the following example. If we assume that a piece of research is being designed to explore the issue of employee empowerment in a tour operating company, this could be assessed using just one unit of analysis – the company itself. Alternatively, you may wish to explicitly design into this situation a comparison of the views or opinions on empowerment of the managers on the one hand and the employees on the other. This would then give us two embedded (within the context of the one case situation) units of analysis – the managers and the employees – that we would use to make direct comparisons. Therefore, the Type 2 design is used to facilitate 'intra-case' comparisons. Examples of this type of design in practice are provided by Hurst and Niehm (2012), who used a rural tourism community in Iowa (USA) as the case context within which they surveyed two distinct groups or samples comprised of resident and tourism customers, and Zhang et al. (2013), who used a company named Home Inns as the case and interviewed corporate executives and unit managers to identify the factors regarded as critical to the success of this budget hotel company. Alternatively, the study conducted by Mackellar (2013) provides an example of a Type 1 design using a single case and unit of analysis, with data collected via participant observation.

The question is, why would we want to complicate matters by having more than one unit of analysis? The answer is because we need to elicit the information that will enable us to answer the research question or test the hypothesis. Again, we only design into the empirical research that which we need. This is at least part of the rationale for the design of the research, which is explained in the methodology section or chapter of the research report or dissertation when it is written up.

More specifically, we may choose a single case study design (Type 1 or 2) because:

- the case in question is regarded as critical to the research – it has all the conditions necessary to test an established theory;

- it is an 'ideal' case – for example, the company or person is regarded as the leading or best in relation to the issue being researched;

- it is a 'unique' case – by definition, it is different from all other possible case situations;

- it is an 'extreme' case – it is very much not a typical, normal case situation, but one in which there are extreme characteristics relating to the phenomenon, such as a company with profit levels way in excess of others operating in the same field or vice versa;

- it is a 'revelatory' case – that is, it is new or perhaps was previously inaccessible for some reason, such as a political regime being in place that previously denied access to outsiders.

Types 3 and 4 in Figure 6.1 are multiple case study designs with, respectively, holistic and embedded units of analysis. Both of these types facilitate 'inter-case' comparisons because they are comprised of more than one case situation. Martin's (2012) study of orientations to work in four small businesses illustrates the application of a Type 3 design using the views etc. of the respective business owners as the unit of analysis. However, the Type 4 design enables both intra- and inter-case comparisons to be made because it includes multiple cases and units of analysis. Taking our example above, we could now not only make a number of intra-case comparisons between the employees and managers in each of the cases but also a number of inter-case comparisons between the managers and the employees in the different cases. This, of course, does increase the power of the design in the sense that multiple cases and units of analysis facilitate more comparisons, but, at the same time, it also increases the complexity of the data collection and analysis processes. Again the decision as to whether or not multiple case design is used should be based on what information is required, as explained above. That said, multiple case designs are explicitly comparative in nature, so, where comparison is explicitly built into the research questions or hypotheses, they may be appropriate.

6.6.4   The principle of replication

To justify the selection of one of these designs, the principle of replication should be referred to. Having multiple cases is analogous to repeating or replicating experiments under either the same or differing conditions. Where cases are selected on the basis that they conform to the same conditions and, therefore, should produce the same results according to the underlying theory, this is known as 'literal replication' – the conditions are literally repeated in the different cases. Conversely, where cases are selected because they are expected to produce contrasting results, but for predictable reasons, this is known as 'theoretical replication'. To illustrate the latter, if the theory predicts that the profitability of companies is strongly influenced by the level of labour turnover they have – the lower the turnover, the higher the profitability and vice versa – then one way to test the validity of this would be to select companies as cases that had different levels of labour turnover. The studies by Ladhari (2012) and Mayr and Zins (2012) illustrate how replication may be used as a purposeful research design to see how prior theories and empirical findings may be explored and validated, or not, in a different time period and a different physical context.

6.7   Observational Research

Observational research can be undertaken by those having a positivistic philosophy and using a deductive approach – that is, the observation takes place in the laboratory and field (quasi-experiments) – but it is more associated with those who have a phenomenological philosophy and use an inductive approach. Where observation occurs within a relatively highly structured and controlled environment and the data are recorded using formal rating techniques, it would be of the former kind. Where it occurs in more naturalistic (less manipulated and controlled) environments and data are recorded using more open-ended, less formal techniques, then it would correspond to the latter kind of approach.

Observation can be conducted either as a participant in what is being observed or indeed as a non-participant. Both of these can have 'distorting' effects on what is being observed, something often referred to as the 'Hawthorne Effect', a phrase derived from the findings of a real-world experiment undertaken over half a century ago which identified that worker's behaviour could be influenced simply by the fact that they knew they were being observed. Although this finding was regarded as quite ground-breaking at the time, it is now regarded as pretty obvious that the act of observing people doing something is likely to change their behaviour in various ways.

Observation can also be conducted overtly or covertly. Overt observation is transparent and conducted with the knowledge, and agreement, of the people who are to be observed whereas covert observation is undertaken secretly, with those being observed having no prior warning or knowledge that they are being observed. While overt observation should not present distinct ethical issues, as long as the basic ethical principles are adopted and followed, covert observation is much more problematical, controversial and ethically dubious (for an interesting discussion of these issues in the context of an actual hospitality research project see Lugosi, 2006).

For example, it is impossible to meet the principle of 'informed consent' if the subjects do not know they are being observed! If you think that this is blindingly obvious and you would not seek to engage in any form of covert observation for good ethical reasons, then good for you, but you could be engaging in this type of research without fully realising it. Given the rise of internet-based research, of either a passive or interactive nature, it is quite likely that you may be observing content on web pages, social media, blogs and other internet formats without those posting this material being aware this is happening, why and who is doing it. Similarly, covert manipulation is possible on interactive sites through the use of hypothetical or deliberately false names. Such anonymity and the potential for covert manipulation on the part of the researcher pose real ethical issues.

6.7.1   Ethnography

Observational research designs are closely associated with what is known as 'ethnography'. Ethnography – from 'ethno', meaning people, and 'graphy', meaning description – is concerned with naturalistic enquiry that has the purpose of being able to describe and understand a particular social entity from the point of view of its inhabitants. In this sense it is vital that the researcher is able to develop an empathy with them, to see the situation through their eyes rather than trying to impose the interpretations of outsiders on them. As this perspective contends that it is only possible to understand the reality of a situation by looking at the ways the participants construct and give meaning to that reality for themselves and this can only be achieved by not contaminating the situation by implementing the research process, its proponents claim that this design can produce highly valid results. However, because of the specificity of the situation any conclusions may be difficult to generalise from.

6.7.2   Visual ethnography

As the term implies, visual ethnography is concerned with the analysis of visual images, largely but not exclusively photographs and video material that is digital or non-digital and available in physical or electronic format. Sometimes referred to as 'visual anthropology', which reveals the disciplinary and methodological roots of ethnography in general, it can also make use of images derived from hypermedia, interactive CDs and virtual reality. However, one of the issues here is whether this approach can be regarded as an empirical research design. If much, if not all, the images used for a visual ethnographic analysis are already published and available in the public domain, either in physical or digital form, then this would be a type of secondary research using data produced and published for purposes other than the research study being conducted. Where this is the case it could not be regarded as an empirical research design unless there are additional elements containing new data (images) created specifically for the research study at hand. For example, what is sometimes referred to as 'visual auto-ethnography', e.g. video diaries, that involve the creation and recording of new audio-visual material, taking photographs and/ or video recording activities or events, would constitute new, empirical data and therefore could constitute an empirical design. The study exploring tourist and resident perceptions of a tourism destination conducted by Garrod (2008) provides a good example of this by using visitors and residents recruited to take photographs using a disposable camera pack and also being asked to complete photologs and questionnaires.

6.7.3   Netnography

Netnography is another branch of ethnography and one that has risen to greater prominence with the expansion of the internet. It is concerned with the same things as ethnography, namely the nature of groups and communities, but which exist online in the virtual world of the internet. Greater internet availability, connectivity, functionality, usage and the potential for more interaction has given rise to 'online communities' who exhibit many of the characteristics and behaviours of communities in the real world. The increasing centrality of the online, virtual world to people's real lives has opened up new avenues of research in this respect. Although netnography appears to be the favoured term for this type of research, with Kozinets (1998) credited as having coined it first, some refer to it as digital or online ethnography or Investigative Research on the Internet (IRI), see Lugosi et al. (2012).

A very good introduction to using netnography for research is the text produced by Kozinets (2009), and the 'Netnography – The Movie' link on the Companion Website (study.sagepub.com/brotherton) will take you to what I think is a really cool video, produced by a student, that explains the different stages of netnography in a clear but very entertaining manner.

Much, though not all, netnographic work in the hospitality and tourism fields has been concerned with communities of consumers and the marketing implications of these, particularly the nature of the hospitality or tourism consumer's experience (see, for example, Mkono, 2011, 2012, and Rageh et al., 2013). In the real, commercial world, monitoring of social media and customer review sites, such as Twitter, Facebook, TripAdvisor etc., is now commonplace, as is the establishment of purposeful Market Research Online Communities (MROCs) or online Community Panels that are set up by companies. These new research designs and techniques are often claimed to be more cost effective, quicker, consistent and more realistic than traditional ways of conducting this type of research.

However, there can be a tendency to forget that the same considerations of sampling, validity and reliability that apply in the traditional world should equally apply in the virtual world. There are some very serious questions and concerns regarding these issues in relation to internet-based research. Given the, at least quasi, anonymity of many internet contributors, the view that people create 'online personas' that may be very different from how these individuals think and behave in the real world and that contributors don't automatically constitute valid samples are all significant threats to validity and reliability. In addition, the virtual world and its communities may not always accurately and fully reflect the real worlds that these communities inhabit. This is at best a part of a person's life and, although it may be an important part, it only provides a partial picture and one that may be unrepresentative of the person's wider existence. In this sense it may be wise to be rather circumspect about drawing definitive conclusions from such a potentially flawed foundation. An example of the value of combining online ethnography (netnography) with more traditional forms of ethnography, in the form of participant observation, is provided by Mkono (2013) in his study of the differences between Western and African tourists regarding the importance of the authenticity of objects experienced in staged cultural experiences in Zimbabwe. Similarly, the study on perceptions of the body at Von Hagen's Body Worlds conducted by Goulding et al. (2013) combined physical ethnography, actually auto-ethnography, from site visits to, and observation of, Von Hagen's Body Worlds and data collected through netnographic methods.

In common with the observation made about visual ethnography earlier, the issue of whether netnography could be regarded as an empirical research design is also one to bear in mind. Simply using material, of whatever kind, that is already posted or published on the internet would be a form of secondary research and could not be regarded as an empirical research design. However, it may be possible to consider netnography as an empirical design if the internet is used as a mechanism to generate new, specific material for the research project in question. For example, simply accessing and using text from existing blogs produced by other people would be secondary research, but active participation in the blog site to specifically generate new material for the research project may be regarded as an empirical design. Similarly, monitoring and recording the proceedings of a chat site would not be an empirical design, but actively interacting in such an environment may be regarded as such. So one of the issues with netnography is the ability to distinguish between primary and secondary data and research designs that may be regarded as empirical or not. In many cases it should be relatively straightforward to distinguish between data on the internet that is clearly primary or secondary in nature; however, as the internet evolves, it may be the case that this dichotomy becomes less clear and distinct. It is likely that new forms of data will emerge that cannot be easily placed into one of these categories and, undoubtedly, this will stimulate researchers to develop new titles for such data from which one will become generally accepted as the preferred nomenclature. What this will be is open to question but I would suggest that something along the lines of 'quasi-primary' or 'intermediate' data may be helpful.

The issue here is to be careful and think about the nature of the research process and the type of data being used. Netnography may be secondary research only but it has the potential to include new, empirical elements. For example, Skype can be used to generate new, original material via either individual or group interviewing, or indeed capturing elements of activities and events (see Technique Tip box – Recording Skype Sessions). Though perhaps this may be regarded as a form of data collection (see Chapter 7), it could equally be seen as a form of empirical research design, especially if combined with other types of interactive data collection via the internet.

Technique Tip	**Recording Skype Sessions**

Although it is not possible to record Skype video and audio through Skype itself, there are various 'recorder' applications available, for both PC and Mac computers, to enable this to be done. These applications essentially allow you to record your Skype conversations to a hard disk and include various options relating to what you wish to record, though see the Note below.

There are numerous versions of these applications/plug-ins available and a quick search will deliver a range of links, but just to give you an idea of what they can enable you to do some brief details on one of these (Evaer) are included below and links to some of the others are provided.

Note: Recording Skype call material without the knowledge, consent or permission of the other participants would certainly be unethical and quite possibly illegal as well. The ethical principles of informed consent and no harm equally apply here.

Evaer – This enables you to capture original Skype video and audio data and to record it in high quality. It supports the recording of single Skype video calls, Skype screen sharing sessions and up to ten-way Skype group video calls. Skype video calls can be recorded directly to hard disk with side-by-side, separate files, audio-only, local-webcam-only and remote-webcam-only modes. There are also

(Continued)

(Continued)

options to record Skype video calls as MP4 or AVI and to record separate MP3 audio files with video calls.

http://evaer.com

Other Recorder Products

Vodburner – www.vodburner.com

Pamela – http://www.pamela.biz/en/

SuperTintin – www.supertintin.com

6.7.4   Is observational research a good option for you?

Due to the limitations of time, access and observer skills, traditional observational research may not be a feasible option for you. Although access may or may not be an issue, the time required to undertake, record and analyse multiple observations is likely to be a potential problem. Similarly, to be an effective observer, as either a participant or non-participant in the situation, requires quite a range of skills that take time to develop and refine.

Bearing all these things in mind, it is a design that is very appropriate for research attempting to develop an in-depth understanding of a group of interacting people within the context of a particular type of location or setting, who are engaging in their normal activities without any outside manipulation. There are, of course, many situations in the hospitality and tourism industries where such interactions could be studied to develop a better understanding of people's perceptions, attitudes, behaviour and so on, but to do this, it is important that you have the necessary time, access and skills which, as indicated above, may not be available. For more guidance on designing and using traditional observational research designs in hospitality see Jauncey (1999) and for newer, netnographic and/or visual approaches see Kozinets (2009) and Pink (2014) respectively.

6.8   Action Research

Action research – sometimes also referred to as 'action learning' – is a very different form of research design to the others reviewed in this chapter. Whereas surveys and experiments tend to emphasise the independent and distanced role of the researcher, and observation and case studies the non-intervention of the researcher, action research, as the name implies, tends to involve the researcher in implementing some change in order to assess and evaluate its effects and impacts.

Action research can take differing guises (see Lashley, 1999), but it can be seen as a form of live experimentation. Although it is concerned with the making of an active intervention to bring about predicted improvements, the intervention is based on an underlying theory or model. Thus, it is not a 'suck it and see' type of approach, based on guesswork, but one flowing from an analysis and understanding of the situation, which is then used to predict what will happen when the change is introduced. This is very much akin to testing a theory or hypothesis by carrying out an experiment. However, although the principles are similar, the practices are not. In particular, the experimental situation may be regarded as naturalistic rather than artificial and the ability of the researcher to control the environment and the process and be an independent, objective observer of the effects of the change is severely limited. Thus, it raises issues concerning how scientific this form of research is and the ability of the researcher to be certain about cause–effect relationships and mechanisms.

In many instances, action research will not be either the most desirable or feasible design for your research project, but there are circumstances where it could be. One of the key issues would be the extent to which you have access to, and the ability to introduce a change or intervention in, the situation or organisation in question. Without the ability to study the situation and be able to introduce the change and evaluate it, your ability to use action research is zero. As a practising manager well beyond graduation, this may well be a desirable and feasible approach to adopt, but as a student with no such organisational position, you are totally reliant on others to give you this access and authorise the introduction of any change.

Therefore, the only circumstances in which you can consider using action research are if you have this type of relationship with an organisation or an organisational unit. This could be the case if you have been employed on a work placement or have a long-standing, part-time employment relationship with such an organisation. Then, it may be possible to develop a project using action research because you could have the necessary degree of access, familiarity and authorisation to do this. However, you need to be aware that you may not have sufficient time to see it through and/or managers can change their minds about letting you do what you need to do to complete the work. Unless you are absolutely certain that there will not be, often irresolvable, problems further down the line, action research is a high-risk choice.

If, after carefully thinking it through, you do decide to adopt this design, then, following a review of the literature relating to your topic, you would need to collect some initial data on the organisational context where you plan to implement the change. This could be achieved by means of a variety of data collection methods. For example, questionnaires, observation, interviewing, examination of company documents – all could be used to help develop an understanding of the present situation.

At this point, using the insights obtained from the literature and the context, you would then need to put together a conceptual framework to summarise your understanding and develop predictions regarding what the effect(s) of the change will be. From this you will see that this is a typical deductive approach in that the actions you plan to take are based on the underlying theory and designed to test this theory and its predictions. Therefore, once the conceptual aspect has been completed, the planned change can be introduced, the data collected and the actual outcomes evaluated in relation to those predicted.

6.9   Mixed-method Designs

Mixed-method research designs are often referred to as those that combine approaches and methods used to collect both qualitative and quantitative data. Although by no means unique, these types of empirical research designs have become more popular in recent years as the 'traditional' schism of quantitative *or* qualitative, but not both, has been viewed as counterproductive in certain research situations. Though there are clearly research designs that are entirely of one type or the other, often for very good reasons, researchers today tend to be more flexible and pragmatic and perhaps less restricted by adherence to one paradigm or set of designs and methods seen to be consistent with the school of thought adopted by the researcher. So, mixed- or multiple-methods designs have become more widespread and acceptable within the academic community in general.

For the views of one of the most authoritative proponents of mixed-method approaches, John Cresswell, on what mixed-methods research is, see the link in the Video Links section of the Companion Website (study.sagepub.com/brotherton).

6.9.1   Which is best – singular or mixed designs?

This does not mean that you should assume this type of design is automatically and always preferable to one of the more singular designs discussed previously in this chapter. In common with the other types of design, mixed-method designs have their own advantages and disadvantages and the nature of the 'mix' can be highly variable with the balance of qualitative to quantitative ranging from major/minor to minor/major. For example, exploratory interviews may be used to supplement the insights gained from a literature review in order to enhance the formulation of a conceptual model to be tested quantitatively. Alternatively, qualitative aspects may be introduced into a study that is primarily quantitative in nature in order to extend understanding. For example, a survey designed to discover which hotel brands are favoured by frequent hotel guests (what), may also include elements designed to obtain information concerning the reasons for their preferences (why).

The point here is that, although empirical research method designs are invariably presented as alternatives to choose between, as indeed is the case in this chapter, implying that if one is chosen others are not, this is not always how it works in reality. Indeed, given the relative strengths and weaknesses of alternative designs it is quite feasible that using a combination of different designs and/or data collection methods may help to offset the weaknesses evident in singular designs. It is also important here to distinguish between empirical research designs and data collection methods. A particular, singular design may utilise a range of different data collection methods designed to collect both qualitative and quantitative data. So, although designs such as experimentation and surveys may be primarily associated with, and used to collect, quantitative data there is no reason why, if appropriate, these designs could not be used to collect qualitative data. Similarly, observational research designs would normally be associated with the collection of qualitative data but enumeration of events, activities, tasks, timings etc. may be included in such a design to add quantitative elements to the study.

The choice of a singular design has the advantage of focus and, quite possibly, a literature base related to the use of this design in previous studies. This may make life a little easier and less complicated but remember the key issue in selecting any empirical design is that it constitutes the best way to obtain the data to answer your research questions etc. In some cases a singular design will be just that, but in others it may be necessary to consider combining aspects of different singular designs to produce one that has the appropriate mix for the task at hand.

6.9.2   Mixed methods vs mixed designs

In addition to a range of different data collection methods used within a particular design, which is often seen to be what mixed-method research involves, there is of course the possibility of using a combination of designs within the same research project. An example of this was provided earlier in this chapter (see Research in Action box – The Nature of Hospitality). In this project the overall design was one of a comparative case study using two different cases (four-star hotels) within which the data was collected by surveying a sample of the guests in each hotel to collect, predominantly but not exclusively, qualitative data through face-to-face interviewing.

This might be regarded as a 'true' mixed design, incorporating aspects of case study, comparative and survey designs rather than the use of a range of methods to collect data within the context of a singular design. Thus, it might be preferable to think in terms of this type as an 'embedded' design rather than a mixed-methods design because, as previously noted, the term 'methods' is normally used to refer to the methods used to collect empirical data. Using this perspective the 'Nature of Hospitality' study would not be one regarded as using 'mixed methods' because only one method was used to collect the empirical data!

6.9.3   Mixed designs in the real world

Similar examples can be envisaged in the real world. If a restaurant company is seeking to develop a new brand or perhaps to revise/update some of its operational formats it may well undertake some research to determine which ideas work and which don't in practice, what the customer response to these will be, which loca-tions are going to be more or less favourable etc. Making substantial changes to an existing format or launching something entirely new and unproven is a potentially risky business that can go dramatically wrong so it seems sensible to try such things out on a smaller scale before committing the investment required to roll this out across the target market/s. This type of new format/product/brand testing is common practice. Certain locations and premises are identified as 'test sites', or case studies in our terminology, within which it is believed (hypothesised) that the new development will work well. To test this, different types of locations and/or premises may be selected to discover which is likely to be more favourable and within these the specific format and operation of the unit may be systematically varied to test alternative options.

In this case, not only do we have elements of a comparative case study design but also those relating to experimentation, where the conditions or parameters (the locations/premises) and the manipulation or treatment (the variations in format and operation) enable a series of 'experiments' to take place. In addition, to collect customer reaction data, a survey design may be incorporated, either via customer questionnaires and/or the use of qualitative interviewing, either in group form (focus groups) or individually (face-to-face). Observational and other non-intrusive designs may also be incorporated. For example, company or independent researchers may act as non-participant observers with each unit to assess customer behaviour and the efficacy of the operational design. Others may engage in aspects of netnography by monitoring relevant social media sites on the internet.

Chapter Summary

There are various ways in which to design the empirical research aspect of a research project, none of which is perfect for all types of project.

This means choices must be made to select the design that is most appropriate for collecting the type of data required to answer the research question and/or test the hypothesis.

Choosing the appropriate design is vital for validity, reliability and credibility reasons and this needs to be explained/justified in the research report.

Experimental and survey research designs are likely to be appropriate for quantitative studies, while observational and case study designs are generally appropriate for qualitative studies.

All empirical research designs can be implemented in differing ways according to the types of data and practical circumstances required and experienced.

Research designs for quantitative studies often take more time and effort to construct and to get right than those for qualitative studies, but this time-to-effort ratio is reversed when the data analysis stage is reached. Often it takes considerably more time and effort to analyse qualitative data than it does to analyse quantitative data.

Replication and comparative research can be useful approaches where previous studies exist and/or explicit comparisons have to be made between units, companies, industries, countries and so on.

References

Brotherton, B. (1999a) 'Case study research', in B. Brotherton (ed.), *The Handbook of Contemporary Hospitality Management Research*. Chichester: John Wiley. pp. 115–42.

Brotherton, B. (1999b) 'Comparative research', in B. Brotherton (ed.), *The Handbook of Contemporary Hospitality Management Research*. Chichester: John Wiley. pp. 143–72.

Brotherton, B. (2000) 'The comparative approach', in B. Brotherton (ed.), *An Introduction to the UK Hospitality Industry: A comparative approach*. Oxford: Butterworth–Heinemann. pp. 1–22.

Brotherton, B. (2003) 'Is your mirror the same as mine? Methodological issues in undertaking and interpreting cross-cultural studies', *Tourism Today*, 3 (Autumn): 26–37.

Brotherton, B. (2005) 'The nature of hospitality: customer perceptions and implications', *Tourism and Hospitality Planning & Development*, 2 (3): 139–53.

Garrod, B. (2008) 'Exploring space perception – a photo-based analysis', *Annals of Tourism Research*, 35 (2): 381–401.

Getz, D., Andersson, T. and Carlsen, J. (2010) 'Developing a framework and priorities for comparative and cross-cultural research', *International Journal of Event and Festival Management*, 1 (1): 29–59.

Goulding, C., Saren, M. and Lindridge, A. (2013) 'Reading the body at Von Hagen's "Body Worlds"', *Annals of Tourism Research*, 40: 306–30.

Guchait, P. and Hamilton, K. (2013) 'The temporal priority of team learning behaviors vs. shared mental models in service management teams', *International Journal of Hospitality Management*, 33 (1): 19–28.

Gueguen, N. and Jacob, C. (2012) 'Lipstick and tipping behavior: when red lipstick enhances waitresses tips', *International Journal of Hospitality Management*, 31 (4): 1333–5.

Hurst, J.L. and Niehm, L.S. (2012) 'Tourism shopping in rural markets: a case study in rural Iowa', *International Journal of Culture, Tourism and Hospitality Research*, 6 (3): 194–208.

Jauncey, S. (1999) 'Observational research', in B. Brotherton (ed.), *The Handbook of Contemporary Hospitality Management Research*. Chichester: John Wiley. pp. 191–206.

Jeong, C., Holland, S., Jun, S.H. and Gibson, H. (2012) 'Enhancing destination image through travel website information', *International Journal of Tourism Research*, 14 (1): 16–27.

Jones, P. (1999) 'Experimental research', in B. Brotherton (ed.), *The Handbook of Contemporary Hospitality Management Research*. Chichester: John Wiley. pp. 97–114.

Jung, H.S. and Yoon, H.H. (2013) 'Is the individual or the organization the cause of hotel employees' stress? A longitudinal study on differences in role stress between subjects', *International Journal of Hospitality Management*, 33: 494–9.

Kozinets, Robert V. (1998) 'On netnography: initial reflections on consumer research investigations of cyberculture', in J. Alba and W. Hutchinson (eds), *Advances in Consumer Research*, Volume 25. Provo, UT: Association for Consumer Research. pp. 366–71.

Kozinets, R.V. (2009) *Netnography: Doing ethnographic research online*. Thousand Oaks, CA: Sage.

Kuo, P.J and Cranage, D.A. (2012) 'Willingness to pay for customization: the impact of choice variety and specification assistance', *International Journal of Hospitality & Tourism Administration*, 13 (4): 313–27.

Ladhari, R. (2012) 'The lodging quality index: an independent assessment of validity and dimensions', *International Journal of Contemporary Hospitality Management*, 24 (4): 628–52.

Lashley, C. (1999) 'Action research', in B. Brotherton (ed.), *The Handbook of Contemporary Hospitality Management Research*. Chichester: John Wiley. pp. 173–90.

Lee, W. and Gretzel, U. (2012) 'Designing persuasive destination websites: a mental imagery processing perspective', *Tourism Management*, 33 (5): 1270–80.

Levy, S.E. (2010) 'The hospitality of the host: a cross-cultural examination of managerially facilitated consumer-to-consumer interactions', *International Journal of Hospitality Management*, 29 (2): 319–27.

Lugosi, P. (2006) 'Between overt and covert research – concealment and disclosure in an ethnographic study of commercial hospitality', *Qualitative Enquiry*, 12 (3): 541–61.

Lugosi, P., Janta, H. and Watson, P. (2012) 'Investigative management and consumer research on the Internet', *International Journal of Contemporary Hospitality Management*, 24 (6): 838–54.

Mackellar, J. (2013) 'Participant observation at events: theory, practice and potential', *International Journal of Event and Festival Management*, 4 (1): 56–65.

Martin, E. (2012) 'Employment relationship in the small firm: revisiting orientations to work', *International Journal of Hospitality Management*, 31 (4): 1318–26.

Mayr, T. and Zins, A.H. (2012) 'Extensions on the conceptualization of customer perceived value: insights from the airline industry', *International Journal of Culture, Tourism and Hospitality Research*, 6 (4): 356–76.

McQuilken, L., McDonald, H. and Vocino, A. (2013) 'Is guarantee compensation enough? The important role of fix and employee effort in restoring justice', *International Journal of Hospitality Management*, 33: 41–50.

Mkono, M. (2011) 'The othering of food in touristic eatertainment: a netnography', *Tourist Studies*, (11) 3: 253–70.

Mkono, M. (2012) 'Using net-based ethnography (netnography) to understand the staging and marketing of "authentic African" dining experiences to tourists at Victoria Falls', *Journal of Hospitality & Tourism Research*, 37 (2): 184–98.

Mkono, M. (2013) 'African and Western tourists: object authenticity quest?', *Annals of Tourism Research*, 41: 195–214.

Pink, S. (2014) *Doing Visual Ethnography*, 3rd edition. London: Sage.

Presbury, R., Fitzgerald, A. and Chapman, R. (2005) 'Impediments to improvements in service quality in luxury hotels', *Managing Service Quality*, 15 (4): 357–73.

Rageh, A., Melewar, T.C. and Woodside, A. (2013) 'Using netnography research method to reveal the underlying dimensions of the customer/tourist experience', *Qualitative Market Research: An International Journal*, 16 (2): 126–49.

Sekaran, U. (2013) *Research Methods for Business: A skill-building approach*, 6th edition. New York: John Wiley.

Skaalsvik, H. (2011) 'Service failures in a cruise line context: suggesting categorical schemes of service failures', *European Journal of Tourism Research*, 4 (1): 25–43.

Wu, L. and Mattila, A. (2013) 'Investigating consumer embarrassment in service interactions', *International Journal of Hospitality Management*, 33: 196–202.

Yin, R.K. (2013) *Case Study Research: Design and methods*, 5th edition. Thousand Oaks, CA: Sage.

Zhang, H.Q., Ren, L., Shen, H. and Xiao, Q. (2013) 'What contributes to the success of Home Inns in China?', *International Journal of Hospitality Management*, 33: 425–34.

7

COLLECTING THE EMPIRICAL DATA

Chapter Content and Issues

Designing and implementing effective questionnaires.
Structured, unstructured and semi-structured questionnaires.
Getting the respondent 'onside'.
Types of question and forms of data.
Questions and measurement scales.
Structured, unstructured, focus group and field interviews.
Participant and non-participant observation.
Use of non-standard approaches and questions – projective techniques.

7.1 Introduction

In the previous chapter we explored the issues and alternatives associated with making the decision as to which overall research design to use in order to structure and organise the collection of the empirical data required for a research project. Once this has been decided, the more detailed decisions regarding how this overall approach and plan are to be put into operation and administered have to be addressed. This means that we have to consider the instruments and procedures we are going to use to actually collect the data and, once again, there are alternative choices available to us that have to be considered before we can make a decision to adopt one, or possibly more, of these as being the most appropriate for our purposes.

It is to these issues that we now turn our attention and consider the use of questionnaires, interviewing, observation and other, non-standard, approaches such as projective techniques that can be utilised to collect valid and reliable data. As these are each considerable topics in their own right, the approach taken here is one of highlighting and exploring the key principles associated with the alternatives and, within each, the different options available to design and implement their data collection instruments and procedures. In addition, the reasoning behind the choices is given to assist you in explaining and justifying the choices you have made in the methodology chapter or section in your research report. Thus, this chapter leads you through the considerations you will have to take into account when making your data collection instrument and process decisions, indicates when and where the alternatives may be more, or less, appropriate and provides discussion and examples of good practice.

7.2 Questionnaires and Questions

Questionnaires, of one form or another, are so prevalent in everyday life that I am sure you have seen many different versions of them and the questions they include. However, regardless of the specific format and context, the main purpose of a questionnaire is to provide a vehicle for obtaining accurate information from a respondent, whether the questionnaire itself is very short or long, comprised of questions that are open-ended or closed and implemented by direct or distributed means.

7.2.1 The nature of questionnaires

All questionnaires are directive in nature as the questions they contain dictate what is to be asked, though some are more restrictive than others in this respect. They also provide some form of structure in terms of the kinds of responses that are desired and allowed and, in many cases, how these are to be recorded. However, whatever the specific format of a questionnaire, it should never be forgotten that it is only a means to achieving certain desired ends. These, of course, are the empirical data requirements of the research question(s), aims or objectives or hypotheses. The questionnaire itself is merely a way of obtaining the data that you require to answer these questions, achieve the aims or objectives or test the hypotheses. Therefore, all the decisions relating to what type of questionnaire to use, what questions to ask and how to implement the process for collecting the data should be made with the aim that they will be the most appropriate and effective ways to achieve the wider purpose. This also needs to be borne in mind when you are constructing a questionnaire, writing the questions and deciding how it will be implemented because the only way you can provide a rationale or justification for the content, structure and implementation choices you make is by clearly indicating that they are consistent with the wider purposes the instrument and processes are designed to achieve.

7.2.2 Designing unstructured/open-ended questionnaires

One of the first issues you need to address when designing a questionnaire is what type of data do you wish to collect? If it is qualitative data – words – the structure and form of the questions will need to be suitable for eliciting this type of response from the respondent. Typically this is likely to lead you towards designing a questionnaire that is not overly structured and has open-ended questions – that is, those where the specific form of the response is not dictated by particular response options that are provided with the question. This may constitute nothing more than a list of interview questions that you wish to put directly to a respondent in a face-to-face situation with, possibly, other 'probes' depending on the responses given as the questionnaire interview progresses. For example, this type of follow-up probing may be brought into play when the respondent says something unexpected that you want to pursue further, something that is not clear so it needs further explanation or something particularly interesting that you would like the respondent to expand on further.

Thus the unstructured, open-ended form of questionnaire allows for a considerable amount of flexibility, in terms of what is asked, what is pursued further and how the data are recorded, and if implemented in a direct manner, it also facilitates the collection and recording of other, non-verbal information, such as body language and so on. This flexibility also enables more in-depth responses to be captured, which are often crucial in the collection of qualitative data. It can also help in situations where you are not sure of the nature and/or breadth of the possible responses that could be given to a question or set of questions. By contrast, questions that elicit closed responses need to meet the criteria we discussed in Chapter 5 – the response options for each question must be both mutually exclusive and collectively exhaustive. To achieve this, the questions invariably have to be quite specific and we will need to know what the possible answers to them could be.

The unstructured, open-ended approach to questionnaire design and implementation is often regarded as being most suitable for relatively small-scale, perhaps exploratory, research studies and/or those where in-depth information is required to generate a 'rich' picture of the issues being investigated. Its inherent flexibility facilitates in-depth enquiry, but this and the nature of the data collected do lead to some potential problems. As the respondents are allowed to provide the responses in their own words and, to a certain extent, on their own terms, it might be expected that the truthfulness, accuracy or validity of the data would be high. This may be true in the sense that respondents are not being forced to select a predetermined option as their response, which they would have to do in a more structured, closed form of questionnaire, but for various reasons people do not always give 'truthful' answers. They may over- or understate certain issues. In some cases they may deliberately give false answers to cover up failures or avoid sensitive issues or they may give answers that they believe, but do not know, to be correct. They may express opinion as fact and they may give responses that they think you are looking for or expect rather than the ones that are really correct. In short, it is wise to be somewhat sceptical rather than simply accept responses of this type at face value.

There is also a reliability issue associated with this form of questionnaire. As the questions are not necessarily asked in the same or a standard way for each respondent and the responses are not recorded using a standard format or scale, then the degree of consistency in the questionnaire's design and implementation can be rather low. This is the downside of flexibility as different researchers may implement the same instrument in differing ways, either within the same research project or at a later date if repeated by other researchers, and such inconsistencies may generate inconsistent and unreliable data. In addition, the nature of the data precludes the type of objective, statistical analysis that can be applied to quantitative data. Words have to be interpreted and people's interpretations of the same collection of words can vary, leading to differing conclusions. The other aspect to this is that unstructured questionnaires generate a high volume of non-standard data from the words provided by the respondents. This can give rise to problems in terms of not only recording and/or transcribing the data but also in being able to cope with this volume of material when trying to analyse it.

7.2.3   Designing structured/closed questionnaires

If it is quantitative data that are required, the questions are likely to be much more specific, the options to answer or respond will be prescribed in the questionnaire, it will have a predetermined structure and instructions for the respondent on how to record their responses and progress through the questionnaire, and because of these features the data it collects will be amenable to some form of statistical analysis. This type of questionnaire is frequently referred to as one that is structured, with closed questions that use one of the measurement scales to prescribe the response options available to the respondents. It is a form usually associated with indirect and distributed implementation strategies where, because there is no direct contact between the person asking the questions and those answering them, the instrument and process have to be more prescribed, detailed and standardised.

The structured questionnaire is likely to be the preferred choice in situations where relatively large-scale surveys are being conducted, where the sample is geographically dispersed and can only be accessed by some form of remote communication, such as by mail, electronically or by telephone, and where quantitative data are required. That said, this form is also used for direct interviews such as market research interviews conducted in public spaces, or situations where the sample is self-selecting such as customer comment/feedback questionnaires left in hotel bedrooms, on restaurant tables, or at tourist destinations and attractions and so on.

7.2.4   Questionnaires and validity/reliability issues

Structured and unstructured questionnaires – usually with predominantly closed or open questions respectively – have different implications for validity and reliability. In general, less structure and more openness in the questions create a less contrived and artificial situation for the collection of data and vice versa. This allows data to be collected in a more naturalistic environment and, hence, validity should be higher, but because it is inherently more flexible in form and application, this can lead to inconsistencies in its implementation that, in turn, will threaten the reliability of the questionnaire and the process of administering it. The reverse is true for more structured, closed forms. They are much more artificial and constrained, but are applied in a consistent manner so they tend to be regarded as more reliable. Even so, there can be problems regarding validity.

7.2.5   Mixed-design questionnaires

Up to this point, it has been at least implicitly suggested that the choice between designing and using a qualitative and unstructured or quantitative and structured questionnaire is mutually exclusive in nature – that is, if one is chosen then the other cannot be. In reality, this is not the case, as questionnaires can, and do, often contain questions that are unstructured *and* structured and designed to collect qualitative *and* quantitative data. This middle route may be described as semi-structured or a hybrid, in that it features both open and closed questions to capture both types of data and, in many cases, to address questions not only of a factual nature – the what, when, where, how often and so on – but also those seeking information relating to underlying reasons – the why and how – for people's behaviour, attitudes, preferences or opinions. It is quite common for more unstructured, open-ended questions to be used as follow-ups or probes to the structured, closed questions in order to obtain information on the reasons for people's responses to the closed questions. For example, if a question asked, 'Which of the following list of holiday destinations would you like to visit the most?' it might be followed up with a request such as, 'Please state the reason(s) for your choice of destination above.'

This can be a very valuable tactic as it can generate data on the reasons certain people prefer certain destinations, in this case, but equally any other form of product, and can be used to elicit the thinking lying behind the attitudes or opinions people have expressed in closed responses. However, it can have negative consequences if it is over-used in a questionnaire. As the respondents have to think about, articulate and physically write responses in these cases, it is more difficult and time-consuming than answering a question where the response options are given and they only have to tick a box. Generally, respondents will not mind answering this type of question on a few occasions, but if they are asked for such statements following many of the questions as they progress through the questionnaire, they may feel that the task is becoming too difficult and time-consuming, become disillusioned and so will then fail to complete and return the questionnaire.

7.2.6   Choosing the appropriate type of questionnaire

So how do you make the decision to choose one of the alternative forms of questionnaire discussed so far? Unfortunately, as with many decisions that have to be taken when designing and conducting a research project, there are no really hard and fast rules for this. Nevertheless, in general terms, the number of people or organisations to be surveyed, how geographically dispersed they are, the nature of the sample respondents, the type of information you need to collect, how you plan to implement the questionnaire and the data analysis methods you intend to use may all have some bearing on this choice.

Other things being equal, the larger the size of the survey and the more geographically dispersed the sample respondents are, which would imply a distributed implementation, then a structured questionnaire with closed questions is likely to be a suitable choice. Similarly, if the respondents are very busy people, then this format will probably be best as it is generally easy and quick to complete. If you need to collect quantitative data and intend to use statistical procedures to analyse it, then once again this format is likely to be best suited to your purposes. If these are not issues for your project, then it may be that a more unstructured, open and qualitative approach to questionnaire design could be a better choice.

7.2.7   Basic questionnaire design and preparation issues

Whichever format is most appropriate for your needs, there are some basic design and preparation issues to be considered and decisions to be made before the questionnaire can be used to collect the data. As previously mentioned, one key issue to be clear about is what information the questionnaire is to be used to collect. This is not just an issue of qualitative or quantitative data but also one of why the information is required and the purpose it will serve in the research project. To address this, as mentioned earlier, you need to be clear about the research question(s), aims and objectives and, possibly, the hypotheses to be tested. These will give you the rationale for needing the data, so it is logical to design a questionnaire that contains questions that are capable of helping you to obtain the particular types of information you need to shed some light on them.

Other key issues to consider are how the questionnaire is to be implemented and what the nature of the target respondents in the sample is. If the questionnaire is to be implemented directly by yourself, in a face-to-face interview situation, then it will be much less important to include instructions in the questionnaire itself than if either a team of different people were to conduct the interviews or it was going to be implemented at a distance via one of the distributed implementation options discussed earlier. Similarly, the format or style of the questionnaire will differ – even though the questions may be written in the same way – when different distribution strategies are used.

If, on the one hand, you are undertaking a direct interview with a respondent, then your ability to talk your interviewee through the questionnaire as the interview progresses is straightforward. On the other hand, if you are implementing the questionnaire by telephone, then the 'talk through' that you can give in a face-to-face situation needs to be written into the questionnaire as a form of script because you cannot see the interviewee and you cannot show him or her the questionnaire and questions you wish to ask. Similarly, when you send a questionnaire by mail, fax or electronic means to a respondent, you need to write 'instructions' into the questionnaire to tell the respondents what you wish them to do and how they should answer the questions. The important thing to do when you are not physically present to articulate the questions and show or explain how you wish the respondents to respond is to include this element of the implementation process in the questionnaire. How this is done will differ depending on whether you have some or no interactive contact with the respondent. The principle here is one of being able to control the implementation process in such a way that it is as consistent as possible across all the respondents which, in turn, helps to avoid or reduce the possibility of error.

In terms of considering the nature of the respondents and how this might affect the way you design the questionnaire and write the questions, you need to try to put yourself in their position as the recipients of the questionnaire. If they are busy managers who have other, more important, priorities to attend to before they can even think about spending time completing your questionnaire, then the way you design your questionnaire should reflect this. The implication here is that you need to try to ensure that it is as easy and quick as possible to complete – otherwise, they may simply decide that they cannot afford to spend the time necessary to complete it, which could dramatically reduce the response rate you are able to achieve. Interestingly, this does not automatically mean that you should attempt to keep the questionnaire as short as possible in terms of the number of questions and/or pages.

It is not the overall length of the questionnaire or the number of questions *per se* that can make it quicker or longer, easier or harder to complete. A questionnaire might be quite long in terms of the number of questions and pages it covers, but relatively quick and easy to complete and vice versa. What is more critical than its physical length or the number of questions is the nature of the questions. In general terms, closed questions are quicker and easier to answer than open ones because the responses are included in the questionnaire and the respondents do not have to think about how they should word the answers – all they have to do is tick a box, circle a number and so on. Hence, a longer questionnaire with a lot of closed questions may be quicker and easier to complete than a shorter one containing mainly open questions.

This is not to say that you should therefore choose closed rather than open questions *per se*. What you choose will depend on the type of data you wish to obtain, so opting for closed questions simply because they are quicker and easier to complete would be like the proverbial tail wagging the dog! Nevertheless, some questions can be asked in either closed or open forms without any detriment to the resulting data. Where this is the case, it would be sensible to choose the former rather than the latter form. For example, you could ask a question about the respondents' gender in an open form, such as 'Please state your gender below' and the respondents would have to write male or female. Alternatively, you could provide these two responses with boxes alongside and ask, 'Please indicate your gender below by ticking the appropriate box'. This involves slightly more effort on your part, but it makes life easier for the respondents. This may also have a positive effect on respondents because they may be more interested in helping you if you show, in the way that the questionnaire is constructed, that you have considered their needs by making it as easy as possible for them to cooperate in completing the questionnaire.

Regardless of whether your target respondents are busy people or not, you are asking them to do you a favour. Generally, there will be no benefit to them in giving up their time and taking the trouble to think about and answer the questions, so why should they bother? A poorly designed questionnaire that does not consider that the respondents may not be particularly interested in your project and its questions is likely to result in a lower than expected, or hoped for, response rate. Thus, in addition to attempts to make the questionnaire as easy and quick to complete as possible, it is important to try to generate some interest, enthusiasm and desire on the part of the respondents to assist you by completing the questionnaire. You would be wise to try to motivate them in some way.

This can be achieved by giving careful consideration to the questionnaire's introduction. The introduction is your opportunity not only to inform the respondents of the nature and purpose of the questionnaire, but also to try to sell the exercise to them in such a way that their interest is generated and they become motivated to engage more enthusiastically with the process. If this is successful, then it is likely to improve the response rate because more questionnaires will be completed and returned. The Research in Action Box – Framing the Questionnaire's Introduction – shows an introductory statement from a postal questionnaire that was cold-mailed to the companies in the sample I used in a research project (Brotherton, 2004a) and that generated a response rate of 38.5 per cent. This is a figure considerably in excess of that normally associated with this questionnaire implementation strategy. Of course, an alternative would be to include this text within a covering, or explanatory, letter sent with the questionnaire, but this may not be as effective because it is a separate piece of paper that could become detached from the questionnaire or not read at all.

Furthermore, you may wish, or need, to put other important information in the introductory statement to explain or clarify certain terms used in the questionnaire that could be open to differing interpretations on the part of the respondents. An example of this is contained in the last two paragraphs of the same Research in Action Box – Framing the Questionnaire's Introduction – which is from the same project and was included as it was important to try to ensure, as far as was reasonably possible, that the people completing the questionnaire all had the same understanding of what a particular term meant in the context of that questionnaire.

Research in Action	**Framing the Questionnaire's Introduction**

Introduction

The primary aim of the research this questionnaire is being used for is to identify the critical success factors (CSFs) within UK Hotels plc and to undertake a comparative analysis of these CSFs to determine the extent to which generic CSFs may be identified for this sector of the hospitality industry. This questionnaire will be the main data collection instrument for this survey. As you will see the questionnaire is divided into two sections as follows: hotel information and departmental CSFs. The responses provided in the first section will be used to structure the responses in section 2 for classificatory and comparative analysis purposes. Those in section 2 will comprise the substantive data for this research study.

I appreciate that you are a busy professional with little free time to engage in an exercise of this nature and that this will certainly not be one of your main priorities, but I sincerely hope that you can find the time to complete and return this questionnaire because without your cooperation it will be impossible to achieve the aim of this project.

Therefore, can I thank you in anticipation of your cooperation and ask that the completed questionnaire be returned to me in the enclosed reply-paid envelope by the date given at the end of the questionnaire. *Please note*: **The information you provide on this questionnaire will be treated in the strictest confidence and will only be used for academic research. Should the results obtained from this questionnaire be published in an academic paper they will not be attributed to any individual. Neither will the results be released to any third party for commercial gain.**

Before completing this questionnaire it is important that all respondents have the same understanding of the terms used in order that consistent results are obtained. Therefore, I would be obliged if you could take a couple of minutes to read the definition of *critical success factors* given below before responding to the questions:

Critical success factors (CSFs) are defined as: the *limited number of factors that have ensured successful performance*. They are not objectives, but the factors critical to successfully meeting business objectives. In short, CSFs are a means to an end.

The same principle, of trying to get the respondents on side, can also be addressed via the style, appearance, layout and structure of the questionnaire by ensuring the following.

- It is easy to understand – it has clear questions and directions.

- It is easy to complete – it has closed rather than open questions where appropriate, with simple response recording techniques that are sequenced from easier to harder, less to more sensitive/personal, and general to more specific.

- It generates sufficient interest to keep respondents going to the finish – achieved by having a suitable introduction and a variety of question formats.

- It is structured using appropriate sections.

All these things can help to improve the chances of the questionnaire being completed and returned.

Much of this is really common sense, yet it often seems to be forgotten when questionnaires are designed. Put yourself in the recipients' shoes and think – if you received a questionnaire that was poorly designed and laid out, with unclear questions sequenced in no apparent order, without any subdivisions, with either no or few useful directions to help you understand how to answer the questions, requiring you to write long answers, how likely is it that you would feel motivated to complete that questionnaire? The answer to this is self-evident – highly unlikely. Similarly, if you are going to take the time and trouble to do someone else a free favour by completing a questionnaire, you might feel happier about doing so if the person who sent it to you thanked you for doing so. A statement to this effect can obviously be included at the end of the questionnaire, but it may also be useful to insert such a statement at the end of the introduction or after it, thanking people in advance or in anticipation of them completing the questionnaire. Finally, the inclusion of a reply-paid envelope may also help to improve the response rate because this again shows you recognise the return of the completed questionnaire incurs a cost and that you do not expect the respondent to bear this.

To make life easier for yourself, once the completed questionnaires have been returned, you may also want to consider 'pre-coding' the closed question response options by entering coding numbers on the questionnaire. This is not always necessary, such as where your questions use a predetermined scale of say 1 to 5 as the numbers to enter into the data analysis software already exist, but, where the questions do not use such a scale, then there is the issue of converting categories or responses into numbers. For example, if you include the gender question mentioned above, respondents are going to indicate whether they are male or female by either writing this or ticking the appropriate box, but entering numbers into data analysis software is easier, quicker and can facilitate other calculations. So, for example, you may choose to code the response of 'male' as the number 1, and that of female as 2.

One thing you should note about this coding is that it is not a good idea to use zeros as a code number because these will contaminate any calculations you may wish to perform on the data. For example, if you wanted to calculate averages or percentages, then zeros would distort the calculations. If you do not want to include code numbers on the questionnaire itself, you can still pre-code the responses by having either a coding sheet that contains the code numbers to be used when the data are entered at a later date or by putting these on to a master, coding copy of the questionnaire that you use to enter the data from the completed questionnaires.

With the increasing speed, connectivity and functionality of the internet it has of course become more feasible in recent years to design and distribute questionnaires via this electronic medium. There are now a large number of examples of hospitality/tourism research surveys being conducted via the internet, or 'online', in the academic journals. However, many of these tend to be rather 'conservative' in terms of actually describing, in any detail, exactly how these have been implemented. There are statements relating to the use of emails sent to target respondents containing web links to the site where the questionnaire can be completed online but details on how all this process is organised and managed are invariably scant or non-existent. In this respect you may find interesting the, highly summarised, but pertinent version of the procedure Chris Dutt, from the Emirates Academy of Hospitality Management in Dubai, used for his MSc research into 'the effects of visiting friends and relatives (VFR) tourism on expatriates' knowledge about the destination' that is contained in the Research in Action box – Designing and Implementing an Online Survey.

Research in Action	Designing and Implementing an Online Survey

The primary focus of this study was to understand the impact VFR tourism has on expatriates' learning about the destination in which they live. The main research question and objectives are highlighted below:

Question

'What influence does the VFR visitor have over the expat-hosts' ability to gain knowledge about the destination?'

Objectives

To gain more insight into the nature of VFR travel

To better understand factors that influence individuals in everyday situations as well as in tourism-specific cases

To improve understanding of how VFR visitors influence expatriate-hosts to learn about the destination

To discover the extent to which VFR visitors promote expatriate-hosts' learning

Designing and Implementing the Online Survey

Having designed the questionnaire, from the results of both a thorough literature review and preliminary interviews conducted with expat-hosts in Dubai, it was felt that, since the survey population comprised of expatriates in Dubai, an online questionnaire would prove the most effective method of capturing a large sample. Next, with an account created on SurveyMonkey (www.surveymonkey.com) a questionnaire was constructed through the built-in functions available

(Continued)

(Continued)

(see examples below). Due to the desired number of questions and expected response rate, a paid account had to be selected. Not only did SurveyMonkey provide an excellent means of designing and distributing an online questionnaire, but it also provided basic descriptive analysis and allowed follow-up questions to be asked, depending on the option the participant selected. Due to the fact that VFR travel is under-researched, especially in Dubai, a lot of the questions focused on collecting descriptive information, which could later be used for running statistical tests.

One of the advantages, for the respondent, of an online questionnaire is that questions can be designed and formatted using a simple 'click' button to record the response. Whether this is a relatively simple question, as the screenshot of question 7 below shows, or a more complicated one potentially involving multiple responses to the same question (see the example of question 19) or a series of statements all using the same interval scale (question 25), the basic principle is the same. Of course, and where appropriate, the design of online questions can follow the same procedure as those created by more traditional means, e.g. where there may be other potential response options not covered by those offered to the respondent, an option to indicate this can be created along with that of entering the text to indicate what this is (see question 19).

7.   My visitors tend to be: (Please select only one)

- Younger than me

- The same age as me

- Older than me

19. While my visitors are in Dubai, I tend to spend more money than usual on... (Please select all that apply)

☐   Food and Beverages in restaurants and bars

☐   Food and Beverages at home

☐   Visiting hotels and resorts

☐   Activities e.g. cinema, SKL Dubai, water parks

☐   Attending events e.g. Dubai Rugby 7s, Dubai Shopping Festival

☐   Transportation (bus, taxis, metro)

☐   Petrol

☐   Other (please specify)

*25. As a result of my family/friends' visit(s), I feel:

	Strongly Agree	Agree	Neutral	Disagree	Strongly Disagree
More confident about living in Dubai.					
More Knowledgeable about Dubai.					
More confident about travelling around the region.					
More Knowledgeable about the region.					
My decision to move to Dubai has been justified.					
That visitors have stimulated my interest in Dubai					
Enthusiastic and I am looking forward to hosting more relatives/friends					

SurveyMonkey allows the user to send a link to potential respondents and a local company created an e-mail to be sent to their database inviting their customers to participate in the questionnaire. This company also offered potential respondents a chance to win prizes, valued at Dhs 100 (US$27), as an incentive to complete the questionnaire. The questionnaire was configured to ensure that no individual could complete it more than once, at least from the same computer, i.e. the computer's IP address was recorded and blocked from accessing the questionnaire again once it was completed from that IP address.

A pilot test for reliability was also conducted with SurveyMonkey with 22 staff in the Dubai-based company who assisted with the questionnaire distribution. The pilot study followed the same methodology as the actual study; the staff were sent the e-mail with a request to complete the questionnaire. The results from the two interval scale questions from the pilot test were then subjected to split-half reliability testing using Cronbach's alpha coefficient. Both these sets of items demonstrated coefficients in the 0.9 range indicating high levels of internal consistency within each set of items.

The final version of the questionnaire was distributed, on the researcher's behalf, by the company. The database was screened to send e-mail invitations only to those expatriate customers who frequently used the services of the company.

(Continued)

(Continued)

Using this method, a final total of 3,058 usable questionnaires were completed: 2,812 questionnaires were completed within the first week with the remaining 246 questionnaires completed in the following 2 weeks.

Mr Chris Dutt

The Emirates Academy of Hospitality Management, Dubai

To explore these issues further go to the Web Links section of the Companion Website (study.sagepub.com/brotherton) which contains a link to an interactive exercise on the design and use of online questionnaires where you can see, in real time, the time required for a respondent to complete different question formats.

7.2.8 Writing questions

By now you should have a good idea of the issues to be considered when compiling and structuring a questionnaire, but we have not yet discussed key issues associated with formulating and writing the questions that are going to form the substantive content of the questionnaire. The term 'questions' is a little misleading, however. Although you may have items that are worded as questions in your questionnaire, you may also have items that are worded as statements. Indeed, it is quite possible to ask essentially the same thing by wording it as either a question or a statement. Individual questionnaires may clearly differ in terms of the specific questions or statements that are included in them because they have different contexts and purposes. That said, questionnaires tend to contain basic types of questions or statements designed to obtain information on the respondents' characteristics, behaviour or perceptions and attitudes.

Questions designed to obtain information on the respondents' characteristics are used to classify or group respondents with the same characteristic. For example, if the respondents are individuals, as opposed to people responding on behalf of an organisation, then you may wish to know their gender, age, occupation, income level, marital status, where they live or work and so on. There are two main reasons for collecting this type of information. One is to help you describe the characteristics of the respondents in your sample. This is often important if you wish to claim that the realised sample is representative of the population as a whole. Second, you may want to compare the responses given to other types of question on the basis of differences in your respondents. For example, you may want to examine whether the behaviour or views of male and female, younger or older, richer or poorer, married or single respondents are the same or different. The Research in Action Box – Questions Designed to Obtain 'Categorical' Data from Individuals – shows a set of questions that were designed to obtain this type of information taken from a study I conducted (Brotherton, 2005).

Research in Action	Questions Designed to Obtain 'Categorical' Data from Individuals				

Q6	What is your gender?	Male	☐	Female	☐
Q7	Have you stayed in this hotel before?	Yes	☐	No	☐
		(Go to Q8)		(Go to Q9)	
Q8	Approximately how many times?	_____			
Q9	What is your stay here for?	Business	☐	Leisure	☐
Q10	Which of the following best describes your ethnic origin?				
White European		☐	Black Afro-Caribbean	☐	
Asian Indian		☐	Oriental	☐	
Q11	Which of the following age groups do you belong to?				
18–24	☐	25–34	☐	35–44	☐
45–54	☐	55–64	☐	65+	☐
Q12	How would you describe your occupation?				
Managerial/professional		☐	Clerical/administrative	☐	
Skilled manual		☐	Unskilled manual	☐	
Q13	Finally, could you tell me what level of education best describes you?				
GCSE (or equivalent)		☐	GCE A level (or equivalent)	☐	
Higher National Diploma/Certificate		☐	Bachelor's degree	☐	
Master's degree		☐	Doctorate	☐	

In the case of a questionnaire addressed to representatives of organisations, you may ask similar types of questions, but the content of these will clearly be different. You may typically want to know about the size of the organisation, where it is located, what brand it belongs to, what standard or quality it is (for a hotel, what star rating it is, for example) and other criteria that might be useful when analysing similarities or differences between the organisations in the sample in their responses to other questions. The Research in Action Box – Questions Designed to Obtain 'Categorical' Data on Companies – provides examples of these types of classificatory questions, used to gather the data for the Brotherton (2004b) study.

Research in Action	**Questions Designed to Obtain 'Categorical' Data on Companies**				

1 Your hotel's brand					
Travelodge	☐	Premier Travel Inn	☐	Holiday Inn Express	☐
Campanile	☐	Comfort Inn	☐	Premier Lodge	☐
Lodge Inns	☐	IBIS	☐		
2 Your hotel's name:					
3 Your position/title:					
4 The hotel's location					
Motorway	☐	A road	☐	Airport	☐
City centre	☐	Town suburb	☐	Rural	☐
5 Number of bedrooms in the hotel					
Fewer than 20	☐	21–30	☐	31–40	☐
41–50	☐	51–60	☐	Over 60	☐
6 Room price: £_____					
7 Average annual room occupancy for the hotel: _____%					
8 Number of staff employed in the hotel:					
Full-time _____ Part-time _____					
9 Approximate breakdown of annual business:					
Business guests _____% Non-business guests _____%					

Behavioural questions are designed to collect information on, not surprisingly, the behaviour of the respondents – what they do, when they do these things, how often they do them, where, in what ways and so on. In the case of an organisation, these may be the types of products and/or services they provide, the standard(s) of them, when and where they are available, how much they cost and so on. Behavioural questions, then, collect factual information on what individuals or organisations do and, possibly, what they own. Typically, in a hospitality or tourism context, you might be interested to know which hotels, destinations or attractions people visit, when they tend to do this, how often or frequently, whether they do this alone or with friends or family, how far they travel to make such visits, how much they spend and so on.

Perceptual or attitudinal questions do not focus on the actual behaviour of individuals or organisations but on how they think of, view or rate particular things. This might be the image they hold of something, their preferences and/or intentions, an explanation of why they make particular choices or their opinions on specific issues. Such questions are widely used to gather information on the extent to which people agree or disagree with certain statements or issues, how important or unimportant the items are to them, how they compare a range of items against one another using criteria given to them and so on. Although many perceptual and attitudinal factors may influence the present and/or future behavioural patterns of individuals and organisations – and thereby will provide information on the reasons for their actual or intended behaviour – these perceptions and attitudes are also formed from their previous behavioural experiences and, as such, can be used to elicit opinions and judgements on these experiences.

7.2.9 Questions and measurement scales

Although, in an unstructured questionnaire, these three types of questions may be asked in an open-ended format, they are more associated with closed formats using a scale to record the responses. From Chapter 5, you will recall that there are four basic types of measurement scale: nominal, ordinal, interval and ratio. Classification questions tend to use nominal and possibly ratio-type scales because all that is required of these questions is that they obtain information to enable you to place the respondents into certain groups or categories based on their characteristics. In the Research in Action Box – Questions Designed to Obtain 'Categorical' Data on Companies – questions 1, 4 and 5 are examples of closed, single response, nominal scale questions; 6 and 7 are single response, ratio scale questions; 8 is a multiple response, ratio scale question; and 9 is a multiple response, nominal scale question.

Behavioural and attitudinal questions may be formulated using either nominal or ratio scales, but ordinal and/or interval scales are more frequently used for these questions because they facilitate the collection of more detailed or fine-grained information on the issue(s) in question. For example, it is possible to ask whether a respondent agrees or disagrees with a statement or regards something as important or not, but these dichotomous, nominal scale questions only collect what is known as bipolar information on the issue. This simply means that a response to the extremes of agreement or disagreement, importance or unimportance, good or bad, expensive or cheap and so on can be obtained, but nothing will be known about the gradations between these extremes.

With questions formulated in this way, you may be able to identify the black and white of the issues, but not any of the shades of grey between the extremes – in the jargon, your measurement scale will lack precision. Also, because you are forcing the respondents to choose an extreme positive or negative position in order to make a response, this raises issues of validity. Simply put, the respondents may not hold such extreme views and would wish to give a response that is slightly positive or negative, but they are not able to because the scale forces them to record a response that is either totally positive or negative. Thus, the data may not be valid or true reflections of people's views and beliefs on the issue(s).

Questions using an ordinal scale ask respondents to place items in order within a given range using a criterion given in the question. For example, 'From the list of ten items below that may influence your satisfaction with the visit to this museum, please place them in order in terms of which would have the greatest influence on your satisfaction to the least by entering a single and different number from 1 (most) to 10 (least) against each.' The important feature of this type of question is that a reason or criterion is given for respondents to make their choices. This provides a basis for the respondents to make relative comparisons between the items. Such criteria could be wide ranging, as the context and content of this type of question can be equally broad. However, criteria such as cost or price, quality, availability, frequency of purchase or visit, desirability, value for money, attractiveness and so on may typically be used.

It is questions using an interval scale that tend to have lots of variations on the specific scale type or form. You will know many of these from your own experiences of seeing and completing questionnaires in your everyday life, though you may not know the more technical terms for them that are used in research methodology jargon. One of the most common forms of interval scale used in questionnaires is known as the Likert scale. Devised by Rensis Likert in the early part of the twentieth century, the Likert scale uses statements to which respondents indicate the extent of their agreement or disagreement. Likert scale questions – or, more accurately, statements – can be written in positive or negative forms regarding the relationship with the variable being investigated. This simply means that the implications of agreement and disagreement are reversed.

The Technique Tip box – Positively and Negatively Worded Likert Scale Statements – shows an example of this. Here the same statement is written in positive and negative forms. Any 'agree' response to the first version would indicate a positive relationship between the independent variable 'loyalty cards' and the dependent variable 'repeat business'. In the case of the second version, this type or relationship would be signified by a 'disagree' response. Therefore, where negatively worded statements are associated with positive independent–dependent variable relationships, the scale scores have to be reversed.

Technique Tip	Positively and Negatively Worded Likert Scale Statements				

	Strongly agree	Agree	Neither agree nor disagree	Disagree	Strongly disagree
Version 1	1	2	3	4	5
Loyalty cards help to increase repeat business in hotels.					
Version 2	1	2	3	4	5
Loyalty cards do not help to increase repeat business in hotels.					

This may sound complicated, but it is quite simple in practice. If respondents indicate that they strongly disagree with the statement in this Technique Tip box that loyalty cards do not help to increase repeat business in hotels, then, logically, they are expressing the opinion that they strongly agree they do have this effect. In Version 1 of the statement, a strong agreement would score 1 on the 1–5 scale, but, in Version 2, effectively the same response would score 5 because of the reversed polarity of the statement. Without converting the response to Version 2 from a score of 5 to 1, effectively the same opinion would be recorded as positive in the first instance and negative in the second. Clearly that would be nonsense.

Varying the polarity of statements in a set of Likert scale items can be useful because it can help to keep the respondent alert, but be careful here as too much changing from positive to negative wordings can be confusing and irritating. However, used judiciously, it can form a type of cross-checking mechanism. In our example, including both versions of the statement in a set of items could help check the consistency of the responses as we would expect both forms of the statement to elicit a consistent underlying response. However, where this tactic is employed, it is not a good idea to place the two forms of the statement adjacent to each other because this could annoy the respondents.

Another common form of interval scale used in contemporary questionnaires is known as the itemised rating scale. Again, you are likely to be familiar with this. It is commonly used to obtain responses within a bipolar range that varies between very positive and very negative. Rather than asking respondents if they are satisfied with an experience or if something is important to them, which invites a simple yes or no answer, this scale explores the intermediate positions between these opposites. Therefore, using this example, an itemised rating scale would ask respondents to indicate the 'extent' to which they are satisfied or the item is important. So, for example, the question might be, 'To what extent have you been satisfied with your visit to this theme park today?' and the response options would be given on a sliding scale of 'Extremely, Very, Fairly, Not very, Not at all'. Alternatively, and using the same response options, a question might ask organisational respondents to indicate the importance of a systematic quality assurance system for customer satisfaction.

Itemised rating scales are really quite straightforward, but there are some issues to be resolved when constructing and using them. One of these is whether to use a balanced or unbalanced scale. If you think about it, this is a simple matter. There are only three possible categories of response – positive, neutral or negative. A balanced scale will have at least one of each, but, more typically, will have at least one neutral option and two or three positive and negative options in the form of five- or seven-point scales. The neutral response option is only ever a single point in the scale, as it is not possible to differentiate between two or more points of indifference between the positive and negative reactions, but it is possible to have more positive or negative points. This would increase the precision of the scale, but as the number of points increases, respondents may find it difficult to produce such finely differentiated responses. In reality, most researchers find that either a five- or seven-point scale is sufficient. The other problem that arises if you increase the number of points in the scale is the difficulty of finding suitably worded descriptions for each point that are sufficiently different from each other to warrant their inclusion. For example, to differentiate between 'extremely' and 'very' is reasonably simple, but to try to find suitably differentiated descriptors for another two or three points between these two would be more problematic.

An unbalanced scale will not have a neutral option but will have equal numbers of positive and negative points. These are therefore also known as even-numbered scales, whereas balanced scales are odd-numbered. An unbalanced scale creates what is known as a forced choice for respondents. In other words they are forced to make a positive or negative response as there is no intermediate option. In the literature, the jury is out over whether a balanced or unbalanced scale is more appropriate. Some commentators argue that everyone has an opinion one way or the other and therefore the neutral option is essentially a cop-out. Others argue that an unbalanced scale denies respondents the opportunity to express a legitimate response where they have no strong opinion in either direction or wish to indicate indifference, so this raises issues of validity. My personal view on this issue is that it is preferable to use a balanced, odd-numbered scale because this avoids the forced choice issue and potential validity criticisms.

What are known as semantic differential scales are also widely used in research questionnaires. The term semantic differential simply means different meanings. In some respects, it is a similar idea to the Likert and itemised rating scales because it facilitates a response between bipolar opposites, such as fast and slow, bright and dark, modern and old-fashioned, hot and cold, expensive and cheap. Although it is used to obtain data on single items or issues, in common with the other types, it is particularly useful for collecting comparative data. For example, if you wanted to compare the characteristics of different hotels, restaurants, theme parks, museums, destination resorts or countries, brands of a product and so on, then a semantic differential scale with a set of suitable bipolar opposites relating to the context could be used to compare quite a range of such entities.

Whatever type of scale is used to provide the response options for the question or statement, it is important to remember that there should be a match between how these are worded. This may sound obvious, but in my experience, it is not always recognised. For example, if you are using a Likert scale, which invites respondents to agree or disagree with statements, then these should not be written as questions. Alternatively, if you are using an itemised rating scale – from extremely to not at all – then you need to ask them a question. In addition, when writing the questions or statements, there are innumerable pitfalls that, if not recognised and addressed, can have significant implications for the clarity and/or validity of the questions. These are highlighted, with illustrative examples, in the Technique Tip box – Writing Questions – Potential Problems to Avoid.

Technique Tip	**Writing Questions – Potential Problems to Avoid**

1. Ask only *one* question at a time – avoid what are known as double-barrelled questions. For example, a question that asks, 'Have you visited this hotel before and were you satisfied with it? Yes ☐ No ☐' is asking two questions in one. The respondent may have visited the hotel previously but was not satisfied with it, so would want to answer 'yes' to one part but 'no' to the other. Splitting the question into two separate ones could easily solve this problem.
2. Questions should not 'lead' a respondent to give a particular response. This introduces bias into the question. For example, a question that asks 'Do you believe that airlines in general should reduce the price of flight tickets?' is likely to attract either a 100 per cent 'yes' response or something very close to it because most people would like to travel more cheaply. It would be in their interests to say yes rather than no!
3. Using partial or incomplete lists of response options is also to be avoided as this partiality may mean that the choices respondents wish to make are not there. For example, a question that asks, 'Which of the following destinations would be your preferred choice for your main annual holiday? Mediterranean ☐ USA ☐ Caribbean ☐' would be very limited. The remedy for this is to provide a much wider listing of possible destinations or to include a catch-all category that respondents could use to indicate an alternative preference, such as 'Another destination ☐ (please specify) _____'.

(Continued)

(Continued)

4. Forcing respondents to take an extreme position, when they may not wish to do so, by asking a question in a 'loaded' manner should also be resisted. For example, a statement such as, 'Trade unions will always reduce labour flexibility in the workplace', inviting agreement or disagreement, is likely to polarise responses, especially if only agree or disagree options are given, as the word 'always' loads this question. Respondents who believe that trade unions may sometimes have this effect, but not always, would have to disagree, even though they believe trade unions may have this effect on some occasions.

5. Questions that are said to be recall-dependent – that is, they rely too much on people's memory – are likely to be problematic because, if respondents cannot remember the real answer, they are likely to guess to provide a response. In this situation, it will be impossible for you to distinguish between accurate answers and those based on guesswork! Therefore, it is advisable to ask only questions relating to contemporary issues, behaviour and so on or to the immediate past. Unfortunately, the term 'immediate past' can be a rather moveable proposition, but some commonsense judgement has to be applied, depending on the context. For example, it may be quite justifiable to ask a person where they have travelled to on holiday for the last two, three or possibly five years, but to ask them more detailed questions on what they did on these trips would be more difficult for them to remember.

6. Bear in mind that not all your respondents will have the same sophisticated language skills as you or will be familiar with the jargon related to the topic, so try to avoid using complicated language and jargon. For example, let's consider the question, 'Would you regard the olfactory nature of the food in this restaurant as inviting or not? Yes ☐ No ☐'. The term 'olfactory' may not be understood by some, perhaps many, of the respondents. This would cast doubt on the validity of the responses because if people do not understand the question, they cannot answer it properly. It would be preferable to ask, 'Was the aroma of the food inviting?' as this is a term understood by all.

7. Direct questions should be exactly that – they should not be phrased in vague or ambiguous terms. Thus, to ask, 'Would it be likely that you might consider making a visit to a museum within the next year? Yes ☐ No ☐', confronts respondents with a number of issues to resolve in their minds before they are able to given an answer. Essentially, what is being asked here is, how likely is it that they will even consider making a visit to any museum, anywhere, in the next 12 months? This is not easy to give a considered answer to because there are so many imponderables, so many conditional factors that make a definitive answer difficult to arrive at.

8. In terms of making questions clear and unambiguous it is a good idea to avoid using double or triple negatives in the wording. For example, a question such as, 'Would you never even consider visiting this destination at any time in the future?' would be a poor one. It would be better to ask,

Would you consider visiting this destination in the future?' because this would elicit the same information – yes or no – but it is stated in positive and much clearer terms than the first question.

9. Hypothetical questions invite hypothetical answers and, as such, are highly suspect in terms of the validity of the data provided in the responses. For example, a question that asks respondents to assess the likelihood of something hypothetical happening, or how they might react to a hypothetical situation, invites speculation and it is extremely difficult, if not impossible, to discern the basis on which such speculative responses are arrived at by respondents.

10. The use of emotive and/or sensitive words in a question is likely to generate either emotive responses, or no responses at all, because respondents may be annoyed that you are asking such questions. For example, asking respondents to give their exact income or age may be resented. Similarly, highly personal questions about people's private thoughts or behaviour or asking companies to answer commercially sensitive questions are likely to remain unanswered on the basis that they are unnecessarily intrusive.

11. Asking questions that require respondents to make calculations before they can answer is fraught with problems because it is invariably impossible to tell whether the calculations they have made are accurate or not and people's abilities to employ such skills are highly variable. Therefore, the accuracy or validity of such responses is likely to be very suspect. For example, a question that asks, 'What proportion of your annual income would you spend on your main holiday?' would be problematic as it is likely respondents would guess the answer rather than take the trouble to actually calculate this accurately. Also, unless another question asks what respondents' annual income is, which would be problematic as it is sensitive, personal information, it would be pointless anyway because, without knowing what the annual income is, you cannot determine the actual value of the proportion indicated.

7.2.10   Standard and non-standard questions

Finally, in terms of the form or type of question to be used, it is worth noting that there are 'standard' and 'non-standard' forms of question. The former is really quite self-explanatory. Standard questions are of the type you will be familiar with from questionnaires you will have generally come into contact with. They are comprised of a direct question or statement that is formulated in words and will have a response option or options formulated in either a similar manner or by utilising some form of graphic(s). Non-standard questions tend to use a different type of stimulus for respondents to react to. This form of questioning is discussed further in Section 7.5, Projective Techniques, later in this chapter, but the non-standard approach may mean the use of stimuli, such as pictures or photographs, cartoons, advertisements, company logos and so on, or more indirect forms of questioning, where purposely vague stimuli are used to provoke respondents into revealing their more subconscious perceptions, feelings, associations and so on.

With these more indirect forms of questioning (see Section 7.5), it is always vital to ask respondents why they have chosen a particular response. Without doing this, it is impossible to know what connotations the responses have for them. Furthermore, this type of follow-up question may also help to reveal which aspects of the stimulus have been particularly instrumental in helping to form or influence the respondents' perceptions or opinions. For example, if pictures of different tourist destinations were used in a questionnaire and respondents were asked to indicate what type of animal they associated with each one, they may respond with a wide variety of animals, from normal domestic dogs and cats to more exotic species. Without asking them why they have chosen those animals, you would not know what they meant to them in that context and, therefore, what their real reactions to the stimuli were.

7.2.11   Questionnaire piloting

Once you have completed your draft questionnaire, you need to evaluate it. This is sometimes referred to as questionnaire piloting or pre-implementation testing. The purpose of this is to identify any potential deficiencies, omissions, errors and so on in the questionnaire and eliminate them before it is used to collect actual data.

There are various ways in which this can be achieved, but the most appropriate is usually regarded as being a pilot test conducted on the same types of people who are going to be the actual respondents. The reason for doing this is fairly obvious. If this small-scale test indicates that there are no problems, then it is highly likely using it on a larger scale with similar people will generate a similar reaction and vice versa. The respondents in the pilot test are asked to complete the questionnaire as though it was a real exercise, but are also asked to indicate any difficulties they encountered – were the questions and response options clear and unambiguous, were the instructions/directions clear and helpful, were any questions worded in a leading or loaded manner, were any of the questions double-barrelled (with two questions in one), were any questions worded in an offensive or insensitive way and so on.

Although using respondents for the pilot who are the same type of people as those you plan to give the actual questionnaire to later is ideal, it may not always be practicable in the context of a student research project. This is because it can take some time and involve additional costs, particularly if the survey's sample is geographically dispersed, which may not be an option or too expensive. Therefore, a more limited form of testing may need to take place, using for example, academic tutors, family members, friends, fellow students or others who are readily available and have the time to help you. Though this may not be the ideal or perfect way to test your questionnaire, it is better than doing nothing at all and it is often surprising when other independent and uninvolved people see something that you have not picked up on because you are so involved in and close to the work.

However you conduct your questionnaire evaluation, this, along with any amendments you make and why you are doing so, should be recorded in the methodology chapter or section of your project report or dissertation because it helps to show that a process has been gone through to try to ensure that the data collection instrument (the questionnaire) is as free from error as possible and, therefore, that the data it has collected should be considered as credible.

Before you implement your questionnaire it may be helpful, as a final check, to consider the items contained in the Key Decision box – Am I Happy with My Questionnaire? – that should help you to decide whether it addresses these issues appropriately or not.

Key Decisions	**Am I Happy with My Questionnaire?**

- Does it explain clearly to the respondent what the purpose of the study and the questionnaire are?

- Will the wording and structure be easy to follow?

- Will it motivate the respondent to complete it?

- Are all the questions really needed to obtain the information you require?

- Are the instructions you have provided for the respondents accurate and clear?

- Have you acted on any feedback from your piloting?

- Have you avoided the potential problems involved in writing questions outlined previously?

- Do all the response choices you have given your respondents match the way the questions have been worded?

- Have you tried to complete the questionnaire yourself in the role of the target respondent to understand how they will experience the task?

- Is the design and layout of the questionnaire economical and easy to follow?

- Is the order of the questions sensible and does this help/encourage the respondent to continue with the task you have given him/her?

7.3 Interviewing

Research interviews can take a variety of forms and can be conducted in a number of ways. An interview may be highly structured, controlled and a specific stimulus–response affair conducted within a formal interviewer–interviewee situation, or may be much more flexible, open-ended, discursive and more like a non-directive, two-way conversation. It may take place face to face or via some form of technology, such as the telephone, video-conferencing, or webcam, that still facilitates real-time interaction between the parties. These interviews can be conducted on a one-to-one basis or in a group environment. Further, as we will see later in this chapter, they may be utilised as one approach to collecting data within field or observational research projects and to facilitate the implementation of non-standard techniques, such as projective techniques. Indeed, Skaalsvik (2011) provides an example of the use of the Critical Incident Technique to analyse data from face-to-face interviews to categorise service failures within the context of cruise line operations.

 For a wider consideration of issues relating to interviewing and interviewing techniques examine the appropriate Web and Video Links for this chapter on the Companion Website (study.sagepub.com/brotherton).

7.3.1   Why choose interviewing?

Whatever the specific form and method of implementation, the basic purpose of an interview remains the same – to obtain the required information from the respondent or respondents. Thus, the interview method shares the same characteristics as other types of data collection, in that it is a means to an end, with the end being defined by the information required to answer the research question(s), achieve the aim or objectives and/or test the hypotheses. In this sense, the primary reference point for determining what should be asked, in what form and how the interview should be conducted is derived from these overall purposes.

That said, we might still ask, why should interviewing be chosen as the preferred form of data collection rather than the other alternatives available? Unfortunately this is not a simple question to answer as there can be many factors affecting such a decision. However, interviewing is generally regarded as a useful approach where qualitative data are required and more in-depth exploration is necessary. Although interviewing can be, and is, used in formal questionnaire-based survey research, where respondents are interviewed on a face-to-face basis with a structured questionnaire, it is perhaps more commonly associated with a more open, less structured instrument and process, within which dialogue between the interviewer and interviewee is guided by the interview questions, but is also allowed to flow around these in a more iterative and interactive manner.

Indeed, one of the advantages of interviewing when compared to other more structured and deterministic methods of data collection is sometimes seen to be the degree of flexibility that exists while the process of collecting the data is taking place. Of course, this varies according to the type of interview and how it is conducted, but regardless of this, as there is real-time contact between the two parties, the opportunity will arise for interaction and, therefore, deviations from a standard script to take place as a consequence of the responses given. This, of course, is not possible at all in the case of a distributed survey questionnaire, where the content and process have to be standardised and contained within the data collection instrument itself, and is often more limited in, say, telephone interviewing, where the recording of responses is frequently more standardised than in face-to-face situations.

On the other hand, as interviewing does tend to attract such idiosyncratic imple-mentation, this very flexibility can be seen as a potential problem. Because it is not standardised, each interview is something of a unique event, due to the varying dynamics that are created between the interviewer and interviewees. This is a feature that is likely to be even more problematic when there are a number of different interviewers, but even where there is only one, the fact remains that the way an interview unfolds and, hence, what happens in it, will vary according to the nature of the relationship established between the interviewer and successive interviewees. It is axiomatic that the different personalities and behavioural characteristics encountered within a set of seemingly similar interviewees will generate different dynamics and relationships in the interview situation, thereby making them different from one another. Therefore, although the flexibility inherent in interviewing can help to explore and probe issues more thoroughly, it can, because of this, make com-paring data from different interviews problematic.

In general terms, interviewing is frequently viewed as a desirable method of data collection where in-depth data are required. Where the purpose is not simply to obtain data relating to questions concerned with what, where, when or how fre-quently but also explanations of the why and how of the issue, interviewing is a method that, relatively easily, facilitates this type of investigation. As explanations of the why or how of some action or behaviour tend to be more idiosyncratic and complex than descriptions of the actions or behaviours themselves, it is not easy to devise standardised questions to elicit this information. Even if it were, the nature of the responses is that they are likely to be conditional, contingent and rather long.

If you have decided to adopt qualitative interviewing as the most appropriate way to collect the data you need then you may wish to take a step back and review your design and implementation decisions before you actually go ahead and begin to conduct the interviews. It is always a good idea to pause at this point to review and evaluate what you are planning to do before you actually do it because the conse-quences of any errors and omissions at this point will become magnified once the process is under way. The Key Decisions box – Have I Planned the Interviewing Process Well? – contains a series of questions to help you test your plans.

Key Decisions	**Have I Planned the Interviewing Process Well?**

- Will the way I plan to introduce and explain the interview, and its role in my research, be clear and informative for the interviewee?

- Do the questions I plan to ask all relate to my research question and/or aim/ objectives?

(Continued)

(Continued)

- Are these going to be the best ones to get the data I need?

- Have I piloted or tested the questions and the interview process with real respondents?

- Are the questions going to be interesting for the respondents and have I built in sufficient opportunities to probe further where this might be required?

- Have I considered what I might do if the interview begins to reveal some unexpected issues and answers?

- Do I know where the interviews will take place and what the conditions are in these places?

- Have I considered and tested the equipment I will need to record the interviews and how this will be used or operated within the interview context?

7.3.2   Group interviewing

Group interviewing – also known as Focus Groups (FGs) – is an interviewing method used where it is important to capture the interactions between the group members and see how these affect the overall response. Though FGs are generally regarded as a non-directed form of interviewing, as the group discussion and interactions flow more freely than in a traditional, scripted, one-to-one interview, they do have a particular focus, hence the name! The focus could be almost anything, but typically, FGs have been used to gauge customers' or employees' feelings about and reactions to new developments, policies, products, advertising messages and identified problems. Whatever its specific nature, this focus provides the basic parameter used to guide the group discussions, though this may also be supplemented with other stimuli to aid the discussion in general and/or provide a vehicle to steer it towards certain desired aspects of the overall purpose.

FGs, typically, are comprised of six to 12 'appropriate' members with a group leader or facilitator to oversee the process. What makes for an 'appropriate' member is difficult to define, but, in order to generate discussion, there is a need to invite or select a range of different members who have some interest in the issues to be discussed. A focus group comprised of very similar people (a homogeneous composition) would not reflect a sufficient variety of views, opinions and reactions and the ensuing discussion may turn out to be limited and rather sterile. On the other hand, a group comprised of people who were all very different (a heterogeneous composition) with nothing at all in common may result in disagreement for disagreement's sake. Therefore, a group composition that lies somewhere between these extremes, with a suitable balance of 'appropriate' members, is likely to be preferable.

As FGs are small and, usually, the members are not selected at random, they are not regarded as representative samples and, therefore, the ability to generalise from their results to the wider population is problematic at best and, realistically, inadvisable. In addition to the characteristics of the sample, the fact that the environment for the focus group may be regarded as artificial, that there is often a high degree of subjectivity in the process itself, its management and in the interpretation of the results, plus that the results can be strongly influenced by the groups' leaders, makes valid generalisations impossible.

As a consequence of these attributes, FGs are often viewed as an interviewing method more suitable for the exploratory and/or initial testing and evaluation stages of a research project than the main empirical data collection phase. Given the nature of the FG environment and process, it is particularly suitable for identifying the issues or aspects of particular phenomena that are important to companies, customers, employees and so on that can then be used to develop more structured data collection instruments or test the validity of such instruments prior to their implementation. That said, because FGs can help to establish insights into underlying thinking and reasoning, they can be used alongside other data collection methods to add this type of information to that which is more descriptive.

So, FGs can be a useful method for collecting certain types of data but, in common with other data collection methods, they need to be planned carefully. Indeed, given the dynamics involved in group interviewing it may be possible to argue that this is even more crucial in the case of FGs. In this respect you may find the issues highlighted in the Key Decisions box – Planning a Focus Group – helpful.

Key Decisions	**Planning a Focus Group**

- Have you thought carefully about who should be invited to be a member of your focus group/s and what size and composition of group/s should you have?

- Are you using FGs alone to obtain the data to answer your research questions or are FGs part of a mixed-method design and, if so, how does the FG element fit with your other data collection methods?

- Have you produced a clear 'guide' for the operation of the FG and, if so, have you piloted or tested this?

- How are you going to encourage people to attend the FG session/s?

- Do you have any contingency plans in place if people do not turn up for the FG session/s?

- Are the questions, activities, stimuli etc. for the FG, all appropriate for the research question/s and have you planned the itinerary and schedule for the session/s?

(Continued)

(Continued)

- Will the questions etc. promote sufficiently the level of thought and discussion you desire?

- What type/s of participant interaction do you want to promote?

- Do you have a back-up plan if the session/s do not work as you planned?

- Have you built in sufficient flexibility to allow unexpected things to happen and/or to be dealt with in the session/s?

- Are you familiar with the place/s the session/s will take place in and have you tested the equipment you are going to use to record the session/s?

- What will you do if some of your equipment fails or malfunctions?

- What is/are your role/s in the sessions?

- What will you do if silences occur?

- How will you encourage people to speak if they are shy or reticent and how will you handle people who tend to monopolise the discussion?

7.4 Observation

If you are an undergraduate undertaking a research project, then data collection using observational methods is likely to be a choice precluded by time and, possibly, access, considerations. If you are a postgraduate student, these may not be such significant issues. That said, if you are interested in this approach to data collection, the chapter written on observational research by Jauncey (1999) would be a useful place to start.

To explore these issues further go to the Web Links section of the Companion Website (study.sagepub.com/brotherton) which contains a link to an interactive exercise on the design and use of online questionnaires where you can see, in real time, the time required for a respondent to complete different question formats.

7.4.1 Observation – validity and reliability issues

Although observational methods of data collection can include laboratory or field experimentation, where the research environment is highly structured, they are more commonly associated with what is often referred to as field research, which takes place in naturalistic settings. In these contexts, observation may be of a participant or non-participant nature. Both contain the same potential problem of contamination that can generate validity issues. In short, the presence of an outsider observing behaviour, whether participating or not, can influence or distort normal patterns of behaviour and, hence, give rise to questions regarding the validity of what is being observed. With regard to the issues associated with participant observation, the study by Mackellar (2013) examining issues arising from the use of this technique in the context of studying events provides a useful discussion of both the technique in general and in relation to the particular case study used.

Such changes in behaviour can occur for a variety of reasons. Those being observed may regard the observer as a potential threat, a type of spy, and may seek to hide behaviour that might be perceived as damaging to them if revealed. Alternatively, they may see the observer as an ally who can be used to serve their purposes to some extent and so overemphasise certain behaviour, such as being more positive than usual or seeking to use the observer as an unwitting agent to further their desire for improvements in the workplace, distorting normality for their own ends. If disturbances to the normal set of conditions in a situation do occur, this is said to reduce the ecological validity of the data being collected, as the presence of the observer has effectively contaminated the true situation.

The reliability of observational data is also an issue. Reliability can be assessed on both an internal and external basis. Internal reliability, or consistency, is concerned with the plausibility and coherence of the picture that is revealed via observation. External reliability is more of a verification process, in that the observations are cross-checked with other sources of data or other researchers to confirm, or otherwise, that this new evidence is consistent with the observational data. As observational data do not solely consist of recording observations as a result of watching, looking, listening, taking notes or making recordings but also include some degree of interaction, in the form of informal conversations or interviews with the people being observed, the credibility of the people and what they say is an issue. As noted earlier, people can, for a variety of reasons, seek to mislead an outsider by means of evasion, misinformation, deception or straightforward lies and these can be individually or group-based, depending on whether the agenda is individual or collective in nature.

7.4.2   Site selection and access

However, before any observational data can be collected, a situation has to be identified and selected and the entry negotiated. Neuman (1994) suggests that there are three key factors to be taken into consideration when selecting a site – richness of data, unfamiliarity and suitability. Not all sites having the same situational setting hold the same potential for richness of interactions, variety and diversity and, therefore, there should be some initial screening of possible sites so that it is possible to select the one with the greatest potential. Other things being equal, selecting a site that is unfamiliar to you is seen to be preferable to one that is more familiar as your observations are less likely to be contaminated with your preconceived ideas. Site suitability is an issue concerned with more than the empirical/theoretical richness it offers. It is also a practical, if not pragmatic, issue. Its proximity, accessibility and potential barriers, such as legal or political restrictions, may be considerations, as indeed may be the ethical restrictions on field research invoked by your institution.

Another key issue is how to secure permission to enter the site. This may also affect the final selection of a site, in the sense that selecting an 'ideal' site that is also one where access cannot be secured is obviously a non-starter. Thus, it may be necessary to identify a shortlist of suitable sites and make the final choice on a more practical basis – considering ones where access can be negotiated. Without an agreement to enter and have appropriate access to those you wish to observe, a site is useless, no matter what its potential richness may be. In negotiating entry to a site, it is important to plan a strategy to secure this before initiating the negotiations. It is also important to recognise that some degree of flexibility and bargaining may be involved in securing such an agreement.

What is equally important is the need to be as honest and comprehensive as possible when explaining what you want access to and how you intend to behave within the situation. Often organisations are suspicious about giving relatively unknown outsiders access to their premises and employees because they can do harm, albeit perhaps unintentionally, to the established condition. Outsiders can be a disruptive influence and do more harm than good, from the organisation's perspective. Similarly, attempting to secure access by deliberately understating the breadth and extent of what you will really require and the time you will need to demand of insiders for interviewing is likely to be disastrous because, when the real extent of these requirements becomes known later, they may well be denied, leaving you with a major problem.

7.4.3 Observational issues

Given a successfully negotiated entry to a site, issues of how you behave and interact within the situation then arise. Observational data collection, unlike surveys or other techniques where the researcher and respondents never actually meet, occurs within a context where you, the observer, is physically present on more than one occasion with the people being observed. In short, you become at least a quasi-member of the situation, with all the implications that has. To collect good-quality observational data, it is important to develop an empathetic understanding of the situation – that is, to be able to see it through the eyes of the insiders – but, at the same time, it is likely you will not be regarded as a fully paid-up member of the group(s) in the situation and, therefore, will be something of an outsider at best. Overlaying this is the paradoxical need to retain the more detached view of an outsider in order not to develop an insular and possibly biased stance and the need to decide what ethical position should be taken in terms of revealing the real purpose(s) of the research. All these aspects raise issues of striking the correct balance between being the detached observer and 'going native', truthfulness versus deception, respecting confidentiality and the desire to disclose information and how to leave the situation without causing any damage when the project ends.

As observational research is contextually contingent – that is, the physical context and what happens within that environment are inseparable – observational data have to include both aspects. The behaviour to be observed occurs within a context and, therefore, the observation of the nature and characteristics of that context are vital elements of the observational data because these will have some impact on the behaviour that occurs within this context. Similarly, the organisational nature of the context also has to be observed. At one level this may be stipulated and defined in company documentation – in an organisational chart indicating responsibilities and relationships between people – but a formal statement of how the situation is structured and seen to operate may not accord with how it actually works in practice.

In terms of people and their actions, the observer should not only record who is present and what they say and do but also what is not said or done, and by whom, as this can reveal valuable information. In addition, non-verbal behaviour, such as body language, can add insights because what people say and do or how they react to others does not always accord with their body language. Also, all situations tend to be idiosyncratic in some respects and one of these is invariably the use of a particular language or jargon specific to the situation. This specialised language is known as the 'argot' or *lingua franca* of the insider and needs to be interpreted by the observer in terms of what these specialised terms mean in the context of the situation and how they may be translated for the outside world.

7.4.4 Recording observational data

The recording of observations normally involves taking notes and constructing maps and diagrams, though these may be supplemented in some cases by audio and/or video recordings. During an observational session, it is usually not possible to take detailed and comprehensive notes because events are unfolding in real time. Therefore, the notes are usually jotted as short memory triggers, sometimes in the researchers' own forms of shorthand, to be used as the basis for writing up the more detailed observational notes after the observational session and it is these that provide an exact, as possible, recording of the session. Maps and diagrams sketched during observation sessions can be useful aids for compiling the observational records as they can add physical, spatial and social, or interaction, dimensions to the records.

Once the descriptive, observational notes for each session have been completed, the raw material for initial analysis and interpretation will be available and further notes can be added. For example, it may be possible to begin to infer wider, more generalised meanings from specific observational records and possibly analyse these in relation to existing theory. In turn, this may suggest further types of observation that would be useful and/or questions that should be asked in future sessions.

As the collection, recording and analysis of observational data are inevitably affected by subjective influences, it is also important to make 'personal' notes for each session. These record the observer's personal states and feelings, as they could have some influence on the observation. For example, if the observer was relaxed or stressed, bored or interested, in a good mood or a bad one, could clearly affect what was perceived and how it was perceived during an observational session.

7.4.5 Observation and interviewing

In observational data collection, field interviews are usually juxtaposed with actual observations. These are somewhat different from survey-type interviews as they are less structured, more informal, flexible and closer to a two-way conversation than a closed question and answer session. Interviewing people in the situation helps to both supplement the observational data and may be iterative with it in the sense that observations may suggest issues to be explored during interview sessions, while responses given in interviews may help to guide future observations. In a similar way, the two might be used to verify or crosscheck conclusions being reached for either type of data. A very useful account and discussion of the extensive use of observation, interviewing and focus groups in food service research is provided by Arendt et al. (2012).

Field interviews are likely to be repeated over time with the same people, but as time progresses the purpose may change, from seeking further background, descriptive information in the beginning, to helping develop a basic understanding, to conversations more concerned with structural and process issues as the researcher's knowledge and understanding of the situation evolve and he or she seeks to analyse issues in more detail and depth.

7.5 Projective Techniques

Projective techniques (PTs) – sometimes also known as 'enabling techniques' – are used to collect qualitative data and, essentially, are an indirect form of questioning that asks respondents to interpret the stimuli they are being presented with. In this sense, they are very different from the normal, standard, direct kinds of questions discussed earlier in the context of questionnaires and questions. In the case of PTs, many of the rules and the dos and don'ts that apply to standard questions do not apply to them. For example, one of the key premises of PTs is that if respondents are presented with a vague stimulus, then they will have to reveal more of their subconscious thinking to be able to articulate an interpretative response. Thus, PTs are often seen as a mechanism for accessing the private worlds of individuals to reveal their innermost thoughts.

In common with other data collection techniques, PTs are not without their advocates and critics. A useful discussion of their usefulness, validity and reliability within the general context of market research is provided by Boddy (2005). PTs have not been used extensively within hospitality or tourism research but they have in some other disciplines, notably those associated with health and the caring professions. They have, however, been used reasonably extensively in market and advertising research, some of which has spilled over into the tourism field. In the more general context PTs have often been used to investigate product/brand image and product/brand personality. Perhaps unsurprisingly some tourism researchers have seen an opportunity to undertake similar studies into destination image and/or personality. Examples of this can be found in the studies conducted by Korstanje (2010),

Prebenson (2007) and Tasci et al. (2007). Similarly, Hofstede et al. (2007) undertook a study using PTs to investigate the personality of four beer brands.

7.5.1 Why use projective techniques?

PTs can be used for descriptive or diagnostic purposes and especially when direct questioning may be regarded as inappropriate, such as in sensitive situations where there may be significant barriers inhibiting open communication. Where respondents may be reluctant to reveal what they really feel because of embarrassment or sensitivity or where the truth may conflict with their rationalised self-image, PTs can be used as an indirect and less threatening or confrontational vehicle to facilitate the revelation of their true feelings and so on. Similarly, many forms of direct questioning, almost by definition, reveal the true purpose of a question to respondents. This can result in them formulating and articulating the response that they feel the questioner wants to receive rather than necessarily the one they truly believe in.

PTs generate a very unstructured form of response because what is important in the process is the freedom given to individuals to respond in their own words. The ambiguous nature of the stimuli used as a vehicle to elicit these responses is important as the more ambiguous it is, the more the respondents have to draw on their experience and inner thoughts to project these on to the stimuli in order to be able to provide an interpretation and, hence, the more they must reveal about the nature of these 'hidden' thoughts in the process. This means that PTs are designed to explore the issue(s) in some depth, to access people's underlying reactions, perceptions and interpretations of the stimuli, revealing what the objects or images really mean to them. Widely used in clinical psychology for some considerable time, PTs have also been used in marketing and advertising research to obtain people's reactions to new products, advertising images and so on. However, there is no particular reason not to use these techniques to explore a wide range of other issues in the hospitality and tourism fields.

PTs in general are very useful where direct questioning may be problematic, such as where there may be some reluctance or resistance on the part of respondents to respond to potentially sensitive or embarrassing questions and more in-depth information is sought concerning how people really think about the issues in question. They are often thought to be particularly useful in the exploratory stages of a research project because of their ability to surface issues and aspects of the phenomena under investigation that may not have been previously considered. However, the downside is that the interpretative nature of the process and data analysis can require considerable ability on the part of the researcher and the nature of the sample used will almost certainly preclude the ability to generalise from the results.

7.5.2 Types of projective techniques

The literature suggests that there are five main types of PT procedures:

- Associative

- Completion

- Construction

- Expressive

- Choice-ordering.

Associative procedures seek to elicit the respondents' associations with the stimuli they are presented with. This may be as simple as word association, where, in its traditional format, respondents react (either orally or in writing) to a rapidly presented series of words with the word(s) they associate with the stimulus words. Alternatively, respondents may be given a single word and invited to record the word(s) they associate with it (see Brotherton, 2005, for an example of this in a hospitality context). The associative stimulus may also be a picture or other type of image, such as a photograph of a tourist destination, a company's logo, or an object, as is the case in new product development, when alternative prototypes of the product are presented to respondents to discover what their associative feelings are or for them to project a personality on to the object in question. In the latter case, respondents are asked to imagine the object as a type of person and describe the personality characteristics of that person. So, for example, a respondent might be asked to describe a brand or an image of a particular hotel, airline, destination etc. as a personality and to indicate this personality's characteristics.

Associative procedures may also utilise metaphors as a vehicle to surface people's feelings about a particular situation or experience (see, Chen, 2010, for an example of the application of the Zaltman Metaphor Elicitation Technique). Metaphors are used in everyday conversation as associative phrases to help interpret and explain relatively unfamiliar situations by transferring knowledge from a relatively familiar situation or domain. For example, we might describe certain types of hotel as 'bed factories' or some forms of transport as 'cattle wagons'. In doing so, we are associating certain characteristics of mass production or crowded forms of animal transportation with other contexts to indicate the nature of the hotel or form of transport we are talking about. However, the metaphor itself, whether given to the respondents to use as an association with the context or elicited from them in their response, can be useless on its own without an explanation being provided by the respondents as to why they chose it.

Brotherton (2005) illustrates this in a study that used certain metaphors as vehicles for respondents in hotels to describe their feelings about the physical and service aspects of hospitality they received as guests in the hotels included in the study. The hotel guests were asked to describe their individual experience of the service they had received in the hotel as if it were an animal. This alone would have been quite useless information without the follow-up questions that asked them to give their reasons for choosing those animals, because it is the reasons for making the associative choice that reveal the thinking or criteria they used to make this choice. Also, in common with Korstanje (2010), who asked respondents to associate colours with their destination experience and to explain why, the Brotherton (2005) study also asked the hotel guests to indicate a colour associated with their experience and to say why they chose that particular colour.

Completion procedures are another form of PT where the stimuli are a little more extensive. Sentence or story completion is a popular form of this type of procedure. Respondents are given the beginning of a sentence or story and then asked to complete it. They freely project their inner feelings, assumptions and perhaps prejudices on to the vehicle, which acts as a form of third party. In other words, the responses given by the respondents are not seen by them as being directly attributable to them as they are simply responding to a situation that is presented. However, the only way they can make such a response is to project their feelings on to the stimulus to complete it and, hence, it acts as a type of neutral vehicle for surfacing this information.

Again, objects, or quasi-objects, can also be used in completion procedures. For example, respondents could be presented with a list of brand names and be asked to group them together into related categories, and then asked to explain their reasoning for the groupings that emerge. This could be used to discover how consumers segment a market for a particular type of hospitality or tourism product, what they see to be related and unrelated or differentiated brands in the marketplace. It could also be used for different types of tourist destinations or attractions.

Construction procedures tend to require more complex and controlled intellectual input from respondents than the procedures described above because they have to construct a response to a limited stimulus. Once again, these procedures use a third person format that enables respondents to record their thoughts, feelings and so on without having to do so directly. These techniques all allow respondents to present their own feelings, but to do so via a neutral third party. These encompass:

- Third person questions, such as, 'What would a businessman think of hotel brand X?'

- 'Thought bubbles', where a picture or cartoon of a situation is presented and respondents have to record the feelings or thoughts of the person or people in the thought bubble(s) in the image.

- Story construction, where a scenario is presented and respondents are asked to describe the characters and how they feel about the situation they are in.

- Persona construction, where certain characteristics of a person, object or quasi-object are given and respondents have to describe the personality of the stimuli type – for example, 'Here is the corporate logo of British Airways. Describe the company's personality' or 'Here is a list of the holiday destinations this person has visited. What is his personality?'

Expressive procedures, such as role-playing or 'give us a clue', can be used to obtain a response without the need for an oral or written question and answer framework. In role-playing, respondents might be asked to play the role of a particular product, brand, type of manager or destination and express the persona of this to an audience. For example, 'Speak to the audience as though you were Disneyland'. In 'give us a clue', respondents may be asked to enact the staff of a particular type of company or brand or perhaps the users of a particular type of product, with the other respondents being invited to guess its real identity. These procedures are designed to illuminate how people view the target stimuli and surface their perceptions, preconceived ideas, prejudices, stereotypes and so on.

Finally, choice-ordering procedures are used to elicit information regarding the priorities and preferences of people. Typically, respondents are presented with a list of stimuli items and asked to group and rank them according to the criteria given to them and explain the reasoning behind the final outcome. For example, given a list of airlines, respondents may be asked to group or rank these in terms of cost, quality, reliability, safety, destination coverage and so on.

 If you believe that projective techniques might be the right choice for you and you want to explore them further then go to 'The Qualitative Mind' link in the Web Links section of the Companion Website (study.sagepub.com/brotherton) as this contains quite extensive links to further information on PTs and examples of different types.

Chapter Summary

Any data collection instrument and procedure is merely a means to an end, but to achieve this end effectively, it must be designed and implemented in a credible manner.

The aim of data collection in general is to obtain sufficient valid and reliable data to be able to answer the research questions and/or test the hypotheses.

Highly structured questionnaires, with closed questions, are best suited to collecting quantitative data, whereas interviewing, observation and projective techniques are more appropriate for collecting qualitative data.

The validity of data is often thought to be greater when more open-ended, naturalistic forms of data collection are used and vice versa, but the reliability of data is invariably low in these cases. It can be much higher where more predetermined, but artificial, forms are used – that is, highly structured questionnaires.

The nature and location – particularly the level of dispersion – of the target respondents may influence the choice of data collection instrument and procedures, due to pragmatic considerations.

Respondents or informants do not always provide true or valid data, as they may distort their responses for various reasons. This factor needs to be recognised and dealt with, as far as is possible, in the design of the instruments and processes.

References

Arendt, S.W., Roberts, K.R., Strobehn, C., Ellis, J., Paez, P. and Meyer, J. (2012) 'Use of qualitative research in foodservice organizations: a review of challenges, strategies, and applications', *International Journal of Contemporary Hospitality Management*, 24 (6): 820–37.

Boddy, C. (2005) 'Projective techniques in market research: valueless subjectivity or insightful reality? A look at the evidence for the usefulness, reliability and validity of projective techniques in market research', *International Journal of Market Research*, 47 (3): 239–54.

Brotherton, B. (2004a) 'Critical success factors in UK corporate hotels', *The Services Industry Journal*, 24 (3): 19–42.

Brotherton, B. (2004b) 'Critical success factors in UK budget hotel operations', *International Journal of Operations and Production Management*, 24 (9): 944–69.

Brotherton, B. (2005) 'The nature of hospitality: customer perceptions and implications', *Tourism and Hospitality Planning & Development*, 2 (3): 139–53.

Chen, P-J. (2010) 'Differences between male and female sport event tourists: a qualitative study', *International Journal of Hospitality Management*, 29 (2): 277–90.

Hofstede, A., van Hoof, J., Walenberg, N. and de Jong, M. (2007) 'Projective techniques for brand image research: two personification-based methods explored', *Qualitative Market Research: An International Journal*, 10 (3): 300–9.

Jauncey, S. (1999) 'Observational research', in B. Brotherton (ed.), *The Handbook of Contemporary Hospitality Management Research*. Chichester: John Wiley. pp. 115–42.

Korstanje, M.E. (2010) 'The power of projective drawings: a new method for researching tourist experiences', e-*Review of Tourism Research (eRTR)*, 8 (5): 85–101.

Mackellar, J. (2013) 'Participant observation at events: theory, practice and potential', *International Journal of Event and Festival Management*, 4 (1): 56–65.

Neuman, W.L. (1994) *Social Research Methods: Quantitative and qualitative approaches*, 2nd edition. Needham Heights, MA: Allyn & Bacon.

Prebensen, N.K. (2007) 'Exploring tourists' images of a distant destination', *Tourism Management*, 27 (3): 747–56.

Skaalsvik, H. (2011) 'Service failures in a cruise line context: suggesting categorical schemes of service failures', *European Journal of Tourism Research*, 4 (1): 25–43.

Tasci, A.D.A., Gartner, W.C. and Cavusgil, S.T. (2007) 'Conceptualisation and operationalisation of destination image', *Journal of Hospitality and Tourism Research*, 31 (2): 194–223.

8

SAMPLING

Chapter Content and Issues

The nature and importance of sampling and why it is necessary.
Representativeness and generalisation.
The population, population elements and population parameters.
The sample frame, subjects, selection, respondents and statistics.
Sample size, composition, response rates and errors.
Confidence levels.
Probability-based, random sampling strategies and techniques for quantitative studies.
Non-probability-based sampling strategies and techniques for qualitative studies.
N = 1 investigations.

8.1 Introduction

In the two previous chapters we considered the decisions involved in selecting the overall research design for the project and the methods, instruments and procedures required to operationalise, or put this design into practice. Having considered how to structure and operationalise the data collection process, the next issue to confront is that discussed in this chapter – who are we going to select as the people or organisations to provide the information we need and why? This means that we have to explore sampling.

Sampling and, in particular, sampling theory and the statistical basis of much of this is something that tends to confuse many students because they can get lost in the mathematical equations and other jargon associated with the subject and lose sight of the key principles that underlie sampling decisions. Therefore, this chapter largely takes a non-mathematical and non-statistical approach to explaining what sampling is and the techniques that can be used to select samples. This does not mean that the mathematical and statistical basis of sampling and sampling theory is ignored, but, rather, that it is explained in a manner that, hopefully, is more readily understandable to the non-mathematician. If you decide that you require a more technical discussion of these issues, Hemmington's (1999) chapter on sampling would be a good choice, as would Dillman et al. (2009).

In addition, many of the video and web links on the Companion Website (study.sagepub.com/brotherton) provide both basic and more advanced material on sampling and the sampling issues and techniques covered in this chapter.

So, here we will consider the nature of sampling and its importance, the relationship between a sample and the population it is obtained from, what would be required for you to be able to generalise from the results of the sample back to the larger population, how the response rate from the sample can be responsible for error and why the expected response rate needs to be taken into account when deciding what the size of sample should be. We will also explore the main sampling strategies and techniques associated with quantitative and qualitative studies, as well as the implications that the size and composition of the sample may have for future decisions concerning the statistical techniques that can be used to analyse the data obtained from those samples.

8.2 What is Sampling and Why is it Important?

8.2.1 Sampling and representativeness

Sampling, or taking a sample, is really very straightforward and simple – certainly in terms of its basic rationale and principles. Essentially, a sample is a smaller version of the whole it is obtained from that reflects the same characteristics as those of the whole (see Figure 8.1). For example, if you were ill and the doctor wanted to take a blood sample for analysis to try to make a diagnosis, the small amount of blood in that sample would be identical to the remainder of the blood in your body. Similarly, if you were asked, in a supermarket, to try a sample of a food item or a drink, then, again, the sample would be a smaller, but identical, version of the full portion or bottle. In each of these cases, the analysis or tasting of the sample would be used to make inferences about the larger entity it was derived from. So, if you liked the sample of food or drink, then you might reasonably infer that you would like that food or drink because the larger entity would have the same characteristics as the sample you tasted. Similarly, if the doctor found a particular abnormality in the blood sample, then he or she might reasonably infer that this would be present in your blood as a whole. However, to make inferences beyond this point may not be justifiable. For example, if your food sample was a particular type of cheese and you liked it, then it would be reasonable to infer that you would like that type of cheese but not that you would then like all types of cheese.

From this we can see that there is an important relationship between the whole the sample is taken from and the sample itself. The whole is known as the 'population' and it is the relationship between this and the sample that is critical for making valid inferences from the sample results to the wider population. Ideally, the sample must

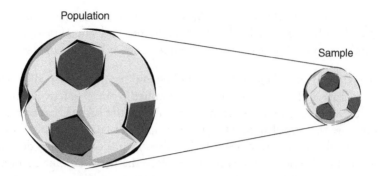

FIGURE 8.1 A representative sample

be as identical as possible to the population it has been obtained from, in terms of its composition and characteristics, for it to be regarded as sufficiently 'representative' to be able to make valid inferences from. On the other hand, if the sample is not representative, then it will be biased in one way or another and so inferences made on the basis of that sample are likely to be wrong. For example, if the population contained 70 per cent males and 30 per cent females and the sample taken from it contained 50 per cent males and females, then the results from the analysis of the sample would be biased in the sense that they would under-represent males and over-represent females in terms of the proportions of these genders found in the real population. However, it is perhaps important to mention at this point that results obtained from a sample not regarded as being sufficiently representative of the wider population from which it has been drawn are not necessarily invalid or useless. Many students get confused over this issue because they do not see the difference between the validity of data and its suitability for generalisation (see Key Concept Box – Validity and Generalisability).

Key Concept	**Validity and Generalisability**
It is extremely important to understand the difference between the validity of sample data and its suitability for generalisation. How valid or accurate the sample data are, in terms of the extent to which they provide a true picture of the views of the respondents, is largely a function of the quality of the data instrument (questionnaire) used to obtain their responses. The use of a valid instrument should produce valid responses regardless of the size, composition or representativeness of any sample these are derived from. Therefore, even very small and/or biased samples can provide valid data. However, certainly biased and, depending on the size of the population, very small samples will not provide data that are suitable to be used for further generalisations.	

This issue of the sample being representative is particularly significant where statistical inferences are to be made, but may be less so in qualitative studies, where the aim is not to generalise results from a sample to the wider population it is drawn from. Sampling in small-scale qualitative studies, such as case studies and observational research, is invariably undertaken for different purposes and in different ways, for both theoretical and practical reasons, to that employed for larger more quantitative work, as we will see later in this chapter. However, in quantitative work, the desire to use a sample to make valid and reliable generalisations about a population is a central purpose of this kind of research, so it is important to understand the issues in order to be able to do this successfully.

8.2.2 Why sample?

Why do we have to have a sample? Why not simply collect information from the population as a whole? The answer is invariably practical in nature, but, conceptually, this is an issue of population heterogeneity. Put another way, because most populations are not comprised of identical (homogeneous) members, they embody at least some degree of variety. If all members of the population were homogeneous or identical, then, logically, a sample of one would be sufficient because the results from this could be generalised to everyone else in the population. This is clearly illustrated by our earlier example of the blood sample. As all the blood in the human body is effectively the same, sharing all the same characteristics, then one sample is fully representative of all the blood. Thus, as we shall see later, the amount of heterogeneity or variation in the population has an implication for the size of sample required. Other things being equal, the greater this is, the greater the need to increase the size of the sample to reflect the extent of variability in the population.

8.2.3 Populations

A population, in research terms, is not necessarily simply comprised of people. Populations may be comprised of particular types of companies, products or brands, destinations, events, processes, photographs, advertisements and so on. 'Population' in this context is a term used to denote a collection of related elements, all of which share some characteristics relevant to the study. This means that the first issue that needs to be addressed is that of defining the population – not only in terms of the type(s) of elements that should be included in it but also its boundaries or parameters. For example, it would be easy to define a population as four-star hotels, but would this mean all the four-star hotels in the world, in Europe, in the UK, in a region of the UK or within a particular UK city? Would it mean all four-star hotels regardless of the type of ownership – independently or corporately owned – and those of any size, from fewer than 10 bedrooms to those with over 1,000 rooms? Defining the population should, in fact, be a relatively simple matter, as long as the parameters of the research have been articulated in the original research question(s) and/or aims or objectives. For example, if the study was specified as one investigating business guest satisfaction in four-star corporate hotels in London, the population, at least in principle, is already defined (see Key Concept Box – Population).

Key Concept	Population

Although the concept of 'population' is generally defined as a set or collection of elements that share some common characteristics it can be defined in different ways.

The 'conceptual' population is one likely to be relevant to your study. For example, all budget hotels in the UK or all front-line service staff in UK five-star hotels would constitute populations that would be appropriate and relevant to research studies focusing on these contexts.

The 'study' population is a part, or sub-set, of the conceptual population. The study population is the one that you are going to use to select your sample, e.g. taking the idea of all budget hotels in the UK as the conceptual population we may, often for very practical reasons, decide to reduce this to one that is more specific and manageable. For example, you might decide that only budget hotels operated by the main budget hotel brands or companies will be used to define the population for your study. Alternatively, you may decide to limit the study population geographically by defining it as all budget hotels within the city of Manchester. These decisions are not random ones, they are taken for good reasons relating either to the nature of the research questions/context defined earlier in the study and/or for more practical, i.e. access, issues.

This also highlights the issue of geographical dispersion. In our earlier example it may not be necessary to sample because, if there are only 200 four-star corporate hotels in London, it could well be quite feasible to send questionnaires to them all. On the other hand, if our population had instead been defined in terms of this type of hotel in the UK as a whole or on a wider basis than that, both the increased numbers of four-star hotels that would be included in the definition and their greater geographical dispersion may well dictate that a sample is needed. In this instance, the greater size and dispersion would make access to the population elements much more expensive and time-consuming and, therefore, perhaps not practicable or feasible in relation to the resources available and the time constraints for the work. This is also a feature of a great deal of commercial research, where budgets are limited and results are required as quickly and as cost-effectively as possible.

Once the population has been defined, taking these matters into consideration, then it is possible to begin thinking about what size of sample should be selected and how to do this. These are issues that we shall address shortly. However, before we do so, it may be helpful for you to become familiar with some of the sampling terminology or jargon (see Key Concept Boxes – The Sample, and Sampling Terminology).

Key Concept	The Sample

The sample you decide to select must be related to the purpose/s or objectives of your research.

Choosing a sample from which you intend to collect data is essentially a 'means to an end' decision. Or, put another way, the sample is a vehicle that you are going to use to help you collect the type and volume of data you need to complete your research.

Although this will be partly a 'theoretical' decision related to the nature of your research objectives, it is also invariably a practical or pragmatic one as well. All research projects have parameters within which they have to operate, even those with large budgets, teams of researchers and extended timescales, so we need to think about the 'practicalities' we face.

This means you have to consider the time you have available, the ease of access you may have to your potential sample respondents and the costs involved.

All sampling is essentially a compromise between the ideal and the achievable and the bottom-line is that all you can do is seek to make your sample as good as it can be given the constraints you face.

Key Concept	Sampling Terminology

All the elements contained within your chosen population are known as the **'sample frame'**, from which the actual sample can be drawn or selected.

Those selected to form part of the sample become known as **'sample subjects'** and the actual people who respond to the questions put to them are the **'sample respondents'**.

The data or values generated from the respondents' responses are known as the **'sample statistics'** and the corresponding values in the population are referred to as the **'population parameters'**.

8.2.4 Sample size

How large does a sample have, or need, to be? In my experience, this is invariably a question that confuses and perplexes students because, for whatever reason, the size of the sample tends to be seen as being directly related to how representative it will be. That is, there is a tendency to think that as the sample gets larger, then it will automatically become more representative. This is a fallacy as it also depends on how the sample has been selected. As indicated earlier, the amount of variation in the population is much more important in this respect. Variation can be measured by using the standard deviation, and the greater the variability in the population, the higher the value of the standard deviation. Hence, a more variable population will tend to indicate that a larger sample size will be required to ensure that the breadth of that variation is reflected in the sample. Similarly, the sample size required may be influenced by the degree of precision desired – that is, the extent to which the sample statistics can be regarded to be a true reflection of the population parameters. However, to increase precision significantly, the sample size would need to be increased quite considerably, which may not be feasible. Indeed, it is claimed that, to double the level of precision, the size of sample may need to be quadrupled.

As precision is concerned with the relationship between the sample statistics and the population parameters, the size of the sample and how it is selected are potential sources of variance between these two. This is known as 'sampling error'. A sample selected on a random basis (see Key Concept Box – Randomness) is likely to have less potential for bias and error than one selected using an alternative technique. Similarly, the larger the size of the sample, the less is the likelihood that alternative samples drawn from the same population would produce different sample statistics or estimates of the population parameters. For example, a sample of 10 drawn from a population of 100 would be quite small and subject to significant error because nine other alternative samples of 10 could be drawn from the same population. On the other hand, if the sample size was 50, only one other sample of the same size could have been drawn. This should illustrate that, generally, as sample size increases the potential for sampling error declines.

Key Concept	**Randomness**

One issue that causes a lot of confusion is that of random sampling or selecting a sample on a random basis.

In everyday life we tend to think that something described as being random is something that happens over which we have no prior knowledge and no control and, because it is random, we cannot predict when, and possibly how, it will occur. Well, of course, this is true but there is something of a paradox when we talk about randomising the process of selecting a sample because to create a randomly selected sample we have to do this in a deliberately random way.

In other words, it is purposeful and planned and we know the likelihood, or probability, of each member of the sampling frame being selected to be included in the sample. We deliberately create a random process to ensure that the selection takes place randomly. So, a random sample is not simply created without prior planning.

The implication of this would appear to be that a high proportion of the population should be included in the sample to minimise error. However, it is not the proportion of the population *per se* included in the sample that is the key issue, but the size of the sample itself. The answer to the question How large a sample do I need for it to be representative of the population as a whole? is rather counter-intuitive. Quite naturally many people take the view that the larger the sample as a proportion of the population the more representative it is going to be. This seems to make sense. If we select a larger proportion of the population then more of the population is included in the sample and hence the sample should be more representative than one that has a smaller proportion, but this is not the issue.

It is the size of the sample rather than the proportion of the population included in this sample that is the key influence on the precision of the results. Some examples may help to illustrate this further. Take a situation where the population is defined as 100 people – how many of these should be included in a sample to make it sufficiently representative, 20, 40, 60, 80? The simple answer is that we cannot tell without more information about the nature or composition of the population. If all the 100 people were exactly the same, or in the jargon were perfectly homogeneous, the amount of variability in the population would be zero. In this case we could select a sample of 1 because this one person is no different from the other 99 in the population. On the other hand, if all the 100 people were totally different and unique (perfectly heterogeneous) then, logically, we would have to select a sample of 100, the whole population. Of course, both of these extremes are very rare indeed and most populations contain more or less variability or heterogeneity. So, as a general rule of thumb, it should be clear that the greater the degree of variability in the population the larger the sample size needs to be to adequately reflect this range of variation.

That said, this relationship is not a simple linear one and the sample size also depends upon the degree of precision, or lack of error, required. Let's explore these two issues. Again, a general rule of thumb is that the greater the degree of precision required the larger the sample needs to be. This is pretty intuitive. So, for example, if we are willing to accept a margin of error of plus or minus 10 per cent the sample size necessary to achieve this for a population of 100 would be around 50, or half the population, but if we wanted to be more precise, i.e. have less margin for error, then at a plus or minus 3 per cent margin for error level we would be looking to almost double this sample size to around 90. What is perhaps slightly less intuitive is the relationship between sample size and population size as we increase the size of population. Intuitively we might expect that as we double the population size then we will need to double the sample size also, but this is not the case because there is a less than proportionate relationship here. If we double our population to 200, at a 10 per cent margin of error we do need to increase the sample size, but not by 100 per cent. If we increased it from 50 to around 65 this would be sufficient. Similarly, with our 3 per cent margin for error, we would increase the sample size from around 90 to somewhere in the region of 170. This is clearly a larger proportionate increase than the former, but it is still not double the original size. For a practical example of how to calculate sample size see the Technique Tip box – Calculating Sample Size.

Technique Tip

Calculating Sample Size

The various sample size calculators available on the internet (see the Companion Website) make this issue relatively straightforward. Using one of these – www.surveysystem.com/sscalc.htm – the following example shows how you can do this.

As you can see you can set the confidence level at the 95% or 99% levels and enter a value for the desired confidence interval. In this case I entered one of 5 and specified the population as 1,000. Hitting the calculate button then delivers the result for sample size needed which, in this case, is 278. In the following box – Find Confidence Interval – you can see the effect that reducing the sample size to 100 has. Now, with this smaller sample, the confidence level has declined to 9.3. It has declined because plus or minus 9.3 provides a wider margin for error, or less precision, than plus or minus 5.

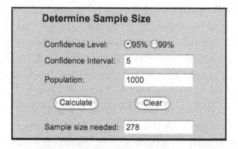

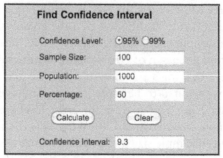

Reproduced with permission of http://www.surveysystem.com/sscale.htm

This relationship is even more pronounced with larger populations. Above a certain point, around the 6,000 mark, there is relatively little to be gained, in terms of increased precision, by increasing the sample size as the population increases. When you see the results from 'national polls' or surveys based on a sample size of, typically, 1,000 to 2,000, that are used to generalise the results to a population of millions, it is this principle that is being enacted. However, the converse of this is true within small populations. Here a larger proportion of the population needs to be sampled to achieve credible estimates within a given margin for error. Similarly, if you want or need to generate sub-groups or sub-samples within your overall sample to analyse similarities or differences between these subdivisions, without compromising the margin for error, then you will need to increase the overall sample size to ensure that the size of these sub-groups is sufficiently large for this to happen. That said, the process of increasing sample size eventually suffers from diminishing returns. As you increase your sample size from a very small proportion of the population to a larger one the gains in greater precision and lower error are quite significant and worthwhile pursuing but, as you take this process further, the gains start to become lower with each increase in size and, eventually, the gain becomes one that is really not worthwhile pursuing because the time and costs involved are likely to offset any benefit obtained.

8.2.5 Sample selection and population characteristics

Returning to the issues of population variability and sample selection, if we want to try to minimise the degree of sampling error we have to take the characteristics or composition of the population into account in selecting the sample. Figures 8.2 and 8.3 illustrate this. Figure 8.2 shows a population of 100 that has 50 per cent males and 50 per cent females. To reflect this we would expect our sample of 40 to be comprised of a similarly equal proportion of males and females, 20/20.

Males					Females				
♂	♂	♂	♂	♂	♀	♀	♀	♀	♀
♂	♂	♂	♂	♂	♀	♀	♀	♀	♀
♂	♂	♂	♂	♂	♀	♀	♀	♀	♀
♂	♂	♂	♂	♂	♀	♀	♀	♀	♀
♂	♂	♂	♂	♂	♀	♀	♀	♀	♀
♂	♂	♂	♂	♂	♀	♀	♀	♀	♀
♂	♂	♂	♂	♂	♀	♀	♀	♀	♀
♂	♂	♂	♂	♂	♀	♀	♀	♀	♀
♂	♂	♂	♂	♂	♀	♀	♀	♀	♀
♂	♂	♂	♂	♂	♀	♀	♀	♀	♀

FIGURE 8.2 Symmetrical population distribution

However where these proportions are different in the population, see Figure 8.3, the proportion of males and females in the sample should reflect this. As you can see, we have now moved from a male/female 50/50 split to one of 70/30 so the respective balance of males and females in the same size sample of 40 is (70% of 40 =) 28 and (30% of 40 =) 12.

Males							Females		
♂	♂	♂	♂	♂	♂	♂	♀	♀	♀
♂	♂	♂	♂	♂	♂	♂	♀	♀	♀
♂	♂	♂	♂	♂	♂	♂	♀	♀	♀
♂	♂	♂	♂	♂	♂	♂	♀	♀	♀
♂	♂	♂	♂	♂	♂	♂	♀	♀	♀
♂	♂	♂	♂	♂	♂	♂	♀	♀	♀
♂	♂	♂	♂	♂	♂	♂	♀	♀	♀
♂	♂	♂	♂	♂	♂	♂	♀	♀	♀
♂	♂	♂	♂	♂	♂	♂	♀	♀	♀
♂	♂	♂	♂	♂	♂	♂	♀	♀	♀

FIGURE 8.3 Asymmetrical population distribution

It is a common misconception to think that there should be an equal, or nearly equal, balance of different respondent characteristics in a sample to make it more representative. This is not a rule that you can universally apply. The Research in Action Box – Critical Success Factors and Budget Hotels – provides an illustration of how this works in practice and how such a situation is explained.

Research in Action	Critical Success Factors and Budget Hotels
The questionnaire package was mailed to the general manager of each budget hotel in the sample. **The population** for the **sample selection** was defined as the leading budget hotel brands in this sector of the UK hotel industry … The **sampling frame** was derived from the literature, i.e. the annual Deloitte & Touche	

UK budget hotel surveys referred to earlier and the recent Mintel (1999) report on budget hotels. The names and addresses of the constituent hotels were obtained from the companies' budget hotel directories and/or their web sites. **A sample of 549 was selected** from this information. This procedure generated **an initial return** of 209 **completed and useable questionnaires.** To address the **validity** issues associated with **non-response** appropriate follow-up action was taken. A reminder letter, with another copy of the questionnaire, was posted to all the non-responding hotels approximately one week after the date given for the return of the original questionnaire. This resulted in a further 30 questionnaires being completed and returned. Thus, **the final useable sample** comprised 239 questionnaires, comprising a very satisfactory **final response rate** of 44 per cent for this type of mailed survey.

The size of the realised sample (n = 239) was very encouraging in terms of providing a representative data set from the budget hotel sector ... the sample was, not unsurprisingly, dominated by the two leading brands, Premier Inn (originally branded Travelinn, then Premier Travel Inn) and Travelodge. Though this did skew the sample in favour of these brands **it nevertheless reflects the population distribution of budget hotel brands in the UK**. The sample was also dominated by budget hotels in motorway and A (trunk road) road locations, with these accounting for almost two-thirds of the respondent hotels. However, this **again reflects the nature of the population distribution for budget hotel locations**. Interestingly, the more recent growth locations of suburban and city centre sites also feature quite strongly, accounting for nearly a further 30 per cent of the sample.

The size distribution shows the 31–40 bedroom range to be the largest single category, followed by the over 60 bedroom group. Cumulatively these two size categories account for 74 per cent of the total. If the 41–50 category were to be added to these this would account for some 90 per cent of the total. **Once again, this is strongly representative of the budget hotel population distribution by size**. Table II [not included here] indicates further characteristics of the sample. This suggests that the sample is very representative of the breadth of budget hotel operations, as it comprises a considerable range of responses in relation to average room occupancy, number of full- or part-time staff and the business mix. Given all of these characteristics it is reasonable to claim that the sample as a whole is highly representative of branded budget hotel operations in the UK.

Source: Brotherton (2004: 949–50). Reproduced with permission from Emerald Group Publishing Limited

8.2.6   Sampling and response rates

A more practical issue is the relationship between the target or planned sample and the realised sample. This is essentially determined by the response rate and has an inverse relationship with initial sample size determination. If the expected response rate is low, then it may be necessary to increase the size of the initial sample to secure a viable realised sample and vice versa. For example, to obtain a final, realised sample of 50 where the expected response rate is 50 per cent, an initial sample of only 100 would be required, but if the response rate were expected to be only 20 per cent, then to secure a realised sample of 50, the initial sample would have to be 250.

Key Concept

Target and Realised Samples

Once you have selected the members from the sampling frame that you wish to include in your sample this can be referred to as your 'target' sample or, put another way, all the potential respondents, individuals or companies, that you would ideally like to collect data from.

However, some of these 'target' respondents may refuse, for a variety of reasons, to take part in your study. Even when individuals or companies have initially indicated that they would be prepared to cooperate and provide you with an opportunity to obtain information from them it is not unknown for some of these to change their minds at a later date!

Therefore, there is likely to be a difference between the selected 'target' sample and the 'actual' or 'realised' sample that you eventually achieve. In short, your actual sample will be comprised of respondents, whereas your target sample is likely to turn out to be a combination of those who did respond (respondents) and those who did not (non-respondents). The relative proportions of these two can be a significant issue (see Non-Response Error).

Another issue is the degree of sub-sample analysis that you may wish to undertake when the data are available. If you wish to explore similarities or differences between sub-groups or categories, each of these will need to be large enough to facilitate such analysis. To obtain sufficient numbers of respondents within each of these sub-groups, it may be necessary to increase the original target sample size. For example, if you wanted to compare the frequency with which different types of people visited an art gallery, based on the age category they belonged to, this may involve five or six separate age categories. With a total realised sample of 30, and assuming the respondents were equally distributed across the age categories, this would only give you five or six cases in each category. However, if the realised sample were to be twice as large, using the same assumption, each category would then have 10–12 cases. However, even this increase is unlikely to be sufficient. It is difficult to be precise about the exact size of sub-groups required for this type of analysis, as different commentators suggest differing minima. That said, a reasonable rule of thumb might be that sub-groups with fewer than 30 members, and preferably 50, are unlikely to be suitable for a range of statistical tests.

Key Concept	**Non-Response Error**

Using the budget hotels scenario we used previously let's say that you identified 50 budget hotels as the 'target' sample, for both theoretical and practical reasons, and that this number and type of hotel were regarded as appropriate to give you the data you need to answer your research question/s. If, however, you manage to interview only 25 of the 50 hotels' general managers then the question arises: how do I know that the responses provided by my realised sample, which is only half of my target sample, are representative of the other half who did not respond? The answer is, unfortunately, you cannot know this with any great certainty either way. In this sense there is an obvious problem.

While it is perfectly reasonable to say that you can be pretty confident that the nature of the responses provided by your actual respondents are accurate and a true reflection of their opinions, views, perceptions, practices etc., it becomes increasingly difficult to extrapolate or generalise this to a wider context the greater the gap between the target and realised samples. This is known as the degree of 'non-response' error that exists.

A simple example can illustrate this. If you had managed to interview 45 of the 50 general managers in your target sample then, both numerically and qualitatively, it would not be unreasonable to suggest that the views of the vast majority, i.e. 45 (90 per cent), of your target sample are more likely than not to be representative of the small minority, i.e. 5 (10 per cent), who did not respond. Hence, any threat to the validity of your sample data would be quite small because the extent of any error in this regard due to a very small number of non-respondents would be negligible.

Alternatively, if the degree of non-response was significantly higher, say 20 (40 per cent) of the 50 general managers refused to be interviewed, I think you may agree that it would now be more difficult to be confident that the opinions of the 30 managers interviewed could be regarded as highly likely to be the same as those held by the 20 who were not. At this point it should be obvious that there is an inverse relationship between the response and non-response rates: the higher the response rate, the lower the non-response rate, and non-response error, will be, and vice versa.

Furthermore, while it is obvious that non-response error has a size or numerical dimension, i.e. the larger the percentage of non-response the greater the threat to overall validity, it may also have a qualitative dimension where the pattern of non-response is uneven. This is an issue related to the composition of the target sample.

Continuing with our budget hotel example, let's say that we designed our original target sample to include 25 female and 25 male general managers, the reasons

(Continued)

(Continued)

for which may be quite obvious, but that the 20 non-responding general managers were comprised of 15 females and 5 males. Now, not only do we have the numerical non-response threat discussed earlier but we also have a final, realised sample that has a much higher proportion of male respondents than females. It is clear to see that this presents a potential problem as the views of male general managers are now over-represented compared to those of females in our realised sample, whereas the intention was to obtain a much more balanced set of views by gender in our original sample design.

See also the Technique Tip box – Dealing with Non-Response Error.

8.2.7   Sampling and confidence intervals

Once you have the sample data and begin the analysis process, it is a relatively simple matter to assess the degree of confidence – that is, the likelihood that the sample statistics are accurate in relation to the population parameters – by computing the 'confidence interval'. As we shall explore in Chapter 9, using a data analysis package such as SPSS, it is straightforward to set the confidence interval for the statistical test to be used. Given the assumption of normally distributed data – that is, the symmetrical, bell-shaped curve – 95 per cent of the cases in such a distribution will lie within two standard deviations above and below the mean, its centre. The same applies to the distribution of sample means, so it is possible to say the same for the sample means or, in other words, that 95 times out of 100 the sample mean will be within this range. In effect, we are saying here that we can be 95 per cent confident that the sample statistics are a true reflection of the population parameters.

Technique Tip	**Dealing with Non-Response Error**

There are two basic types of non-response: unit or item. The former refers to a nil-return, or non-completion, of the questionnaire, while the latter is concerned with missing responses to some question items. Unit non-response frequently occurs due to an inability to contact the potential respondent, a lack of willingness, ability or refusal to respond. Item non-response can also occur for similar reasons and also be due to errors in the construction of the questionnaire.

The best strategy for dealing with potential non-response error is to try to avoid or reduce it happening in the first place. This can be achieved by ensuring that the questionnaire being used is clear, concise and easy to complete to encourage more target respondents to become actual respondents. Put simply, the more interesting the questions and the easier they are to understand and answer the more likely it is that people will willingly cooperate. Ensuring that the target respondents have been properly and accurately identified in the first place, both in terms of who they are and where/how they can be contacted, can help to increase questionnaire return rates. If you are intending to conduct a survey within an organisation, recruiting a supporter, or champion, can help. Such a person will encourage his/her colleagues to cooperate and may even help you with part of the distribution/collection process.

In the case of item non-response this is often relatively insignificant. If there are just a few missing responses to a few questions on your questionnaire, which is quite common, then you can effectively ignore these because the degree of error they are likely to generate will be insignificant. Where this is more widespread it is possible to use a range of weighting, or re-weighting, procedures to deal with these issues but these are really beyond the scope of this text and are not likely to be relevant to the vast majority of student research work, particularly at undergraduate level.

Finally, when you come to write up your results do not ignore or try to hide any non-response, either unit or item, that has occurred because the people who are supervising and/or marking your work will be smart enough to recognise it and will assume that you have not if you don't deal with it. Be honest and record where it has arisen and explain what you believe the effects of this may have been on your results and the conclusions you can draw from these.

8.2.8 Sampling and reality

Before we move on to consider the various quantitative and qualitative sampling strategies and methods available to you it is important to remember that the process of sampling is invariably one in which various trade-offs have to be made. In reality, sampling rarely turns out to be a perfect process that meets all the 'ideal' criteria relating to sample selection. In my experience this is often something recognised by students and is an issue that tends to develop significant anxiety because, given the time, resource and access constraints most student research work operates under, student researchers quickly realise that they are not going to be able to adopt a sampling procedure regarded as ideal and that this will lead to them being penalised in the marking of their work. This may, but should not, be the case (see Key Decisions Box – Dealing with Your Sampling Demons).

Key Decisions	**Dealing with Your Sampling Demons**

Most sensible researchers recognise that sampling is hardly ever a perfect process and, frequently, is one that is driven by a combination of ideal and realistic decisions, and by various compromises and trade-offs. Any supervisor or marker of your work should be aware of this and will understand the constraints you are working under. The key point here is that you will not be expected to create the 'perfect' sample for your work but the best one you can manage given the constraints you face. So, although in many cases random sample selection is ideal, being able to achieve this may be difficult, if not impossible. Not being able to achieve this is not the key issue. What is of vital importance is to explain why this has been the case and what would have been required to do this. Explain and justify why you were not able to achieve such a sample and be clear and honest about what your alternative was. If you didn't manage to achieve as large a sample as you intended explain why this happened and recognise what limitations this has created for the analysis of the data and the generalisability of the results.

If you make sampling decisions that are illogical and cannot be justified in any reasonable manner then you might rightly expect to be criticised for this. A more common sampling problem encountered by students, for which they are likely to be correctly penalised, is what is claimed on the basis of the sample. I cannot recall the number of occasions when I have read student dissertation work that claims the results derived from a convenience sample can be generalised! In the general pecking order of sampling, convenience sampling is regarded as distinctly inferior to random sampling but this is only the case if the aim is to generalise the results from the sample back to the population it was drawn from.

There is nothing inherently wrong with convenience sampling *per se* and, as this is often the most feasible choice for student researchers, you should not feel that this will somehow be regarded as such by your supervisor or marker. As long as you provide a sensible explanation for why you made, or had to make, this choice and do not make unjustifiable claims about being able to generalise the results from this you should not be penalised. In fact, you are likely to receive credit for recognising the limitations of convenience sampling because this shows you are aware of them.

8.3 Quantitative Data Sampling

Sampling in quantitative studies is known as probability-based sampling. In this approach, each population element has a known, non-zero and, usually equal, chance of being selected for inclusion in the sample. A process of selecting the elements for the sample in a random manner ensures that this is the case and biased selection cannot occur because, by definition, randomness cannot be predicted or controlled. Unsurprisingly, this is commonly referred to as random sampling and is used where generalisation from the results for a sample back to the population as a whole is critical and it is intended to use statistical techniques to analyse the sample data.

To select a target sample from a sampling frame on a random basis we may want to generate a series of random numbers that we can then apply to our list of potential respondents contained in the frame. Indeed, ideally, unless there are other good reasons for not doing so, we will have arranged the entries in our sampling frame randomly before the final sample selection takes place. A good analogy to illustrate this is playing cards. To try to ensure that there is no inherent or systematic bias involved in dealing cards, say for a game of poker, the pack is shuffled in such a way that ensures, as far as is reasonably possible, that the cards are dealt at random, thereby not providing any one player with a biased advantage. In either case, being able to easily generate a set of random numbers to enable us to do this with less time and trouble would be useful. This may sound a complicated and time-consuming process but actually it can be achieved relatively quickly and simply. The generation of an appropriate list of random numbers can be easily achieved using the random number generator function in Excel or in SPSS, but there are also random number generators available on websites (see Technique Tip box – Generating Random Numbers).

Technique Tip	Generating Random Numbers

Using Excel to generate random numbers

[1] Open a new worksheet, go to the Tools menu and select 'Data Analysis'.

[2] Select 'Random Number Generation', click on 'OK' and this will open a dialogue box so that you can set the requirements.

[3] For the 'Number of variables', enter '1'. This will provide a list of random numbers in one column of the spreadsheet.

[4] In the 'Number of Random' option, enter the number of random numbers you need. For example, if you want to select a sample of 50 from a sampling frame of 300, then enter '50' here.

[5] In the 'Distribution' option, select 'Uniform'.

[6] In the 'Between' option, enter the lowest and highest values between which you want the random selection to be made. So, in our example above, this would have been between 1 and 300.

(Continued)

(Continued)

[7] Click on the 'OK' button and you should have a list of 50 random numbers in the column on your spreadsheet.

[8] You may want to tidy up the output as it will be displayed to a number of decimal places, unless you have previously specified the cell output to be different to this. To do this, go to the Format menu and select 'Cells' to open the cell formatting options box. In the 'Number' option, simply change the output to one with no decimal places and you will get whole numbers in the column.

Using SPSS to generate random numbers

Let's say you want 200 random numbers between 1 and 1000.

[1] Start up SPSS and go to the Variable View, choose a variable, and type in a name for it (e.g. 'Rand'). Now format the 'Decimals' to 0 to make SPSS produce the random numbers to the nearest whole number.

[2] Remaining in the Variable View, set the column labelled 'Measure' to 'Scale'.

[3] Now return to the Data View. Go to your 'Rand' column (variable) and enter any number in the 200th row of this column to inform SPSS you want 200 random numbers.

[4] In the Transform menu, click 'Compute variable' and in the 'Target Variable' box, type the name of the column ('Rand') where your random numbers are to go.

[5] Go to the 'Function group' box, and select 'Random Numbers'. A list of types of random numbers will appear. Double-click 'Rv.Uniform' in the list of types of random numbers and RV.UNIFORM(?,?) will appear in the 'Numeric Expression' box.

[6] The (?,?), is designed to specify the range of random numbers, so for 200 random numbers between 1 and 1,000 you simply replace the two question marks with a 1 and a 1,000, thus (1,1,000).

[7] Click 'OK' and a message pop-up will appear, asking if you want to 'Change the existing variable'.

[8] Click 'OK' and you will see that your 'Rand' column now has 200 numbers in it, between 1 and 1,000.

Using websites to generate random numbers

As you might expect, there are a range of online random number generators available. A simple search using the search term 'online random number generator' will deliver many hits, such as that to be found at www.random.org/integers/. The opening page for this is shown in the following screenshot:

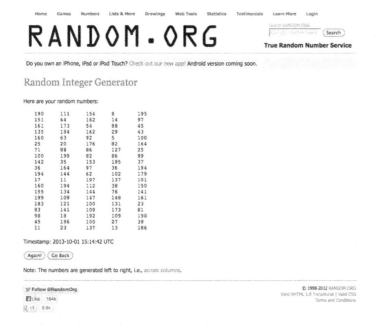

The results page (which appeared in a flash!) of a request for 100 random numbers between 1 and 200 is shown below.

Screenshots reproduced with permission of www.random.org/integers

The main probability-based sampling strategies will now be discussed in turn.

8.3.1   Simple random sampling

This is a relatively straightforward procedure, but it does demand that the sampling frame is known and each item in the frame is numbered or coded. Each item has an equal chance of being, or not being, selected. The chance of an item being selected to be included in the sample cannot be influenced by the person selecting the sample because it is made on a random basis. Random number tables can be used for this, but using Excel, SPSS or website random number generators is a quick and easy way to generate a set of random numbers for this purpose as it can be tailored to the size of the sampling frame and the size of sample to be selected from this. Useful examples of the application of simple random sampling in actual research studies are provided by Han et al. (2011), Pantelidis (2010) and Victorino and Bolinger (2012).

8.3.2   Systematic random sampling

This is conducted by selecting the items for inclusion in the sample at systematic or regular intervals by means of the sampling frame, using a randomised starting point. For example, to select a sample of 30 restaurants from a sampling frame containing 270, the sampling interval would have to be 270/30 = 9. If the random number selected to start the process was 4, then the 4th, 13th, 22nd, 31st ... would be selected until the total of 30 had been reached. Ideally, the items in the sampling frame should be organised randomly before selection takes place, to avoid the problem of 'periodicity'. This happens because the items in the sampling frame are likely to be ordered in some way, so a systematic selection may result in some types being over-, or under-represented, even though the selection proceeds from a random point. To avoid this, it is necessary to mix, shuffle or randomise the list comprising the sampling frame before selection takes place. For examples of how this sampling method is used in practice see Ottenbacher and Harrington (2010) or Pike and Mason (2011).

8.3.3   Stratified random sampling

This technique assumes some prior knowledge of the population that can be used to separate it into distinct, mutually exclusive groups or strata. This may be on the basis of age, location, gender, occupation and so on or, in the case or organisations, size, location, brand, quality and other such aspects. This may be done where it is hypothesised that a particular characteristic could constitute a source of variance. In such circumstances a proportional representation of the strata would be desired. So, if it were proposed that men and women would have significantly different opinions on certain issues, then it would be important to ensure that the correct proportions of each gender were included in the sample. For example, if it was known that the population was comprised of 60 per cent males and 40 per cent females, it would be important to ensure that these groups were proportionately represented in the sample by selecting 1.5 more male subjects than female in order to explore the 'between-group' variations. Once the sample frame is organised into the relevant groupings the desired degree of proportionality can be identified. Following this it is a relatively simple matter to then apply either a simple or systematic random selection procedure for each strata. Applications of this method can be seen in the studies produced by Gallardo et al. (2010) and Michel et al. (2012).

8.3.4 Cluster sampling

Geographic area cluster sampling can be used to alleviate costly and time-consuming access to a sample where it is very geographically dispersed and/or where it is impossible or not practical to put together a full list of the target population elements. It is most suitable where the clusters contain the same variability as the population and where they are relatively homogeneous. If there proved to be a high degree of between-cluster variability, then a much larger number of clusters would need to be included in the sample because the population would be exhibiting a greater degree of homogeneity.

The sampling frame is comprised of the list of clusters rather than individual cases. From this, a number of clusters are selected on a random basis and data are collected from every case contained in the clusters selected. This is known as one or single-stage cluster sampling. It is possible to go beyond this and employ two-stage cluster sampling. Here data are collected from selected members of each cluster rather than all the members of each. So, for example, if the membership of the clusters was numerically large then it may be decided that it would be too time-consuming, and perhaps costly, to try to include each of these in the sample. In such circumstances a random selection, either simple or systematic, of the members from each cluster to be included in the sample may be employed. For a number of examples of how cluster sampling is used in practice see the studies by Draper et al. (2011), Kastenholz et al. (2013), Obonyo et al. (2013) and Rittichainuwat (2013).

The random selection of clusters effectively makes this form of sampling probability-based, but the nature of cluster sampling is likely to generate a sample that is inherently less representative than one selected using the stratified random procedure. More recently, multistage cluster sampling has been advocated as a way to minimise such an eventuality. This approach is essentially a repeated form of cluster sampling within which, at successive stages, sub-groups within each cluster are selected as further samples. This is akin to an 'ever-decreasing circles' approach to sampling as the sample focus moves to ever smaller sub-groups within the clusters.

8.4 Qualitative Data Sampling

Sampling in a qualitative study is less concerned with sample size and the external validity of the data collected. In general, quantitative studies are not designed to collect data that have the primary purpose of being generalised from the sample to a wider population. The aim of most qualitative studies is not to use the data collected from a sample to predict the behaviour of the wider population; qualitative studies are more concerned with a specific context, which is studied in-depth by collecting information from a relatively small sample of respondents, who may, or may not, be representative of a wider population. It is the internal (contextual) validity and meaningfulness within this context that is the overwhelming focus whereas, in a quantitative study the emphasis is placed upon the external validity and reliability of the data that enables it to be generalised back to the wider population. In this sense the justification for a qualitative sample is not that it has been selected using a predetermined, and previously validated, procedure such as random sampling, but that it is appropriate and relevant to the purpose of the study. So, sampling strategies, decisions and procedures in qualitative research are often less 'prescribed' than those associated with quantitative studies. They tend to be emergent rather than predetermined and, consequently, have more flexibility. This is illustrated by the use of 'snowball' or 'chain' sampling (see Section 8.4.3).

Nevertheless, this still leaves the question of how large should the qualitative sample be. If there is little point in trying to quantify this, as we have established, then how do we know when the sample is sufficiently large to stop? The answer to this is that we continue until we reach 'saturation'. But what does this mean in reality? Basically it means that we continue to develop and increase the size of the sample until we get to a point where there is no good reason to continue. But how do we know when we have got to this point? This is not always a clear black-and-white point but when it becomes clear that increasing the sample size further is unlikely to yield additional new and relevant data, when it already embodies sufficient and appropriate coverage and variation, and when it has allowed the theoretical relationships to be sufficiently developed and explained, a justifiable argument may be advanced to claim that taking this process further is not required or sensible.

Sampling designs and strategies to collect qualitative data are known as non-probability-based sampling, although they can also be used to collect quantitative data where statistical extrapolation (generalisation) is not a primary concern. It may be that your research aim and objectives do not require generalisation from sample estimates to the population these are from, but perhaps an in-depth case study relating to the issues under investigation. Similarly, if your study is being pursued via an inductive approach, then it is highly likely you will not be able to identify a population as such and sensibly apply a probability-based approach to selecting a sample. Indeed, if you are working within the confines of a relatively small and limited empirical situation, then it is probable that the people within it will not be equally valuable to you in terms of collecting the data required. For example, there may be just a few people who hold the information you require in general and there may be only single individuals who hold specific types of information (see Key Concept Box – Key Informants).

Key Concept	Key Informants

In qualitative, or indeed mixed-method, research it is frequently recognised that not all potential respondents are equal. Some are likely to be more knowledgeable, experienced and/or be in positions that enable them to have insights that others do not. Such people may be referred to as 'Key Informants' and are likely to be primary data collection targets for the qualitative researcher.

Although, by definition, these people are likely to be limited numerically, there may be situations where a relatively high number of these could be identified. In such circumstances it may be necessary to select a sample of these rather than try to collect data from all of them. Of course, this raises the question of how this sample should be determined. One way of addressing this issue can be to select them at random to avoid potential criticisms of bias. Hence, although the overall sampling strategy is non-random, certain components of this might be selected by using random procedures.

Often in such situations you may be feeling your way into the issues as you go along and so the sampling strategy and selection of subjects proceeds as you gain more knowledge and understanding of them. Such an approach is frequently known as 'grounded theory' because the evolution of the empirical data collection strategies and techniques and the development of theoretical understanding take place in conjunction with each other. In short, as data are collected, this helps to generate theory grounded in the empirical reality and, in turn, the emerging theory helps to inform the data collection process as it begins to indicate what information would be required, and from whom, to develop the theory further (see Section 8.4.5 Theoretical Sampling).

8.4.1   Convenience sampling

This is the simplest form of non-probability-based sampling. It is, as the name implies, a way of selecting a sample that is convenient – that is, one available at the time and place of your choice. This may be as straightforward as using your student peers as a sample because they are conveniently available to collect the data from. Alternatively, it might constitute stopping people in the street and asking for their cooperation or approaching visitors at a tourist destination or attraction and asking them if they would complete a questionnaire or be interviewed.

Given that your ability to determine or control the selection of the sample is extremely limited under these circumstances, as it is essentially dependent on people's goodwill, the likelihood of the sample being representative of the population is extremely low, so you should be very circumspect about trying to make generalisations based on such a 'self-selecting' sample. Though the data you collect via this form of sampling may be valid, the nature of the sample makes it unreliable for generalisation purposes. Despite this, many hospitality and tourism organisations use a 'self-selecting' procedure to obtain feedback information from their customers by, for example, leaving questionnaires in guest bedrooms, on restaurant tables and so on. They then, erroneously, extrapolate the results from these to make claims about the percentage of their customers who are happy or satisfied. This alone would be suspect enough, but they then also may use this information to make business decisions! Examples are provided by Gu and Siu (2009), Ladhari (2012) and Prayag and Ryan (2012).

8.4.2 Purposive, judgemental or criterion sampling

These procedures can be used to select sample subjects on the basis of some important characteristic(s) they possess. For example, as referred to earlier, a person may be regarded as a 'key informant' because of the position they hold. Alternatively, particular types of operation, destination or event may be regarded as 'key' because they possess the relevant characteristics. What is regarded as 'key' may vary from situation to situation. It may be that an extreme or atypical case is desired, such as studying the brand or market leader to help understand why other competitors are less successful. On the other hand, selecting a typical case may be viewed as a way to generate a more representative view. Cases may also be chosen on the basis that they are regarded as one likely to confirm or disconfirm the theory and hypotheses being tested. It could also be that those individuals or organisations to be included in the sample need to meet a certain criterion or a wider range of criteria. For example, it might be deemed necessary to select only those employees who have direct and substantial contact with customers, to select only types of tourist destination that meet certain criteria, or hotels that meet a minimum size criterion.

So, essentially, a judgement is made for justifiable reasons to purposely choose and include certain individuals, organisations, destinations, events etc. in the sample. The key phrase here is 'for justifiable reasons', as you need to be able to convince the reader/s of your study that they can have confidence in the reasoning behind your sample selection and that, in turn, this is more likely than not to produce valid results. In these respects, this form of sampling is essentially a purposeful strategy. Sample elements are chosen for a justifiable reason not simply because they are readily available, i.e. convenience sampling. For applications of this approach see Khodr (2012), Kwok and Yu (2012) and Milman (2011).

8.4.3 Snowball and expert-choice sampling

In some situations, who should be included in the sample as key informants is quite obvious from the outset, but in others this may not be the case. Where it is not, and assistance is required to identify potentially valuable sample subjects, it is possible to employ either the 'snowball' or 'expert choice' approaches. These are essentially referral mechanisms whereby, in the former, initial sample subjects are asked to suggest or recommend others who could provide the information required and, in the latter, experts are asked to recommend potential subjects who have the desired characteristics. Both these approaches can be helpful, but they have the disadvantage that sample selection can become rather haphazard and dependent on the subjective opinions of the people making the recommendations. See Kim et al. (2009) for an example of the use of this type of sampling.

8.4.4 Quota sampling

This is a quasi-representative sampling strategy. Although the sample subjects are not selected randomly, so the sample is less representative than probability-based strategies, it is closer to these strategies than other forms of non-probability-based sampling. Proportionate quotas for subjects to be included in the sample are devised so that the proportions are the same in the sample as they are in the population. Thus, if the population were comprised of 50 per cent males and females, then the sample would need to include equal quotas of the two genders. Or, in the case of organisations, the sample should include the same proportions of larger and smaller companies, however defined, that exist in the population as a whole. This makes selection relatively easy, but has the disadvantage that the influence of the selector or researcher over exactly which people or companies are selected can introduce bias. Examples using this approach can be found in the studies by Chen et al. (2012), Fesenmaier et al. (2011) and Pena et al. (2013).

Although quota sampling is a form of stratified sampling, the sample selection is not made randomly, so it cannot be as representative. That said, it is a quicker and cheaper form of sampling, within which control over the sample is quite high, and it has a reasonable degree of representativeness. The downside is that it can be a difficult strategy to employ where the characteristics that are used to determine the quotas or proportions are numerous. For example, to sample proportionate numbers on the basis of gender, three occupation types and three age ranges (2 x 3 x 3) would create 18 categories of subjects to select. If a category such as a previous or new guest or visitor were added, then the number of categories would double to 36!

8.4.5 Theoretical sampling

This is a very different sampling strategy and one that is often necessary to use in inductive investigations. Because inductive investigation is designed to develop or create new theory it should be clear that there is no existing theory to inform the researcher about what the nature of the sample should be. Of course, there may be an element of initial judgemental sampling to begin with because potentially valuable informants are unlikely to be totally unknown at the outset. For an example of the use of theoretical sampling in practice see the Park and Allen (2013) study that uses a comparative case study design with the cases selected using this strategy.

That said, it is equally true that the scope, scale and nature of the eventual sample will not be fully known because the surfacing of concepts and the building of consequent theoretical insights proceeds hand-in-hand with the collection of the empirical data. In this sense, where the sampling process goes as the work progresses is informed by the iterative process of data collection, analysis and the emergent theory. In short, as the researcher learns more about the phenomenon this then informs and leads him or her to seek out and include further sampling units that have the potential to assist the further development of the theory.

8.5 N = 1 Investigations

These often tend to have a combination of more positivistic, experimental, research designs using either quantitative or qualitative methods. The sample size is 1 and the idea is usually to assess the effect/s of doing something to a person or a situation. In this sense it is analogous to the presence, or application, of the 'treatment' within a controlled experimental environment to answer the questions of what happens when the treatment is present and what happens when it is not? Or alternatively, what are the outcomes when it exists and when it does not? For example, what are the levels of alcohol sales in the bar during 'happy hour' and outside of this time? Or, again alternatively, if we have a 'happy hour' with reduced prices will this lead to higher alcohol sales? This is an example of the use of a quantitative method where the respective sales volumes/values can be directly compared.

This approach using qualitative methods may be employed to explore reactions, perceptions, feelings, emotions etc. For example, the Human Resources Manager reads some research that suggests providing more natural lighting in an office environment makes employees feel happier and increases team interactions. So, she decides to give this a try by changing the lighting system in one office. The question then is: how will she know if this has worked in the way it was predicted to? While there may be some 'objective' data available on the office's work output before and after the change it is likely that most of the possible effects of the change are likely to be difficult to quantify in any systematic way. Therefore, talking to, or interviewing, the office staff to ask them about how they were affected, or not, by the change is likely to be the type of qualitative approach used in this situation.

N = 1 investigations may also be used by organisations seeking to test or trial new products, brands, operating procedures or systems. Although many such 'trials' often use more than one relevant site or location the use of a single site may precede this to limit potential adverse consequences if the issue in questions fails to deliver the expected benefits. Working on the basis of 'if it works in the original test site then we can proceed to see if it will work in others' may be a sensible strategy. Not only will the original trial indicate whether modifications need to be made before this is extended to other sites, it will also provide the basis for this 'experiment' to be repeated under different market/operating conditions.

Chapter Summary

Samples are necessary where populations are large, exhibit heterogeneity and/or they are geographically dispersed.

To be able to make reliable generalisations from the sample data back to the population as a whole the characteristics and proportions within the sample must be sufficiently representative of those in the population.

The size of sample that needs to be selected depends on the degree of variability or homogeneity in the population and its size. Where there is quite a bit of variety, the sample needs to be large to reflect and cope with this variability.

The size of sample selected and, perhaps more importantly, that realised, will have implications for the type of data analysis techniques that can be used to analyse the sample data.

Sampling in quantitative studies is probability-based and random in nature. It uses established statistical formulae and techniques to address the key sampling questions.

Sampling in qualitative studies is not based on statistical probability theory and is more flexible and emergent in nature. This does not mean that the data collected will be less valid – it may even have greater validity – but it does limit the extent to which it is possible to generalise from the results.

References

Brotherton, B. (2004) 'Critical success factors in UK budget hotel operations', *International Journal of Operations & Production Management*, 24 (9): 944–69.

Chen, C.C., Lin, Y.H. and Petrick, J.F. (2012) 'Social biases of destination perceptions', *Journal of Travel Research*, 52 (2): 240–52.

Dillman, D.A., Smyth, J.D. and Christian, L.M. (2009) *Internet, Mail and Mixed-Mode Surveys – The Tailored Method*, 3rd edition. Hoboken, NJ: John Wiley and Sons.

Draper, J., Woosnam, K.M. and Norman, W.C. (2011) 'Tourism use history: exploring a new framework for understanding residents' attitudes toward tourism', *Journal of Travel Research*, 50 (1): 64–77.

Fesenmaier, D.R., Xiang, Z., Pan, B. and Law, R. (2011) 'A framework of search engine use for travel planning', *Journal of Travel Research*, 50 (6): 587–601.

Gallardo, E., Sanchez-Canizares, S.M., Lopez-Guzman, T. and Jesus, M.M.N. (2010) 'Employee satisfaction in the Iberian hotel industry: the case of Andalusia (Spain) and the Algarve (Portugal)', *International Journal of Contemporary Hospitality Management*, 22 (3): 321–34.

Gu, Z. and Siu, R.C.S. (2009) 'Drivers of job satisfaction as related to work performance in Macao casino hotels: an investigation based on employee survey', *International Journal of Contemporary Hospitality Management*, 21 (5): 561–78.

Han, H., Back, K.J. and Kim, Y.H. (2011) 'A multidimensional scale of switching barriers in the full-service restaurant industry', *Cornell Hospitality Quarterly*, 52 (1): 54–63.

Hemmington, N. (1999) 'Sampling', in B. Brotherton (ed.), *The Handbook of Contemporary Hospitality Management Research*. Chichester: John Wiley & Sons. pp. 245–62.

Kastenholz, E., Eusebio, C. and Carneiro, M.J. (2013) 'Studying factors influencing repeat visitation of cultural tourists', *Journal of Vacation Marketing*, 19 (4): 343–58.

Khodr, H. (2012) 'Exploring the driving factors behind the event strategy in Qatar: a case study of the 15th Asian Games', *International Journal of Event and Festival Management*, 3 (1): 81–100.

Kim, Y.G., Eves, A. and Scarles, C. (2009) 'Building a model of local food consumption on trips and holidays: a grounded theory approach', *International Journal of Hospitality Management*, 28 (3): 423–31.

Kwok, L. and Yu, B. (2012) 'Spreading social media messages on Facebook: an analysis of restaurant business-to-consumer communications', *Cornell Hospitality Quarterly*, 54 (1): 84–94.

Ladhari, R. (2012) 'The lodging quality index: an independent assessment of validity and dimensions', *International Journal of Contemporary Hospitality Management*, 24 (4): 628–52.

Michel, J.W., Kavanagh, M.J. and Tracey, J.B. (2012) 'Got support? The impact of supportive work practices on the perceptions, motivation, and behavior of customer-contact employees', *Cornell Hospitality Quarterly*, 54 (2): 161–73.

Milman, A. (2011) 'The symbolic role of postcards in representing a destination image: the case of Alanya, Turkey', *International Journal of Hospitality & Tourism Administration*, 12 (2): 144–73.

Obonyo, G.O., Ayieko, M.A. and Kambona, O.O. (2013) 'An importance-performance analysis of food service attributes in gastro-tourism development in Western Tourist Circuit, Kenya', *Tourism and Hospitality Research*, 12 (4): 188–200.

Ottenbacher, M.C. and Harrington, R.J. (2010) 'Strategies for achieving success for innovative versus incremental new services', *Journal of Services Marketing*, 24 (1): 3–15.

Pantelidis, I.S. (2010) 'Electronic meal experience: a content analysis of online restaurant comments', *Cornell Hospitality Quarterly*, 51 (4): 483–91.

Park, S-Y. and Allen, J.P. (2013) 'Responding to online reviews: problem solving and engagement in hotels', *Cornell Hospitality Quarterly*, 54 (1): 64–73.

Pena, A.I.P., Jamilena, D.M.F. and Molina, M.A.R. (2013) 'Antecedents of loyalty toward rural hospitality enterprises: the moderating effect of the customer's previous experience', *International Journal of Hospitality Management*, 34: 127–37.

Pike, S. and Mason, R. (2011) 'Destination competitiveness through the lens of brand positioning: the case of Australia's Sunshine Coast', *Current Issues in Tourism*, 14 (2): 169–82.

Prayag, G. and Ryan, C. (2012) 'Visitor interactions with hotel employees: the role of nationality', *International Journal of Culture, Tourism and Hospitality Research*, 6 (2): 173–85.

Rittichainuwat, B.N. (2013) 'Tourists' perceived risks toward overt safety measures', *Journal of Hospitality & Tourism Research*, 37 (2): 199–216.

Victorino, L. and Bolinger, A.R. (2012) 'Scripting employees: an exploratory analysis of customer perceptions', *Cornell Hospitality Quarterly*, 53 (3): 196–206.

9

ANALYSING QUANTITATIVE DATA

Chapter Content and Issues

Tidying up your raw data.
Setting up SPSS and entering the data.
Getting a feel for your data using descriptive statistics –
frequencies, distributions, measures of dispersion and
central tendency.
Establishing the reliability of your measurement scales.
Analysing associations and differences between two variables –
cross-tabulation, correlation, regression and statistical
significance.
Inferential statistics and hypothesis testing – parametric and
non-parametric tests.
Data reduction techniques – developing a more parsimonious
solution using principal components (factor) analysis.

9.1   Introduction

Having progressed through the prior stages of the research process, you now have your reward in the form of the quantitative data from your completed questionnaires and, hopefully, this is of sufficient quantity and quality for you to begin analysing what it is telling you. However, after the initial euphoria you may have felt as you received all this data and knowing that your earlier design and implementation decisions have now been validated, you may be asking yourself what you can do with all this. Obtaining the data is one thing, but now you have to analyse and interpret it, and that involves statistics!!

However, fear not, you do not need to have a detailed understanding of the mathematical and statistical formulae that underlie the type of quantitative data analysis you may wish to do. Of course, such an understanding is useful, but, what is more important in this context is a knowledge of the types of statistical techniques and procedures that you can use to conduct this analysis, what these can be used for and how to set these up and interpret the results. It is the purpose of this chapter to explain, in straightforward language, all these aspects of quantitative data analysis so that you can utilise software such as SPSS to do all the hard work of calculating the results for you and be confident in interpreting and using the results.

Although, of course, there are other software packages that can be used for quantitative data analysis, including Microsoft Excel, SPSS is perhaps the one most commonly subscribed to by higher education institutions and is therefore the one most likely to be available to you to help you undertake this type of analysis. In addition to the hints, tips, advice and guidance contained within this chapter there are also valuable support resources available via both the Video and Web Link sections of the Companion Website (study.sagepub.com/brotherton) covering the use of SPSS specifically and also on more general aspects of statistical analysis.

9.2 General Issues

When all the data are available for processing and analysis, the first task is to tidy, clean up or edit the raw data. This is necessary because all the questions on a questionnaire may not have been answered, so there will be missing responses, and/or perhaps respondents have recorded their responses to some questions in an unclear or inappropriate manner. Where there are missing responses, because not all the respondents have chosen to answer all the questions, there are a number of options available. These may be simply ignored, if you are prepared to accept a lower response rate to the question(s) concerned. If the number of non-responses is low, this is probably the easiest way to deal with them. Alternatively, where there is a higher non-response rate, you may wish to enter a 'proxy' response. This could be based on the mid-point value in the case of an interval scale or the mean value of all the responses to the question. In cases where the recording of the response is unclear or not in the form asked for, then you have to make a judgement as to whether it is possible to edit these responses to make the response clear and/or appropriate or to ignore them if it is not, effectively treating them as non-responses.

9.2.1 Coding the data

If the questionnaire has not been pre-coded, then you will need to code the questions, both in terms of the variables they address and the values of the responses to them that are to be entered into the data analysis software. This is a relatively simple procedure because all you are trying to do here is to ensure that each question or variable is differentiated from the others and that the numbers to be entered relating to the response options are logical and mutually exclusive. For example, in the case of a question asking for a respondent's gender, where the response will be either male or female, it would be sensible to give the variable a title of 'Gender' and code the two responses as male = 1 and female = 2.

In general, it is not a good idea to use zero as a code number because, if you wish to calculate average values at a later date, these will be distorted, for obvious reasons, if zeros are included in such a calculation. If the responses to a question are organised using an interval scale, perhaps from 1 to 5, then the coding is quite simple as the numbers 1 to 5 can be used for the five response descriptors employed in the question.

If a question has used an ordinal scale, for respondents to rank items using the criterion given in the question it may be necessary to regard each of the items as a separate variable in order to record the rankings given to them by all the respondents. For example, a question asking respondents to indicate the most to least important influences on their degree of satisfaction with a visit to a restaurant might include items such as the portion size, speed of service, ambience, cost of the meal and friendliness of the staff. Each of these could be ranked as 1, 2, 3, 4, or 5. By treating each one as a separate variable, any of these ranking numbers can be recorded against each one for later analysis. Where a ratio scale has been used, this will have generated ungrouped, or raw, data that, at least theoretically, could range from zero to infinity. Probably the best way to deal with this type of data is to simply enter it in its raw form, then, following an initial evaluation of its distribution and range of the data, to order or recode it on the basis of sensible groupings. The SPSS data analysis software procedure for recoding data using new variables is shown in the Technique Tip box – Using SPSS to Recode Data.

Technique Tip

Using SPSS to Recode Data

[1] Go to the Transform menu, select 'Recode', then select 'Into Different Variables' (see the note below) to open this dialogue box.

[2] Select the variable you wish to recode from the list and move it into the 'Numeric Variable > Output Variable' box. Then type the name for the new variable into the 'Output Variable/Name' box. Click on 'Change' and it will be inserted in the 'Numeric Variable > Output Variable' box.

[3] Now you need to tell SPSS how to change the values of the original variable to the new one. To do this, click on the 'Old and New Values' button to open this dialogue box. There you have options to change single values or ranges of values from the original to the new variable (see the example below). Whichever option you choose, you need to enter the new value in the 'New Value' box and then click on the 'Add' button to add it to the new values list in the adjacent window.

[4] When you have entered all the old for new values, click on the 'Continue' button to return to the main dialogue box, and then click on 'OK'. A new variable with the name you have given it will then appear in the datasheet in the Data View window.

Note: It is possible to recode a variable without creating a new variable by using the 'Into Same Variable' option *but* this will mean that you will lose your original data, as it will be changed into the new format.

Example: If you have a range of raw, or ungrouped, data values and wish to recode them into categories, then you will need to specify the ranges to be included in each new category. So, you might inform SPSS that the old values up to 20 should be the first category by checking the 'Range (Lowest Through)' option and entering 20 in that box. This will place all the values up to and including 20 into the first new category you specify. For the highest category, you follow essentially the same procedure, but use the 'Range (Through Highest)' option, entering the lowest value of this category. So, if you want this category to be from 70 upwards, enter '70' in the box. For intermediate categories between the lowest and highest, you need to use the 'Range (Through)' boxes to enter the lowest and highest values for the category.

9.2.2   Setting up SPSS for data entry

Once all the data has been coded, the next task is to set up the data analysis package so that it can be entered. Again, the most commonly used package, widely available in most institutions, is SPSS. The first stage in using SPSS is to set up, or configure, the 'data sheet'. The SPSS data sheet is similar to an Excel spreadsheet, in that it is a blank matrix of columns and rows into which the data are entered. However, before this is done, the columns, which constitute the variables, have to be named or numbered according to the codes they have been given on the questionnaire. You can simply give each column a variable number (Var1, Var2, Var3 and so on) or else a more descriptive name (Gender, Age, Occupation and so on, for example). Whichever option is chosen will make no difference to later analyses of the data, but it may have implications for ease of use. By this I mean that using descriptors rather than numbers for the variables is likely to make life easier later when analysis output is produced because the output will bear the variable name. Thus, something headed 'Gender' will be easier to recognise than something headed 'Var1'.

The SPSS data sheet, from versions 10.5 onwards, has two views that can be selected from the opening screen. The opening view will be the Data View, as this is the data sheet that the data are entered into. To name or configure the variables (each column in the data sheet), you need to select the Variable View by clicking on the tab at the bottom of the screen. This screen provides various options for you not only to name each variable but also specify the type of data to be entered, descriptors relating to the code numbers to be entered, how missing responses should be treated and so on. In the Variable View, each row is a separate variable and the columns contain the options for formatting the data to be entered for each one. The Technique Tip box – Using SPSS to Format Variables for Data Entry – details what these options are.

Technique Tip

Using SPSS to Format Variables for Data Entry

[1] In the first column – 'Name' – type the name you wish to give the variable. This is limited to eight characters or fewer, but you will have the option later to provide a longer name or description for the variable (see 3 below).

[2] In the second column – 'Type' – you need to specify whether the type of data is of a numeric or string form – that is, numbers or words. The default for this is numeric. To change it to a particular type of numeric value, a string format or specify the format of the numeric value, click on the button to the right of the word 'Numeric'. This opens the 'Variable Type' box, which contains these options. Assuming that you do not wish to specify a particular type, all you may wish to change are the default numbers of 8 and 2 in the 'Width' and 'Decimal Places' boxes. If you have data with more than eight digits, then you may wish to adjust this value. Similarly, if all your data are comprised of whole numbers, then you might want to set the 'Decimal Places' number to zero. If you make changes to any of the default values, then these will appear in the third ('Width') and fourth ('Decimal Places') columns once you have clicked on 'OK' and returned to the Variable View window.

[3] In the fifth column – 'Label' – you have the opportunity to enter a longer description for each variable, which can be useful when you produce some output. For example, the variable name might be 'Occ', for 'occupation'. Here, the complete word can be entered as a fuller description to facilitate identification of the variable when output statistics are produced. To do this, simply click on the cell and type in the longer name.

[4] The sixth column – 'Values' – gives you the opportunity to enter value labels, or descriptors, for the categories or scale intervals in your data. For example, in the case of the variable 'Gender' there will be categorical values for males and females. You may have decided to code these as 1 for males and 2 for females, but, unless you tell SPSS what the 1s and 2s mean, it will not know. Similarly, in the case of a scale, say a five-point Likert scale, you will be entering numbers between 1 and 5, but, again, SPSS will not know what these relate to unless it is told. Clicking on the right-hand side of the 'Values' cell will open the 'Value Label' box. In it you can enter the value and its corresponding label. So, from the example above, if you type '1' in the 'Value' box and then 'Male' in the 'Value Label' box, then click on 'Add', this will appear in the 'Summary' box below as '1 = Male'. You then simply repeat this procedure for the remaining items until you have labelled them all, then click on 'OK' to return to the Variable View window. There you will see that these values are displayed in the relevant 'Values' cell.

[5] The seventh column – 'Missing' – enables you to specify how SPSS should deal with any missing values in the data. Unless you wish to provide a specific instruction to deal with missing values in a particular way, this can be ignored.

[6] The eighth column – 'Columns' – is used to set the width of the columns in the data sheet. The default for this is eight characters wide and this is usually sufficient. So, unless you have long numeric or string data, it is best to leave this as it is.

[7] The ninth column – 'Align' – sets the alignment of the data in the cells of the data sheet. The default setting is 'Right' and, once again, there is little to be gained by changing this, unless you have particular reasons for doing so.

[8] The final column – 'Measure' – enables you to specify the type of data relating to the variable. The default setting for this is 'Scale', which is for interval or ratio data, but this can be changed to 'Nominal' or 'Ordinal' if your data for the variable are one of these types. To make the change, simply click on the right-hand side of the cell and select the appropriate option.

Shortcuts: Once you have set up all the attributes for a variable, it is possible to save time and effort in setting up others that have either all or some of the attributes. If other variables have all the same attributes except the name and label, then you can copy and paste them to save entering all the same information again for each one.

Where you want to copy and paste all the variable's attributes, you can do this as follows. In the Variable View, click on the row number of the variable you wish to copy the attributes from. This should highlight the whole row. Then press 'Control-C' to copy the information and click on the empty row you want to use for the new variable. Now press 'Control-V' to paste the information in. All you will have to change is the variable name and its label.

Where you only want to copy and paste the attributes from one or two cells, then you can simply select the cell(s) concerned, copy their contents, select the cell(s) you want to put this information into and paste it in.

When all the variables and their formats have been specified, a return to the Data View will show that each column now has a distinctive number or descriptor relating to the variable concerned. The detail relating to the formatting of the data entries for each will not be shown, but the software will have been informed what this is from the options chosen in the Variable View.

9.2.3 Entering data into SPSS

You are now ready to start entering your data on the basis that each column is a variable and each row is a case – effectively one completed questionnaire. Therefore, the first row will have all the responses recorded from the first completed questionnaire, the second row those from the second questionnaire and so on. Either before or as you enter the data from each completed questionnaire it is a good idea to simply number each questionnaire so that, at a later date, if you need to identify which data row has been entered from which questionnaire, this is easy to do. You may need to do this if, later, you find that errors have been made typing in the data. If you have previously decided to ignore any missing responses, then you simply do not enter anything in the cells relating to these on the data sheet as SPSS will recognise empty cells as missing values.

9.2.4   Checking the data

With all the data entered, the next task is to check that these have been entered correctly and the data sheet does not contain errors as a result of typing mistakes. This can be done by carefully reviewing the data sheet entries on screen or by printing out the sheet and proofreading it. Either of these actions should help you to identify rogue entries and correct them before any analysis is undertaken. When you are sure that the data are 'clean' – correct – then you are ready to begin using the software to analyse these.

9.2.5   Selecting cases and/or variables

In the following sections of this chapter we will consider various options for producing basic, descriptive, bivariate (associations or differences between two variables), inferential and data reduction statistics from your data, but first, it may be helpful for you to be aware of the 'Split Files' and 'Select Cases' options available within SPSS. When you are using any of the statistical techniques that follow, you may wish to set these up to deal with particular cases meeting certain conditions and/or for the calculation to be repeated for separate categories or groups relating to a particular variable.

For example, you may wish to test to see if the responses given by males and females are both statistically significant or whether one set is and another is not. Similarly, you may wish to pick out certain cases from your total data set to perform a particular analysis on those that meet certain conditions, e.g., you may wish to analyse all the coastal resort destinations but not the other types of destination. To do the former, you would need to use the split file option, and for the latter, the select cases option. The SPSS procedures for using these options are outlined in the Technique Tip box – Using SPSS to Split Files or Select Cases.

Technique Tip	**Using SPSS to Split Files or Select Cases**

Splitting files

Splitting files enables you to repeat an analysis for all the categories or groups within a variable.

[1] In the Data View go to the Data menu and select the 'Split File' option.

[2] In the 'Split File' dialogue box, your list of variables will be displayed in the left-hand window. Select which one(s) you wish to use to split the file and move these to the window headed 'Groups Based On'.

[3] From the three options above this box, if you click on 'Compare Groups' this will produce the groups' results together, or, if you click on 'Organise Output by Groups', the results for each group will be presented separately and successively.

[4] Click on 'OK' to return to the Data View window.

Selecting cases

Where you wish to select particular values for your variable or categories rather than repeating the same analysis for all the variable's categories, then this option will enable you to do exactly that.

[1] Go to the Data menu and click on the 'Select Cases' option.

[2] In the 'Select Cases' dialogue box, there are various options to specify the basis on which the cases should be selected, but perhaps the most commonly used one is the 'If' option. Selecting this opens the 'If' dialogue box for you to specify the conditions to be used to select the cases.

[3] To inform SPSS which variable the cases are to be selected from, highlight this in the left-hand window and press the button to move it into the window at the top of the 'If' dialogue box. Now you have to specify the condition or value of the variable to be used to select the cases. This can be done using the keypad or 'Functions' options below the window. For example, if you only want the analysis to apply to the category of male respondents and this has previously been coded as 1, from the variable 'Gender', then you need to set the window as 'gender = 1'. It is also possible to set the condition to include more than one category for selecting the cases using the 'And' or 'Or' operators.

[4] Once the condition has been set, click on 'Continue' to return to the 'Select Cases' dialogue box, then click 'OK' to return to the Data View window.

Note: When you return from the 'Split File' or 'Select Cases' boxes, you will see that changes have occurred to the organisation of your data in the data sheet and, in the bar at the bottom of the screen, either the words 'Split File on' or 'Filter on' will be displayed, respectively. These changes are not permanent, but once you have completed the analysis for the split file or selected cases you need to turn off the function, otherwise any further analyses will only be conducted on this basis.

To turn off the split file and return the data sheet to a normal format, go to the Data menu, select 'Split File', click on the first option – 'Analyse all cases, do not create groups' – and click on 'OK'. To turn off select cases, go to the Data menu, choose 'Select Cases', click on the 'All cases' option, then Click on 'OK'. You can tell when these options are switched on or off by looking at the display in the status bar at the bottom of the Data View window.

9.3 Descriptive Statistics

The first stage in quantitative data analysis is to produce some relatively simple output to get an initial feel for the data. This is likely to address questions such as does the data provide the type of picture expected, does it contain possible relationships that weren't expected, does it indicate a fairly normal distribution or is it skewed in a particular direction, what does it tell me about the characteristics of the sample?

9.3.1 Frequency distributions

So, how do you set about doing this? Essentially, you need to produce some statistics or output that summarises or describes the characteristics of your data. Perhaps the easiest way to achieve this is to use SPSS to produce some frequency distributions for your data and, if appropriate, some measures of central tendency and dispersion. The procedure you need to follow to do this is contained in the Technique Tip box – Using SPSS to Obtain Frequency Distributions/Tables.

Technique Tip	**Using SPSS to Obtain Frequency Distributions/Tables**

[1] Go to the Analyse menu, select 'Descriptive Statistics', then 'Frequencies'.

[2] In the 'Frequencies' dialogue box, select the name(s) or number(s) you have given to the variable(s) you wish to see the frequencies for and press the arrow key to place these in the 'Variables' window.

[3] If you then click on 'OK', without changing the other options available, SPSS will do the calculations and display these as tables in an 'Output' window that you can save as a separate file using the 'Save As' command.

Simply by looking at the relative proportions, or distribution, of the values across any nominal categories in a frequency table, you will get a feel for whether they are even or uneven and, in the case of tables containing interval or ratio data, whether they are fairly evenly dispersed or skewed towards one extreme or the other. An alternative way to do this is to produce some charts (see Technique Tip box – Using SPSS to Produce Charts and Graphs).

Technique Tip	**Using SPSS to Produce Charts and Graphs**

[1] In SPSS you can do this quite easily by going to the Graphs menu and selecting the type of chart you wish to produce. There you will be given the options to produce bar or pie charts, histograms, line graphs and other types of chart.

[2] Selecting one of these will open the appropriate dialogue box for you to specify the variable to be charted or graphed and the format for this.

[3] You can also produce bar and pie charts and histograms at the same time as you request frequencies from within the 'Frequencies' dialogue box. Having selected the variable(s) you wish to chart, click on the 'Charts' button, select the desired type in the options box this opens, click on 'Continue' to return to the 'Frequencies' box and click on 'OK' to activate the process.

9.3.2 Measures of central tendency

However, as useful as frequency distributions and charts and graphs may be for getting an idea as to what your data are indicating, there is often value in trying to summarise the key characteristics in a more parsimonious manner. Working out the 'average' value in the data and providing an indication of its variability or spread and the nature of its distribution, is often helpful. This requires you to consider the measures of location, or the central tendency, dispersion and skewness.

There are three commonly used measures of central tendency: the mode, median and mean. The modal value is simply the one that occurs most frequently in a data set and is the simplest measure of central tendency. This can be used for all types of data, from nominal to ratio, but it is rarely used for data above nominal level. It can be misleading if the modal value is extreme and it is possible to have more than one modal value in a set of data – that is, when the same frequency is evident for different values. By contrast, the median is not influenced by extreme values and there can be only one median value. This is because the median is the middle value within a set of data. The median can be used for ordinal data upwards.

The third measure of central tendency is known as the mean. Most people would generally refer to this as the average. The mean is calculated by taking the sum of the values in the data set and then dividing this by the number of values in the set. The mean can only be used for interval or ratio data and its advantage lies in the fact that all the data in the set are used to calculate it. However, extreme values can 'pull' the mean value towards one end of the distribution or the other, providing a somewhat distorted picture. Therefore, the amount of skew in the data set influences the mean value. If the data are very skewed, in either direction, this will tend to pull the mean value up or down. This is particularly true where there is a limited amount of data in the set, but far less true when there is a large amount. In view of this, it may be advisable, with a very skewed data set, to consider using the median value as a more appropriate measure of central tendency for the data.

9.3.3   Data range and dispersion

To obtain an indication of the variability within the data set, you can examine the range and dispersion of the data. The range is a very simple and crude statistic, it is the difference between the smallest and largest value in the data set. As the range can be distorted by a single extreme value in the set, it may provide a misleading picture of the distribution of the data.

This problem can be avoided by using the interquartile range instead of the simple range, but this cannot be used with nominal data. If you have ordinal data, however, the interquartile range can be used and it is really quite a straightforward concept. A quartile is a quarter, thus the data set is divided up into four equal parts, two each side of the middle value (the median) in the set. This means that 50 per cent of the data have values above the median and 50 per cent below it. By taking the two central quarters, the interquartile range provides an indication of the range of data falling between the second quarter and the third quarter in the set or, in other words, the 50 per cent of the data clustered immediately above and below the median. Although the interquartile range avoids the distortion caused by extreme values, it uses only half of the data in the set and this may give a misleading picture of the degree of clustering in the set.

The standard deviation statistic, for interval or ratio data, eliminates this partiality problem because it is calculated using all the values in the data set, which are then compared with the mean. However, it is possible that extreme values can distort it. That said, the standard deviation is a widely used statistic for representing a measure of dispersion within a data set. Generally, the smaller the standard deviation, the more clustered the values are around the mean and vice versa. However, you need to remember that the actual value of the standard deviation statistic is related to the value of the mean, which, in turn, is related to the range of the data set.

This may sound complicated, but it is really quite simple. Taking two hypothetical examples, if you had a data range of 5 because the question asked used a five-point scale and the mean was 3, you would not expect a large standard deviation value. If the standard deviation value for this data were to be 1, then it would mean that approximately just over two-thirds of your data would be clustered within the range of 2 to 4 – the value of one standard deviation above and below the mean of 3. On the other hand, if your data ranged between 1 and 100 and the mean was 50, you might expect the value of one standard deviation above and below this to be greater than 1. So, if the value was 10, you would say that one standard deviation above and below the mean indicated that just over two-thirds of the data would be clustered between 40 and 60. In turn, two standard deviations above or below the mean would account for around 95 per cent of all the data, three standard deviations, almost 100 per cent (actually 99.7 per cent).

Therefore, in the range of 1 to 100 used in the example above, the value of two standard deviations would be 20, as the value of one was 10, so 95 per cent of the data would lie between the values of 30 and 70. The values for the mean and standard deviation used in these examples would suggest that the distribution of these values is symmetrical or, in the jargon, approximates to a 'normal distribution', where the mean lies in the centre of the distribution with 50 per cent of the data above it and 50 per cent below it.

One way to determine whether or not the distribution is normal in shape is to examine the values for the mode, median and mean. If these are the same, it indicates that the distribution is symmetrical and normal in shape. Where the mean is higher or lower than the median, then the distribution will be skewed in a positive or negative direction and it will be asymmetrical in shape. The procedure used to obtain these measures of central tendency, dispersion and skewness in SPSS is outlined in the Technique Tip box – Using SPSS to Obtain Measures of Central Tendency, Dispersion and Skewness.

Technique Tip	**Using SPSS to Obtain Measures of Central Tendency, Dispersion and Skewness**

[1] Go to the Analyse menu, select 'Descriptive Statistics', then 'Descriptives'.

[2] In the 'Descriptives' dialogue box, you then need to place the variables you wish to have these measures calculated for into the 'Variables' box.

[3] Click on the 'Options' button, select the statistics you require, then click on 'Continue' to return to the 'Descriptives' box.

[4] Click on 'OK' and the results will then appear in an 'Output' window.

Note: The interpretation of these results should be straightforward, but if you have selected 'Skewness' and/or 'Kurtosis' to get a feel for the shape of the data distribution, these may not be so familiar.

Skewness provides an indication of how symmetrical the distribution is and kurtosis how peaked or flat it is. If the distribution is normal, both of these will have a value of zero. A positive skewness value would indicate a clustering of data to the left of the distribution, while a negative value would be the reverse of this. Kurtosis values that are positive indicate the distribution is peaked and those that are negative indicate a flatter distribution.

9.3.4   Uses of descriptive data

These types of exploratory data analysis will give you some idea about what your data can tell you and may help to indicate whether they are suitable for further statistical analysis. They can also form the basis for presenting a descriptive picture of your data where this might be required in the report or thesis. This could be useful for providing the reader with a background picture or context of the scope and scale of the situation you have been investigating that can then be used to relate other analytical results to. Also, you may wish to use some of the univariate (single variable) data relating to your respondents' characteristics to indicate the representativeness, if that is possible, of your sample. The Research in Action box – Expressing Sample Representativeness – contains a piece of text taken from one of my papers, which we also looked at in Chapter 8 (Brotherton, 2004), that indicates how this might be approached.

Research in Action	Expressing Sample Representativeness

The size of the realised sample (n = 239) was very encouraging in terms of providing a representative data set from the budget hotel sector. Not unsurprisingly, it was dominated by the two leading brands Premier Travel Inn (originally Travelinn, now Premier Inn) and Travelodge. Though this did skew the sample in favour of these brands, this nevertheless reflects the population distribution of budget hotel brands in the UK.

The sample was also dominated by budget hotels in motorway and A (trunk road) road locations, with these accounting for almost two-thirds of the respondent hotels. However, this again reflects the nature of the population distribution for budget hotel locations. Interestingly, the more recent growth locations of suburban and city centre sites also feature quite strongly, accounting for nearly a further 30 per cent of the sample.

The size distribution shows the 31–40 bedroom range to be the largest single category, followed by the over 60 bedroom group. Cumulatively these two size categories account for 74 per cent of the total. If the 41–50 category were to be added to these, this would account for some 90 per cent of the total. Once again, this is strongly representative of the budget hotel population distribution by size.

Other categorical data also indicates that the sample is very representative of the breadth of budget hotel operations, as this is comprised of a considerable range of responses in relation to average room occupancy, number of full- and part-time staff and the business mix. Given all of these characteristics it is reasonable to claim that the sample as a whole is highly representative of branded budget hotel operations in the UK.

Source: Brotherton (2004: 949–50). Reproduced with permission from Emerald Group Publishing Limited

9.3.5 Scale reliability

One other issue that you may also wish to address at this stage is the reliability, or otherwise, of the scale(s) you have used to collect the data. There are a number of different aspects to the issue of reliability, but perhaps the main one is the internal consistency of the set of scale items used – that is, whether or not they are all measuring the same construct. There are a number of ways to assess reliability, but perhaps the most common statistic is Cronbach's alpha coefficient. The Technique Tip box – Using SPSS to Calculate Split-Half Reliability – outlines the SPSS procedure to obtain this.

Essentially, the calculation lying behind this overall statistic is one of inter-item correlations in a two-dimensional matrix or, in other words, all the items in the scale are correlated with each other and an overall value (the alpha coefficient) is produced to summarise all these relationships. Given that a perfect, positive correlation between a set of items would be 1, it follows that the closer to 1 the alpha value is, the better the correlation is between all the items in the set and vice versa. It is generally accepted that the alpha value should be at least 0.7, but preferably higher. A value in the 0.8 or 0.9 range would be regarded as indicative of adequate to very satisfactory scale reliability.

Technique Tip	**Using SPSS to Calculate Split-Half Reliability**

[1] Go to the Analyse menu, select 'Scale' and then 'Reliability Analysis'.

[2] Select all the variables that are included in the set or scale and move these into the 'Items' box.

[3] Select 'Alpha' in the 'Models' section of the box.

[4] Click on the 'Statistics' button and select 'Item, Scale and Scale If Item Deleted' in the 'Descriptives For' section. Click on 'Continue' to return to the 'Reliability Analysis' box.

[5] Click on 'OK' and the results will appear in an 'Output' window.

Note: This can produce a lot of data, especially if there are many items included in the scale, but the key results to examine are as follows. First, at the end of the output, there will be a figure for the alpha value. This is the Cronbach's alpha coefficient and it indicates the internal consistency or coherence of the set of items. It is the sum of all the correlations between the items and, the closer it is to 1 (remember, a correlation coefficient of 1 indicates a perfect correlation), the greater the relatedness or consistency of the set of items.

It is generally accepted that, for the scale to be considered reliable, the alpha value should be at least 0.7, with higher values moving towards 1 indicating greater reliability. If the alpha value is less than 0.7, then you may be able to

(Continued)

(Continued)

improve it by removing items that have a low correlation with others in the set. The column headed 'Alpha if Item Deleted' will indicate what the alpha value would be if an item was deleted from the scale. If, when doing this for any of the items, it shows that the overall alpha value would be higher than 0.7 if it were to be removed, then you may wish to consider doing this. You can also examine such a column even if the alpha is 0.7 or greater to see if it could be improved by removing any of the items.

However, you need to be careful because you may find that removal of one or more items only improves the alpha value by a very small amount, which may not be a price you are prepared to pay to gain a small increase in reliability. In other words, some of the items may have already been found to be statistically significant and removing these would involve trading off some validity for greater reliability.

9.4 Bivariate Analysis

Earlier in this chapter we examined some of the issues associated with producing basic descriptive statistics for individual variables to get an initial feel for the data, but you are likely to want to ask questions concerning whether there are differences between, say, the behaviour or opinions of males and females, larger and smaller companies, public and private sector organisations and so on. Similarly, you may wish to explore if there are connections or associations between two or more of your variables – that is, to what extent the frequency of visits to an art gallery, for example, is associated with the price of admission. This leads us into what is known as bivariate (two variables) analysis.

9.4.1 Cross-tabulation

In everyday life, we might ask the question, is there a connection between people's incomes and the number of holidays they take each year? What we are really asking here is, does the level of income affect or influence the number of holidays people take? Lying behind this may be the unstated assumption that, the greater the level of income people enjoy, the more holidays they are likely to take, simply because they have the economic means to do so. In research terms, we might have expressed this as a hypothesis that postulated an association between income levels and frequency of holidays purchased in the form 'People with higher incomes will go on holiday more frequently than those with lower incomes' or, alternatively, 'There is no relationship between people's incomes and the frequency with which they go on holiday'. This type of data is likely to be nominal in nature – that is, it will be the result of a question in the questionnaire that simply asked respondents to tick a box to indicate their annual income levels and another question that asked them to tick the appropriate box to indicate how many holidays they take in a year.

To establish whether or not an association exists between income levels and the frequency with which people go on holiday using this type of data, a cross-tabulation procedure can be used. We have already hypothesised what the dependent and independent variables are in this case – the former is the frequency of holidays and the latter the level of income. If we now put the values for these two variables into the columns and rows of a table, we can begin to see if the frequency of holidays does vary with income level. However, a table with actual values across, say, five income groupings and five holiday frequency categories may be difficult to interpret. Also, because the number of responses within each of the two sets of groupings may be very unequal, viewing a table with the frequency values displayed may give a misleading picture.

To avoid this problem, it is a good idea to format the output from a cross-tabulation analysis in percentages rather than actual values. This makes interpretation easier, but the type of percentage formatting you use depends on where you have placed the dependent and independent variables. If the columns have been designated for the dependent variable and the rows for the independent variable, then the percentage values in each cell should be set for the rows and vice versa because it is the effect of the variation in the independent variable on the dependent variable that you are interested in. This will enable you to make comparisons down the table for holiday frequency categories to identify whether or not there are large differences between the rows, which are the levels of income. It is the size of the differences between these percentages that indicates the strength of any association between the two variables. The closer this gets to the maximum (100 per cent difference), the greater the association and vice versa. As a basic rule of thumb, 100 per cent difference can be regarded as a perfect association and 0 per cent difference as no, or zero, association, while something in the region of 50 per cent difference indicates a moderate association. The SPSS procedure for this is shown in the Technique Tip box – Using SPSS to Produce Cross-Tabulation Results.

Technique Tip

**Using SPSS to Produce
Cross-Tabulation Results**

[1] Go to the Analyse menu, select 'Descriptive Statistics', then 'Crosstabs' to open this dialogue box.

[2] There, you need to select the dependent and independent variables from the list of variables in the box on the left. This is done by specifying which variables are to be used for the rows and which for the columns of the table. You can choose to enter the dependent variables in either the rows or the columns, but it may be preferable to enter the independent variables in the rows and the dependent variables in the columns. This is done by simply selecting the appropriate variable from the list and pressing the relevant arrow key to place it in either the 'Rows' or 'Columns' boxes.

(Continued)

(Continued)

[3] Once you have completed this task, click on the 'Cells' button and check the 'Row' and 'Total' boxes in the 'Percentages' section to ensure that the percentages are calculated by rows – the independent variables. If you have decided to place the independent variables in the columns of the table, then, of course, you need to check the 'Columns' box.

[4] Click on 'Continue', then, when the display has returned to the 'Crosstabs' dialogue box, click on 'OK' and the results will appear in an 'Output' window.

It is also possible to use the 'Crosstabs' option in SPSS to produce more summarised statistics relating to the degree to which the covariance of the two variables is related, or correlated. These statistics are correlation coefficients and measure the strength of the statistical association between the two variables.

The phi coefficient is one such statistic used for two-by-two tables – that is, where both the independent and dependent variables have two categories each. Its value will range from zero to +1 and the interpretation of the value is the same as the percentage difference referred to earlier, so the closer it is to zero the weaker the association, and the closer it is to +1 the stronger the association.

In situations where the table is larger than two-by-two categories, then Cramer's V coefficient can be used. Once again, the value of Cramer's V will vary between zero and +1 and its interpretation is the same as that specified for the phi coefficient. Both of these correlation coefficients are suitable for nominal and/or ordinal data.

9.4.2   Scatter graphs and correlation

Where association is being explored for variables comprised of interval or ratio data, producing a scatter graph or diagram is often a useful first step in being able to visualise whether the two variables might be associated. This should indicate whether the distribution of the data points on the graph are clustered together in some way or scattered with no discernible pattern. The Technique Tip box – Using SPSS to Produce Scatter Graphs – outlines the procedure used to produce a scatter graph in SPSS.

Technique Tip

Using SPSS to Produce Scatter Graphs

[1] Go to the Graphs menu and select 'Scatter'. In the dialogue box, ensure that 'Simple' is highlighted and click on the 'Define' button.

[2] From the list of variables displayed, select the one you wish to be the independent variable and add this to the X-axis box, and then do the same for the dependent variable, adding this to the Y-axis box.

[3] If you wish to add titles and labels to the graph, you can do this using the 'Titles' button. Click on 'OK' to activate the calculation and open the output window containing the scatter graph.

If a perfect correlation exists between the two sets of data, then all the points would sit in a straight line on the graph. However, as a correlation can be positive or negative (which indicates an inverse relationship between the two variables) the slope of this line can differ accordingly. Given that the independent variable is always placed on the X (horizontal) axis of the graph and the dependent on the Y (vertical) axis, in the case of a perfectly positive relationship, the line would slope upwards from left to right at an angle of 45 degrees, indicating that a given change in the value of the independent variable would be associated with the same change in the value of the dependent variable. For example, a 10 per cent increase in the number of bed spaces available at a destination would be accompanied by a 10 per cent increase in the number of overnight stays at that destination and vice versa.

This is also known as a 'unitary' relationship, as the unit of change for both variables is the same in either direction – a 10 per cent increase/decrease in the independent variable is accompanied by a 10 per cent increase/decrease in the dependent one. Where the association is perfectly negative, the line will slope downwards from left to right, indicating an inverse relationship. For example, a 10 per cent increase in the price of airline tickets would be associated with a 10 per cent reduction in the number of airline passengers and vice versa.

However, in many cases the association will not be perfectly positive – with a correlation coefficient of +1 – or perfectly negative – with a value of –1. Indeed, where no association exists between the two, the coefficient will have a value of zero. To interpret the intermediate values, a useful rule of thumb is that a value of either +0.5 or –0.5 indicates, respectively, a moderately strong positive or negative association. Therefore, values between plus or minus 0.5 and zero indicate a weak positive or negative association, with this becoming weaker the closer the value gets to zero in each case. The same logic applies to intermediate values lying between plus or minus 0.5 and plus or minus 1, except here, as the value moves closer to these extremes, it indicates a stronger association. For example, a correlation coefficient of 0.6 would not indicate a very strong association, but one of 0.8 would. Producing correlation coefficients to assess possible association between variables in SPSS is quite straightforward; see the Technique Tip box – Using SPSS to Produce Correlation Coefficients.

Technique Tip	Using SPSS to Produce Correlation Coefficients

[1] Go to the Analyse menu, select 'Correlate' and then 'Bivariate'(for two variables).

[2] In the dialogue box, select the two variables to correlate, add these to the 'Variables' box, and then select the appropriate correlation calculation – either Pearson's or Spearman's – in the 'Correlation Coefficients' section (see the note below). Also at this point select the '2 Tail' box, unless you have good reasons to support the view that the correlation will take a specific direction, in which case you can choose the '1 Tail' option.

[3] Next, click on the 'Options' button and, in the window that opens, select 'Exclude Cases Pairwise' under 'Missing Values'. If you wish to include the means and standard deviations in the output, then you can also select those there.

[4] Click on 'Continue' and then 'OK' when you return to the previous window to produce the results in an 'Output' window.

Note: If all of your data are of the interval or ratio kind, then the preferred choice of correlation coefficient should be Pearson's product moment correlation coefficient. However, this does assume that the data for both variables are normally distributed. If they are not, or any of your data are ordinal or ranked, then choose the Spearman's rank correlation coefficient. Both methods produce the same type of output, but they may not produce the same value for the coefficient!

9.4.3   Statistical significance

The matrix produced in the output will indicate the correlation coefficient between the two variables and something known as a p value. Essentially this indicates the probability that the result (correlation coefficient) may have occurred by chance rather than being a true reflection of the association between the two variables. If the p value is small, then this indicates a small probability that the result has occurred due to chance and so it can be regarded as statistically significant. Generally, a value of 0.05 is used as the decision point for this. This indicates we can be confident that, 95 times out of 100, the same result would be obtained or, in other words, that we can state a confidence level of 95 per cent for the result. However, the accepted practice is to be a little more circumspect than this and to demand a p value of less than 0.05 before regarding the result as being statistically significant. In other words, we can say that a different result would only occur less than 5 times in 100 repeat occasions. This, in turn, gives us reasonable confidence that, on the balance of probabilities, our result can be regarded as a true one.

One thing that you need to be careful about here when examining the implications of a correlation coefficient and its p value is that the two statistics are not related – they express different things. It is possible to get a very weak correlation coefficient of, say, 0.22 with a corresponding p value of less than 0.05, which would be regarded as statistically significant. However, as the two are unrelated or, strictly speaking have a very weak level of association, the latter does not improve the former. Therefore, in this case, all you could say is that the degree of association between the two variables is very weak, with a correlation coefficient of 0.22, and that you could be 95 per cent confident that this weak association is applicable to the population from which the sample was taken.

Where only categorical data are available to investigate any possible association between two variables, the chi-square test for independence can be used to test for this. It compares the actual frequencies of cases in the categories of one categorical variable with those in another with the values that might be expected if the two sets of data were totally independent. The test calculates the probability that the data could have occurred by chance and, therefore, whether there is a statistically significant association between the variables or not – that is, whether the relevant p statistic is less than 0.05 or not. The Technique Tip box – Using SPSS to Obtain the Chi-Square Test for Independence – outlines the SPSS procedure to obtain the chi-square statistic.

Technique Tip

**Using SPSS to Obtain the
Chi-Square Test for Independence**

[1] Go to the Analyse menu, then 'Descriptive Statistics' and select 'Crosstabs'.

[2] In the 'Crosstabs' dialogue box, select and move your variables into the 'Rows' and 'Columns' boxes.

[3] Next, click on the 'Statistics' button, select 'chi-square' and then click on 'Continue' to return to the 'Crosstabs' dialogue box.

[4] Now, click on the 'Cells' button and, in the 'Counts' box, click on the 'Observed' and 'Expected' options. In the 'Percentage' section, click on 'Column, Row and Total'. Click on 'Continue' and then 'OK' after returning to the 'Crosstabs' dialogue box.

[5] The results will now appear in an 'Output' window.

If you have remained alert as you have been reading the material in this section then you will have noticed that, in the discussion on correlation, the term 'association' will have always been used to refer to any possible connection between two variables. This has been deliberate because a correlational association is not the same as a cause–effect relationship, or causation. In other words, even though we may be able to establish that there is a *statistical* association between two variables, it does not prove that a change in one is the cause of a change in the other. All we can say, with certainty, is that they co-vary and the strength of this covariant relationship is stronger or weaker. Of course, we may have made assumptions about the cause–effect nature of the identified relationship and this may have been specified further in the research hypotheses, but correlation alone does not provide proof of the existence of such a relationship and it does not tell us the size of the impact that one variable has on the other. This can be determined by means of regression analysis.

9.4.4   Regression analysis

This type of analysis is something that often seems daunting to students not well versed in statistical methods, but it is not necessary to have a detailed understanding of the underlying theory and computation required to generate a regression value and produce a result. What is more important is the interpretation of what the regression value means. In short, a regression line is one that best fits the distribution of data on a scatter graph, which is why it is often referred to as the 'line of best fit'.

As we saw earlier, it is unlikely that a scatter graph will have a distribution of data points that are perfectly correlated – that is, all on a straight line – but they may be distributed in a pattern suggesting a relationship between the two variables that can be identified by establishing the strength of the correlation coefficient. Thus, regression analysis is an extension of correlation. Where correlation analysis produces a coefficient of association (the R value), regression takes this one stage further by calculating the square of R (the R^2 value) to produce a line that best fits the distribution of data points.

Logically, the closer the data points are to lying in a straight line on a scatter graph, the more accurate the regression analysis can be, as the values it estimates to produce the line will be closer to the true values represented by the data points. If you think of this as a type of averaging, then the regression line represents an average path through the data points. Now, remember our earlier consideration of the mean and how this could be affected by extreme values. A similar issue arises here in that, if there are some of what are called residual outliers – values lying some distance away from most of the others on the graph – then the average that is calculated, the regression line, is a good indication of the true values near to this line but a poorer one of those lying much further away from it. Thus, the greater the number of outliers and the further they are away from the line, the less robust the regression value is. See the Technique Tip box – Using SPSS to Produce Simple (Two Variable) Regression Analysis – for the steps you need to take to produce a regression value.

Technique Tip

Using SPSS to Produce Simple (Two Variable) Regression Analysis

---

[1]   Go to the Analyse menu, select 'Regression' and then 'Linear'.

[2]   In the 'Linear Regression' dialogue box, select and move the independent and dependent variables into the respective boxes.

[3] Before clicking on 'OK' to produce the regression results, it is possible to request other statistics by pressing the 'Statistics' button. In the box this opens, a range of options is available, but unless you are very familiar with regression analysis, it may be advisable to select only 'Estimates', 'Model Fit' and 'Descriptives'. You may also wish to select 'Casewise Diagnostics' and set the 'Outliers' value to 3 standard deviations in the 'Residuals' section (see the note below).

Note: The 'Casewise Diagnostics' option allows you to identify whether or not there are any very large residuals or outliers that could be eliminated from the analysis to improve it.

The output this produces may appear to be complex and confusing at first glance, but you do not need to consider all the values SPSS produces. The key statistics are the multiple R and R^2 figures. The former indicates the correlation between the variables and the latter the regression value. We saw earlier in our discussion of correlation that the closer the correlation coefficient value is to -1 or $+1$, the stronger the negative or positive association is between the two variables, and the same logic applies here, except that the regression value, or coefficient, will have a value between zero and $+1$. Therefore, the closer to $+1$ the regression coefficient, or R^2 figure, is, the closer the 'fit' of the regression statistic. For example, if the correlation coefficient, the multiple R value, is 0.85 and the regression coefficient, the R^2 value, is 0.75, this tells you that there is a strong, positive correlation between the two variables and that 75 per cent of the variance in the dependent variable can be accounted for by the independent variable.

Conversely, if the multiple R value is 0.3 and the R square value is 0.2, then you have to conclude that there is an extremely weak correlation between the variables and only 20 per cent of the variation in the dependent variable could be explained by the independent variable or, in other words, the vast majority (80 per cent) of any change in the dependent variable is being caused by something else. Again, the SPSS output for regression analysis will provide an indication of the statistical significance of the result and this should be interpreted in the same way as discussed earlier.

9.5 Inferential Statistics

The very term 'inferential statistics' may be off putting if you do not understand what it means. It often appears to be complicated and so may not be considered. However, making or drawing inferences from statistics is really quite a simple concept.

Inferential statistics are concerned with how confident you can be about making valid inferences about the population from your sample data. Logically, the greater the degree of error in the sample data, the less confident you can feel about generalising from the results to the population as a whole. Alternatively, think of it as trying to answer the question 'How likely is it that I can apply the sample statistics to the population?' What inferential statistics do is provide you with an objective basis for making such a claim, as opposed to one based on pure speculation.

9.5.1   Hypothesis testing

The inferential statistical tests available for this purpose are varied, as we shall see, but essentially they are all designed to determine the degree of statistical significance of the results obtained by using recognised statistical procedures. What does this mean? As mentioned earlier, the idea is to determine the extent to which the results could have been due to chance – that is, some form of error – or the likelihood that they are a true reflection of the population from which the sample was obtained. In terms of testing a hypothesis, a statistically significant result indicates that you can be confident about making a decision to accept or reject the hypothesis and have the evidence to support that decision.

Earlier it was stated that the cut-off point for deciding whether a result can be regarded as statistically significant or not is if the relevant statistic has a value of less than 0.05 (the 95 per cent confidence level). It is also the case that higher confidence levels can be claimed or may be evident in the statistic. The other p values commonly used for this are 0.01 and 0.001. These indicate the higher confidence levels, of 99 per cent and 99.9 per cent respectively. Therefore, if the statistical significance of the result was 0.002, you could state that this is a significant result at the 99 per cent confidence level, but not at the 99.9 per cent level as the value of 0.002 is not less than the value of 0.001, used for that confidence level.

As we saw in Chapter 5, the accepted convention in research is to operate from an assumption that there is no association or difference between the variables specified in the negative, or null, form of the hypothesis and, if this can be disproved or rejected, then the positive, or alternative, form of the same hypothesis, which states that there will be an association or difference, is accepted.

Another way to think about this is to use the analogy of a legal trial. The assumption is that the accused is innocent until proven guilty on the basis of the evidence presented. This is very similar to the process of accepting and rejecting hypotheses. In the trial situation, either sufficient evidence is presented to reject the defendant's innocence and, hence, accept the opposite condition of guilty or the evidence supports the innocence of the person concerned and they are found to be not guilty. In short, there are only two outcomes, and if one is accepted the other must be rejected.

When testing a hypothesis, there are two general types of tests that can be conducted. These are known as directional or non-directional and one-tailed or two-tailed tests respectively. They are really quite straightforward as the difference between the two, which will decide for you what test you will use, is embodied in the hypothesis you wish to test. For example, a non-directional hypothesis might state that the respondents will not indicate that the price of a holiday is extremely important or unimportant in influencing their decision to book it. In other words, they will effectively be indifferent to the price. To test this it would be necessary to use a two-tailed test because you would want to know whether the pattern of responses to the question asked indicated that they did regard it as important or unimportant to be able to reject the hypothesis. If, however, the hypothesis stated that the respondents will not indicate that the price of a holiday is extremely important in influencing their decision to book it, then a one-tailed test could be used as only one side of the frequency distribution needs to be explored to establish whether the data support the hypothesis or not.

In choosing the type of statistical test to use in order to assess association or difference, the type of data you have for the variables concerned is a major influence. Inferential statistics fall into two basic types, known as parametric and non-parametric. Parametric tests can only be used on interval or ratio data, but there are non-parametric equivalents available for nominal and ordinal data (see Table 9.1). Parametric tests are also based on the assumptions that the sample data have been derived from a population with a normal distribution, and if there is more than one sample, each has the same variance. Non-parametric tests are not constrained by these assumptions, but both types do assume that the sample data have been obtained from a probability-based sampling procedure.

TABLE 9.1 Parametric and non-parametric tests for confirmatory analysis

Parametric (P) and non-parametric (NP) tests	Type of data	Purpose
Confidence intervals (P)	Normally distributed univariate	Estimating from samples
Pearson's product moment correlation coefficient (P)	Bivariate (interval or ratio data)	Measuring association and exploring relationships
Spearman's rank order correlation coefficient (NP)	Bivariate (at least ordinal data)	Measuring association and exploring relationships
Independent samples t-tests (P) (NP equivalent is the Mann–Whitney U test)	Bivariate (at least interval data for the dependent variables)	Measuring difference and comparing independent groups
Paired samples t-test (P) (NP equivalent is the Wilcoxon signed-rank test)	Bivariate (at least interval data for the dependent variables)	Measuring difference and comparing the same subjects on more than one occasion
One sample t-test (P)	Bivariate (at least interval data)	Measuring difference and comparing the sample subjects to a test value
Chi-square test for independence (NP)	Bivariate (nominal data)	Measuring difference and comparing groups
Chi-square test for goodness of fit (NP)	Bivariate (nominal data)	Measuring difference and comparing groups

9.5.2   t-Tests

As there are many parametric and non-parametric tests available, it is not possible to discuss all of them here. Details on those not included here, and how to use them in SPSS, can be found in the excellent books by Kinnear and Gray (2011) and Pallant (2013). One widely used parametric test is the Student's t-test and versions of this are available for independent samples, paired samples and just one sample. The independent samples test would be used where two different and independent samples, say males and females, were asked the same questions separately and you wished to establish whether or not there was a statistically significant degree of difference between them. Where, for example, the same sample of people were asked the same questions before and after some intervention or 'treatment' or asked different questions in an attempt to measure the same variable, then these samples would be paired or related and the paired t-test would be appropriate. The procedure to access these tests in SPSS is outlined in the Technique Tip box – Using SPSS to Conduct Student's t-tests.

Technique Tip

Using SPSS to Conduct Student's t-Tests

Independent Samples t-Tests

These tests are used to compare the mean score, from a continuous variable, with two separate groups of sample subjects.

[1]   Go to the Analyse menu and click on 'Compare Means', then select 'Independent samples t-test'.

[2]   In the dialogue box that opens, select the dependent variable – the continuous variable – from the list of variables in the box on the left and click on the button to move this into the 'Test Variable(s)' box.

[3]   Next, select the independent variable from the list and click on the button to move this into the 'Grouping Variable' box.

[4]   Then click on 'Define Groups' to enter the numbers used to code each group in the data file. For example, if the variable were 'Gender' and 1 = males and 2 = females, then you would enter 1 in the 'Group 1' box and 2 in the 'Group 2' box. Click on 'Continue'.

[5]   Back in the main dialogue box, you will now see the two group numbers in brackets after the name of the variable in the 'Grouping Variable' box – in our example, 'Gender (1 2)'. Click on 'OK' to produce the results.

Note: In the output for this test, you need to examine the significance (sig.) figure for Levene's test for equality of variances first. This examines whether

---

the variation in scores across the two groups is the same. If the sig. figure for this is greater than 0.05, which indicates no significant difference, then the 'Equal Variances Assumed' results can be used. If it is less than 0.05, then this assumption is not valid and the 'Equal Variances Not Assumed' results should be used. In both cases, the 'Sig. Two-Tailed' column is the one you are interested in as the result there shows whether there is a significant difference (p <0.05) between the groups or not (p >0.05).

Paired Samples *t*-Tests

These tests are also sometimes referred to as 'repeated measures' tests and are used where you have two samples from exactly the same respondents – that is, when you have collected data from them on two separate occasions or under different conditions. For example, in an experiment where a pre-test is undertaken before any 'treatment' is applied and where a post-test occurs after the treatment.

[1] Go to the Analyse menu, click on 'Compare Means' and then 'Paired Samples t-test'.

[2] Click on the two variables you wish to use for the analysis in the left-hand box and these will appear, highlighted, in the 'Current Selections' area under the variables list box.

[3] Click on the button to place these into the 'Paired Variables' box on the right, then click on 'OK' to produce the results.

Note: The table entitled 'Paired Samples Test' is the one you are interested in. In the final column of this, labelled 'Sig. (Two-tailed)', you have the p values to indicate whether the test has found any statistically significant differences between the two variables (p <0.05) or not (p >0.05). To establish the nature of this difference, examine the 'Mean' scores for the two variables in the 'Paired Samples Statistics' table.

One Sample *t*-Tests

These are used to test the confidence interval for the mean of a single population. Here, as there is only one sample and one mean, we do not have other sample means to make comparisons with, but this is dealt with by establishing a test value to represent another mean.

[1] Go to the Analyse menu, click on 'Compare Means' and then 'One Sample t-test'.

[2] In the dialogue box that opens, select from the list of variables in the box on the left the variable you wish to use for the test and click on the button to move this into the 'Test Variable(s)' box.

[3] In the 'Test Value' box, enter the figure to be used as the comparator for your variable's mean. For example, if the variable had scores based on a

(Continued)

(Continued)

> 1–5 scale, the null hypothesis could be rejected if this was very close to the 'indifference' point in this scale of 3. Therefore, in this case, to establish if the data indicate that you can reject the null hypothesis, you set the 'Test Value' to 3 so that the mean of the variable is compared to it to establish whether it is significantly different or not.
>
> [4] Click on 'OK' to produce the results.
>
> *Note:* The most important figure in these results is the sig. two-tailed figure in the one sample test table. If it is >0.05, then the difference between the variable's mean and the test value is not statistically significant and the null hypothesis cannot be rejected and vice versa.

There is another version of independent samples *t*-test where the two samples are not drawn from exactly the same sample frame. This is known as a 'matched samples' test. The idea here is to 'match' the composition and characteristics of the two samples so that they are as identical as possible in these respects even though they have been obtained from different groups of people. This test should be used when the two samples are not drawn from the same sample frame. For example, a hotel organisation may conduct a survey of its guests and discover they have some concerns. After making changes and improvements to address these it will probably want to know if these have been successful. However, it may be impossible to survey the same guests and a new, 'matched', sample might have to be determined using other guests who reflect the same characteristics as the original ones.

In situations where only one sample exists, the one sample *t*-test would be used. This operates slightly differently from the independent or paired sample tests because, in this case, there is only one mean value from the single sample. In the other *t*-tests, there are two means – one from each of the samples – for the test to compare in order to establish if there is any statistically significant difference between the two, but this is obviously not the case where there is only one sample. Therefore, the one sample *t*-test uses what is called a 'test value' to compare the mean from the sample. Unless the population mean is known, in which case this can be used as the test value comparator, it is the nature of the scale that enables you to identify what the appropriate test value figure should be.

This test value should be set at the midpoint value in the scale used. The reason for this is that, if you have a five-point scale, then two of these points will lie at the negative end of the scale or distribution, two will lie at the positive end and the midpoint then becomes the null or indifferent point in the scale. If this sounds complicated, consider the following example and it should become clearer.

If a question such as 'How important is the cleanliness of the hotel in determining guest satisfaction?' had been asked using a five-point scale (ranging from 1 = Extremely unimportant, 2 = Unimportant, 3 = Not really important or unimportant, 4 = Important and 5 = Extremely important), then if all or a large majority of the respondents indicated a value of 3, they would effectively be saying that cleanliness had no real relationship with guest satisfaction. Now, consider the null hypothesis that this question was designed to collect the data to test. It may well have been something like, 'There will be no relationship between cleanliness and hotel guest satisfaction', or alternatively, 'The respondents will not indicate cleanliness to be either very important or very unimportant as a factor influencing guest satisfaction'. For either of these to be accepted, the pattern of responses would have to cluster strongly around the value of 3 on the scale. Thus, the midpoint of the scale effectively embodies a mean test value that will support acceptance of the null hypothesis.

Therefore, logically, if the actual mean from your sample data lies some distance from this midpoint test value, it is likely that the t-test, in comparing these two means, will find that this difference is large enough to be regarded as statistically significant and produce a p value that is less than 0.05. So, for example, if your sample data mean for the above question is 4.5 indicating an average response between 'Important' and 'Extremely important', then you might reasonably expect that, when this is compared with the test value of 3, it will be found to be a statistically significant difference or result.

To further illustrate this, consider the data in Table 9.2. These show a selection of the summarised one sample t-test results for a piece of research that I conducted (see Brotherton, 2004) using questions based on a five-point scale similar to the one referred to above, which were designed to identify the factors budget hotel operators regarded as being most critical to their success. As you can see from the table, most of the actual sample means lie in the 4–5 range of the 1–5 scale and, therefore, not surprisingly, the t-test results indicated that most of these were statistically significant. Interestingly, you can see that the two factors not found to be statistically significant by the t-test have mean values very close to 3 and are less clustered than the others – that is, their standard deviations (SDs) are larger.

TABLE 9.2 Summarised one sample t-test results

Critical success factors	Mean	SD
1 Central sales/reservation system	4.13	0.82
2 Convenient locations	4.43	0.65
3 Standardised hotel design	3.81	0.90
4 Size of hotel network	3.92	0.90
5 Geographic coverage of hotel network	4.09	0.81
6 Consistent accommodation standards	4.76	0.43
7 Consistent service standards	4.75	0.50
8 Good-value restaurants	4.03	0.81
9 Value for money accommodation	4.68	0.57

(Continued)

TABLE 9.2 (Continued)

Critical success factors	Mean	SD
10 Recognition of returning guests	4.43	0.69
11 Warmth of guest welcome	4.71	0.52
12 Operational flexibility/responsiveness	4.05	0.75
13 Corporate contracts	3.12	1.2
14 Smoking and non-smoking rooms	4.14	0.85
15 Design/look of guest bedrooms	3.99	0.79
16 Size of guest bedrooms	3.77	0.83
17 Guest bedrooms' comfort level	4.33	0.69
18 Responsiveness to customers' demands	4.42	0.64
19 Customer loyalty/repeat business	4.56	0.60
20 Disciplined operational controls	4.13	0.76
21 Speed of guest service	4.35	0.69
22 Efficiency of guest service	4.50	0.60
23 Choice of room type for guests	3.71	0.92
24 Guest security	4.46	0.71
25 Low guest bedroom prices	3.79	0.95
26 Limited service level	3.07	1.0
27 Hygiene and cleanliness	4.86	0.37
28 Quality audits	4.23	0.87
29 Staff empowerment	3.91	0.88
30 Strong brand differentiation	4.08	0.90
31 Customer surveys/feedback	4.08	0.92
32 Staff training	4.74	0.47
33 Added-value facilities in guest rooms	3.55	1.0
34 Staff recruitment and selection	4.27	0.72
35 Standard pricing policy	4.11	0.88
36 Quality standards	4.73	0.56

Note: All the CSFs are significant, in a positive direction, at the $p < 0.001$ level, except factors 13 (Corporate contracts) and 26 (Limited service level), which are not significant.

Source: Brotherton (2004: 952). Reproduced with permission of Emerald Publications

9.5.3 The chi-square test

A non-parametric alternative to *t*-tests is the chi-square (χ^2 – 'chi' is a letter of the Greek alphabet) test. This assumes that the data have been collected using a random sampling procedure and that they are in numerical form – frequencies as opposed to percentages – but not that the data are of interval or ratio status. This means that it can be used on nominal data where the categories are mutually exclusive and where one respondent cannot be counted in more than one category. Earlier, we saw that the chi-square test for independence can be used to establish whether two categorical variables are associated with each other. Here, we are concerned with the chi-square test being used to determine whether or not there are statistically significant differences between two or more categorical variables or between two or more samples.

This is known as the chi-square test for one sample data or the test for goodness of fit. This test compares the actual set of frequencies in your data with an expected distribution, which is usually defined by the data analysis software on the basis that each category in the set would have the same, minimum number of cases. The Technique Tip box – Using SPSS for the Chi-square Goodness of Fit Test – outlines the SPSS procedure for this test. The output it produces is fairly straightforward to interpret. There is a table with the actual and expected frequencies for the categories and one headed 'Test Statistics', which contains the chi-square statistic, the degrees of freedom (df) associated with this and the statistical significance of the result (Asymp. Sig.). The key figure here is the latter and you are looking for this to have a value of less than 0.05 for it to be statistically significant.

Technique Tip

Using SPSS for the Chi-square Goodness of Fit Test

[1] Go to Analyse, Non-Parametric Tests and select 'chi-square'.

[2] In the 'chi-square' dialogue box, place the variable you wish to use for the test in the 'Test Variable List' box and make sure that the 'Get From Data' option is ticked in the 'Expected Range' settings and the 'All Categories Equal' option is ticked in the 'Expected Values' settings.

[3] Click on 'OK' and the results will appear in an 'Output' window.

9.6 Data Reduction Techniques

Data reduction techniques are somewhat different from those discussed thus far in this chapter, but are useful when you wish to seek a more parsimonious solution from a large range of explanatory variables or respondents. Cluster analysis is one of these techniques and it seeks to identify groups or clusters of related respondents based on the responses they have given to the questions. This can be a powerful analysis, but is often complex to interpret and somewhat controversial. Cluster analysis will not be dealt with here, but if you wish to explore it further a useful discussion is provided by Ryan (1995).

9.6.1   Principal components analysis

The other technique is perhaps the one you are more likely to use. It concentrates on grouping variables together to produce a solution that concentrates on the variables explaining the greatest amount of variance and is often referred to as 'factor analysis'. One of the most commonly used techniques in this category is known as Principal Components Analysis (PCA). PCA reflects the notion that certain variables might be facets of the same concept and that high scores on one of these may also be found on others that comprise a 'group'. PCA uses an underlying model to divide the set of variables into such separate 'components' or groupings. Each of these explains a certain proportion of the variance, with the first explaining the most and successive ones less. Therefore, the first component contains the variables that explain the highest percentage of the variance, making them the most important, explanatory ones.

PCA can produce a small number of components – say three or four – but may produce a much larger number – possibly eight, nine or more – as it uses all the variables in the original set to explain all the variance. However, the explanatory power of the later components will be much less than that of the first or second, which gives rise to the issue of how many components should be used. This can be determined by using the eigenvalue produced in the PCA output statistics. The eigenvalue is an index of the amount of variance the component accounts for in the original set of variables and it is generally agreed that retaining the components having an eigenvalue greater than one is sensible.

However, before conducting a PCA, it is important to assess the quality or suitability of your data for this type of analysis. The two tests generally accepted to be indicative of this are known as the Bartlett's Test of Sphericity (BTS) and the Kaiser–Meyer–Olkin (KMO) test of sampling adequacy. These may sound complicated, but they are really quite simple to set up and interpret. See the Techniques Tip box – Using SPSS to Assess Data Suitability for PCA.

Technique Tip	**Using SPSS to Assess Data Suitability for PCA**

[1]   Go to the Analyse menu, select 'Data Reduction' and then 'Factor' to open the 'Factor analysis' dialogue box.

[2]   Select the variables that you intend to use for the analysis and move these into the 'Variables' window in the dialogue box.

[3]   Click on the 'Descriptives' button, then, in the 'Correlation Matrix' section, click on the 'KMO and Bartlett's test of sphericity' option.

[4]   Click on 'Continue' to return to the main 'Factor Analysis' dialogue box and then click on 'OK'.

[5]   The results will appear in an 'Output' window.

OK, so you have your BTS and KMO results but what do these mean, how do you interpret them? This is not at all complicated. What you are looking for in the output from these tests is as follows. In the BTS, you are looking for the significance level to be less than 0.05, and in the KMO test, for the KMO value to be close to 1. Pallant (2013) suggests that a minimum KMO value of 0.6 is required to justify undertaking PCA, while Ryan (1995: 256) provides a useful categorisation of KMO values as follows:

KMO >0.9	'Marvellous'	KMO in the 0.8s	'Meritorious'
KMO in the 0.7s	'Middling'	KMO in the 0.6s	'Mediocre'
KMO in the 0.5s	'Miserable'	KMO <0.5	'Unacceptable'

If you have successful results for the BTS and KMO tests, then conducting a PCA can be justified. To do this in SPSS, follow the instructions in the Technique Tip box – Using SPSS to Conduct a PCA. The PCA procedure produces quite a lot of output data, even when you have not selected more of the additional options, and this can be quite confusing at first glance. The 'Correlation Matrix' simply indicates the correlation coefficients for the combinations of items and the 'Total Variance Explained' table contains the eigenvalues referred to above, from which you can decide how many components should be retained, as explained previously. The 'Communalities' table contains information, in the 'Extraction' column, on the proportion of the variance that is accounted for by each of the variables. The 'Component Matrix' indicates which component the variables have been initially allocated to before 'rotation' has taken place. Finally, the 'Rotated Component Matrix' shows the allocations of the variables to each component after rotation.

Technique Tip

Using SPSS to Conduct a PCA

[1] Go to the Analyse menu, select 'Data Reduction' and then 'Factor' to open the 'Factor Analysis' dialogue box.

[2] Select the variables you wish to use for the analysis and move these into the 'Variables' window in the dialogue box.

[3] Click on the 'Descriptives' button and then select the 'Coefficients' and 'Reproduced' options in the 'Correlation Matrix' section. These will produce the correlation matrix and communalities in the output. Click on 'Continue'.

[4] Now you are back to the main 'Factor Analysis' dialogue box. Click on the 'Extraction' button. In this box, make sure that, in the 'Methods'

(Continued)

(Continued)

> section, 'Principal Components' is selected, in the 'Analyse' section select 'Correlation Matrix', in the 'Extract' section ensure the 'Eigenvalue over' option is ticked and set it to '1', then click on 'Continue'.
>
> [5] Next, click on the 'Rotation' button, and in the box that opens click on the 'Varimax' option in the 'Methods' section, and the 'Rotated Solution' in the 'Display' section and then on 'Continue'.
>
> [6] Now, click on the 'Options' button and select the 'Exclude Cases Pairwise' in the 'Missing Values' section. In the section called 'Coefficient Display Format' click on 'Sorted by Size', and in the box for 'Suppress Absolute Values Less Than' enter the figure '.3' and click on 'Continue' (see the note below).
>
> [7] Click on 'OK' to produce the results in an 'Output' window.
>
> *Note:* Setting a value of .3 here will make the output easier to interpret because this will mean that any variables not meeting this minimum criterion for 'loading' will not be displayed. It is also logical because that is the value below which you would probably not consider conducting PCA when you inspect the correlation coefficients in the correlation matrix table. However, you can set this to a higher level, such as .4 or .5, if you wish, but this may exclude some variables that possibly should be included in the solution.

The 'rotation' does not change the component solution produced in PCA, but makes the interpretation of this solution easier because the figures in each component column in this table indicate the 'loading', or strength, of membership of the variables for each component. As any variable may be allocated to, or 'load', on to more than one component in this table, what you need to look for is the highest loading value for each variable to decide which component it should be allocated to. For example, if the variable 'Price' has loading figures of 0.2 for component one, 0.6 for component two and 0.8 for component three in the rotated component matrix table, then it should be allocated to component three.

Although PCA will usually produce a solution for you, it will not always produce the solution you may have been expecting, and sometimes it produces a set of components that don't make sense as it may allocate seemingly unrelated variables to a particular component. The other issue here, of course, is that although PCA will group the variables together to create the components, it will not tell you what these components are or what they mean. In short, it will not give you descriptive headings for the components and this is where you have to interpret what each of the components is. In other words, you have to examine the variables that comprise the components and decide whether or not these are sensible groupings and what they should be called.

For example, in a piece of research that I conducted to establish the most critical factors for successful budget hotel operations in the UK (see Brotherton, 2004), the original 34 possible variables in the questionnaire were reduced by the data analysis, including use of PCA, to the five most critical, which were allocated to two components or categories. One of these had the variables 'Convenient location' and 'Central reservation systems' and it was decided that both of these were essentially concerned with making the hotels easy to access for the customer or guest. Hence, these were combined to form the component labelled 'Accessibility'. The other had the variables 'Consistent accommodation standards', 'Value-for-money accommodation' and 'Hygiene and cleanliness'. These three were interpreted as being aspects of how well the hotels performed their basic operational purpose and so formed the category named 'Performance'. Therefore, at the end of this research exercise, it was concluded that the two most critical components or dimensions influencing the success of budget hotel operations were how accessible they were and how well they performed and these, in turn, were determined by the five variables.

Chapter Summary

Data invariably need to be cleaned up before they are entered into an analysis package.

Once they have been entered, the first task is to produce some basic, descriptive statistics to get a feel for its characteristics – in the form of frequencies, graphs, charts, measures of dispersion and central tendency – and, perhaps, some indication of the reliability of any scales used.

Following this, to explore the extent to which variables may be associated and/or if there are any differences between some sub-aspects of your sample, the use of appropriate bivariate analyses, such as cross-tabulation, correlation, regression, and establishing if any associations or differences can be regarded as valid (statistically significant) or have merely occurred due to chance, and therefore cannot be regarded as significant, is an important task.

Inferential statistics are used to indicate how confident you can be when making inferences about the population as a whole from your sample statistics.

The use of Student's t-tests or chi-square can help to establish whether your sample results are statistically significant or not and if the null hypothesis can be rejected.

Data analysis techniques, such as factor analysis (PCA), can help to reveal underlying categories in your data and provide a more parsimonious solution.

References

Brotherton, B. (2004) 'Critical success factors in UK budget hotel operations', *International Journal of Operations & Production Management*, 24 (9): 944–69.

Kinnear, P.R. and Gray, C.D. (2011) *SPSS for Windows Made Simple: Release 19*. Hove: Psychology Press.

Pallant, J. (2013) *SPSS Survival Manual: A step-by-step guide to data analysis using SPSS for Windows*, 5th edition. Buckingham: Open University Press.

Ryan, C. (1995) *Researching Tourist Satisfaction: Issues, concepts, problems*. London: Routledge.

10

ANALYSING QUALITATIVE DATA

Chapter Content and Issues

Is the qualitative data quantifiable or not?
Has it been collected deductively or inductively?
Unitising, coding and categorising the data.
Content analysis and semiotics.
Computer-assisted analysis.
Dealing with objectivity, validity and reliability issues
   in qualitative data analysis.
Displaying qualitative data.
Justifying your data analysis choices.

10.1 Introduction

In general, analysing qualitative data tends to be more challenging than analysing quantitative data. This is largely because the latter benefits from established techniques and procedures that can be applied in standard ways to the data. That said, there are reasonably well-established techniques for analysing qualitative data that can be used as a basis or framework to help guide and structure the analytical process. However, the main problem with analysing qualitative data is its inherent variability. Not only are the types of qualitative data potentially more variable than numeric data – it can be text, pictures and so on – but the form these types take is also highly variable. This means that the analysis of qualitative data has to be much more flexible and interpretative in nature than is the case for numeric data.

Given the breadth and diversity of qualitative data and the types of analysis that can be employed to interpret these, it is not possible to cover all of this ground in this chapter. Therefore, here we shall concentrate on issues concerned with the type of qualitative data you possess, how it has been collected and for what purpose. We will also consider the basic principles and processes used in this type of analysis, along with two techniques – content analysis and semiotics – that are often used to analyse qualitative data. Finally, in common with quantitative data analysis, there is a need to address validity and reliability issues to ensure that the analysis and consequent interpretative results are seen to be credible.

10.2 What Kind of Qualitative Data Do You Have?

On the one hand this may seem a rather silly question to ask, but on the other, it is relevant to the type and nature of analysis you may wish, or are able, to apply to the data. At a simple level, qualitative data may be comprised of words or text, still or moving visual images, such as photographs or video material, or other observational recordings, such as maps, diagrams and so on. Regardless of the form, these may have been collected inductively or deductively. This, of course, has implications for the purpose of the data – whether it is to build a theory or test it – and for how the analysis is organised and proceeds.

TABLE 10.1 Words associated with hospitality

Behavioural	Physical	Temporal
Welcoming (34)	Comfort (7)	Leisure (5)
Warmth of		
Service		
Friendly		
Accommodating		
Feeling welcome		
Service (32)		
Customer		
Good		
Polite		
Welcoming		
Excellent		
Friendliness (32)		
Warmth (13)		
Of welcome		
Of service		
Looked after (12)		
Being well		
Pleasantness/Politeness/Manners (9)		
Attention (3)		

Source: Brotherton (2005: 144); www.tandf.co.uk/ journals. Reproduced with permission of Taylor and Francis Ltd

Where the data has been collected inductively for theory-building purposes, it is likely to be far more voluminous, wide-ranging and disparate than data collected deductively to test specific hypotheses. In addition, some qualitative data may be quantifiable, in the sense that it can be enumerated, usually in the form of frequencies and percentages. However, you may ask, 'Why would I want to convert qualitative data into some quantified format?' The short answer to this is that it may help you to identify patterns within the data that, in turn, may begin to indicate the existence of categories or dimensions in the data as a whole.

This is usually referred to as 'quanticising' the data. An example of this is provided by Brotherton (2005) where, within the context of a comparative case study research project conducted in two four-star hotels to identify how hotel guests thought about or perceived the concept and experience of hospitality, textual data were converted into frequencies. The result of one part of this process is shown in Table 10.1. Here, the data relate to the question, 'What word or words do you associate with hospitality?' Given the relative frequencies of the occurrence of the words proffered by the respondents, the analysis of these frequencies clearly indicated that the overwhelming majority were concerned with behavioural aspects of hospitality, while small minorities indicated some association with its physical and temporal aspects.

This quantitative weight of evidence suggests then that when people think freely about what hospitality means to them, the first, and most important, feature for them is the behaviour of the people providing the hospitality. Similarly, when two sets of hotel guests were asked to indicate the words they would use to describe the physical aspects of hospitality they had experienced in the respective hotels, the enumeration of their responses clearly indicated that they could be categorised as words expressing either an impression of, or passing a judgement on, these physical aspects (see Table 10.2).

TABLE 10.2 Words used to describe the physical aspects of hospitality in the hotels

Impression	[Performance]
Modern (14)	Very nice/Good/Excellent (16)
Clean (8)	
Comfortable (8)	Adequate/Mediocre/Quite basic (3)
Bright (3)	
Old-fashioned (12) but, nice/quite nice, classical/ornate, traditional, historical, colonial, classy, charming, clean	Very nice/Good/Excellent (8)
	OK/Adequate/Average (4)
On the other hand, drab and faded glory	
Comfortable (5)	
Pleasant/relaxing (8)	

Source: Brotherton (2005: 144); www.tandf.co.uk/ journals. Reproduced with permission of Taylor and Francis Ltd

In addition to using 'seasons of the year' (see later) this project also used other vehicles to indirectly question the hotel guests. For example, they were asked to indicate a colour and, separately, an animal that they would use to describe both the physical and service aspects of their experience at the hotel, and to explain why they chose the particular colour and animal they associated with these experiences because, of course, the reasons for their choices were crucial to understanding the nature of these associations. To see how the project was developed further from this initial study see the Research in Action Box – Hospitality in a Fast Food Environment.

The production of quantitative frequencies from the original qualitative data can be achieved very simply by using SPSS. The qualitative data are entered into SPSS as string variables – that is, the words themselves are typed in rather than numbers – and then the software is simply asked to produce the output frequencies for the relevant variables in the same way that it would be for numeric data, as described in Chapter 9. In cases where qualitative response options are predetermined, rather than open-ended as they are here, then it is a straightforward matter to code them to facilitate enumeration. For example, in the project referred to above, the respondents were also asked to choose the season – spring, summer, autumn or winter – that they most associated with the experience of the service they had received in the hotel. In SPSS, all that is required to process the respondents' answers to this question is that the variable 'season' has its values defined in the variable view window for the data sheet as spring = 1, summer = 2, autumn = 3 and winter = 4. In this and other such cases, therefore, the data can be entered in numeric form from the outset.

Where the response option is not predetermined, but the actual responses exhibit clear sets of commonalities, then it may be possible to code the data before entry or recode the string data into numeric form after entry. For example, if when initially examining interview or questionnaire data it is clear that the same words or phrases occur frequently, it may be sensible to consider coding these numerically to make data entry and analysis simpler. Even when this is not undertaken before data entry, but it becomes evident once the basic frequencies have been produced, it can still be achieved by recoding the string variable into numeric form using the procedure for recoding numeric variables described in Chapter 9.

This quanticising of qualitative data can also offer further analytical opportunities. For example, in the project referred to earlier personal, or respondent characteristics, data were collected from each interviewee, i.e. age, income, educational level, gender, ethnicity etc., because it was felt at the outset that these may be potential sources of variation. In short, that people of differing ages, education, income, gender or ethnicity may hold different views and perceptions in relation to the more substantive questions they were asked. As this type of nominal data lends itself readily to quantitative coding it is not surprising that these data were entered into SPSS in numeric form, e.g. males = 1 and females = 2. So, when the qualitative data were quanticised in the same nominal format it was possible to conduct a quantitative, chi-square, analysis to ascertain if indeed there were any statistically significant variations in this respect. This confirmed that there were not and allowed the claim to be made that the data were not sensitive to different respondent characteristics.

Research in Action	Hospitality in a Fast Food Environment

Having tested and found the instrument and procedures to be sound in the initial study, referred to earlier in this chapter (Brotherton, 2005), this was then repeated or replicated in a follow-up study conducted within fast food establishments (for the full results from this, see Brotherton and Wood, 2008). This addressed the question: would the same study conducted in a very different hospitality setting produce similar or very different results? Or put another way; how sensitive was the instrument to the environment it was being used in? By retaining the original questionnaire, with appropriate wording changes to reflect the different context, and using the same interview procedure and data analysis techniques it would be possible to directly compare the two sets of results to answer this question.

OK, you may say; but why bother? There were perhaps two main reasons. First, one of the underlying questions being addressed in this study was whether hospitality could be regarded as a generic or context-specific concept. Second, the usefulness of the approach underlying the instrument and procedures would be enhanced if they proved to be robust in different contexts. In other words, to determine if this research process could be generalised across different contexts rather than being limited to just one.

Space does not permit an extended explanation of the results from this here but, in summary, the results showed strong consistency across the two environments that, in turn, provided an encouraging picture to suggest that further extensions of the work to other environments would be appropriate.

10.3 Basic Principles and Stages in Qualitative Data Analysis

It should be evident from the previous section that, regardless of the type of qualitative data you have, the basic principles and process of analysing this type of data are generic, whether you are testing or building a theory. Given that, whatever the form, the volume of qualitative data you have collected is likely to be considerable, the first problem is to address how this raw data can be organised to reduce its scale and complexity. Unitising and coding the data are the first stages in this process.

If you have interview data that you wish to unitise and code then viewing the video material entitled 'Qualitative Analysis of Interview Data: A Step-by-Step Guide', available via the Video Links section of the Companion Website (study.sagepub.com/brotherton) would be helpful to get an understanding of the process from beginning to end.

10.3.1   Unitising and coding

Unitising the data simply means choosing the unit, or focus, for the analysis. This might be individual words, ideas, phrases, events, images or even the questions used in an interview or on a questionnaire. The latter may be particularly appropriate where different people have been asked the same question and you wish to compare their answers. Table 10.3 contains an example of the value of this approach for revealing very different views from the staff in one hotel, which, in turn, surfaced a key issue – why is there not unanimous agreement over the simple issue of who the yield manager is? Liang et al. (2012) provide an interesting and illuminating discussion of a number of these issues relating to the problem of having a clear and unambiguous view of what the unit of analysis is and the difficulties encountered in achieving this within the context of international tourism studies.

TABLE 10.3   Who is the yield manager in the hotel?

Respondent	Reponse
DGM	The Rooms Division Manager
Res. M	We don't have one as such, although the Rooms Division Manager assumes that role with my assistance
RDM	The Reservations Manager and I do a bit of work between us, and the Reception Manager is beginning to get involved now as well
HR	The Rooms Division Manager, well she maintains the system
RM	We haven't got one, but the Rooms Division Manager, the Reservations Manager and myself are involved in it
RC	I assume it's the Rooms Division Manager and the Reservations Manager
	The Rooms Division Manager is actually managing it and the Reservations Manager helps with it
R	The Reservations Manager

DGM = Deputy General Manager; Res. M = Reservations Manager; RDM = Rooms Division Manager; HR = Head Receptionist; RM = Reception Manager; RC = Reservations Coordinator; R = Receptionist.

Source: Brotherton and Turner (2001: 36). Reproduced with permission of *Journal of Services Research*

Coding in general is a matter of attaching operational and/or conceptual identities to the data in order for these to be organised, categorised, then broken down and reassembled into a more meaningful form. In short, it is a process of ordering, reducing and summarising the data, whether this is purely an administrative task in the initial stages of the analysis or one more concerned with identifying themes and relationships later in the process. Once the data have been converted into a more manageable form by means of the coding process, the next step is either to examine this to identify any emergent structure or categories, if the data have been collected inductively, or to examine how the data relate to the conceptual framework used as the basis for the deductive research design and data collection. Once this structure has been established, either prior to data collection or as a consequence of its analysis, the data can be examined further to identify possible patterns, themes and relationships between the categories to either build or test theoretical propositions.

OK, this all sounds very logical and straightforward in principle but how does it work in practice? The reality is that moving from a mass of raw data at the outset to a more refined thematic form at the end does not happen in one step. This would simply be far too complex a leap. So, coding is not a one-stop exercise. You may wish to think of it as a layered pyramid, with the mass of raw data forming the base and the themes and concepts that eventually emerge from this as the apex. To get from the base to the apex you may need to go through a number of coding stages. Qualitative data analysis is essentially an iterative process, involving a number of stages, that moves from unorganised raw data through stages that progressively reduce and focus the key message/s that the 'processed' data eventually reveal.

10.3.2   Open coding

The use of 'open' coding initially to place some structure on the data provides a starting point for this. This is essentially a questioning exercise that needs to be conducted with an open mind in order that 'unexpected' instances and/or categories can be identified. So you look at your data and ask a series of questions. This is likely to involve asking whether there are any similarities in the data that essentially relate to the same thing. This does not mean that you have to identify and group together 'identical' words, phrases, images etc., but those that may be different in form but are sufficiently similar in meaning. You can see this in Table 10.1. Here a series of different words are grouped together under one heading (Behavioural) because they all imply that this aspect of hospitality is represented by each of them. So, for example, being looked after, warmth of welcome, friendliness, pleasantness all reflect the behaviour of the people providing the hospitality experienced by the guest. Conversely, where the words people associated with hospitality do not relate to this aspect they are clearly saying something different. So difference is equally important as this now allows other categories to be identified. Again, in this example, where people have responded with words such as comfort or leisure they are clearly not trying to communicate anything to do with the behaviour of those providing the hospitality. They are indicating that they associate hospitality with other things, with the physical provision (comfort) and the type of 'time' (leisure) when they normally experience hospitality.

Another issue is the frequency of occurrence. Where particular words, phrases or images appear more frequently than others it may be reasonable to tentatively conclude that these could be more significant than those occurring only relatively infrequently. This aspect is also illustrated by Table 10.1, which clearly shows that the relative incidence of words associated with hospitality used by the respondents is far greater in the behavioural category than the other two. Given the free and open way these data were offered by the respondents who were interviewed it might be reasonable to conclude that this aspect of hospitality is of overwhelming importance in the mind of those receiving it. In some situations you may also wish to ask questions concerning sequencing, correlation and possibly causation. However, it is likely that these are reserved for the next level of coding (see Section 10.3.3).

This initial questioning and categorising is essential in an inductive analysis but is also important in a deductive one, where the data are being examined to ascertain whether they 'fit' or support the prior conceptual framework that has been established from a literature review, because it is entirely possible that new categories and concepts may be identified which, in turn, may help to extend or strengthen the existing theory. So, open coding helps to identify and open up possible lines of enquiry suggested by the data and this initial stage of processing it. For a useful description of how the coding process was conducted to analyse semi-structured interview data and to open up such lines of enquiry see Crawford (2013).

Of course this can be a time-consuming and, sometimes, a tedious exercise. However, it is the foundation upon which further conceptualisation is based and therefore an extremely important aspect to get right because the quality of everything developed from, or built on, this foundation will depend upon the strength of this beginning. This also begs the question; when should I stop this process, or when do I know that it is not worthwhile continuing further? This is often referred to as having reached the point of 'theoretical saturation'. Essentially this occurs when further consideration of the data yields no additional categories or concepts. This is an intuitive, rather than formulaic, point because in some instances this will be achieved quite quickly and in others it may take more time and thought.

10.3.3 Axial coding

With this rudimentary structure in place a re-examination of it, using more 'focused' coding, should enable you to begin to identify major patterns and categories, and identify possible relationships between these. This more sophisticated structure should then be examined once again, using axial coding, to identify overarching themes and concepts. Again, the study by Crawford (2013), referred to earlier provides a useful example of how such themes can be identified, as does that of Curtin (2010) that used a number of qualitative data collection methods to bring together different types of data into common themes and categories.

Axial coding enables you to identify connections and relationships between the categories and concepts identified during the open coding stage of the process. Essentially this is a matter of 'putting the flesh on the bones' of the structure established in the previous stage by inserting the connections and links between the structural elements. This enables you to identify which of the categories or concepts are connected to each other. In turn, this raises questions concerning sequencing and possible cause–effect relationships and begins to deepen the analysis beyond a simple identification of discrete categories. Now issues associated with actions and interactions, and their possible effects and consequences, start to be identified and explored. In addition, as the more detailed picture emerges questions regarding the potential importance and influence of the context(s) the data relate to can be pursued and, depending upon the complexity of the emerging picture, the existence and relevance of any intervening elements can be identified. If there is a sequence, or chain, of connected elements in the emerging picture then it now becomes possible to add even more detail by articulating how this process works.

It is possible that this process of axial coding may evolve into what is referred to as 'selective' coding. Some commentators see this as a distinct type of coding, which technically it is, but it invariably arises as a consequence of the outcomes from the axial coding process employed within an inductive approach to analysing the data. Selective coding entails identifying a 'core' category or concept to which all the others are related and specifying what these relationships are. Within a deductive context of course this would arise if the conceptual framework contained a core concept and others related to it. This is highly likely because such a framework would identify the dependent and independent variables.

10.4 Qualitative Data Analysis Techniques

There are basically two main options for managing your qualitative data: manual or computerised methods. These are self-explanatory in some respects and not mutually exclusive. Depending upon the volume and variety of your data, and your ability to access and use computer-aided analysis software, you may find that pragmatism rules the day. In short, the nature of your data and the availability of time and resources are likely to be the major influences on which method/s you can realistically employ.

The techniques used to analyse qualitative data may be subdivided into those applicable to data obtained inductively or deductively. However, while it is true to say that there are techniques that are appropriate for one of these approaches and not the other, some can be used for each category or have their equivalents in the other category. Though it is possible that you have adopted an inductive approach to your research project, it is far more likely that you will have chosen a deductive route because of time and other constraints. Consequently, well-known inductive techniques such as grounded theory, analytic induction, narrative, conversation and discourse analysis will not be discussed here, but details of these can be obtained from the sources listed in the Further Reading section of the Companion Website (study.sagepub.com/brotherton) if required.

Content analysis and semiotics are perhaps the techniques most commonly applied to qualitative data obtained deductively, though they may be used to analyse such data obtained inductively. They are similar, but not synonymous, techniques in that they seek to derive meaning and make inferences from textual or visual data.

10.4.1 Content analysis

This is a technique that has been around for a century or so and hence there is a considerable body of knowledge relating to its methodological development and application over this period. It is often viewed as a quantitative method of data analysis, that employs a deductive approach to analysing qualitative data because it tends to emphasise the counting, or enumeration, of key words, phrases, images and so on to produce frequencies, which can then be objectively compared to an exiting conceptual framework. An interesting and contemporary example of this is provided by Titz and Dawson (2011), who undertook a study designed to explore the nature of online hotel guest review comments using the standard SERVQUAL dimensions, or constructs, as the framework to code, and subsequently enumerate, these comments. By contrast, the research project referred to earlier in this chapter (Brotherton, 2005) did not take a deductive approach to the collection of analysis of the data. The qualitative data was obtained by conducting face-to-face interviews in the two case study hotels, using open-ended, free-response questions the results from which were then subjected to content analysis to ascertain the frequencies and identify emergent categories.

However, this use of content analysis is limited to identifying the denotative, or surface, meaning and can result in these meanings being decontextualised. That said, it is possible to counteract this by considering the underlying, latent or connotative meaning of the data by ensuring that the context or contexts are taken into account when inferences are made.

If content analysis is your data analysis method of choice then you may wish to utilise some of the resources contained in the Companion Website (study.sagepub.com/brotherton). Here you will find both video and textual material, in the Video and Web Links sections, that will enable you to develop a more extensive and detailed understanding of content analysis and how it is used.

10.4.2   Semiotics

This sees the issue of context as a more fundamental consideration, that meaning can only be established by taking the context into account. It is concerned with the analysis of signs and what they are signs of. Semiotics, then, focuses on audible or visible cues and their underlying meanings. Given that the significance of a particular sign is contextually dependent, it follows that the same sign may have a different significance or meaning when it appears in different contexts. Thus, semiotics cannot be conducted in an acontextual manner. Furthermore, in addition to the signs and their significance varying according to their incidence in differing contexts, there is another element – the 'interpreter', who perceives, interprets and gives meaning to them. This contributes another dimension in that different interpreters may interpret the significance of a given sign in the same context differently.

In common with content analysis the Companion Website (study.sagepub.com/brotherton) also contains additional video and textual material on semiotics and semiotic analysis.

10.4.3 Computer-assisted qualitative data analysis (CAQDAS)

Though much, if not most, qualitative data analysis and interpretation is likely to be conducted via written means, it is possible to utilise computing power to assist this process. As we noted earlier, SPSS, for example, can be used to quantify qualitative data, but more specialised qualitative data analysis software packages do exist to support many of the inductive and deductive techniques referred to earlier. For example, the NVIVO, ATLAS.ti, The Ethnograph, HyperResearch and MAXQDA packages tend to be the ones most commonly referred to in the literature. The extent to which you will have access to any of these, however, will depend on whether or not your institution has any of them available for you to use. Even if it does not, it is often possible to obtain trial or demo versions of them and these may be sufficient for your needs, so it is worth checking out the web addresses listed below. All of these sites will offer trial versions, demos, associated tutorials and 'how-to' videos.

You may also wish to consult the web links on the Companion Website (study. sagepub.com/brotherton) specifically dealing with CAQDAS issues.

- NVIVO: www.qsrinternational.com
- ATLAS.ti: www.atlasti.com
- The Ethnograph: www.qualisresearch.com
- HyperResearch: www.researchware.com
- MAXQDA: www.maxqda.com

Although there is no doubt that CAQDAS packages such as these offer a range of analysis options it is likely, certainly at undergraduate dissertation level, that the investment of time and effort to learn how to use a package may be disproportionate to the returns obtained. Qualitative studies with relatively small samples, or numbers of cases, limited interviews and comparatively small amounts of data may not justify the investment required.

10.5 Displaying Qualitative Data

At each stage of the coding and analysis process the results need to be displayed in one form or another. During the earlier stages of the process this is more likely to involve forms utilising static or discrete categorisation to place some order upon the abstracted data. Typically, lists, tables and matrices are used to do this, often organised to identify the similarities and/or differences between different types of interview respondent, different types/sources of data etc. This, for example, facilitates an identification of possible agreement/disagreement across such categories. Sometimes the use of a map can be helpful in locating and identifying potential similarities and differences in the data, something that is obviously useful when there may be spatial aspects important to the study.

Of course, this may well pose the question, why do they agree/disagree? In turn, this may well provide opportunities for the data to be re-configured and displayed differently. For example, a flowchart, fishbone or cause–effect diagram might now be helpful to represent this. Similarly, although cross-tabulation is something normally associated with quantitative analysis, this is a technique that can be used in qualitative analysis to help identify and display similarities/differences. Figure 10.1 provides a hypothetical example of how this may be used. This shows the individual interview respondents (the numbers in each oval) grouped into three distinct categories. Two of these may have been expected – the high income/never use and the low income/almost always use groups – but the third one may have been unexpected and this representation now helps to raise questions concerning why this may be the case and what the nature/characteristics of the interviewees are who populate this group.

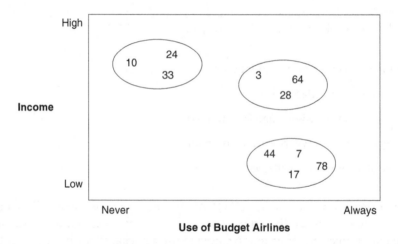

FIGURE 10.1   Budget airline usage and income levels

10.6   Justifying Qualitative Data Analysis Choices

Just as there is a need to explain and justify the selection and use of techniques and procedures when analysing quantitative data, these same issues have to be addressed with qualitative data analysis. In the case of quantitative data analysis, this is relatively straightforward because statistical techniques tend to be regarded as fairly objective and proven. As the analysis and interpretation of qualitative data are much more subjective and interpretative, however, it is not possible, in the main, to cite a particular statistic to claim validity or reliability. Similarly, the feasibility of any attempt to generalise from sample results to a wider population, if desired, is also problematic because it is unlikely that the sample used will have been determined statistically to facilitate the making of such inferences valid and reliable. These features can be serious threats to any qualitative data analysis and interpretation because they are likely to compromise the objectiveness, internal and external validity and reliability of the results.

How objective an interpretation is relates to whether or not it is possible for someone else to apply the same techniques and procedure and confirm that they are able to produce the same results. How internally valid the results are raises the issues of authenticity and credibility – that is, how true they are and whether or not they can be believed. How externally valid qualitative data analysis results are depends on how transferable they are to other contextual conditions. How reliable such results are depends on their dependability over time or space.

Given that it may not be desirable, or indeed feasible, to claim that a set of qualitative results is externally valid or totally objective, the key issues are usually those of internal validity and reliability. By resisting the desire to claim that the results are generally applicable and accepting that subjective elements will have played a role in the interpretation of the data – explicitly documenting this by including a reflexive account of your views and beliefs and the potential impact of these on the analysis – you will make your claims more credible.

If you are to convince anyone that your results should be accepted as reliable, you need to ask the question, 'If someone else had conducted this research, would they have arrived at the same conclusions?' The issue here is that a minimisation of subjective bias is achieved in both the instruments and procedures of data collection and analysis. This can be demonstrated by ensuring that there is an audit trail for the whole process. This is akin to writing up the method used for an experiment which, if followed by another, should produce reliable results.

10.6.1 Triangulation

This is another approach to dealing with validity and reliability issues. Essentially, triangulation is a technique used to increase confidence in the accuracy and dependability of the results by utilising more than one data analyst or interpreter, source of data or data collection method. The idea of this is that if the interpretations of more than one person analysing the same data independently, or the data produced in different locations by different people or at different times, or else different methods used to collect data relating to the same issue or question, e.g. 'questionnaire and interview data', all arrive at or point to the same conclusions, then this type of confirmatory process increases confidence in the research process and results. In short, the results are validated from a number of different directions. For an example of this in practice see the study by Matteucci (2013), which triangulates data from photographic images, participant observation and in-depth interviews.

A good analogy would be the evidence provided at a criminal trial that then has to be evaluated by the jury to determine whether the accused is guilty or innocent. Various types of evidence – eye witness, forensic, motivation, the means of committing the crime, the opportunity etc. – are presented by both the prosecution and the defence and 'tested' during the trial process that builds the two narratives of guilt or innocence. During this process each side will suggest that the evidence, and its interpretation, supports its position, which is, of course, diametrically opposed to that of the other side. When this process is complete it is then the task of the jury to evaluate these two alternative conclusions to decide which is the more believable or credible given the evidence presented and the arguments/explanations advanced by each side. Clearly, it is the strength, or weight, of evidence, and its credibility, that then should lead the jury to conclude one way or the other. The point here being that it is unlikely that one single piece of data or evidence will be sufficient to make a decision. However, this does not imply that all the data or evidence will be equally important in influencing the final decision. Some may be stronger and more pertinent than others, and vice versa.

Chapter Summary

Qualitative data collected as part of a deductive study will generally be easier to analyse than quantitative data because a conceptual framework already exists to structure and compare these.

Some forms of qualitative data can be quantified to assist analysis, but care needs to be taken when doing this as it can lead to the context(s) being ignored.

Computer software can assist analysis of either enumerated or non-enumerated qualitative data, but once again, these aids tend to decontextualise the analysis.

Data structuring, summarising and reduction are key tasks within the process of analysing qualitative data as they all assist the identification of categories, patterns, themes and relationships in the data.

Techniques such as content analysis and semiotics are useful for analysing textual and/or pictorial data, particularly in deductively designed studies.

A major issue in qualitative data analysis is the ability of the researcher to instil confidence in the reader as to the credibility of the methods and processes used to produce the final interpretation of the data.

References

Brotherton, B. (2005) 'The nature of hospitality: customer perceptions and implications,' *Tourism and Hospitality Planning & Development*, 2 (3): 139–53.

Brotherton, B. and Turner, R. (2001) 'Introducing yield management in hotels: getting the technical–human balance right', *Journal of Services Research*, 1 (2): 25–47.

Brotherton, B. and Wood, R.C. (2008) 'The nature and meanings of hospitality', in B. Brotherton and R.C. Wood (eds), *The SAGE Handbook of Hospitality Management*. London: Sage. pp. 37–61.

Crawford, A. (2013) 'Hospitality operators' understanding of service: a qualitative approach', *International Journal of Contemporary Hospitality Management*, 25 (1): 65–81.

Curtin, S. (2010) 'What makes for memorable wildlife encounters? Revelations from "serious" wildlife tourists', *Journal of Ecotourism*, 9 (2): 149–68.

Liang, C-H.J., Chen, H-B. and Wang, M-W. (2012) 'Units, populations and valid analyses', *International Journal of Culture, Tourism and Hospitality Research*, 6 (1): 70–80.

Matteucci, X. (2013) 'Photo elicitation: exploring tourist experiences with researcher-found images', *Tourism Management*, 35: 190–7.

Titz, K. and Dawson, M. (2011) 'The efficacy of Servqual constructs to code online hotel guest reviews: a content analysis', *International CHRIE Conference-Refereed Track. Paper 10.* http://scholarworks.umass.edu/refereed/ICHRIE_2011/Friday/10.

11

WRITING UP THE RESEARCH PROJECT

Chapter Content and Issues

Who is going to be the reader and what will be important to him or her?
What questions will he or she have in mind when reading the work?
What do I have to do to convince him or her that my work is credible?
How do I write in an academic style?
What has to be included in the final, written version?
Why do I need to include references in my work?
How do I make sure I reference correctly?

11.1 Introduction

In this final chapter we consider some key aspects of writing up the research study. Rather than trying to provide a model for writing the research report or dissertation, which in fact is a rather pointless exercise because different institutions will have different preferences and requirements, the approach taken here is concerned with encouraging you to make sure that some of the technical aspects of writing up, such as the references, are done correctly and to consider how issues of style and presentation should be approached, taking into account who the reader of this work will be and what is likely to be important to him or her. The purpose of this is not to provide you with a prescriptive blueprint to follow when writing up the work, but to supply a series of key thoughts to bear in mind when you are planning how to structure and present your arguments and evidence.

11.2 Style, Presentation and the Reader

One of the first questions you should consider when beginning to write up your research project or dissertation is, 'Who is going to read this and what are their expectations?'

11.2.1   The nature of academics

Normally, your audience is going to be one or more of the academic tutors who will be marking the work. You may have previously been given information from the tutors concerning the purpose of the research work, in educational terms, and possibly an indication of the criteria they intend to use to mark or grade it. You may also have other information concerning what their expectations are in relation to the required content and preferred style of different aspects or parts of the work and the final report or dissertation. This type of guidance is invaluable as it tells you what is expected, what will gain credit, what you will be penalised for and so on. You ignore these things at your peril!

Given that you should have this type of specific guidance, which, as mentioned, does vary from institution to institution, there are no examples of this type of information here. It is more useful to consider the nature of the academics who will read your work and what is likely to be important to them. Of course, this still has to be something of a generalisation because individual academics have their own unique educational and experiential backgrounds, beliefs and priorities. Nevertheless, academics in general are sceptical people because scepticism lies at the heart of an academic's being. It will have been instilled in them during their own training as academics.

This means that they are not predisposed to take anything they are told at face value – they need to be convinced by force of argument and supporting evidence. Thus, the academic who reads your work will not just accept or believe what you have written simply because you have written it. Therefore, one question you should bear in mind when writing up your report or dissertation is, 'Will the content and style of what I am writing enable the reader to accept what I say as convincing and therefore accept my results, conclusions and the method used to obtain these?' In other words, will it be credible enough to withstand the critical scrutiny of the reader?

11.2.2   Credibility

So, what makes something credible in the eyes of the reader? There are a number of things to consider from the reader's point of view. Is this a worthwhile topic, and does it have the potential to add something new to what is known already? Does it have an appropriate focus or is it far too general? Is there a convincing rationale provided for undertaking the research? Does it have a clear and feasible research question to answer or an aim and objectives to achieve? The answer given to all these questions should be 'yes' because these are all issues that should have been resolved before the work began.

Second, the academic may ask the following. Does this student demonstrate a sound and critical knowledge of antecedent (previous) work conducted in relation to this question or issue in the same field? In other words, is the student sufficiently aware of what came before, has this been evaluated in a critical manner, have obvious gaps or omissions in this been recognised and does the literature review contain a logical argument and substantive evidence to support a 'yes' answer to these questions? Does the review form a sound basis for the decisions that have been made regarding the conceptual framework used to inform the design of the empirical aspect of the research?

To put this in simpler terms, is the foundation for the work sufficiently strong for me to be confident that what is derived from or built on this basis is likely to be consistent and strong? If the foundations are seen to be weak, then this is likely to lead to the perception that whatever is built on these is weak also. In turn, this increases the academic's scepticism quotient and is likely to make him or her view the remainder of the work more critically.

Third, if, as the reader, I am happy with the foundations for the empirical work, the next question is, has this work been suitably informed by the conceptual thinking lying behind it and have appropriate data collection and analysis methods and procedures been adopted that will enable the researcher to answer the research question or achieve the aim or objectives? That is, is there a logical link between the conceptual view of the issue and how this is to be investigated in the real world or are these two elements unconnected and living in separate worlds? The element that should connect the conceptual and empirical aspects of your work is the 'conceptual framework' and associated methodology. As we saw in Chapter 5, this is derived from or built on the review of the literature and is then used as the basis for designing the empirical investigation. Therefore, whoever is reading, and marking, your work will want to see that this framework is a logical synthesis of the existing state of knowledge on the issues being researched and the methods used to investigate them have been clearly explained and justified.

To give the reader confidence in your empirical research design, you not only need to explain fully what methods and procedures you have chosen to use and how these have been used, but you should also provide evidence to convince him or her that these decisions have a logical basis, are consistent and that there is evidence to support their validity. This is why the methodology section or chapter in a research report or dissertation is so important. It is another aspect of the process of convincing the sceptical reader that the results you have obtained should be regarded as valid and reliable because the methods and processes used to obtain them are sound. You may remember, from your school science lessons, that when you were asked to write up the results obtained from laboratory experiments you were required to include not only what the results obtained were but also the type of apparatus used and the procedure or method adopted. Why were you asked to include these elements? Because your teacher could then determine whether the experiment was designed and conducted correctly, or not, as a basis for evaluating whether the results you obtained could be regarded as valid or not. Exactly the same principle applies here. If you can convince the person reading and marking your work that the approach you have taken to designing and conducting it has been sensible, logical and appropriate then s/he will have more confidence in the potential validity of its outcomes.

Fourth, the results and their significance are a key part of the whole investigation and the reader will be very interested in what results have been obtained and what you believe they show or mean. The reader is likely to be asking questions such as, 'What are the results, are they presented clearly, can I understand them, has the author explained what types of data analysis have been used to obtain them and produced interpretations of what they mean, is there an indication of their significance, do they support any claims made about their significance?' Again, the reader will be trying to see if the results are believable in terms of the method(s) and process(s) used to obtain them and what you claim they show or prove. To be successful in these respects, they have to be clear and used in a sensible and credible manner.

What is vitally important in this respect is the need to be truthful about what your results show. It is tempting to think that your work will be regarded as failing if the results do not support your prior assumptions or hypotheses or if you try to ignore what they do show in order to claim that your work does support what you hoped to prove. This is always a mistake, which will be recognised by the reader and probably will be heavily punished in terms of marks.

You should not feel that if your results do not allow you to prove what you set out to prove this is an automatic admission of failure and that it will lead to a loss of marks. Indeed, the reverse is more likely to be true. Honesty is always the best policy here because the reader will be looking to see if you are aware of the implications of your results whether these are favourable or not – and your credibility will be enhanced if you evaluate them honestly.

Finally, in the conclusions section of your work, the reader will be looking to see if you can 'close the circle'. By this I mean bring together the conceptual and empirical parts of the investigation, identify and reflect on any errors that became evident after the event and highlight any remaining and/or new questions, inconsistencies, problems and so on that only became evident once the research had been completed. So, the reader will have questions such as, 'Are the conclusions justified, is there sufficient evidence to support them, are they sensible, have any omissions or errors been recognised and commented on appropriately and are there sensible suggestions for future work that needs to be done as a consequence of the findings from this work?'

In general, what the reader is looking for here is a clear indication that you have developed a suitable insight into not only the results and what they show but also into what you have learned from the process of actually conducting the research. Given that it is rare for a research project to go totally to plan, and that decisions made in designing and conducting it are not always the correct ones with hindsight, you should not be afraid to admit to any problems you encountered or mistakes made because how you dealt with them and/or recognised the implications of them will indicate that you have reflective insight.

11.2.3 Academic style

On the question of the style of writing to use and the technicalities of formatting and presenting the document, once again you will undoubtedly have received some type of document from your institution outlining the style and format it requires you to use. Because such requirements do vary from place to place, again it does not seem sensible to make prescriptive comments on such issues here. However, one aspect is worthy of further comment because it is generally applicable and you may have some doubts about it. It is the requirement that the document is written in an 'academic style'. What does this mean in practice?

Writing in an academic style is not an intuitive thing for many people as it is not how we would normally speak or write – it is quite formal and dispassionate. In technical terms, the academic style of writing involves using the third person rather than the first as it tries to convey an objective approach to the issues in question. In other words, it is a narrative based on evidence rather than subjective opinion or speculation. This means that you have to write as though you are an independent, uninvolved observer.

Your personal, subjective opinion is not required – only your objective and logical use and analysis of the evidence, whether you personally agree with it or not. So, using 'I' or 'we' is not permissible. Instead of 'I think' or 'I believe', use phrases such as, 'the evidence shows' or 'in the light of the available evidence it appears to be clear that'. Similarly, phrases such as 'my results' or 'my conclusions are' should be avoided. Use 'the results' and 'the conclusions' instead.

An academic style of writing also demands explicitness; accuracy and precision in the use of language so do not be vague and imprecise. For example, the phrase 'some researchers have found that ...', is likely to have markers such as myself writing 'who are they?', 'when did they discover this?', 'were their methods sound?' etc. – and deciding to mark you down as a consequence. Similarly, phrases such as 'it has been found that ...', are likely to drive your marker equally crazy! Another practice that will antagonise a marker is the non-standard use of standard terms. Many terms in academic subjects have highly specific meanings and usage that can vary from how we might use these terms in everyday language. Remember our discussion of the difference in meaning between significant and statistically significant in Chapter 9. Another common mistake is to use the word 'survey/s' to refer to questionnaires. The term survey refers to the overall approach, strategy or research design; it should not be used to refer to the questionnaires that are used to collect the survey data. So, to say, '324 completed surveys were used in the analysis', is totally incorrect. You did not undertake 324 surveys; you undertook one survey that yielded 324 completed questionnaires.

Being cautious in what you claim and the language you use to do this is also a feature of academic writing. This is often referred to as 'hedging'. Hedging means that you 'hedge your bets' by not taking too extreme a position. So, for example, rather than saying, 'this proves that x causes y', which is a very definitive statement, it may be preferable to be a little more circumspect and say, 'this constitutes quite strong evidence to suggest that x may be a primary cause of y', or alternatively, 'the available evidence suggest that, on the balance of probabilities, x is more likely than not to be a cause of y'. There is, of course, a sound reason for adopting this type of approach; it is not just, as some may see it, to be merely a silly convention invented by academics. If you think back to Chapter 2, and our discussion of the 'what can we know' issue, you will recall that it is difficult to be certain of anything; there is always the possibility, however small, that what you think you know may not be correct.

A dispassionate, objective approach to writing up a research report involves stating the purpose(s) of it and providing a rationale to justify undertaking the research (see Chapters 1 and 3), comparing, contrasting and commenting on the evidence that already exists in the literature (see Chapter 4), explaining and justifying your conceptual conclusions and the methodological decisions underlying your empirical research design and procedures (see Chapters 2, 5, 6, 7 and 8), stating the results and the analytical techniques and procedures used to obtain these (see Chapters 9 and 10) and the conclusions derived from this process.

11.3 The Contents

As most institutions will have their own guidelines concerning the structure and sequence of a research report or dissertation, there is, once again, little point in trying to prescribe a particular format here. That said, the content of these types of documents is fairly, though not totally, universal in terms of the type of sections or chapters that must be included. What does, of course, vary is the particular order that these should be presented in and whether or not certain aspects should be separated or can be dealt with in one subdivision of the work. For an extended version of what follows, including useful examples, see Baum (1999).

11.3.1 The introduction

This should be the first chapter or section of the document. Its purpose is to paint in the general background for the study – that is, locate the specific issue(s) being investigated within their wider context. Here you are trying to explain where you are coming from in terms of arriving at the specific focus of the research from the more general context it is derived from. This is sometimes thought of as the rationale for undertaking the study – why it is important, what benefits it will bring, who will be interested in the findings, what it will add to what is already known. Within the introduction it is also usual to include the study's focus – the research question(s) to be answered or the aim/objectives to be achieved – to give the reader a clear indication of what it is designed to achieve. It is often regarded as helpful to conclude the introduction with a short summary of the chapters or sections included in the document to give the reader an indication of what is to come.

Along with further information covering issues associated with a number of aspects of writing up the research the Companion Website (study.sagepub.com/brotherton) also contains links to video material focusing specifically on the introduction and conclusions parts of the final report or dissertation.

11.3.2 The literature review

The literature review invariably follows the introduction, though some commentators suggest that the methodology section or chapter should precede it. However, my personal view is that the methodology section should follow the literature review as the question of what methodological approach should be adopted and the methods employed can really only be answered once the existing state of knowledge has been considered and reviewed. Whichever order is preferred or indeed demanded, the review of the literature, as discussed in Chapter 4, is your opportunity to demonstrate that you are aware of and have critically considered the current state of knowledge relating to your research topic or question. The literature review will not reproduce text from the original sources in a verbatim manner and, in this sense, will contain a considerable amount of summarising and paraphrasing from the original sources. This is often something students encounter some difficulty in doing effectively (see Technique Tip box – Summarising and Paraphrasing).

Technique Tip	**Summarising and Paraphrasing**

A summary is obviously a shortened version of the original but summarising does not mean simply cutting out certain words, phrases or sentences from the original and using what remains. When you summarise something it will obviously be shorter than the original but it is also transformed into your own words. This raises some issues.

Accuracy is one. When you transform the original into a shorter version and state this in your own words it is critical that you do this accurately. Your ability to achieve this depends upon your understanding and interpretation of the original so you must make sure that you understand what the original is saying and reproduce this accurately in your summarised interpretation.

Attribution is another. Although you are converting the original into your own words you were not the originator of the ideas or results you are summarising. This was someone else and therefore you have to recognise this by attributing these things to their originator by using an appropriate citation.

Paraphrasing is similar to summarising but the latter tends to be more general in providing an overall view or stance on the topic, whereas the former tends to be more specific dealing with a more limited and particular aspect that is to be explored in greater detail. The same principles of converting the original to your own words and providing suitable attribution apply equally to paraphrasing.

This, of course, can be subdivided into sections, but they should be few in number and limited to major subdivisions because the review should be a discursive treatment of the material. Breaking the review into too many sections disrupts the flow of your argument and helps to create the impression that you may be merely describing, rather than critically evaluating, the material.

At the end of the review, there needs to be a summary or a concluding section that synthesises the discussion and highlights the key issues and questions that your empirical investigation is to focus on. This also serves as a useful link or bridge for the next chapter on methodology.

11.3.3   The methodology chapter

This is the chapter where you begin to make the transition from what is known already to your intentions regarding what you intend to do to add to this. Working from the review of the literature, you have both substantive and methodological inputs to help you formulate a conceptual framework and hypotheses that can be explained and justified by reference to the literature. You must also explain the methods and processes used to action the empirical data collection and analysis phases of your research and justify those choices. This is your opportunity to convince the reader that your results and findings should be taken seriously because you have obtained them in a systematic and credible way.

The video material on writing a methodology chapter, available via the Companion Website (study.sagepub.com/brotherton), may help you to get a firmer understanding of these issues and how to deal with them.

11.3.4   The results or findings chapter

This chapter comes next, but its format may differ from institution to institution. In some cases this is purely a chapter that reports the results or findings from the empirical investigation, followed by another chapter that interprets and discusses the significance and implications of these findings. However, some institutions may favour putting these two aspects together into one single chapter. Whichever format is preferred clearly has implications for how these two aspects are organised and dealt with. Where separate chapters are specified in the guidelines issued the results chapter purely deals with the presentation of the results. In this sense it is a factual statement of the results obtained from the analysis of the empirical data, be this quantitative or qualitative in nature. The results chapter is then followed by the 'discussion' chapter that should seek to indicate what these results mean and what their implications are. Where a single results/discussion chapter is preferred this provides more flexibility in how the results and their implications can be dealt with. In this case there may be options to either separate these two elements to 'ape' the two chapter model by presenting the results at the beginning and then discussing them later in the chapter. Alternatively, it may be possible to weave these two elements together as the chapter progresses.

Although your institution may indicate its preference in these respects within the guidelines provided it equally may not. If it does then you should adhere to its stated preference and if it does not then you need to think about which approach would be the most appropriate. Remember, what you are trying to do here, in both of these respects, is to tell the reader what has been discovered as a result of your research and then what this means or what implications it has. In doing this your guiding principle should be to adopt a format and style that is the most appropriate to communicate these things as clearly and concisely as possible.

The use of tables, charts and diagrams is invariably a good strategy because in producing these you will be demonstrating that you have not simply decided to present the raw data but have engaged with it to analyse and summarise what it says. Furthermore, presenting your results, when appropriate, using contemporary data visualisation techniques and software can further indicate that your analysis has been conducted in a more extensive and thoughtful manner. In this respect the web link to the 'Flowing Data' website in the Companion Website (study.sagepub.com/brotherton) would be particularly helpful to obtain ideas of how you could do this.

11.3.5   The conclusions

Finally, this chapter – which may also include an opportunity to make recommendations or suggestions for future research – is where you bring your work to a close and state if the original question has been answered or whether the aim/objectives have been achieved totally, partially or not at all. In other words, you can now comment on the relative success or failure of the project and reflect on what were good and bad decisions, which problems you encountered and any ongoing uncertainties. See Technique Tip box – Writing Better Conclusions.

Technique Tip	Writing Better Conclusions

Firstly, make sure that your 'conclusions' really do conclude the work that has been conducted and reported in the earlier sections or chapters of the piece. Striking out on a tangent, introducing new material not referred to before and/ or deciding it is appropriate to have a personal rant are all strategies that will disadvantage you. So, make sure that your conclusions are based upon, and derived from, what you have said previously in your work because if you start making assertions that do not have an evidence base the marker is going to ask 'where has this come from – out of the blue?' – and will penalise you accordingly.

Secondly, ensure you summarise, without repeating large pieces of the prior text, the key aspects, the main themes and the most important, significant and interesting findings. You need to avoid the marker writing on your work – 'merely repetition'! This is your last chance to convince the reader that your work really does contain things that are valuable and, as not everything will be equally interesting or valuable, you need to pick out, and highlight, the aspects that have the greatest value. Think about someone trying to convince you that a certain product is the one you should buy: they are not going to tell you everything about this, they will focus on, and emphasise, the key aspects that they believe are going to be of greatest interest and relevance to you. This is how you should think about this aspect of your conclusions.

Thirdly, do not over-claim. Academics are going to be very sceptical of conclusions that claim the work has been perfect, that all the questions have been fully answered and that there are no further questions or issues to explore on the topic. Again, think about this. If someone tried to convince you that something is perfect you may well be a little sceptical, you may not believe them. Remember the old adage; if it sounds too good to be true it probably isn't!

Fourthly, you can be personal but don't go overboard. It is permissible in the conclusions to give your opinion/s *but* do not do this in a dogmatic manner.

Fifth, be honest but not suicidal. Academics know that research projects rarely, if ever, go entirely to plan. There are always limitations, expected or unexpected, decisions can be made that, with the benefit of hindsight, may be seen to be mistaken. In my experience many students feel that it is a sign of weakness to admit any errors or limitations because they think this will count against them. This is rarely the case. In fact the reverse is more often that not the case. Recognising errors and limitations, and identifying their impacts and effects, is honesty. Going to town and over-emphasising these and their effects will be counterproductive. Honesty is a virtue but self-flagellation is foolishness, so take a balanced approach. The key thing to remember here is that, whatever else it might be, the research project is a learning exercise or vehicle. Looking back, recognising and reflecting upon the process you have gone through in terms of its success and failures is a very important part of the whole process. Doing this demonstrates that you have developed insight, reflexivity and have learned from the experience.

Finally, remember that the pursuit of knowledge does not end with your contribution. It is virtually certain that your work will not have fully answered all the questions it was designed to address and it is highly likely that new questions will have been generated by what you have done. Therefore, while you can, and should, make clear what your work has contributed to the topic, you also need to recognise and state what needs to be done from this point onwards. So, identifying fruitful areas, new issues, emergent questions and possibilities for future research is an important part of the research process. Just as reviewing the literature produced by previous research studies helped to inform the nature of your project, you should 'return the favour' by suggesting where the research agenda might go from this point onwards. Just as you stood on the shoulders of those who came before you – you need to provide a similar platform for those who are going to come after you.

11.4   References in the Text and Bibliography

Referencing the sources of information used and cited in the text of your work, and producing the corresponding full version in the bibliography, is something that seems to confuse many students in terms of understanding what to do (how to reference in a technically correct manner) and why it is necessary in the first place (its purpose). Hopefully, both of these issues will become clearer once you have read this section.

11.4.1   Why reference?

Taking the rationale for referencing first, one reason for it is that it demonstrates what is known as appropriate attribution. This means that if you are using another person's work, you make sure that the source of the work is properly recorded – you acknowledge that it belongs to that person. He or she is the original author and the intellectual effort that this individual has put into producing the work should be explicitly recognised by citing the appropriate details. Technically, whether you overtly intend to or not, if you do not do this then you are likely to be accused of an unacceptable practice that may attract a penalty from your institution. This may be referred to as poor attribution practice, cheating or plagiarism, depending on how serious and endemic it is in your work. I shall not discuss these issues further here as your institution will undoubtedly have informed you of how such practices are defined, how to avoid committing these sins and the penalties attached to them if you do and are caught.

A second reason for referencing is to present evidence that you are aware of, and are knowledgeable about, other work that has been produced relating to the topic or research question(s) you are dealing with. A good analogy here is that of a court trial. If a lawyer, representing either party, can refer to previous cases that are relevant to the one in question, supporting the point he or she is trying to make, then this strengthens his or her argument.

11.4.2   How to reference correctly

Moving on to the issue of how to reference correctly, there are many referencing styles or systems that have their own conventions regarding what should be included in the text and the references section for written or other types of sources. Indeed, you may have encountered these in the different books, journals and periodicals you have read as part of your research because different publishers have different 'house styles' for the referencing format they prefer to use in their publications. Whatever the particular style and format adopted, it is generally the case that the information required to produce a reference using one system will be sufficient to produce a similar reference using another system, even though how this is organised and presented will differ. Therefore, you should not feel that if your sources have used different referencing systems and formats this will stop you converting them into the system you are using.

Perhaps the most widely used referencing system is the Harvard system and this may well be the one your institution recommends or even insists that you use. If it is not, then I am sure you will have been provided with the details of an alternative system that the institution prefers and how to produce references using that system. Rather than waste time and space here discussing the alternative referencing systems, I intend to concentrate on the Harvard system as a vehicle to illustrate how textual and bibliographic references should be produced.

11.4.3   Text citations

Taking text citations first, there are two main types of reference. These are commonly known as indirect, passing references or direct quotations. The difference between the two is that an indirect reference is used when you are writing the text using your own words but these have been derived from or influenced by another source. For example, you may be summarising findings from previous studies in your own words, but need to record the source of these studies to indicate where these conclusions can be found. Alternatively, you may want to note the source of the evidence you have used to produce your summary. In the case of a direct quotation, you are using someone else's words and not your own – you are reproducing directly what someone else has previously said or written.

In the Harvard system, there is little difference between these two forms of text citation. Both require the author(s) surname(s) and the year of publication of the source cited. For a direct quotation, the page number(s) where the original text is located in the source are also included. Where the actual citation, whether it is indirect or direct, should appear in your text and the format it should take can vary slightly depending on how it fits into the flow of the narrative and whether it is a citation for a table or figure. Technique Tip box – Direct and Indirect Text Citations Using the Harvard System – contains some examples of these variations.

Technique Tip

Direct and Indirect Text Citations Using the Harvard System

The information that should be included in a standard, indirect text citation is the author(s) surname(s) and the year of publication. All of this information or only the date may be contained within brackets, such as '(Brotherton, 2004)' or 'Brotherton (2004)', or with multiple authors, '(Brotherton and Wood, 2004)' or 'Brotherton and Wood (2004)'.

Often, the fully bracketed form is used where the citation appears at the end of a sentence and the other where it appears within the sentence because this tends to fit in well with the flow of the text. However, it is possible to use the bracketed form within a sentence where this is more appropriate. For example, 'some

(Continued)

(Continued)

authors argue that hospitality is a multifaceted concept (Brotherton and Wood, 2004) but other authors disagree (Smith and Jones, 2003)'. If the sentence had been worded differently, then the non-bracketed form might have been more appropriate. For example, 'While Brotherton and Wood (2004) argue that hospitality is a multifaceted concept, Smith and Jones (2003) disagree'.

The same principles apply to direct quotations, but then the start and finish of the quotation must be indicated and the page number(s) where this appeared in the original source must be included. It is also sometimes regarded as good practice to italicise the text of a quotation to make it even clearer where it begins and ends and to show that it is something other than your own words. For example, 'according to Brotherton and Wood (2004: 45) *"the research evidence clearly indicates that hospitality is a multifaceted concept that requires more sophisticated investigation than has hitherto been undertaken"*.'

If the quotation is a long one – two to three sentences or a paragraph – then it is also often regarded as good practice to separate it from the main text by presenting it as a separate paragraph and possibly indenting it on the left and right sides.

Where you are producing a citation for a table, diagram or figure taken from an original source, the normal conventions and format for a direct quotation apply, but with one small difference. It is regarded as good practice to locate the citation under the table, diagram or figure and to include the word 'source'. For example, 'Source: Brotherton and Wood (2004: 52)'.

So, as we have seen above, normally the difference between a direct quotation and an indirect reference is quite obvious in terms of whose words are being used – yours or someone else's – but there can be something of a grey area between these two where most of the words used are your own but you want to quote one, two or a few words directly from the original source. In these circumstances, it is normal practice to use the standard, indirect form of citation – that is without including the page number(s). You simply indicate which of the words are not your own by using quotation marks around them. For example, 'Brotherton and Wood (2004) take a different view of hospitality from many other authors and suggest that it is "a multifaceted concept".'

You may also encounter some types of source that differ from the standard ones referred to above. Some examples of these are provided in the Technique Tip box – Solving Possible Citation Problems in the Harvard System. These may include sources with no named author, government publications, secondary and electronic sources or other types of media, such as film, television or radio, and other variations on the standard formats. The same Technique Tip box, and the one that follows – Bibliographic Citations Using the Harvard System – contain examples of how these can be cited in the text and bibliography using the Harvard system.

Technique Tip	Solving Possible Citation Problems in the Harvard System

More than one publication by the same author(s) published in the same year

This is a problem because both the text and bibliographic citation use the year of publication as a differentiating indicator. However, this problem is easy to solve. All you need to do is place a suffix after the year to differentiate one publication from another. For example, 'Brotherton and Wood (2004a)' and 'Brotherton and Wood (2004b)' indicate that there are two separate publications produced by these authors in the same year and that there are two separate entries in the bibliography or references section for these two different publications.

When can you use 'et al.'?

Et al., an abbreviated version of the Latin *et alia*, simply means 'and others'. It is a form of shorthand to avoid having to cite all the authors' surnames in the text. For example, 'Brotherton, Wood, Smith and Jones (2004)' can become 'Brotherton et al. (2004)'. It cannot be used where there are fewer than three authors or in the corresponding entry in the bibliography or references section.

Dealing with quotations that flow over two pages or are discontinuous

In some circumstances, you may wish to cite a quotation that begins on one page and ends on the next or you may wish to pick out and combine two or more pieces from different pages in the original text. The conventions for dealing with these are as follows. First, with a continuous quotation flowing over two pages, you cite the reference in the same way as you would for a normal quotation, but indicate the starting and finishing pages for the quote, inserting a dash between the two, such as 'Brotherton (2004: 19–20)'. Second, when the quotation is discontinuous, the page numbers the separate pieces of text appear on in the original are separated by commas, so for example it could read 'Brotherton (2004: 21, 25, 32)'. In the quotation itself, the pieces are separated by a series of dots (known as an ellipsis), such as, 'hospitality as a concept … is multifaceted … and one lacking sufficient explanation'.

Citing multiple works by one author or different authors in the text

Where you wish to summarise evidence and/or ideas from more than one source, then it is normal practice to string these citations together. For example, in the case of multiple works by one author, you might say, 'All the work on this issue by Green (1998, 2000, 2004) has arrived at the same conclusion' or 'Green's work (1998, 2000, 2004) has arrived at the same conclusion' or 'Green has arrived at the same conclusion in all of his work (1998, 2000, 2004)'.

(Continued)

(Continued)

In the case of multiple authors, you may say, 'All the work on this issue has come to the same conclusion (Blue, 2004; Brown, 1996; Green, 1994; Yellow, 2000)' or 'all the work conducted on this issue (Green, 1994; Brown, 1996; Yellow, 2000; Blue, 2004) has come to the same conclusion'. You may arrange the list of citations in either alphabetical (in the first example here) or ascending chronological (in the second example) order. If your institution does not specify, you may choose which you prefer but you *must be consistent* throughout the whole of your write-up. You may feel chronological order is more relevant should you wish to indicate how study in a particular field has developed over time.

What do I do when the source I've read cited another author but did not give the reference for this?

This is known as secondary referencing and should be used sparingly as it may reduce the credibility of your writing or argument. However, in cases where you have no other option, the following formats should be used. For example, in the text, this may appear as, 'Wood (cited by Brotherton, 2003) contends that ...' or, in the case of a quotation, '"hospitality is a defunct concept" (Wood, cited by Brotherton, 2003: 45)'. In the bibliography, use the same format as for a chapter from an edited book.

11.4.4   Bibliographic citations

The text citations you include in your write-up are essentially condensed, or shortened, versions of the full citation included in the bibliography or references section. However, there is a crucial relationship between these two beyond the difference in their length. It is, first, that the two must exist and, second, that the full bibliographic details must be identifiable from the version in the text. As we have seen already, the reference in the text follows the format of author(s) surname(s) and year of publication, so logically the full bibliographic details in the references section should initially follow the same format because we only have these two pieces of information in the text reference from which we need to be able to find the full reference. Technique Tip box – Bibliographic Citations Using the Harvard System – has examples of how different types of source should be cited in the bibliography.

Technique Tip	**Bibliographic Citations Using the Harvard System**
	The first principle to apply when creating a bibliography using the Harvard system is to organise the entries in alphabetical order by the author(s) surname(s) and initial(s). This is the first detail given in references in the text so it is logical

that this is the first piece of information given in the full bibliographic entry. Similarly, as the corresponding references in the text only have one more piece of information – the year of publication – it is also logical that this comes next. Hence, the text reference 'Brotherton and Wood (2004)' becomes 'Brotherton, B. and Wood, R.C. (2004)' in the bibliography.

What are now required are the remaining details about the publication to enable those viewing the citation to obtain the source if they so desire. The ways in which these details are recorded differ slightly according to the type of source – that is, whether it is a book, paper in a journal, article in a magazine or newspaper, a dissertation or thesis, a sound or video recording, a website – but all follow the same basic principle of containing sufficient information to enable the source to be identified and obtained. Hypothetical examples of each of these and a way of setting each one out are shown below.

For books

Author(s) surname(s), initials (year of publication) title, place of publication, name of publisher. For example, 'Brotherton, B. and Wood, R.C. (2004) *Hospitality: A radical view*. London, Sage.'

For papers in journals

Author(s) surname(s), initials (year of publication) title of the paper, name of the journal, volume number, issue number, pages the paper appears on. For example, 'Brotherton, B. and Wood, R.C. (2004) 'Hospitality – a radical view', *International Journal of Hospitality Management*, 22 (4), pp. 234–50.'

For a chapter from an edited book

Chapter author(s) surname(s), initials (year of publication) title of the chapter, editor(s) initials and surname(s), title of the book, place of publication, name of publisher, pages the chapter appears on. For example, 'Brotherton, B. and Wood, R.C. (2004) 'Hospitality – a radical view', in G. Hathaway (ed.), *Hospitality in the Twenty-first Century*. London, Sage, pp. 45–60.'

For an article from a magazine or newspaper

This format described here applies to these types of publication, which do not have volume and issue numbers. Where magazines have such pieces of information, the format given above for papers in journals can be used. Author(s) surname(s), initials (year of publication), title of the article, name of the magazine or newspaper, date of publication, page(s) the article appears on. An example from a newspaper would be 'Brotherton, B. and Wood, R.C. (2004) 'Hospitality – a radical view', *The Times*, 22 January, p. 6.' For an article from a magazine, an example would be, 'Brotherton, B. and Wood, R.C. (2004) 'Hospitality – a radical view', *Contemporary Hospitality*, January, pp. 6–8.'

For work by an unidentifiable author

In such cases, either the normal format for the type of publication is used and the word 'Anon.' or the title of the publication can be used in place of the

(Continued)

(Continued)

author's name. For example, 'Tourism Today (2011) 'Who believes traditional destinations are dead?', *Tourism Today*, 4 (1), pp. 1–2'.

For government publications

Use the format given for books and, if there is no identifiable author, put the name of the organisation that commissioned the report. For example, 'Department of Culture (2002) *Reorganising the UK's Tourism Organisations*. London, TSO.'

For theses or dissertations

Follow the same basic procedure that you would for books, but here, of course, there will be no publisher or location information as these are unpublished works. However, the equivalent information exists in the form of the name of the institution that conferred the award and its location. For example, 'Jones, B. (1999) 'Service quality in UK restaurants', PhD thesis, Department of Hospitality Management, John Wrasse University, Boston, UK'.

For electronic sources

There are many different types of electronic sources for documents, but the general principles for citing them are the same as those for more conventional publications. What is required is for sufficient details to be provided to allow the source to be identified and accessed.

The general format for this type of source is author(s) surname(s), initial(s) (where there is no identifiable author, 'Anon.' or the website name can be used) (year of publication) title, location (that is, name of website), place (if applicable), URL (that is, website address), date accessed. For example, 'Hogg, T. (2012) 'Ruritania's tourism future', University of Ruritania, Real City. Available at: http/ ur.ac.ru/ruritania-tourism-research-institute/research-papers/july-2001/html [accessed 30 September 2014]'.

The statement that both forms of the citation (i.e. in the text and in the bibliography) should exist may sound rather obvious, but experience suggests that this does not always happen. It is easy, when writing the text and citing sources as you go, to forget to also enter the full reference in the bibliography. Similarly, it is tempting to pad out a bibliography with more citations than have been recorded in the text to make it look as though you have read more widely than you actually have. Both these things should be avoided, for fairly obvious reasons, but there is another reason, one that is rooted in the use of the Harvard system. It is a basic tenet of this system that all the bibliographic citations have corresponding citations in the text and vice versa. If there is a mismatch between them, then the reader may become suspicious and, more importantly, you may lose marks!

Note also that there are some differences of opinion regarding the nature of the bibliography in this system. Some regard it as a complete record of all the sources consulted, regardless of whether they have been cited in the text or not. Thus what I have referred to earlier as the bibliography they would call a list of references, as it contains only sources cited in the text. Where this is the desired practice, you would have a references section and a bibliography may contain those sources listed in the reference section *plus* others consulted but not cited in the text. Personally I find this rather confusing and illogical and would suggest that you regard the bibliography as the definitive list of references cited in the text. If you wish, it is possible to have another list entitled 'Other sources consulted' that would give details of sources not cited in the text.

If you need further guidance on how to reference other types of sources, there are many websites that have guidance documents. By entering 'Harvard referencing system' as the search term into Google, you can access these easily.

11.5 A Final Check

Once you feel that you have completed a final draft of the work then it is always a good idea to review this to ensure that you have not left out any crucial material and that you have produced the work in the appropriate manner and format. The review-type questions contained in the Research Action Checklist – Checking Your Write-Up – will help you to do this in a reasonably systematic and comprehensive manner. In addition, these are the key questions that any marker of your work will have in mind as they are reading it, so, if you address these appropriately, you are likely to put yourself in an advantageous position.

Research Action Checklist	Checking Your Write-Up

Introduction/Rationale

✓ Will the reader have a clear and unambiguous understanding of your research topic?

✓ Have you explicitly stated what the context and boundaries of the topic are?

✓ Is there a sound rationale and justification for researching this topic?

✓ Is the main research question or aim clearly stated?

✓ Are the subsidiary questions or objectives clear, achievable and directly related to the overall purpose of the research?

✓ Will the reader 'get' what you are proposing to do?

(Continued)

(Continued)

The Literature Review

✓ Is your literature review structured and organised to ensure that your argument/analysis flows logically and clearly?

✓ Have you made clear how the literature you have reviewed is relevant and related to your research question/s and/or aim/objectives?

✓ Will your literature review, as a whole, convince the reader that you have sufficiently covered the existing knowledge relating to your topic?

✓ Is your literature review written in an analytical, critical manner, or is it merely a descriptive summary of what has gone before?

✓ Does your review have a clear 'end point', i.e. is there a synthesis or summary of the key points and issues?

✓ Will the review provide a sound basis for you to develop a conceptual model and hypotheses to link the secondary and primary research activities?

The Methodology

✓ Have you developed an appropriate conceptual model, and associated hypotheses, to link the literature review and the design and conduct of the empirical research?

✓ Does this provide sufficient guidance for your empirical research design decisions?

✓ Have you used your model/hypotheses to explain and justify why you have chosen to design and structure your empirical research in the way you have done?

✓ Will the reader be convinced that your choice of design/approach is the most appropriate one?

✓ Are all the variables clearly stated and explained and are the relationships between these stated explicitly?

✓ Have you made clear what measures you used and why these are vital to achieve a successful outcome?

✓ Is your sampling strategy clear and have you adequately explained the procedures used to implement this?

✓ Have you detailed and justified the instruments and procedures used to collect the data?

✓ Are your data analysis choices clearly stated and justified?

✓ Are any ethical aspects dealt with appropriately?

✓ Were there any difficulties encountered in the research process and have you explained the implications of these and how you dealt with them?

The Findings/Results and Discussion

✓   Are your findings presented in a clear and parsimonious manner or do the key findings get lost amongst a lot of unnecessary detail?

✓   If there is too much data that is obscuring the main points could you remove some of this and place it in an appendix?

✓   Have you chosen the most appropriate formats to present your data?

✓   Are your results presented so that they relate directly to your research question/s, aim/objectives and hypotheses?

✓   Will the reader clearly see the main points you are trying to highlight in your results?

✓   Are your interpretations of the implications and significance of the results logical and consistent?

✓   Does your discussion connect the findings to your research question/s, aim/ objectives and hypotheses?

✓   If you have made assertions and inferences on the basis of your results are these fully explained and justified by reference to the evidence that supports them?

The Conclusions

✓   Are your conclusions merely a summary of what you've said before?

✓   Do your conclusions make it clear which of your research questions, or aims/ objectives, have been answered or achieved, and which have not, and why?

✓   Have you reflected on the process of your research and identified its successes, limitations and any failures?

✓   Do your conclusions 'close the circle' by making it clear how your research has added something to the existing body of knowledge relating to your topic?

✓   Is there a recognition, and statement, of the implications of your findings for further research on the topic, i.e. have you included a tentative future research agenda for those who follow you indicating where and how future research effort might usefully be focused?

General Style and Format Issues

✓   Are your sentences and paragraphs a suitable length to make your message clear?

✓   Have you used appropriate chapter/section headings and sub-headings to signal changes in content and emphasis?

✓   Is your writing style appropriate?

✓   Have you included clear signposts in the text to guide the reader from one aspect to another?

(Continued)

(Continued)

✓ Have you avoided using any potentially racist or sexist language?

✓ Are all your figures, tables, charts and diagrams labelled appropriately, clearly and consistently?

✓ Spelling and grammar checkers are not foolproof, so have you carefully proofread your text to ensure that typos and other errors that would not be picked up by these checkers have been eliminated?

✓ Is your referencing accurate, complete and compliant with the referencing style you have been required to use?

✓ Have you ensured that everything that should have been attributed has been, so that you cannot be accused of poor attribution practice or plagiarism?

✓ Do the text and bibliographic citations match exactly?

✓ Is there a clear and logical structure to the work as a whole and does the text 'flow' from beginning to end?

✓ Have you made sure that your work complies with the guidance you have been given regarding things such as maximum word length, inclusion of a contents list, list/s of figures, tables etc., the layout of the title page, the line spacing and font size required, the type of binding that is acceptable?

✓ If you have included any appendices have you placed these at the end of the work, after any bibliography or reference list, and numbered them appropriately?

Chapter Summary

Before you start writing, consider the nature of who is going to read your work and what is likely to be important to him or her.

Remember, you have to convince the reader that your study is worthwhile and has been designed and conducted in a credible manner.

Make sure that you adopt the right style of writing and presentation for the nature of the work and its audience.

Structure and sequence the document in a logical manner.

Ensure that you have referenced all your sources correctly, both in the text and in your reference section or bibliography.

Don't forget to review your final draft to ensure you have not left out anything crucial and that you have addressed all the questions in the review checklist fully.

References

Baum, T. (1999) 'Presentation of research findings', in B. Brotherton (ed.), *The Handbook of Contemporary Hospitality Management Research*. Chichester: John Wiley. pp. 305–30.

INDEX

academic writing style 282, 283, 285, 286
access 17, 52–53, 142, 147, 150, 156, 157,
    192–194, 206, 207, 223
action research 126, 156–158, 161
aims 46, 50, 55–57, 61, 79, 129, 149, 164,
    168, 205, 301
alternate hypotheses 111,
analytic induction 275
analytical survey 137
applied research 1–2, 12, 14–15, 22
argot 195
artificiality 34, 36, 126, 131
association, measures of
    Cramer's V coefficient 248
    Cross-tabulation 232, 246–247, 265, 278
    Pearson's r 250, 255
    phi coefficient 248
    Spearman's r 2 250, 255
average *see* mean
axial coding 274–275

balanced scales 120, 182
Bartlett's Test of Sphericity 262
between-group variation 223, 257
bias 6, 10, 20, 27, 73, 123, 194, 204,
    219, 279
    questionnaire design and 138, 141, 183
    respondent 140
    sampling 87, 138, 208, 225, 227
bibliographic referencing 85, 293, 296, 302
bipolar scale 180, 182–183
bivariate
    data analysis 238, 246, 255, 265
Boolean logic 77–78

case studies
    embedded 149, 151, 159
    holistic 149, 151
    multiple 149, 151
    single 149, 224
case study
    design 42, 52, 53, 126, 141, 146–151,
        160, 162, 228
    research 141, 146–151, 161, 276

cases
    atypical 226
    critical 150
    extreme 18, 150, 226
    revelatory 150
    unique 150
categorical variables 104, 107, 118, 236,
    251, 261
causal relationships 95, 107, 109, 131
causality, conditions for 110, 131
central tendency 232, 240–243, 265
characteristics of scientific research 1,
    6–12, 22
    confidence 9–10
    generalisable 10–11
    objective 10
    parsimonious 11
    precision 9
    purposeful 7
    replicable 8–9
    rigorous 7
    testable 8
chi-square test 251, 255, 260–261, 265
    for goodness of fit 255, 261
    for independence 251, 255, 261
citations
    Harvard system 293–299
classification questions 179
closed questions 30, 87, 168–169, 164–167,
    171–172, 179, 200
cluster
    analysis 261
    sampling 223
coding 172, 233–235, 267, 270, 272–275,
    271, 277
    axial 274–275
    open 273–274
    selective 275
collective exhaustion 117
comparative research 43, 52, 93, 126, 133,
    136, 141–146, 149, 151, 159–161, 171,
    228, 269
    case-oriented approaches 146
    negative approach 144

comparative research *cont.*
  positive approach 143–144
  variable-oriented approaches 146
comparisons
  inter-case 145, 151
  intra-case 145, 151
computer assisted qualitative data
    analysis 267, 277
concepts 17, 38, 53, 88, 90, 94–100, 105,
    108–109, 114–117, 122, 124–125,
    133–134, 228, 273–276
  dimensions and 115
  elements and 116
  indicators and 116
conceptual framework 7, 57, 92, 94, 95–98,
    100–102, 109, 114, 121, 124–125,
    129–130, 157, 280, 284, 289
  its relationship to constructs and variables
    97–98
  what it does 96–97
  what it is 95
  where it appears in a research study 96
  why it is necessary 96
conclusion section, research report and 285,
    290–291, 301
concurrent validity 123
confidence 9–10, 33, 127, 129, 226, 279, 284
confidence intervals 202, 210, 216, 250,
    254, 255, 257
construct validity 122
constructs 17, 94, 96–98, 100, 109, 114,
    117, 124, 125, 276
content analysis 267, 275–276, 280
content validity 122
control
  experimental design and 32, 128,
    130–131, 133
  groups 128, 146
convenience sampling 218, 225–226
convergent validity 122
correlation 13, 33, 94, 95, 110, 124, 232,
    245–246, 248–253, 255, 264–265, 274
correlation coefficients 248–250, 263–264
Cramer's V coefficient 248
criterion related validity 123
critical realism 24, 41, 43
Cronbach's alpha coefficient 124, 175, 245
cross-national studies 145
cross-sectional studies 137, 143
cross-tabulation 246–248, 265, 278

data
  collection 14–18, 37, 41, 59, 71, 126–127,
    130, 155, 157–159, 163–200, 225,
    228, 273–274, 279
  empirical 7, 13–16, 34, 57, 71, 73,
    96–97, 127, 130, 126, 159, 163–200,
    225, 289
  interval 118–121, 179–180, 240–241,
    248 255
  nominal 118, 179, 241–242, 246, 248,
    255, 261, 270
  observational 192–196,
  ordinal 118–119, 179–180, 234, 241–242,
    248, 250, 255
  primary 14–15, 72–73, 154–155
  qualitative 12, 17, 37, 41–42, 123,
    147, 158–160, 164–165, 167–168,
    188–189, 196, 223–228, 267–280
  quantitative 12, 17, 37, 41–43, 158–159,
    166–168, 218–224, 232–265,
    269–270, 280
  ratio 120, 179, 234, 242, 290
  raw 13, 120, 233–235, 273,
  secondary 14–15, 72–73, 153–155
  tertiary 72–73
data analysis methods
  qualitative 42, 267–280
  quantitative 232–265, 268
data coding 172, 233–235, 267, 270,
    271–275, 277
data reduction 106, 232, 238, 261–264
deduction 3, 15, 16, 18, 22, 71–72
deductive
  approaches 1, 16–17, 34, 44, 71, 89, 96,
    124, 129–131, 157, 275–276
  research 16–18, 90, 97, 106, 133, 280
dependent variable 90, 100–107, 110–111,
    124, 143–144, 180, 247–249, 252–253,
    255–256, 258, 275
descriptive
  research 1, 12–13, 22
  statistics 232, 240–246, 265
  surveys 136–137
determining
  reliability 94, 123–124
  validity 94, 122–123
developing aims and objectives 46, 55–57
differences, measuring
  chi-square test 251, 255, 260–261, 265
  student *t*-test 256, 265

dimensions 97, 106, 109, 115, 265, 269, 276
directional hypotheses 109–110, 112, 254
discriminant validity 122
dispersion, measurement of
  interquartile range 242
  standard deviation 208, 216, 242–243,
    250, 253, 259
distributing questionnaires 168, 175,
  212–213, 217
double-barrelled questions, and
  questionnaire design 183, 186

ecological validity 263
eigenvalues 202–3
empirical
  data 7, 13–16, 34, 57, 71, 73, 96–97, 127,
    130, 126, 159, 163–200, 225, 289
  evidence 3, 13, 18, 34, 56, 85, 88–89, 94,
    109, 113, 130, 284
  research 7, 13, 14–16, 31–32, 34, 43–44,
    73, 89–90, 92, 94, 96–97, 99–100,
    103, 105, 114, 116–117, 124,
    126–160, 284, 300
epistemology 23, 26–29, 40, 43
equivalence
  conceptual 144–145
  measurement 144–145
error
  administrative 141
  non-response 139–140, 214–217
  response 138, 140–141, 169, 187
  sampling 138, 208–209 211
  systematic 138
ethical considerations 62–65, 193
ethnography 152–154
  visual 153
experimental research 32, 130–134, 146,
  157, 228
experiments
  field 151
  laboratory 27, 32, 131, 284
explanatory research 12–13, 15, 22
exploratory research 12–13, 22
external validity 122, 131, 224, 279
extreme cases, sampling and 226

face-to-face questionnaires 138, 160, 165
face validity 122, 165
factor analysis 105–106, 123, 262–263, 265
field interviews 188, 193, 196

field studies, research process and 16, 37, 196
focus groups 160, 190–191, 196
framework, conceptual 7, 57, 92, 94, 95–98,
  100–102, 109, 114, 121, 124–125,
  129–130, 157, 280, 284, 289
frequency distributions 240–241

generalisability 10–11, 15, 204, 218
generalisation 98, 108, 135, 146, 191,
  204–205, 219, 224, 226, 229, 283

Harvard system of referencing 292–299
hypothesis
  development 109, 112
  null and alternate 111, 254
  one and two-tailed 254–255, 258
  testing 3, 109–110, 112, 134, 157, 160,
    254–255
hypotheses 3, 7–8, 17–18, 34, 38, 57, 92,
  94–97, 106, 109–114, 125–126, 128,
  130–131, 133, 164, 188, 200, 226, 254,
  269, 289, 300–301
  causal 95, 109–111, 125
  correlational 95, 109–111, 125
  directional 109–110, 112, 254
  non-directional 109–110, 254

ideographic methodology 16
independent samples *t*-test 255–256, 258
independent variable 90, 100–107, 110–111,
  124, 143–144, 180, 247–249, 252–253,
  255–256, 275
indicators 109, 115–116, 125
induction 3, 15–18, 38, 71–72, 97, 275
inductive research 15–18, 36, 44, 71–72,
  89–90, 92, 96–97, 106, 124, 131–132,
  146–147, 151, 224, 228, 269, 272,
  274–275
inferential statistics 3, 253–261, 265
information
  primary 14–15, 72–73, 154–155
  secondary 14–15, 72–73, 153–155
  tertiary 72–73
information gathering *see* data collection
itemised rating scale 181–183
internal consistency 40, 124, 175, 193, 245
internal validity 124, 131, 193, 224, 279
internet-based research 152, 154
interpretivist paradigm 7, 146
interquartile range 242

interval
   data 118–121, 179–180, 240–241, 248 255
   scale 107, 118–121, 125, 174–175,
       179–183, 233–234, 236–237, 242
intervening variable 100–105, 107, 124
interviewing 37, 87, 137–138, 155, 157,
   159–160, 187–192, 194, 196, 229
interviews
   face-to-face 137–138, 159–160, 188
   field 188, 193, 196
   group 155, 160, 190–192, 196
   individual 160
   semi-structured 168, 188, 274
   structured 163, 166, 168, 187–188
   telephone 166, 168, 187
   unstructured 163, 166, 168

judgement sampling 226, 228

Kaiser–Meyer–Olkin test of sampling
   adequacy 262–263
knowledge and reality 6, 24–28, 32, 34, 39
kurtosis 243

laboratory experiments 27, 32, 131, 284
layout, questionnaire 168–176, 187
leading questions, questionnaire design
   and 186
level of confidence 202, 210, 216, 250,
   254, 255, 257
Levene's test for equality of variances 256
Likert scale 119, 180–183, 236
literature
   accessing and obtaining 76–80
   evaluating and reviewing 86–89
   reading and note taking 80–86
   searching and sourcing 76–80
   what is it? 72–73
literature review
   role and placement in inductive and
       deductive studies 71–72, 89–90
   what is it? 73–76
   why is it necessary? 68–72
   writing it up 89–92
loaded questions, questionnaire design
   184, 186
location, measuring
   mean 241–242
   median 241–242
   mode 241–242
longitudinal study 137, 143

mailed questionnaires 19, 139, 170, 213
manipulation 130–131, 152, 160
mean 241–242
measurement
   of variables 97, 117–124, 133, 144
   reliability 121–122, 124, 245–246
   scales 117–124
   validity 20, 121–123, 166–167, 180
measuring association
   Cramer's V coefficient 248
   cross-tabulation 246–248, 265, 278
   Pearson's r 250, 255
   phi coefficient 248
   Spearman's r 2 250, 255
measuring differences
   chi-square test 251, 255, 260–261, 265
   student t-tests 256, 265
measuring dispersion
   interquartile range 242
   standard deviation 208, 216, 242–243,
       250, 253, 259
measuring location 241–242
median 241–242
metaphors 198
method section, of research report 289
methodologies
   phenomenological 35–39
   positivistic 31–35
   post-modernism 39–40
   pragmatism 40–42
mixed-design 41, 167
mixed-methods 41, 158–160
mode 241–242
models 54, 89, 108–109
moderating variable 100–107, 124
multi-stage cluster sampling 223
mutual exclusivity 117

naturalistic enquiry 36,152
nature of literature 72–73
nature of research 2–6
netnography 153–156, 160
nominal
   data 118, 179, 241–242, 246, 248, 255,
       261, 270
   scales 118, 120, 179
non-parametric tests 255–256, 260–261
non-participant observation 16, 37, 152,
       156, 160, 192
non-probability based sampling 223–229
non-response error 139–140, 214–217

normal distribution 216, 240, 243, 255
note-taking 80–86

objectives 7, 55–58, 61, 76, 99, 129–130, 164,
    168, 171, 173, 188, 205, 207, 224, 283
objectivity, scientific research and 6, 10,
    34, 41
observation
    participant 16, 27, 37, 150, 152, 154,
        156, 163, 192–193, 279
    non-participant 16, 37, 152, 156, 160, 192
observational data
    recording 195
observational research 146, 151–156,
    159–160, 188, 192–196,
one sample *t*-test 255–259
one-tailed hypotheses 254
online surveys 172
ontology 26–28
open coding 273–274
open-ended questions, questionnaire design
    and 42, 164–165, 167, 276
operational definition 17, 100, 114–116,
    121–122
operationalisation 34, 94, 114–116
ordinal
    data 118–119, 179–180, 234, 241–242,
        248, 250, 255
    scales 118–119, 179
outliers 252–253

paired samples *t*-test 255–258
paradigms
    interpretivist 7, 146
    phenomenological 16, 30, 33, 35–40,
        43–44
    positivistic 18, 30–37, 39–40, 44
paradigms and methodology 28–29
parametric tests 255–256
parsimony, scientific research and 11,
    241, 261
participant observation 16, 27, 37, 150,
    152, 154, 156, 192–193, 279
Pearson's product moment correlation
    coefficient (r) 250, 255
periodicity 222
phenomenology 16, 30, 33, 35–40, 43–44
phi coefficient 248
philosophies
    phenomenology 16, 30, 33, 35–40, 43–44
    positivism 18, 30–37, 39–40, 44

philosophies *cont.*
    post-modernism 39–40
    pragmatism 40–42
piloting questions 186–187
plagiarism 70, 292, 302
population
    defining 205–206
    elements 205–207, 219, 223, 226
    heterogeneity 205, 209, 229
    homogeneity 223, 229
    parameters 205, 207–208, 216
    variability 205, 208–209, 211, 223, 229
positivism 18, 30–37, 39–40, 44
postal questionnaires 170
post-modernism 39–40
pragmatism 40–42
precision 9, 38, 120–121, 180, 182,
    208–211, 286
predictive validity 123
primary
    data 14–15, 72–73, 154–155
    research 14–15, 73, 155, 225, 300
principal components analysis 262–265
probability-based sampling 218–224,
    229, 255
projective technique procedures 185, 188,
    196–200
    association 198–199
    choice ordering 200
    completion 199
    construction 199
    expression 119–200
pure research 14–15
purposive sampling 226
p values 250–251, 254, 257, 259

Q-methodology 42
qualitative
    data analysis 42, 267–280
    sampling 203, 205, 217, 223–229
qualitative data
    displaying 277–278
    quanticising 269–270
    what kind? 268–271
qualitative data analysis
    basic principles and stages 271–274
    justifying choices 278–79
    techniques 275–277
quantitative
    data analysis 232–265, 268
    sampling 205, 217–224, 228–229

questionnaire
  design 164–185
  piloting 186–187
  preparation 164–185
questionnaire surveys 134–142, 164–187
  direct implementation 137–138, 141,
    168–170, 188
  distributed implementation 19, 138,
    166, 188
questionnaires
  semi-structured 167
  structured 166, 200
  unstructured 164–167
questions
  attitudinal 179
  behavioural 179
  categorical/classificatory 118, 176–179
  closed 30, 87, 168–169, 164–167,
    171–172, 179, 200
  coding 172, 233–235, 270,
  double-barrelled 183, 186
  leading 186
  loaded 184, 186
  measurement scales and 119, 120–121,
    166, 179–185
  non-standard forms 185–186, 188,
    196–200
  open 42, 164–165, 167, 276
  perceptual 179
  problems to avoid 183–185
  projective 185, 188, 196–200
  recall-dependent 184
  standard forms 15–186
  writing 176–179
quota sampling 227

random numbers 219, 220–222
random sampling 138, 208–209, 218–219,
  222–225, 229
randomisation 208–209, 222
range 242–243
ratio
  data 120, 179, 234, 242, 290
  scales 120, 179
raw data
  cleaning up 13, 195, 233–235, 271–275
realism 36, 41, 43
recall-dependent questions, questionnaire
  design and 184
recoding data 234–235

reductionism 35
referencing 291–302
  bibliographic 296–299
  text 293–296
regression 252–253, 265
reliability 73, 116, 121–124, 133, 154,
  165–167, 175, 192–193, 196, 224,
  245–246, 279
  inter-rater 123
  split-half 124, 175, 245–246
  test-retest method 123
replication 11, 70, 136, 151, 160
  literal 151
  theoretical 151
replicative studies 46, 69–70
representativeness, sampling and
  202–205, 227
research
  aims 46, 50, 55–57, 61, 79, 129, 149,
    164, 168, 205, 301
  ethics 62–65, 193
  nature of 2–6
  paradigms 7, 16, 18, 28–40, 43–44
  plan 46–64
  problems 5, 14–15, 18–22, 24, 49,
    69, 128
  proposals 46–64
  purposes 1, 12, 14, 15, 69, 71, 126, 130,
    132, 136, 145, 149
  questions 18–22, 54–55
  topics 21, 47–54, 68, 80, 86
  types 12–18
research designs
  action 126, 156–158, 161
  case study 141, 146–151, 161, 276
  comparative 43, 52, 93, 126, 133, 136,
    141–146, 149, 151, 159–161, 171,
    228, 269
  experimental 32, 130–134, 146, 157, 228
  observational 146, 151–156, 159–160,
    188, 192–196
  survey 134–140
research report
  conclusions 285, 290–291, 301
  introduction 287
  literature review 287–289
  methodology 289
  style, presentation and the reader
    282–287
  results 289–290

respondents 8, 19–21, 63, 75, 87, 99,
    117–118, 135–142, 165–172, 175–176,
    179–188, 190, 196–200, 204, 207,
    214–216, 217, 220, 224–225, 233–234,
    244, 246, 254–255, 257, 259, 261,
    269–270, 273, 278
response
    bias 140
    rates 19–20, 139, 213–215, 217
results section of research report 289–290
rigour, the scientific method and 8, 15

sample
    composition 75, 87, 118, 135, 140,
        203–204, 209, 211, 215, 258
    frame 207, 209, 212, 214, 219,
        222–223, 258
    inferences 203–205, 253, 265, 279
    initial 139, 213–214, 227
    precision 9, 208–211
    realised 176, 213–216, 229, 244
    representativeness 140, 203–204, 227, 244
    respondents 19, 117–118, 135, 137–141,
        166–168, 170, 176, 186, 190, 197,
        207, 214–217, 219, 224–225, 244, 259
    selection 9, 35, 133, 140, 201, 209, 211–
        213, 217–219, 222–223, 225–227
    size 75, 85, 87, 135, 139, 203–206,
        208–215, 222–224, 226, 228–229, 244
    statistics 207–208, 216, 240, 253–255, 265
    subjects 207, 223, 225–227, 255–256
sampling 202–231
    area 138, 223
    bias 87, 138, 208, 225, 227
    cluster 223
    confidence intervals and 202, 210, 216,
        250, 254, 255, 257
    convenience 218, 225–226
    criterion 226
    error 138, 208–209, 211
    expert choice 227
    frame 207, 209, 212, 214, 219,
        222–223, 258
    judgement 226, 228
    multi-stage 223
    non-probability based 223–229
    population and 205–209, 211, 216, 219,
        223, 226, 229
    probability based 218–224, 229, 255
    purposive 226

sampling *cont.*
    quota 227
    reality and 217–218, 224
    response rates and 19–20, 139,
        213–215, 217
        simple random 222
    size and 75, 85, 87, 135, 139, 203–206,
        208–215, 222–224, 226, 228–229, 244
        snowball
        strategies 164–73
        stratified random 222–223
        systematic random 222
    techniques 218–228
    theoretical 228
scale reliability 121–122, 124, 165–166,
    175, 245–246, 265
scales
    balanced 120, 182
    interval 107, 118–121, 125, 174–175,
        179–183, 233–234, 236–237, 242
    itemised rating 181–183
    Likert 119, 180–183, 236
    nominal 118, 120, 179
    ordinal 118–119, 179
    ratio 120, 179
    semantic differential 182–183
    unbalanced 182–183
scatter graphs 248–249
selective coding 275
scientific research 6–12, 15, 30–32, 37,
    43–44, 111, 130, 157
schools of thought 23, 28–31, 37, 39,
    43–44
secondary
    data secondary 14–15, 72–73, 153–155
    research 14–16, 73, 153–155, 300
semantic differential scale questions
    182–183
semiotics 267, 275–276, 280
semi-structured questionnaires 167
sequencing, questionnaire design and 274
skewed data 240–243
Spearman's rank correlation coefficient
    (r2) 250, 255
split-half reliability 124, 175, 245–246
spread *see* dispersion
SPSS
    association, measuring 118, 254–255
    Bartlett's Test of Sphericity 262
    bivariate data analysis 238, 246–255, 265

SPSS *cont.*
  central tendency, dispersion and skewness
      208, 216, 232, 240–243, 250, 253,
      259, 265
  charts and graphs 240–241, 265
  chi-square test for goodness of fit 255, 261
  chi-square test for independence 251,
      255, 261
  cluster analysis 261
  correlation coefficient analysis 245,
      252–253, 255, 263
  Cramer's V coefficient 248
  cross-tabulation 246–248, 265, 278
  data range 234, 242–243
  data recoding 234–235, 270
  data reduction 261–265
  data sheet 234–235, 237–239, 270
  data view 235–239
  defining variables 233–237
  descriptive statistics 238, 240–247, 251,
      262, 265
  eigenvalues 202–3
  entering data 237–238
  factor analysis 105–106, 123, 262–263, 265
  formatting data 233–237
  frequency distributions and tables 240–241
  hypothesis testing 254–255
  inferential statistics 253–261, 265
  interquartile range 242
  Kaiser–Meyer–Olkin test of sampling
      adequacy 262–263
  kurtosis 243
  Levene's test for equality of variances 256
  missing responses 216, 233, 235, 237–238
  non-parametric tests 255–256, 260–261
  output window 240, 243, 245, 248–251,
      261–262, 264
  parametric tests 255–256
  phi coefficient 248
  principal components analysis 262–265
  p values 250–251, 254, 257, 259
  regression analysis 252–253
  residual outliers 252–253
  scatter graphs 248–249
  select cases option 238–239
  skewness 240–243
  split file option 238–239
  standard deviation 242–243, 250, 253, 259,
      250, 253, 259
  string variables 236,–237, 270
  student *t*-tests 256–260, 265

SPSS *cont.*
  t-test values 256–260
  univariate data analysis 240–246, 255
  variable view 235–239
  standard deviation 208, 216, 242–243,
      250, 253, 259
  statistical significance 250–254, 256, 261
  statistics
      data reduction 106, 232, 238, 261–264
      descriptive 232, 240–246, 265
      inferential 3, 253–261, 265
  structured interview 163, 166, 168,
      187–188
  structured questionnaires 166, 200
  student *t*-tests 256–260, 265
  survey
      design 134–136
      error 131, 133, 135, 138–142, 186,
          210–211, 217
      implementation 19, 137–138, 141,
          168–170, 188
      questions 30, 87, 168–169, 176–186, 200
      research 134–143, 164–187
      response rate 19–20, 53, 139–140, 172,
          174, 213–217
  surveys
      advantages and disadvantages 136
      analytical 136–137
      descriptive 136–137
      online 172
      types 136–137

telephone interviews 166, 168, 187
telephone questionnaires 138–140, 166
tertiary data 72–73
test–retest reliability 123
text referencing 92, 291–294, 296, 299, 302
theoretical
    framework 7, 17–18, 57, 89, 95–98,
        109, 114, 127
    models 89, 108–109
    research 14–15
theories and theory 108–109
topics
    finding and refining 47–54
triangulation
    data 41, 279–280
    methods 279–280
t-tests 256–260
    two-tailed 255, 257–258

unbalanced scales 182
unit of analysis 146, 149–151, 272–273
univariate
  data 244, 255
  data analysis 240–246
unstructured
  interviews 163, 166, 168
  questionnaires 164–167

validity
  concurrent 123
  construct 122
  content 122
  convergent 122
  criterion-related 123
  discriminant 122
  ecological 263
  external 122, 131, 224, 279
  face 122, 165
  internal 124, 131, 193, 224, 279
  predictive 123

variability
  between clusters 223
  population 205, 208–209, 211, 223, 229
variables
  categorical 104, 107, 118, 236, 251, 261
  dependent 90, 100–107, 110–111, 124,
    143–144, 180, 247–249, 252–253,
    255–256, 258, 275
  exploring relationships between 86–90
  independent 90, 100–107, 110–111,
    124, 143–144, 180, 247–249,
    252–253, 255–256, 275
  intervening 100–105, 107, 124
  moderating 100–107, 124
  re-coding 234–235, 270
visual ethnography 153–154

wording principles, questionnaire design
    and 120, 138, 176, 181, 184, 187, 271
writing the literature review 89–92
writing the research report 282–302

194917